PISA 2000 TECHNICAL REPORT

EDITED BY RAY ADAMS AND MARGARET WU

OECD
ORGANISATION FOR ECONOMIC CO-OPERATION AND DEVELOPMENT

FOREWORD

Are students well prepared to meet the challenges of the future? Are they able to analyse, reason and communicate their ideas effectively? Do they have the capacity to continue learning throughout life? Parents, students, the public and those who run education systems need to know the answers to these questions.

Many education systems monitor student learning in order to provide some answers to these questions. Comparative international analyses can extend and enrich the national picture by providing a larger context within which to interpret national results. They can show countries their areas of relative strength and weakness and help them to monitor progress and raise aspirations. They can also provide directions for national policy, for schools' curriculum and instructional efforts and for students' learning. Coupled with appropriate incentives, they can motivate students to learn better, teachers to teach better, and schools to be more effective.

In response to the need for internationally comparable evidence on student performance, the OECD launched the Programme for International Student Assessment (PISA). PISA represents a new commitment by the governments of OECD countries to monitor the outcomes of education systems in terms of student achievement on a regular basis and within a common framework that is internationally agreed upon. PISA aims at providing a new basis for policy dialogue and for collaboration in defining and operationalising educational goals – in innovative ways that reflect judgements about the skills that are relevant to adult life. It provides inputs for standard-setting and evaluation; insights into the factors that contribute to the development of competencies and into how these factors operate in different countries, and it should lead to a better understanding of the causes and consequences of observed skill shortages. By supporting a shift in policy focus from educational inputs to learning outcomes, PISA can assist countries in seeking to bring about improvements in schooling and better preparation for young people as they enter an adult life of rapid change and deepening global interdependence.

PISA is a collaborative effort, bringing together scientific expertise from the participating countries, steered jointly by their governments on the basis of shared, policy-driven interests. Participating countries take responsibility for the project at the policy level through a Board of Participating Countries. Experts from participating countries serve on working groups that are charged with linking the PISA policy objectives with the best available substantive and technical expertise in the field of international comparative assessment of educational outcomes. Through participating in these expert groups, countries ensure that the PISA assessment instruments are internationally valid and take into account the cultural and curricular contexts of OECD Member countries, that they provide a realistic basis for measurement, and that they place an emphasis on authenticity and educational validity. The frameworks and assessment instruments for PISA 2000 are the product of a multi-year development process and were adopted by OECD Member countries in December 1999.

First results from the PISA 2000 assessment were published in *Knowledge and Skills for Life - First Results from PISA 2000* (2001). This publication presents evidence on the performance in reading, mathematical and scientific literacy of students, schools and countries, provides insights into the factors that influence the development of these skills at home and at school, and examines how these factors interact and what the implications are for policy development.

PISA is methodologically highly complex, requiring intensive collaboration among many stakeholders. The successful implementation of PISA depends on the use, and sometimes further development, of state-of-the-art methodologies. The PISA Technical Report describes those methodologies, along with other features that have enabled PISA to provide high quality data to support policy formation and review. The descriptions are provided at a level of detail that will enable review and potentially replication of the implemented procedures and technical solutions to problems.

The PISA Technical Report is the product of a collaborative effort between the countries participating in PISA and the experts and the institutions working within the framework of the International PISA Consortium that was contracted by the OECD with the implementation of PISA. The report was prepared by the International PISA Consortium, under the direction of Raymond Adams and Margaret Wu. Authors and contributors to the individual chapters of this report are identified in the corresponding chapters.

TABLE OF CONTENTS

CHAPTER 1. THE PROGRAMME FOR INTERNATIONAL STUDENT ASSESSMENT: AN OVERVIEW.......15
   Managing and implementing PISA 17
   This report 17

READER'S GUIDE..19

SECTION ONE: INSTRUMENT DESIGN

CHAPTER 2. TEST DESIGN AND TEST DEVELOPMENT 21
   Test scope and test format..21
   Timeline 21
   Assessment framework and test design..22
      Development of the assessment frameworks 22
      Test design 22
   Test development team..23
   Test development process..23
      Item submissions from participating countries 23
      Item writing 23
      The item review process 24
      Pre-pilots and translation input..24
      Preparing marking guides and marker training material 25
   PISA field trial and item selection for the main study 25
   Item bank software 26
   PISA 2000 main study...26
   PISA 2000 test characteristics 27

CHAPTER 3. STUDENT AND SCHOOL QUESTIONNAIRE DEVELOPMENT 33
   Overview..33
   Development process...34
      The questions 34
      The framework 34
   Coverage 36
      Student questionnaire...36
      School questionnaire 36
   Cross-national appropriateness of items..37
   Cross-curricular competencies and information technology 37
      The cross-curricular competencies instrument..37
      The information technology or computer familiarity instrument 38

SECTION TWO: OPERATIONS

CHAPTER 4. SAMPLE DESIGN 39
   Target population and overview of the sampling design...39
   Population coverage, and school and student participation rate standards 40
      Coverage of the international PISA target population...40
      Accuracy and precision 41
      School response rates 41
      Student response rates...42
   Main study school sample...42
      Definition of the national target population..42
      The sampling frame 43

    Stratification 43
    Assigning a measure of size to each school 48
    School sample selection 48
    Student samples...53

CHAPTER 5. TRANSLATION AND CULTURAL APPROPRIATENESS OF THE TEST AND SURVEY MATERIAL 57
Introduction 57
Double translation from two source languages 57
Development of source versions 59
PISA translation guidelines 60
Translation training session 61
International verification of the national versions 61
Translation and verification procedure outcomes..63
    Linguistic characteristics of English and French source versions of the stimuli 64
    Psychometric quality of the French and English versions 66
    Psychometric quality of the national versions 67
Discussion 69

CHAPTER 6. FIELD OPERATIONS 71
Overview of roles and responsibilities 71
    National Project Managers 71
    School Co-ordinators 72
    Test administrators 72
Documentation 72
Materials preparation..73
    Assembling test booklets and questionnaires..73
    Printing test booklets and questionnaires 73
    Packaging and shipping materials 74
    Receipt of materials at the National Centre after testing 75
Processing tests and questionnaires after testing..75
    Steps in the marking process 75
    Logistics prior to marking..77
    How marks were shown 78
    Marker identification numbers..78
    Design for allocating booklets to markers 78
    Managing the actual marking 81
    Multiple marking...82
    Cross-national marking 84
    Questionnaire coding 84
Data entry, data checking and file submission...84
    Data entry 84
    Data checking 84
    Data submission 84
    After data were submitted 84

CHAPTER 7. QUALITY MONITORING 85
Preparation of quality monitoring procedures..85
Implementing quality monitoring procedures 86
    Training National Centre Quality Monitors and School Quality Monitors 86
    National Centre Quality Monitoring 86
    School Quality Monitoring 86
    Site visit data..87

SECTION THREE: DATA PROCESSING

CHAPTER 8. SURVEY WEIGHTING AND THE CALCULATION OF SAMPLING VARIANCE 89
Survey weighting 89
The school base weight 90
The school weight trimming factor 91
The student base weight 91
School non-response adjustment 91
Grade non-response adjustment 94
Student non-response adjustment 94
Trimming student weights 95
Subject-specific factors for mathematics and science 96
Calculating sampling variance 96
The balanced repeated replication variance estimator 96
Reflecting weighting adjustments 97
Formation of variance strata 98
Countries where all students were selected for PISA 98

CHAPTER 9. SCALING PISA COGNITIVE DATA 99
The mixed coefficients multinomial logit model 99
The population model 100
Combined model 101
Application to PISA 101
National calibrations 101
Item response model file (infit mean square) 102
Discrimination coefficients 102
Item-by-country interaction 102
National reports 102
International calibration 105
Student score generation 105
Computing maximum likelihood estimates in PISA 105
Plausible values 105
Constructing conditioning variables 107
Analysis of data with plausible values 107

CHAPTER 10. CODING AND MARKER RELIABILITY STUDIES 109
Examining within-country variability in marking 109
Homogeneity analysis 109
Homogeneity analysis with restrictions 112
An additional criterion for selecting items 114
A comparison between field trial and main study 116
Variance component analysis 116
Inter-country rater reliability study - Design 124
Recruitment of international markers 125
Inter-country rater reliability study training sessions 125
Flag files 126
Adjudication 126

CHAPTER 11. DATA CLEANING PROCEDURES 127
Data cleaning at the National Centre 127
Data cleaning at the International Centre 128
Data cleaning organisation 128

Data cleaning procedures 128
  National adaptations to the database 128
  Verifying the student tracking form and the list of schools 128
  Verifying the reliability data 129
  Verifying the context questionnaire data 129
Preparing files for analysis 129
  Processed cognitive file 130
  The student questionnaire 130
  The school questionnaire 130
  The weighting files 130
  The reliability files 131

SECTION FOUR: QUALITY INDICATORS AND OUTCOMES

CHAPTER 12. SAMPLING OUTCOMES 133
Design effect and effective sample size 141

CHAPTER 13. SCALING OUTCOMES 149
International characteristics of the item pool 149
  Test targeting 149
  Test reliability 152
  Domain inter-correlations 152
  Reading sub-scales 153
Scaling outcomes 153
  National item deletions 153
  International scaling 154
  Generating student scale scores 154
Differential item functioning 154
Test length 156
Magnitude of booklet effects 157
  Correction of the booklet effect 160

CHAPTER 14. OUTCOMES OF MARKER RELIABILITY STUDIES 163
Within-country reliability studies 163
  Variance components analysis 163
  Generalisability coefficients 163
Inter-country rater reliability study - Outcome 174
  Overview of the main results 174
  Main results by item 174
  Main study by country 176

CHAPTER 15. DATA ADJUDICATION 179
Overview of response rate issues 179
Follow-up data analysis approach 181
Review of compliance with other standards 182
Detailed country comments 182
  Summary 182
  Australia 182
  Austria 183
  Belgium 183
  Brazil 184
  Canada 184
  Czech Republic 184

Denmark	184
Finland	185
France	185
Germany	185
Greece	185
Hungary	185
Iceland	185
Ireland	185
Italy	185
Japan	185
Korea	186
Latvia	186
Liechtenstein	186
Luxembourg	186
Mexico	186
Netherlands	186
New Zealand	187
Norway	189
Poland	189
Portugal	189
Russian Federation	189
Spain	190
Sweden	190
Switzerland	190
United Kingdom	191
United States	191

SECTION FIVE: SCALE CONSTRUCTION AND DATA PRODUCTS

CHAPTER 16. PROFICIENCY SCALES CONSTRUCTION 195
Introduction 195
Development of the described scales 195
    Stage 1: Identifying possible sub-scales 195
    Stage 2: Assigning items to scales 196
    Stage 3: Skills audit 196
    Stage 4: Analysing field trial data 196
    Stage 5: Defining the dimensions 196
    Stage 6: Revising and refining main study data 196
    Stage 7: Validating 197
Defining proficiency levels 197
Reading literacy 199
    Scope 199
    Three reading proficiency scales 199
    Task variables 200
    Task variables for the combined reading literacy scale 200
    Task variables for the retrieving information sub-scale 201
    Task variables for the interpreting texts sub-scale 201
    Task variables for the reflection and evaluation sub-scale 202
    Retrieving information sub-scale 204
    Interpreting texts sub-scale 205
    Reflection and evaluation sub-scale 206
    Combined reading literacy scale 207

  Cut-off points for reading 207
 Mathematical literacy 208
  What is being assessed? 208
  Illustrating the PISA mathematical literacy scale 210
 Scientific literacy 211
  What is being assessed? 211
  Illustrating the PISA scientific literacy scale 213

CHAPTER 17. CONSTRUCTING AND VALIDATING THE QUESTIONNAIRE INDICES 217
 Validation procedures of indices 218
 Indices 219
  Student characteristics and family background 219
  Parental interest and family relations 221
  Family possessions 224
  Instruction and learning 226
  School and classroom climate 228
  Reading habits 230
  Motivation and interest 232
  Learning strategies 234
  Learning style 237
  Self-concept 238
  Learning confidence 240
  Computer familiarity or information technology 242
  Basic school characteristics 244
  School policies and practices 245
  School climate 246
  School resources 249

CHAPTER 18. INTERNATIONAL DATABASE 253
 Files in the database 253
  The student files 253
  The school file 254
  The assessment items data file 254
 Records in the database 254
  Records included in the database 254
  Records excluded in the database 254
 Representing missing data 254
 How are students and schools identified? 255
 The student files 255
 The cognitive files 256
 The school file 256
 Further information 257

REFERENCES 259

APPENDIX 1. Summary of PISA reading literacy items 262

APPENDIX 2. Summary of PISA mathematical literacy items 266

APPENDIX 3. Summary of PISA scientific literacy items 267

APPENDIX 4. The validity studies of occupation and socio-economic status (Summary) 268
    Canada 268
    Czech Republic 268
    France 268
    United Kingdom 269

APPENDIX 5. The main findings from quality monitoring of the PISA 2000 main study 270
    School Quality Monitor Reports 270
    Preparation for the assessment 272
    Beginning the testing sessions 273
    Conducting the testing sessions 273
    The student questionnaire session 274
    General questions concerning the assessment 274
    Summary 275
    Interview with the PISA school co-ordinator 275
    National Centre Quality Monitor Reports 277
    Staffing 277
    School Quality Monitors 278
    Markers 278
    Administrative Issues 278
    Translation and Verification 279
    Adequacy of the manuals 280
    Conclusion 281

APPENDIX 6. Order effects figures 282

APPENDIX 7. PISA 2000 Expert Group membership and Consortium staff 286
    PISA Consortium 286
        Australian Council for Educational Research 286
        Westat 286
        Citogroep 286
        Educational Testing Service 286
        Other experts 286
    Reading Functional Expert Group 287
    Mathematics Functional Expert Group 287
    Science Functional Expert Group 287
    Cultural Review Panel 287
    Technical Advisory Group 287

APPENDIX 8. Contrast coding for PISA 2000 conditioning variables 288

APPENDIX 9. Sampling forms 305

APPENDIX 10. Student listing form 316

APPENDIX 11. Student tracking form 318

APPENDIX 12. Adjustment to BRR for strata with odd numbers of primary sampling units 320

LIST OF FIGURES

1. PISA 2000 in a Nutshell..16
2. Test Booklet Design for the Main Survey...23
3. Mapping the Coverage of the PISA 2000 Questionnaires 35
4. School Response Rate Standards - Criteria for Acceptability 42
5. Student Exclusion Criteria as Conveyed to National Project Managers 56
6. Allocation of the Booklets for Single Marking of Reading by Cluster............................79
7. Booklet Allocation for Single Marking of Mathematics and Science by Cluster, Common Markers 80
8. Booklet Allocation for Single Marking of Mathematics and Science by Cluster, Separate Markers .80
9. Booklet Allocation to Markers for Multiple Marking of Reading...................................82
10. Booklet Allocation for Multiple Marking of Mathematics and Science, Common Markers...........83
11. Booklet Allocation for Multiple Marking of Mathematics 83
12. Example of Item Statistics Shown in Report 1 103
13. Example of Item Statistics Shown in Report 2 103
14. Example of Item Statistics Shown in Report 3 104
15. Example of Item Statistics Shown in Report 4 104
16. Example of Item Statistics Shown in Report 5 105
17. Notational System...110
18. Quantification of Categories..111
19. H* and H** for Science Items 114
20. Homogeneity and Departure from Uniformity..116
21. Comparison of Homogeneity Indices for Reading Items in the Main Study and the Field Trial in Australia..117
22. Comparison of Reading Item Difficulty and Achievement Distributions...................151
23. Comparison of Mathematics Item Difficulty and Achievement Distributions 151
24. Comparison of Science Item Difficulty and Achievement Distributions 152
25. Items Deleted for Particular Countries 153
26. Comparison of Item Parameter Estimates for Males and Females in Reading...........155
27. Comparison of Item Parameter Estimates for Males and Females in Mathematics ...155
28. Comparison of Item Parameter Estimates for Males and Females in Science 155
29. Item Parameter Differences for the Items in Cluster One 161
30. Plot of Attained PISA School Response Rates 181
31. What it means to be at a Level 198
32. The Retrieving Information Sub-Scale..204
33. The Interpreting Texts Sub-Scale...205
34. The Reflection and Evaluation Sub-Scale..206
35. The Combined Reading Literacy Scale 207
36. Combined Reading Literacy Scale Level Cut-Off Points 207
37. The Mathematical Literacy Scale 209
38. Typical Mathematical Literacy Tasks 211
39. The Scientific Literacy Scale..212
40. Characteristics of the Science Unit, Semmelweis 214
41. Characteristics of the Science Unit, Ozone 215
42. Item Parameter Estimates for the Index of Cultural Communication (CULTCOM) 221
43. Item Parameter Estimates for the Index of Social Communication (SOCCOM) 222
44. Item Parameter Estimates for the Index of Family Educational Support (FAMEDSUP) 222
45. Item Parameter Estimates for the Index of Cultural Activities (CULTACTV)..............................222
46. Item Parameter Estimates for the Index of Family Wealth (WEALTH) 224
47. Item Parameter Estimates for the Index of Home Educational Resources (HEDRES)................224
48. Item Parameter Estimates for the Index of Possessions Related to 'Classical Culture' in the Family Home (CULTPOSS) 225

49. Item Parameter Estimates for the Index of Time Spent on Homework (HMWKTIME) 226
50. Item Parameter Estimates for the Index of Teacher Support (TEACHSUP) 226
51. Item Parameter Estimates for the Index of Achievement Press (ACHPRESS) 227
52. Item Parameter Estimates for the Index of Disciplinary Climate (DISCLIM) 228
53. Item Parameter Estimates for the Index of Teacher-Student Relations (STUDREL) 229
54. Item Parameter Estimates for the Index of Sense of Belonging (BELONG) 229
55. Item Parameter Estimates for the Index of Engagement in Reading (JOYREAD) 231
56. Item Parameter Estimates for the Index of Reading Diversity (DIVREAD) 231
57. Item Parameter Estimates for the Index of Instrumental Motivation (INSMOT) 232
58. Item Parameter Estimates for the Index of Interest in Reading (INTREA) 233
59. Item Parameter Estimates for the Index of Interest in Mathematics (INTMAT) 233
60. Item Parameter Estimates for the Index of Control Strategies (CSTRAT) 235
61. Item Parameter Estimates for the Index of Memorisation (MEMOR) 235
62. Item Parameter Estimates for the Index of Elaboration (ELAB) 235
63. Item Parameter Estimates for the Index of Effort and Perseverance (EFFPER) 236
64. Item Parameter Estimates for the Index of Co-operative Learning (COPLRN) 237
65. Item Parameter Estimates for the Index of Competitive Learning (COMLRN) 237
66. Item Parameter Estimates for the Index of Self-Concept in Reading (SCVERB) 239
67. Item Parameter Estimates for the Index of Self-Concept in Mathematics (MATCON) 239
68. Item Parameter Estimates for the Index of Academic Self-Concept (SCACAD) 239
69. Item Parameter Estimates for the Index of Perceived Self-Efficacy (SELFEF) 241
70. Item Parameter Estimates for the Index of Control Expectation (CEXP) 241
71. Item Parameter Estimates for the Index of Comfort With and Perceived Ability to Use Computers (COMAB) 242
72. Item Parameter Estimates for the Index of Computer Usage (COMUSE) 243
73. Item Parameter Estimates for the Index of Interest in Computers (COMATT) 243
74. Item Parameter Estimates for the Index of School Autonomy (SCHAUTON) 245
75. Item Parameter Estimates for the Index of Teacher Autonomy (TCHPARTI) 245
76. Item Parameter Estimates for the Index of Principals' Perceptions of Teacher-Related Factors Affecting School Climate (TEACBEHA) 247
77. Item Parameter Estimates for the Index of Principals' Perceptions of Student-Related Factors Affecting School Climate (STUDBEHA) 247
78. Item Parameter Estimates for the Index of Principals' Perceptions of Teachers' Morale and Commitment (TCMORALE) 247
79. Item Parameter Estimates for the Index of the Quality of the Schools' Educational Resources (SCMATEDU) 249
80. Item Parameter Estimates for the Index of the Quality of the Schools' Physical Infrastructure (SCMATBUI) 249
81. Item Parameter Estimates for the Index of Teacher Shortage (TCSHORT) 250
82. Duration of Questionnaire Session, Showing Histogram and Associated Summary Statistics 271
83. Duration of Total Student Working Time, with Histogram and Associated Summary Statistics 272
84. Item Parameter Differences for the Items in Cluster One 282
85. Item Parameter Differences for the Items in Cluster Two 283
86. Item Parameter Differences for the Items in Cluster Three 283
87. Item Parameter Differences for the Items in Cluster Four 283
88. Item Parameter Differences for the Items in Cluster Five 284
89. Item Parameter Differences for the Items in Cluster Six 284
90. Item Parameter Differences for the Items in Cluster Seven 284
91. Item Parameter Differences for the Items in Cluster Eight 285
92. Item Parameter Differences for the Items in Cluster Nine 285

LIST OF TABLES

1. Test Development Timeline..22
2. Distribution of Reading Items by Text Structure and by Item Type.................................27
3. Distribution of Reading Items by Type of Task (Process) and by Item Type...................27
4. Distribution of Reading Items by Text Type and by Item Type..27
5. Distribution of Reading Items by Context and by Item Type...28
6. Items from IALS...28
7. Distribution of Mathematics Items by Overarching Concepts and by Item Type............28
8. Distribution of Mathematics Items by Competency Class and by Item Type..................29
9. Distribution of Mathematics Items by Mathematical Content Strands and by Item Type..............29
10. Distribution of Mathematics Items by Context and by Item Type...................................29
11. Distribution of Science Items by Science Processes and by Item Type............................30
12. Distribution of Science Items by Science Major Area and by Item Type.........................30
13. Distribution of Science Items by Science Content Application and by Item Type.........30
14. Distribution of Science Items by Context and by Item Type..31
15. Stratification Variables...45
16. Schedule of School Sampling Activities...51
17. Percentage of Correct Answers in English and French-Speaking Countries or Communities for Groups of Test Units with Small or Large Differences in Length of Stimuli in the Source Languages..65
18. Correlation of Linguistic Difficulty Indicators in 26 English and French Texts..............66
19. Percentage of Flawed Items in the English and French National Versions 67
20. Percentage of Flawed Items by Translation Method...68
21. Differences Between Translation Methods..69
22. Non-Response Classes..92
23. School and Student Trimming..95
24. Some Examples of Δ..115
25. Contribution of Model Terms to (Co) Variance..120
26. Coefficients of the Three Variance Components (General Case)...................................122
27. Coefficients of the Three Variance Components (Complete Case)................................123
28. Estimates of Variance Components (x100) in the United States....................................123
29. Variance Components (%) for Mathematics in the Netherlands....................................124
30. Estimates of ρ_3 for Mathematics Scale in the Netherlands...124
31. Sampling and Coverage Rates 135
32. School Response Rates Before Replacements..138
33. School Response Rates After Replacements..139
34. Student Response Rates After Replacements...140
35. Design Effects and Effective Sample Sizes for the Mean Performance on the Combined Reading Literacy Scale..143
36. Design Effects and Effective Sample Sizes for the Mean Performance on the Mathematical Literacy Scale 144
37. Design Effects and Effective Sample Sizes for the Mean Performance on the Scientific Literacy Scale...................145
38. Design Effects and Effective Sample Sizes for the Percentage of Students at Level 3 on the Combined Reading Literacy Scale 146
39. Design Effects and Effective Sample Sizes for the Percentage of Students at Level 5 on the Combined Reading Literacy Scale 147
40. Number of Sampled Students by Country and Booklet 150
41. Reliability of the Three Domains Based Upon Unconditioned Unidimensional Scaling 152
42. Latent Correlation Between the Three Domains...153
43. Correlation Between Scales...153
44. Final Reliability of the PISA Scales...154
45. Average Number of Not-Reached Items and Missing Items by Booklet and Testing Session 156

46. Average Number of Not-Reached Items and Missing Items by Country and Testing Session 157
47. Distribution of Not-Reached Items by Booklet, First Testing Session 157
48. Distribution of Not-Reached Items by Booklet, Second Testing Session 158
49. Mathematics Means for Each Booklet and Country 158
50. Reading Means for Each Booklet and Country 159
51. Science Means for Each Booklet and Country 160
52. Booklet Difficulty Parameters 161
53. Booklet Difficulty Parameters Reported on the PISA Scale 161
54. Variance Components for Mathematics 164
55. Variance Components for Science 165
56. Variance Components for Retrieving Information 166
57. Variance Components for Interpreting Texts 167
58. Variance Components for Reflection and Evaluation 168
59. ρ_3-Estimates for Mathematics 169
60. ρ_3-Estimates for Science 170
61. ρ_3-Estimates for Retrieving Information 171
62. ρ_3-Estimates for Interpreting Texts 172
63. ρ_3-Estimates for Reflection and Evaluation 173
64. Summary of Inter-Country Rater Reliability Study 174
65. Summary of Item Characteristics for Inter-Country Rater Reliability Study 175
66. Items with Less than 90 Per Cent Consistency 176
67. Inter-Country Reliability Study Items with More than 25 Per Cent Inconsistency Rate in at Least One Country 177
68. Inter-Country Summary by Country 178
69. The Potential Impact of Non-response on PISA Proficiency Estimates 180
70. Performance in Reading by Grade in the Flemish Community of Belgium 183
71. Average of the School Percentage of Over-Aged Students 184
72. Results for the New Zealand Logistic Regression 188
73. Results for the United States Logistic Regression 193
74. Reliability of *Parental Interest and Family Relations* Scales 223
75. Reliability of *Family Possessions* Scales 225
76. Reliability of *Instruction and Learning* Scales 227
77. Reliability of *School and Classroom Climate* Scales 230
78. Reliability of *Reading Habits* Scales 232
79. Reliability of *Motivation and Interest* Scales 234
80. Reliability of *Learning Strategies* Scales 236
81. Reliability of *Learning Style* Scales 238
82. Reliability of *Self-Concept* Scales 240
83. Reliability of *Learning Confidence* Scales 242
84. Reliability of *Computer Familiarity* or *Information Technology* Scales 244
85. Reliability of *School Policies and Practices* Scales 246
86. Reliability of *School Climate* Scales 248
87. Reliability of *School Resources* Scales 250
88. Validity Study Results for France 268
89. Validity Study Results for the United Kingdom 269
90. Responses to the School Co-ordinator Interview 276
91. Number of Students per School Refusing to Participate in PISA Prior to Testing 277
92. Item Assignment to Reading Clusters 282

CHAPTER 1

THE PROGRAMME FOR INTERNATIONAL STUDENT ASSESSMENT: AN OVERVIEW

Ray Adams

The OECD Programme for International Student Assessment (PISA) is a collaborative effort among OECD Member countries to measure how well 15-year-old young adults approaching the end of compulsory schooling are prepared to meet the challenges of today's knowledge societies.[1] The assessment is forward-looking: rather than focusing on the extent to which these students have mastered a specific school curriculum, it looks at their ability to use their knowledge and skills to meet real-life challenges. This orientation reflects a change in curricular goals and objectives, which are increasingly concerned with what students can do with what they learn at school.

The first PISA survey was conducted in 2000 in 32 countries (including 28 OECD Member countries) using written tasks answered in schools under independently supervised test conditions. Another 11 countries will complete the same assessment in 2002. PISA 2000 surveyed reading, mathematical and scientific literacy, with a primary focus on reading. Measures of attitudes to learning, and information on how students manage their own learning were also obtained in 25 countries as part of an international option. The survey will be repeated every three years, with the primary focus shifting to mathematics in 2003, science in 2006 and back to reading in 2009.

In addition to the assessments, PISA 2000 included Student and School Questionnaires to collect data that could be used in constructing indicators pointing to social, cultural, economic and educational factors that are associated with student performance. Using the data taken from these two questionnaires, analyses linking context information with student achievement could address differences:

- between countries in the relationships between student-level factors (such as gender and social background) and achievement;
- in the relationships between school-level factors and achievement across countries;
- in the proportion of variation in achievement between (rather than within) schools, and differences in this value across countries;
- between countries in the extent to which schools moderate or increase the effects of individual-level student factors and student achievement;
- in education systems and national context that are related to differences in student achievement across countries; and
- in the future, changes in any or all of these relationships over time.

Through the collection of such information at the student and school level on a cross-nationally comparable basis, PISA adds significantly to the knowledge base that was previously available from national official statistics, such as aggregate national statistics on the educational programs completed and the qualifications obtained by individuals.

The ambitious goals of PISA come at a cost: PISA is both resource intensive and

---

[1] In most OECD countries, compulsory schooling ends at age 15 or 16; in the United States it ends at age 17, and in Belgium, Germany and the Netherlands, at age 18 (OECD, 2001).

methodologically highly complex, requiring intensive collaboration among many stakeholders. The successful implementation of PISA depends on the use, and sometimes further development, of state-of-the-art methodologies. This report describes some of those methodologies, along with other features that have enabled PISA to provide high quality data to support policy formation and review.

Figure 1 provides an overview of the central design elements of PISA. The remainder of this report describes these design elements and the associated procedures in more detail.

Sample size
- More than a quarter of a million students, representing almost 17 million 15-year-olds enrolled in the schools of the 32 participating countries, were assessed in 2000. Another 11 countries will administer the same assessment in 2002.

Content
- PISA 2000 covered three domains: reading literacy, mathematical literacy and scientific literacy.
- PISA 2000 looked at young people's ability to use their knowledge and skills in order to meet real-life challenges rather than how well they had mastered a specific school curriculum.
- The emphasis was placed on the mastery of processes, the understanding of concepts, and the ability to function in various situations within each domain.
- As part of an international option taken up in 25 countries, PISA 2000 collected information on students' attitudes to learning.

Methods
- PISA 2000 used pencil-and-paper assessments, lasting two hours for each student.
- PISA 2000 used both multiple-choice items and questions requiring students to construct their own answers. Items were typically organised in units based on a passage describing a real-life situation.
- A total of seven hours of assessment items was included, with different students taking different combinations of the assessment items.
- Students answered a background questionnaire that took about 30 minutes to complete and, as part of an international option, completed questionnaires on learning and study practices as well as familiarity with computers.
- School principals completed a questionnaire about their school.

Outcomes
- A profile of knowledge and skills among 15-year-olds.
- Contextual indicators relating results to student and school characteristics.
- A knowledge base for policy analysis and research.
- Trend indicators showing how results change over time, once data become available from subsequent cycles of PISA.

Future assessments
- PISA will continue in three-year cycles. In 2003, the focus will be on mathematics and in 2006 on science. The assessment of cross-curricular competencies is being progressively integrated into PISA, beginning with an assessment of problem-solving skills in 2003.

Figure 1: PISA 2000 in a Nutshell

MANAGING AND IMPLEMENTING PISA

The design and implementation of PISA 2000 was the responsibility of an international Consortium led by the Australian Council for Educational Research (ACER). The other partners in this Consortium have been the National Institute for Educational Measurement (Cito Group) in the Netherlands, the Service de Pédagogie Expérimentale at Université de Liège in Belgium, Westat and the Educational Testing Service (ETS) in the United States and the National Institute for Educational Research (NIER) in Japan. Appendix 7 lists the many Consortium staff and consultants who have made important contributions to the development and implementation of the project.

The Consortium implements PISA within a framework established by a Board of Participating Countries (BPC) which includes representation from all countries at senior policy levels. The BPC established policy priorities and standards for developing indicators, for establishing assessment instruments, and for reporting results. Experts from participating countries served on working groups linking the programme policy objectives with the best internationally available technical expertise in the three assessment areas. These expert groups were referred to as Functional Expert Groups (FEGs) (*see Appendix 7* for members). By participating in these expert groups and regularly reviewing outcomes of the groups' meetings, countries ensured that the instruments were internationally valid and that they took into account the cultural and educational contexts of the different OECD Member countries, that the assessment materials had strong measurement potential, and that the instruments emphasised authenticity and educational validity.

Participating countries implemented PISA nationally through National Project Managers (NPMs), who respected common technical and administrative procedures. These managers played a vital role in developing and validating the international assessment instruments and ensured that PISA implementation was of high quality. The NPMs also contributed to the verification and evaluation of the survey results, analyses and reports.

The OECD Secretariat had overall responsibility for managing the programme. It monitored its implementation on a day-to-day basis, served as the secretariat for the BPC, fostered consensus building between the countries involved, and served as the interlocutor between the BPC and the international Consortium.

THIS REPORT

This Technical Report does not report the results of PISA. The first results from PISA were published in December 2001 in *Knowledge and Skills for Life* (OECD, 2001) and a sequence of thematic reports covering topics such as: Social Background and Student Achievement; The Distribution and Impact of Strategies of Self-Regulated Learning and Self-Concept; Engagement and Motivation; and School Factors Related to Quality and Equity is planned for publication in the coming months.

This Technical Report is designed to describe the technical aspects of the project at a sufficient level of detail to enable review and potentially replication of the implemented procedures and technical solutions to problems. The report is broken into five sections:

- *Section One—Instrument Design:* Covers the design and development of both the questionnaires and achievement tests.
- *Section Two—Operations:* Covers the operational procedures for the sampling and population definitions, test administration procedures, quality monitoring and assurance procedures for test administration and national centre operations, and instrument translation.
- *Section Three—Data Processing:* Covers the methods used in data cleaning and preparation, including the methods for weighting and variance estimation, scaling methods, methods for examining inter-rater variation and the data cleaning steps.
- *Section Four—Quality Indicators and Outcomes:* Covers the results of the scaling and weighting, reports response rates and related sampling outcomes and gives the outcomes of the inter-rater reliability studies. The last chapter in this section summarises the outcomes of the PISA 2000 data

adjudication—that is, the overall analysis of data quality for each country.
- *Section Five—Scale Construction and Data Products:* Describes the construction of the PISA 2000 described levels of proficiency and the construction and validation of questionnaire-related indices. The final chapter briefly describes the contents of the PISA 2000 database.
- *Appendices*: Detailed appendices of results pertaining to the chapters of the report are provided.

READER'S GUIDE

LIST OF ABBREVIATIONS

The following abbreviations are used in this report:

ACER	Australian Council for Educational Research
AGFI	Adjusted Goodness-of-Fit Index
BPC	PISA Board of Participating Countries
BRR	Balanced Repeated Replication
CCC	PISA 2000 questionnaire on self-regulated learning
CFA	Confirmatory Factor Analysis
CFI	Comparative Fit Index
CIVED	Civic Education Study
DIF	Differential Item Functioning
ENR	Enrolment of 15-year-olds
ETS	Educational Testing Service
FEG	Functional Expert Group
I	Sampling Interval
IALS	International Adult Literacy Survey
ICR	Inter-Country Rater Reliability Study
IEA	International Association for the Evaluation of Educational Achievement
ISCED	International Standard Classification of Education
ISCO	International Standard Classification of Occupations
ISEI	International Socio-Economic Index
IT	PISA questionnaire on computer familiarity
MENR	Enrolment for moderately small schools
MOS	Measure of size
NCQM	National Centre Quality Monitor
NDP	National Desired Population
NEP	National Enrolled Population
NFI	Normed Fit Index
NNFI	Non-Normed Fit Index
NPM	National Project Manager
PISA	Programme for International Student Assessment
PPS	Probability Proportional to Size
PSU	Primary Sampling Units
RMSEA	Root Mean Square Error of Approximation
RN	Random Number
SC	School Co-ordinator
SD	Standard Deviation
SEM	Structural Equation Modelling
SES	Socio-Economic Status
SQM	School Quality Monitor
TA	Test Administrator
TAG	Technical Advisory Group
TCS	Target Cluster Size
TIMSS	Third International Mathematics and Science Study
TIMSS-R	Third International Mathematics and Science Study - Repeat
TOEFL	Test of English as a Foreign Language
VENR	Enrolment for very small schools
WLE	Weighted Likelihood Estimates

FURTHER INFORMATION

For further information on the PISA assessment instruments, the PISA database and methods used see also:

Knowledge and Skills for Life – First Results from PISA 2000 (OECD, 2001);

Knowledge and Skills for Life – A New Framework for Assessment (OECD, 1999a);

Manual for the PISA 2000 Database (OECD, 2002a);

Sample Tasks from the PISA 2000 Assessment – Reading, Mathematical and Scientific Literacy (OECD, 2002b); and

The PISA Web site (*www.pisa.oecd.org*).

SECTION ONE: INSTRUMENT DESIGN

CHAPTER 2 { TEST DESIGN AND TEST DEVELOPMENT

Margaret Wu

TEST SCOPE AND TEST FORMAT

PISA 2000 had three subject domains, with reading as the major domain, and mathematics and science as minor domains. Student achievement in reading was assessed using 141 items representing approximately 270 minutes of testing time. The mathematics assessment consisted of 32 items, and the science assessment consisted of 35 items, representing approximately 60 minutes of testing time for each.

The materials used in the main study were selected from a larger pool of approximately 600 items tested in a field trial conducted in all countries one year prior to the main study. The pool included 16 items from the International Adult Literacy Survey (IALS, OECD, 2000) and three items from the Third International Mathematics and Science Study (TIMSS, Beaton *et al.*, 1996). The IALS items were included to allow for possible linking of PISA results to IALS.[1]

PISA 2000 was a paper-and-pencil test, with each student undertaking two hours of testing (i.e., answering one of the nine booklets). The test items were multiple-choice, short answer, and extended response. Multiple-choice items were either standard multiple-choice with a limited number (usually four or five) of responses from which students were required to select the best answer, or complex multiple-choice presenting several statements from which students were required to give one of several possible responses (true/false, correct/incorrect, etc.). Closed constructed-response items generally required students to construct a response within very limited constraints, such as mathematics items requiring a numeric answer, or items requiring a word or short phrase, etc. Short response items were similar to closed constructed-response items, but had a wide range of possible responses. Open constructed-response items required more extensive writing, or showing a calculation, and frequently included some explanation or justification.

Pencils, erasers, rulers, and, in some cases, calculators, were provided. The Consortium recommended that calculators be provided in countries where they were routinely used in the classroom. National centres decided whether calculators should be provided for their students on the basis of standard national practice. No items in the pool required a calculator, but some items involved solution steps for which the use of a calculator could facilitate computation. In developing the mathematics items, test developers were particularly mindful to ensure that the items were as calculator-neutral as possible.

TIMELINE

The project started in January 1998, when some initial conception of the frameworks was discussed. The formal process of test development began after the first Functional Expert Groups' (FEGs) meetings in March 1998. The main phase of the test item development finished when the items were distributed for the field trial in November 1998. During this eight-month period, intensive work was carried out in writing and reviewing items, and on pre-pilot activities.

---

[1] Note that after consideration by the Functional Expert Groups (FEGs), National Project Managers (NPMs) and the Board of Participating Countries (BPC), a link with TIMSS was not pursued in the main study.

The field trial for most countries took place between February and July 1999, after which items were selected for the main study and distributed to countries in December 1999.

Table 1 shows the PISA 2000 test development timeline.

Table 1: Test Development Timeline

Activity	Date
Develop frameworks	January-September 1998
Item submission from countries	May-July 1998
Develop items	March-November 1998
Pre-pilot in Australia	October and November 1998
Distribution of field trial material	November 1998
Translation into national languages	November 1998-January 1999
Pre-pilot in the Netherlands	February 1999
Field trial marker training	February 1999
Field trial in participating countries	February-July 1999
Select items for main study	July-November 1999
Cultural Review Panel meeting	October 1999
Distribute main study material	December 1999
Main study marker training	February 2000
Main study in participating countries	February-October 2000

ASSESSMENT FRAMEWORK AND TEST DESIGN

DEVELOPMENT OF THE ASSESSMENT FRAMEWORKS

The Consortium, through the test developers and expert groups, and in consultation with national centres, developed assessment frameworks for reading, mathematics and science. The frameworks were endorsed by the Board of Participating Countries (BPC) and published by the OECD in 1999 in *Measuring Student Knowledge and Skills: A New Framework for Assessment* (OECD, 1999a).

The frameworks presented the direction being taken by the PISA assessments. They defined each assessment domain, described the scope of the assessment, the number of items required to assess each component of a domain and the preferred balance of question types, and sketched the possibilities for reporting results.

TEST DESIGN

The 141 main study reading items were organised into nine separate clusters, each with an estimated administration time of 30 minutes. The 32 mathematics items and the 35 science items were organised into four 15-minute mathematics clusters and four 15-minute science clusters respectively. These clusters were then combined in various groupings to produce nine linked two-hour test booklets.

Using R_1 to R_9 to denote the reading clusters, M_1 to M_4 to denote the mathematics clusters and S_1 to S_4 to denote the science clusters, the allocation of clusters to booklets is illustrated in Figure 2.

The BPC requested that the majority of booklets begin with reading items since reading was the major area. In the design, seven of the nine booklets begin with reading. The BPC further requested that students not be expected to switch between assessment areas, and so none of the booklets requires students to return to any area after having left it.

Reading items occur in all nine booklets, and there are linkages between the reading in all booklets. This permits all sampled students to be assigned reading scores on common scales. Mathematics items occur in five of the nine booklets, and there are links between the five booklets, allowing mathematics scores to be reported on a common scale for five-ninths of the sampled students. Similarly, science material occurs in five linked booklets, allowing science scores to be reported on a common scale for five-ninths of the sampled students.

In addition to the nine two-hour booklets, a special one-hour booklet, referred to as Booklet zero (or the SE booklet) was prepared for use in schools catering exclusively to students with special needs. The SE booklet was shorter, and designed to be somewhat easier than the other nine booklets.

The two-hour test booklets, sometimes referred to in this report as 'cognitive booklets'

Booklet	Block 1	Block 2	Block 3	Block 4
1	R_1	R_2	R_4	$M_1\ M_2$
2	R_2	R_3	R_5	$S_1\ S_2$
3	R_3	R_4	R_6	$M_3\ M_4$
4	R_4	R_5	R_7	$S_3\ S_4$
5	R_5	R_6	R_1	$M_2\ M_3$
6	R_6	R_7	R_2	$S_2\ S_3$
7	R_7	R_1	R_3	R_8
8	$M_4\ M_2$	$S_1\ S_3$	R_8	R_9
9	$S_4\ S_2$	$M_1\ M_3$	R_9	R_8

Figure 2: Test Booklet Design for the Main Survey

to distinguish them from the questionnaires, were arranged in two one-hour parts, each made up of two of the 30-minute time blocks from the columns in the above figure. PISA's procedures provided for a short break to be taken between administration of the two parts of the test booklet, and a longer break to be taken between administration of the test and the questionnaire.

TEST DEVELOPMENT TEAM

The core of the test development team consisted of staff from the test development sections of the Australian Council for Educational Research (ACER) in Melbourne and the Cito Group in the Netherlands. Many others, including members of the FEGs, translators and item reviewers at national centres, made substantial contributions to the process of developing the tests.

TEST DEVELOPMENT PROCESS

Following the development of the assessment framework, the process of test development included: calling for submissions of test items from participating countries; writing and reviewing items; pre-piloting the test material; preparing marking guides and marker training material; and selecting items for the main study.

ITEM SUBMISSIONS FROM PARTICIPATING COUNTRIES

An international comparative study should draw items from a wide range of cultures and languages. Thus, at the start of the PISA 2000 test development process, the Consortium called for participating countries to submit items.

A document outlining submission guidelines was prepared stating the purpose of the project, and the working definition of each subject domain as drafted by the FEGs. In particular, the document described PISA's literacy orientation and its aim of tapping *students' preparedness for life*. The Consortium requested *authentic* materials in their original forms, preferably from the news media and original published texts. The submission guidelines included a list of variables—such as, text types and formats, response formats and contexts (and situations) of the materials—according to which countries were requested to classify their submissions. A statement on copyright status was also sought. Countries submitted items either directly to the Consortium, or through the FEG members who advised on their appropriateness before sending them on. Having FEG members act as liaison served the purpose of addressing translation issues, as many FEG members spoke languages other than English, and could deal directly with items written in languages other than English.

A total of 19 countries contributed materials for reading, 12 countries contributed materials for mathematics, and 13 countries contributed materials for science. For a full list of country and language source for the main study items, see Appendix 1 (for reading), Appendix 2 (for mathematics) and Appendix 3 (for science).

ITEM WRITING

The Consortium test development team reviewed contributed items from countries to ensure that they were consistent with the frameworks and had no obvious technical flaws. The test developers also wrote many items from scratch to ensure that the pool satisfied the framework specifications for the composition of the assessment instruments. There were three separate teams of test developers for the three domains, but some integrated units were developed that included both reading and science items.[2] In all, 660 minutes of reading material, 180 minutes of mathematics material, 180 minutes of science

---

[2] An *Integrated Unit* contained a stimulus text that usually had a scientific content. A number of reading items and science items followed the stimulus.

material, and 60 minutes of integrated material were developed for the field trial.[3]

To ensure that translation did not change the intentions of the questions or the difficulty of the items, the test developers provided translation notes where appropriate, to underline potential difficulties with translations and adaptations and to avoid possible misinterpretations of the English or French words.[4] Test developers also provided a summary of the intentions of the items. Suggestions for adaptations were also made to indicate the scope of possible changes in the translated texts and items. During the translation process, the test developers adjudicated lists of country adaptations to ensure that the changes did not alter what the items were testing.

THE ITEM REVIEW PROCESS

The field trial was preceded by an extensive review process of the items including panelling by the test development team, national reviews in each country, reviews by the FEGs, pre-pilots in Australian and Dutch schools, and close scrutiny by the team of translators.

Each institution (ACER and Cito Group) routinely subjected all item development to an internal item panelling process[5] that involved staff from the PISA test development team and test developers not specifically involved in the PISA project. ACER and Cito Group also exchanged items and reviewed and provided comments on them.

After item panelling, the items were sent in four batches[6] to participating countries for national review. The Consortium requested ratings from national subject matter experts of each item and stimulus according to (i) students' exposure to the content of the item (ii) item difficulty (iii) cultural concerns (iv) other bias concerns (v) translation problems, and (vi) an overall priority rating for inclusion of the item. In all, 27 countries provided feedback; the ratings were collated by item and used by the test development team to revise and select items for the field trial.

Before the field trial, the reading FEG met on four occasions (March, May, August, October 1998), and the mathematics and science groups met on three occasions (March, May, October 1998) to shape and draft the framework documents and review items in detail. In addition to bringing their expertise in a particular discipline, members of the expert groups came from a wide range of language groups and countries, cultures and education systems. For a list of members of the expert groups, see Appendix 7.

PRE-PILOTS AND TRANSLATION INPUT

In the small-scale pre-pilot conducted in Australian and Dutch schools, about 35 student responses on average were obtained for each item and used to check the clarity of the stimulus and the items, and to construct sample answers in the *Marking Guides (see next section)*. The pre-pilot also provided some indications about the necessary answer time. As a result of the pilots, it was estimated that, on average, an item required about two minutes to complete.

Translation also provided another indirect, albeit effective, review. Translations were made from English to French and *vice versa* to provide the national translation teams with two source versions of all materials *(see Chapter 5)* and the team often pointed out useful information such as typographical errors, ambiguities and translation difficulties, and some cultural issues. The group of experts reviewing the translated material detected some remaining errors in both versions. Finally one French-speaking member

---

[3] However, for the main study, no integrated units were selected.
[4] The PISA instruments were distributed in matching English and French source versions.
[5] In test development literature, *item panelling* is sometimes referred to as *item shredding* or a *cognitive walk-through*.

[6] Referred to as *item bundles*.

and one English-speaking member of the reading FEG reviewed the items for linguistic accuracy.

PREPARING MARKING GUIDES AND MARKER TRAINING MATERIAL

A *Marking Guide* was prepared for each subject area with items that required markers to code responses. The guide emphasised that markers were to *code* rather than *score* responses. That is, the guides separated different kinds of possible responses, which did not all necessarily receive different *scores*. The actual *scoring* was done after the field trial data were analysed, which provided information on the appropriate scores for each different response category.[7]

The *Marking Guide* was a list of response codes with descriptions and examples, but a separate training workshop document was also produced for each subject area. Marker training for the field trial took place in February 1999. Markers used the workshop material as exercises to practise using the *Marking Guides*. Workshop material contained additional student responses: the correct response codes were in hidden texts, so that the material could be used as a test for markers and as reference material. In addition, a *Marker Recruitment Kit* was produced with more student responses to be used as a screening test when recruiting markers.

PISA FIELD TRIAL AND ITEM SELECTION FOR THE MAIN STUDY

The PISA Field Trial was carried out in most countries in the first half of 1999. An average of about 150 to 200 student responses to each item were collected in each country. During the field trial, the Consortium set up a marker query service. Countries were encouraged to send queries to the service so that a common adjudication process was consistently applied to all markers' questions.

Between July and November 1999, national reviewers, the test development team, FEGs and a Cultural Review Panel reviewed and selected items.

---

[7] It is worth mentioning here that as data entry was carried out using KeyQuest®, many short-responses were entered directly, which saved time and made it possible to capture students' raw responses.

- Each country received an item review form and the country's field trial report (*see Chapter 9*). The NPM, in consultation with national committees, completed the forms.
- Test developers met in September 1999 to (i) identify items that were totally unsuitable for the main study, and (ii) recommend the best set for the main study, ensuring a balance in all aspects specified in the frameworks. FEG chairs were also invited to join the test developers.
- The FEGs met with the test developers in October 1999 and reviewed and modified the recommended set of selected items. A final set of items was presented to the National Project Managers Meeting in November 1999.
- A Cultural Review Panel met at the end of October 1999 to ensure that the selected items were appropriate for all cultures and were unbiased for any particular group of students. Cultural appropriateness was defined to mean that assessment stimuli and items were appropriate for 15-year-old students in all participating countries, that they were drawn from a cultural milieu that, overall, was equally familiar to all students, and that the tests did not violate any national cultural values or positions. The Cultural Review Panel also considered issues of gender and appropriateness across different socio-economic groups. For the list of members in the Cultural Review Panel, see Appendix 7. Several sources were used in the item review process after the field trial.
- Participant feedback was collected during the translation process, at the marker training meeting, and throughout each country's marking activity for the field trial. The Consortium had compiled information about the wording of items, the clarity of the *Marking Guides*, translation difficulties and problems with graphics and printing which were all considered when items were revised. Furthermore, countries were asked once again to rate and comment on field trial items for (i) curriculum relevance, (ii) interest to 15-year-olds, (iii) cultural, gender, or other bias, and (iv) difficulties with translation and marking.
- A report on problematic items was prepared. The report flagged items that were easier or harder than expected; had a positive non-key point-biserial or a negative key point-biserial;

non-ordered ability for partial credit items; or a poor fit. While some of these problems could be traced to the occasional translation or printing error, this report gave some statistical information on whether there was a systematic problem with a particular item.
- A marker reliability study provided information on marker agreement for coding responses to open-ended items and was used to revise items and/or *Marking Guides*, or to reject items altogether.
- Differential Item Functioning (DIF) analyses with regard to gender, reading competence and socio-economic status (SES). Items exhibiting large DIF were candidates for removal.
- Item attributes. Test developers monitored closely the percentage of items in each category for various attributes. For example, open-ended items were limited to the percentages set by the BPC, and covered different aspects of the area in the proportions specified in the framework.

ITEM BANK SOFTWARE

To keep track of all the item information and to facilitate item selection, the Consortium prepared item bank software that managed all phases of the item development. The database stored text types and formats, item formats, contexts, and all other framework classifications, and had a *comments* field for the changes made throughout the test development. After the field trial, the item bank stored statistical information such as difficulty and discrimination indices. The selection process was facilitated by a module that let test developers easily identify the characteristics of the selected item pool. Items were regularly audited to ensure that the instruments that were developed satisfied framework specifications.

PISA 2000 MAIN STUDY

After items for the PISA 2000 Main Study were selected from the field trial pool, items and *Marking Guides* were revised where necessary, clusters and booklets were made, and all main study test instruments were prepared for dispatch to national centres. In particular, more extensive and detailed sample responses were added to the *Marking Guides* using material derived from the field trial student booklets. The collection of sample responses was designed to anticipate the range of possible responses to each item requiring expert marking, to ensure consistency in coding student responses, and therefore to maximise the reliability of marking. These materials were sent to countries on December 31, 1999.

Marker training materials were prepared using sample responses collected from field trial booklets. Double-digit coding was developed to distinguish between the *score* and the response *code* and used for 10 mathematics and 12 science items. The double-digit codes allowed distinctions to be retained between responses that were reflective of quite different cognitive processes and knowledge. For example, if an algebraic approach or a trial-and-error approach was used to arrive at a correct answer, a student could score a '1' for an item using either method, and the method would be reflected in the second digit. The double-digit coding captures different problem-solving approaches by using the first digit to indicate the score and the second digit to indicate method or approach.

Marker training meetings took place in February 2000. Members of the test development team conducted separate marker training sessions for each of the three test domains.

As in the field trial, a marker query service was established so that any queries from marking centres in each country could be directed to the relevant Consortium test developer, and consistent advice could be quickly provided.

Finally, when cleaning and analysis of data from the main study had progressed sufficiently to permit item analysis on all items and the generation of item-by-country interaction data, the test developers provided advice on items with poor measurement properties, and where the interactions were potentially problematic. This advice was one of the inputs to the decisions about item deletion at either the international or national level (*see Chapter 13*).

PISA 2000 TEST CHARACTERISTICS

An important goal in building the PISA 2000 tests was to ensure that the final form of the tests met the specifications as given in the PISA 2000 framework (OECD 1999a). For reading, this meant that an appropriate distribution across: *Text Structure, Type of Task (Process), Text Type, Context* and *Item Type* was required. The attained distributions, which closely matched the goals specified in the framework, are shown by framework category and item type[8] in Tables 2, 3, 4 and 5.

Table 2: Distribution of Reading Items by Text Structure and by Item Type

Text Structure	Number of Items	Multiple-Choice	Complex Multiple-Choice	Closed Constructed-Response	Open Constructed-Response	Short Response
Continuous	89 (2)	42	3	3	34 (2)	7
Non-continuous	52 (7)	14 (2)	4 (1)	12	9 (1)	13 (3)
Total	141 (9)	56 (2)	7 (1)	15	43 (3)	20

Note: The numbers in parentheses indicate the number of items deleted after the main study analysis.

Table 3: Distribution of Reading Items by Type of Task (Process) and by Item Type

Type of Task (Process)	Number of Items	Multiple-Choice	Complex Multiple-Choice	Closed Constructed-Response	Open Constructed-Response	Short Response
Interpreting	70 (5)	43 (2)	3 (1)	5	14 (2)	5
Reflecting	29	3	2	-	23	1
Retrieving Information	42 (4)	10	2	10	6 (1)	14 (3)
Total	141 (9)	56 (2)	7 (1)	15	43 (3)	20 (3)

Note: The numbers in parentheses indicate the number of items deleted after the main study analysis.

Table 4: Distribution of Reading Items by Text Type and by Item Type

Text Type	Number of Items	Multiple-Choice	Complex Multiple-Choice	Closed Constructed-Response	Open Constructed-Response	Short Response
Advertisements	4 (3)	-	-	-	1	3 (3)
Argumentative/Persuasive	18 (1)	7	1	2	8 (1)	-
Charts/Graphs	16 (1)	8 (1)	-	2	3	3
Descriptive	13 (1)	7	1	-	4 (1)	1
Expository	31	17	1	-	9	4
Forms	8	1	1	4	1	1
Injunctive	9	3	-	1	5	-
Maps	4	1	-	-	1	2
Narrative	18	8	-	-	8	2
Schematics	5	2	2	-	-	1
Tables	15 (3)	2 (1)	1 (1)	6	3 (1)	3
Total	141 (9)	56 (2)	7 (1)	15	43 (3)	20 (3)

Note: The numbers in parentheses indicate the number of items deleted after the main study analysis.

---

[8] Item types are explained in section "Test Scope and Test Format".

Table 5: Distribution of Reading Items by Context and by Item Type

Text Context	Number of Items	Multiple-Choice	Complex Multiple-Choice	Closed Constructed-Response	Open Constructed-Response	Short Response
Educational	39 (3)	22	4	1	4	8 (3)
Occupational	22	4	1	4	9	4
Personal	26	10	-	3	10	3
Public	54 (6)	20 (2)	2 (1)	7	20 (3)	5
Total	141 (9)	56 (2)	7 (1)	15	43 (3)	20 (3)

Note: The numbers in parentheses indicate the number of items deleted after the main study analysis.

Table 6: Items from IALS

Unit Name	Unit and Item ID
Allergies Explorers	R239Q01
Allergies Explorers	R239Q02
Bicycle	R238Q02
Bicycle	R238Q01
Contact Employer	R246Q01
Contact Employer	R246Q02
Hiring Interview	R237Q01
Hiring Interview	R237Q03
Movie Reviews	R245Q01
Movie Reviews	R245Q02
New Rules	R236Q02
New Rules	R236Q01
Personnel	R234Q02
Personnel	R234Q01
Warranty Hot Point	R241Q02
Warranty Hot Point	R241Q01

For reading it was also determined that a link to the IALS study should be explored. To make this possible, 16 IALS items were included in the PISA 2000 item pool. The IALS link items are listed in Table 6.

For mathematics an appropriate distribution across: *Overarching Concepts (main mathematical theme)*, *Competency Class*, *Mathematical Content Strands*, *Context* and *Item Type* was required. The attained distributions, which closely matched the goals specified in the framework, are shown by framework category and item type in Tables 7, 8, 9 and 10.

Table 7: Distribution of Mathematics Items by Overarching Concepts and by Item Type

Overarching Concepts	Number of Items	Multiple-Choice	Closed Constructed-Response	Open Constructed-Response
Growth and Change	18 (1)	6 (1)	9	3
Space and Shape	14	5	9	-
Total	32 (1)	11 (1)	18	3

Note: The numbers in parentheses indicate the number of items deleted after the main study analysis.

Table 8: Distribution of Mathematics Items by Competency Class and by Item Type

Competency Class	Number of Items	Multiple-Choice	Closed Constructed-Response	Open Constructed-Response
Class 1	10	4	6	-
Class 2	20 (1)	7 (1)	11	2
Class 3	2	-	1	1
Total	32 (1)	11 (1)	18	3

Note: The numbers in parentheses indicate the number of items deleted after the main study analysis.

Table 9: Distribution of Mathematics Items by Mathematical Content Strands and by Item Type

Mathematical Content Strands	Number of Items	Multiple-Choice	Closed Constructed-Response	Open Constructed-Response
Algebra	5	-	4	1
Functions	5	4	-	1
Geometry	8	3	5	-
Measurement	7 (1)	3 (1)	4	-
Number	1	-	1	-
Statistics	6	1	4	1
Total	32 (1)	11 (1)	18	3

Note: The numbers in parentheses indicate the number of items deleted after the main study analysis.

Table 10: Distribution of Mathematics Items by Context and by Item Type

Context	Number of Items	Multiple-Choice	Closed Constructed-Response	Open Constructed-Response
Community	4	-	2	2
Educational	6	2	3	1
Occupational	3	1	2	-
Personal	12 (1)	6 (1)	6	-
Scientific	7	2	5	-
Total	32 (1)	11 (1)	18	3

Note: The numbers in parentheses indicate the number of items deleted after the main study analysis.

For science an appropriate distribution across: *Processes*, *Major Area*, *Content Application*, *Context* and *Item Type* was required. The attained distributions, which closely matched the goals specified in the framework, are shown by framework category and item type in Tables 11, 12, 13 and 14.

Table 11: Distribution of Science Items by Science Processes and by Item Type

Science Processes	Number of Items	Multiple-Choice	Complex Multiple-Choice	Closed Constructed-Response	Open Constructed-Response	Short Response
Communicating to Others Valid Conclusions from Evidence and Data	3	-	-	-	3	-
Demonstrating Understanding of Scientific Knowledge	15	9	1	-	3	2
Drawing and Evaluating Conclusions	7 (1)	1	2 (1)	1	3	-
Identifying Evidence and Data	5	2	1	-	2	-
Recognising Questions	5	1	3	-	1	-
Total	35 (1)	13	7 (1)	1	12	2

Note: The numbers in parentheses indicate the number of items deleted after the main study analysis.

Table 12: Distribution of Science Items by Science Major Area and by Item Type

Science Major Area	Number of Items	Multiple-Choice	Complex Multiple-Choice	Closed Constructed-Response	Open Constructed-Response	Short Response
Earth and Environment	13	3	2	1	6	1
Life and Health	13	6	1	-	5	1
Technology	9 1)	4	4 (1)	-	1	-
Total	35 (1)	13	7 (1)	1	12	2

Note: The numbers in parentheses indicate the number of items deleted after the main study analysis.

Table 13: Distribution of Science Items by Science Content Application and by Item Type

Science Content Application	Number of Items	Multiple-Choice	Complex Multiple-Choice	Closed Constructed-Response	Open Constructed-Response	Short Response
Atmospheric Change	5	-	1	1	3	-
Biodiversity	1	1	-	-	-	-
Chemical and Physical Change	1	-	-	-	1	-
Earth and Universe	5	3	1	-	-	1
Ecosystems	3	2	-	-	1	-
Energy Transfer	4 (1)	-	2 (1)	-	2	-
Form and Function	3	1	-	-	2	-
Genetic Control	2	1	1	-	-	-
Geological Change	1	-	-	-	1	-
Human Biology	3	1	-	-	2	-
Physiological Change	1	-	-	-	-	1
Structure of Matter	6	4	2	-	-	-
Total	35 (1)	13	7 (1)	1	12	2

Note: The numbers in parentheses indicate the number of items deleted after the main study analysis.

Table 14: Distribution of Science Items by Context and by Item Type

Context	Number of Items	Multiple-Choice	Complex Multiple-Choice	Closed Constructed-Response	Open Constructed-Response	Short Response
Global	16	4	3	1	7	1
Historical	4	2	-	-	2	-
Personal	8	4	2	-	2	-
Public	7 (1)	3	2 (1)	-	1	1
Total	35 (1)	13	7 (1)	1	12	2

Note: The numbers in parentheses indicate the number of items deleted after the main study analysis.

Chapter 3: Student and School Questionnaire Development

Adrian Harvey-Beavis

OVERVIEW

A Student and a School Questionnaire were used in PISA 2000 to collect data that could be used in constructing indicators pointing to social, cultural, economic and educational factors that are thought to influence, or to be associated with, student achievement. PISA 2000 did not include a teacher questionnaire.

Using the data taken from these two questionnaires, analyses linking context and information with student achievement could address differences:

- between countries in the relationships between student-level factors (such as gender and social background) and achievement;
- between countries in the relationships between school-level factors and achievement;
- in the proportion of variation in achievement between (rather than within) schools, and differences in this value across countries;
- between countries in the extent to which schools moderate or increase the effects of individual-level student factors and student achievement;
- in education systems and national contexts that are related to differences in student achievement among countries; and
- in any or all of these relationships over time.

In May 1997 the OECD Member countries through the Board of Participating Countries (BPC) established a set of priorities and their relative individual importance to guide the development of the PISA context questionnaires. These were written into the project's terms of reference. For the Student Questionnaire, this included the following priorities, in descending order:

- basic demographics (date of birth and gender);
- global measures of socio-economic status (SES);
- student description of school/instructional processes;
- student attitudes towards reading and reading habits;
- student access to educational resources outside school (*e.g.*, books in the home, a place to study);
- institutional patterns of participation and programme orientation (*e.g.*, the student's educational pathway and current track/stream);
- language spoken in the home;
- nationality (*e.g.*, country of birth of student and parents, time of immigration); and
- student expectations (*e.g.*, career and educational plans).

The Member countries considered that all of these priorities needed to be measured in each cycle of PISA. Two other measures—in-depth measure of student's socio-economic status and the opportunity to learn—were also considered important and were selected for inclusion as focus topics for PISA 2000.

The BPC requested that the Student Questionnaire be limited in length to approximately 30 minutes.

For the School Questionnaire, the BPC established the following set of priorities, in descending order of importance:
- quality of the school's human and material resources (*e.g.*, student-teacher ratio, availability of laboratories, quality of teachers, teacher qualifications);
- global measures of school-level SES (student composition);
- school-level variables on instructional context;
- institutional structure/type;
- urbanisation/community type;
- school size;
- parental involvement; and
- public/private control and funding.

The BPC considered that these priorities needed to be covered in each cycle of PISA. Four other measures considered important and selected for inclusion as *focus* topics for the PISA 2000 School Questionnaire were listed in order of priority:
- school policies and practices;
- school socio-economic status and quality of human and material resources (same ranking as staffing patterns);
- staffing patterns, teacher qualifications and professional development; and
- centralisation/decentralisation of decision-making and school autonomy.

The BPC requested that the School Questionnaire be limited in length to approximately 20 minutes.

Questions were selected or developed for inclusion in the PISA context questionnaires from the set of BPC priorities. The choice of questions, and the development of new ones, was guided by a questionnaire framework document, which evolved over the period of the first cycle of PISA.[1] This document indicated what PISA could or could not do because of its design limitations, and provided a way to understand key concepts used in the questionnaires. As the project evolved, the reporting needs came to play an increasingly important role in defining and refining BPC priorities. In particular, the needs of the initial report and the proposed thematic reports helped to clarify the objectives of the context questionnaires.

---

[1] The questionnaire framework was not published by the OECD but is available as a project working document.

DEVELOPMENT PROCESS

THE QUESTIONS

The first cycle of the PISA data collection could not always benefit from previous PISA instrumentation to guide the development of the context questionnaires. The approach therefore was to consider each BPC priority and then scan instruments used in other studies, particularly those that were international, for candidate questions. Experts and Consortium members also developed questions. A pool of questions was developed and evaluated by experts on the basis of:
- how well questions would measure the dimensions they purported to tap;
- breadth of coverage of the concept;
- ease of translation;
- anticipated ease of use for the respondents;
- cultural appropriateness; and
- face validity.

National centres were consulted extensively before the field trial to ensure meeting a maximum number of criteria. Further review was undertaken after the consultation and a set of questions was decided upon for the field trial and reviewed for how well they covered BPC priorities. In order to trial as many questionnaire items as possible, three versions of the Student Questionnaire were used in the field trial, but only one version of the School Questionnaire. This was due partly to the small number of field trial schools and to the fact that the domains to be covered were less challenging than some in the Student Questionnaire.

While the question pool was being developed, the questionnaire framework was being revised. This was reviewed and developed on an ongoing basis for providing guidance to the theoretical and practical limits of the questionnaires.

To obtain further information about the response of students to the field trial version of the questionnaire, School Quality Monitors (*see Chapter 7*) interviewed students after they had completed them. This feedback was incorporated into an extensive review process after the field trial. For the main study, further review and consultation was undertaken involving the analysis of data captured during the field trial which gave an indication of:
- the distribution of values, including levels of missing data;

- how well variables hypothesised to be associated with achievement correlated with, in particular, reading achievement;
- how well scales had functioned; and
- whether there had been problems with specific questions within individual countries.

Experts and national centres were again consulted in preparation for the main study.

THE FRAMEWORK

The theoretical work guiding the development of the context questionnaires focused on policy-related issues.

The grid shown in Figure 3 is drawn from the work of Travers and Westbury (1989) [see also Robitaille and Garden (1989)] and was used to assist in planning the coverage of the PISA 2000 questionnaires. The factors that influence student learning in any given country are considered to be contextually shaped. Context is the set of circumstances in which a student learns and they have *antecedents* that define them in fundamental ways. While antecedents emerge from historical processes and developments, PISA views them primarily in terms of existing institutional and social factors.

A context finds expression in various ways—it has a *content*. Content was seen in terms of curriculum for the Third International Mathematics and Science Study (TIMSS). However, PISA is based on a dynamic model of *lifelong learning* in which new knowledge and skills necessary for successful adaptation to a changing world are continuously acquired throughout life. It aims at measuring how well students are likely to perform beyond the school curriculum and therefore conceives content much more broadly than other international studies.

The antecedents, context and content represent one dimension of the framework depicted in Figure 3. Each of these finds expression at a different level—in the educational system, the school, the classroom, and the student.

These four levels constitute the second dimension of the grid. The bold text in the matrix represent the core elements that PISA could cover given its design. The design permits data to be collected for seven of the 12 cells depicted in Figure 3 and marked in bold. The PISA design best covers school and student levels but does not permit collecting much information about class level. PISA does not collect information on system level directly either, but this can be derived from other sources or by aggregating some PISA variables at the school or country level.

Questionnaires were developed through a process of review, evaluation, and consultation and further refined by examining field trial data, input from interviews with students, and developing the questionnaire framework.

	Antecedents	Context	Content
System	1. Country features	2. **Institutional settings and policies**	3. Intended Schooling Outcomes
School	4. **Community and school characteristics**	5. **School conditions and processes**	6. Implemented curriculum
Class	7. Teacher background characteristics	8. **Class conditions and processes**	9. Implemented curriculum
Student	10. **Student background characteristics**	11. **Student classroom behaviours**	12. **Attained Schooling Outcomes**

Figure 3: Mapping the Coverage of the PISA 2000 Questionnaires

COVERAGE

The PISA context questionnaires covered all BPC priorities with the exception of Opportunity to Learn, which the BPC subsequently removed as a priority.

STUDENT QUESTIONNAIRE

Basic demographics

Basic demographics information collected included: date of birth; grade at school; gender; family structure; number of siblings; and birth order.

Family background and measures of socio-economic status

The family background variables included: parental engagement in the workforce; parental occupation (which was later transformed into the PISA International Socio-Economic Index of Occupational Status, ISEI); parental education; country of birth of students and parents; language spoken at home; social and cultural communication with parents; family educational support; activities related to classical culture; family wealth; home educational resources; use of school resources; and home possessions related to classical culture.

Student description of school/instructional processes

For the main study, data were collected on class size; disciplinary climate; teacher-student relations; achievement press; teacher support; frequency of homework; and time spent on homework. This group of variables also covered instruction time; sense of belonging; teachers' use of homework; and whether a student attended a remedial class, and provided data on students' marks in mathematics, science and the students' main language class[3].

Student attitudes towards reading and reading habits

Attitudes to reading and reading habits included frequency of borrowing books; reading diversity; time spent in reading; engagement in reading; and number of books in the home.

Student access to educational resources outside school

Students were asked about different types of educational resources available in the home including books, computers and a place to study.

Institutional patterns of participation and programme orientation

The programme in which the student was enrolled was identified within the Student Questionnaire and coded into the International Standard Classification of Education (ISCED) (OECD, 1999b), making the data comparable across countries.

Student career and educational expectations

Students were asked about their career and educational plans in terms of job expectations and highest education level expected.

SCHOOL QUESTIONNAIRE

Basic school characteristics

Administrators were asked about school location; school size; hours of schooling; school type (public or private control and funding); institutional structure; and type of school (including grade levels, admission and transfer policies; length of the school year in weeks and class periods; and available programmes).

School policies and practices

This area included the centralisation or decentralisation of school and teacher autonomy and decision-making; policy practices concerning assessment methods and their use; and the involvement of parents.

School climate

Issues addressed under this priority area included perception of teacher and student-related factors affecting school climate; and perception of teachers' morale and commitment.

School resources

This area included the quality of the schools' educational resources and physical infrastructure including student-teaching staff ratio; shortage of teachers; and availability of computers.

---

[3] Because of difficulties associated with operationalising the question on 'marks', this topic was an international option.

CROSS-NATIONAL APPROPRIATENESS OF ITEMS

The cross-national appropriateness of items was an important design criterion for the questionnaires. Data collected within any one country had to allow valid comparisons with others. National committees through NPMs reviewed questions to minimise misunderstandings or likely misinterpretations based on different educational systems, cultures or other social factors.

To further facilitate cross-national appropriateness, PISA used typologies designed for use in collecting international data; namely, the International Standard Classification of Education (ISCED), and the International Standard Classification of Occupations (ISCO). Once occupations had been coded into ISCO, the codes were re-coded into the International Socio-Economic Index of Occupational Status (*ISEI*), which provides a measure of the socio-economic status of occupations in all countries participating in PISA (*see Chapter 17*).

CROSS-CURRICULAR COMPETENCIES AND INFORMATION TECHNOLOGY

In addition to these two context questionnaires developed by the Consortium, there were two other instruments, available as international options,[4] that were developed by OECD experts or consultants.

THE CROSS-CURRICULAR COMPETENCIES INSTRUMENT

Early in the development of PISA, the importance of collecting information on a variety of cross-curricular skills, knowledge and attitudes considered to be central goals in most school systems became apparent. While these skills, knowledge, and attitudes may not be part of the formal curriculum, they can be acquired through multiple, indirect learning experiences inside and outside of school. From 1993 to 1996, the Member countries conducted a feasibility study on four cross-curriculum domains: Knowledge of Politics, Economics and Society (Civics); Problem-Solving; Self-Perception/ Self-Concept; and Communication Skills.

Nine countries participated in the pilot: Austria, Belgium (Flemish and French Communities), Hungary, Italy, the Netherlands, Norway, Switzerland and the United States. The study was co-ordinated by the Department of Sociology at the University of Groningen, on behalf of the OECD. The results (published in the OECD brochure, *Prepared for Life* (Peschar, 1997)) indicated that the *Problem-Solving* and the *Communication Skills* instruments required considerable investment in developmental work before they could be used in an international assessment. However, both the *Civics* and the *Self-Perception* instruments showed promising psychometric statistics and encouraging stability across countries.

The INES General Assembly, the Education Committee and the Centre for Educational Research and Innovation (CERI) Governing Board members were interested by the feasibility study and encouraged the Member countries to include a Cross-Curriculum Competency (CCC) component in the Strategic Plan that they were developing. The component retained for the first cycle of PISA was *self-concept*, since a study on civic education was being conducted at the same time by the IEA (International Association for the Evaluation of Educational Achievement) and it was decided to avoid possible duplications in this area. The CCC component was not included in the PISA General Terms of Reference, and the OECD subcontracted a separate agency to conduct this part of the study.

From various aspects of self-concept that were included in the pilot study, the first cycle of PISA involved the use of an instrument that provided a self-report on self-regulated learning, based on the following sets of constructs:
- *strategies of self-regulated learning*, which regulate how deeply and systematically information will be processed;
- *motivational preferences and goal orientations*, which regulate the investment of time and mental energy for learning purposes and influence the choice of learning strategies;
- *self-regulated cognition mechanisms*, which regulate the standards, aims, and processes of action in relation to learning;

---

[4] That is, countries could use these instruments, the Consortium would support their use, and the data collected would be included in the international data set.

- *action control strategies*, particularly effort and persistence, which prevent the learner from being distracted by competing intentions and help to overcome learning difficulties; and
- *preferences for different types of learning situations*, learning styles and social skills that are required for *co-operative learning*.

A total of 52 items was used in PISA 2000 to tap these five main dimensions.

A rationale for the self-regulated learning instrument and the items used is presented in DEELSA/PISA/BPC (98)25. This document focuses on the dynamic model of continuous lifelong learning that underlies PISA, which it describes as:

> 'new knowledge and skills necessary for successful adaptation to changing circumstances are continuously acquired over the life span. While students cannot learn everything they will need to know in adulthood they need to acquire the prerequisites for successful learning in future life. These prerequisites are both of cognitive and motivational nature. This depends on individuals having the ability to organise and regulate their own learning, including being prepared to learn independently and in groups, and the ability to overcome difficulties in the learning process. Moreover, further learning and the acquisition of additional knowledge will increasingly occur in situations in which people work together and are dependent on one another. Therefore, socio-cognitive and social competencies will have a directly supportive function.'

THE INFORMATION TECHNOLOGY OR COMPUTER FAMILIARITY INSTRUMENT

The PISA 2000 *Information Technology* (IT) or *Computer Familiarity* instrument consisted of 10 questions, some of which had several parts. The first six were taken from an instrument developed by the Educational Testing Service (ETS) in the United States. ETS developed a 23-item questionnaire in response to concerns that the *Test of English as a Foreign Language* (TOEFL), taken mostly by students from other countries as part of applying to study in the United States, may have been producing biased results when administered on a computer because of different levels of computer familiarity (see Eignor *et al.*, 1998). Since the instrument proved to be short and efficient, it was suggested that it be added to PISA. Network A and the BPC approved the idea.

Of the 23 items in the ETS instrument, 14 were used in the PISA 2000 questionnaire, some of which were grouped or slightly reworked. For example, the ETS instrument asks *How would you rate your ability to use a computer?* and the PISA questionnaire asks, *If you compare yourself with other 15-year-olds, how would you rate your ability to use a computer?*

The last four questions in the PISA questionnaire (*ITQ7* to *ITQ10*) were added to provide a measure of students' interest in and enjoyment of computers, which are not covered in the ETS questionnaire.

SECTION TWO: OPERATIONS

CHAPTER 4 { SAMPLE DESIGN

Sheila Krawchuk and Keith Rust

TARGET POPULATION AND OVERVIEW OF THE SAMPLING DESIGN

The desired base PISA target population in each country consisted of 15-year-old students attending educational institutions located within the country. This meant that countries were to include (i) 15-year-olds enrolled full-time in educational institutions, (ii) 15-year-olds enrolled in educational institutions who attended on only a part-time basis, (iii) students in vocational training types of programmes, or any other related type of educational programmes, and (iv) students attending foreign schools within the country (as well as students from other countries attending any of the programmes in the first three categories). It was recognised that no testing of persons schooled in the home, workplace or out of the country would occur and therefore these students were not included in the International Target Population.

The operational definition of an age population directly depends on the testing dates. The international requirement was that the assessment had to be conducted during a 42-day period[1] between 1 March 2000 and 31 October 2000. Further, testing was not permitted during the first three months of the school year because of a concern that student performance levels may be lower at the beginning of the academic year than at the end of the previous academic year.

The 15-year-old International Target Population was slightly adapted to better fit the age structure of most of the Northern Hemisphere countries. As the majority of the testing was planned to occur in April, the international target population was consequently defined as all students aged from 15 years and 3 (completed) months to 16 years and 2 (completed) months at the beginning of the assessment period. This meant that in all countries testing in April 2000, the national target population could have been defined as all students born in 1984 who were attending a school or other educational institution.

Further, a variation of up to one month in this age definition was permitted. For instance, a country testing in March or in May was still allowed to define the national target population as all students born in 1984. If the testing was to take place at another time, the birth date definition had to be adjusted and approved by the Consortium.

The sampling design used for the PISA assessment was a two-stage stratified sample in most countries. The first-stage sampling units consisted of individual schools having 15-year-old students. In all but a few countries, schools were sampled systematically from a comprehensive national list of all eligible schools with probabilities proportional to a measure of size.[2] The measure of size was a function of the estimated number of eligible 15-year-old students enrolled. Prior to sampling, schools in the sampling frame were assigned to strata formed either explicitly or implicitly.

---

[1] Referred to as the *testing window*.

[2] Referred to as Probability Proportional to Size (or PPS) sampling.

The second-stage sampling units in countries using the two-stage design were students within sampled schools. Once schools were selected to be in the sample, a list of each sampled school's 15-year-old students was prepared. From each list that contained more than 35 students, 35 students were selected with equal probability and for lists of fewer than 35, all students on the list were selected.

In three countries, a three-stage design was used. In such cases, geographical areas were sampled first (called first-stage units) using probability proportional to size sampling, and then schools (called second-stage units) were selected within sampled areas. Students were the third-stage sampling units in three-stage designs.

POPULATION COVERAGE, AND SCHOOL AND STUDENT PARTICIPATION RATE STANDARDS

To provide valid estimates of student achievement, the sample of students had to be selected using established and professionally recognised principles of scientific sampling, in a way that ensured representation of the full target population of 15-year-old students.

Furthermore, quality standards had to be maintained with respect to (i) the coverage of the international target population, (ii) accuracy and precision, and (iii) the school and student response rates.

COVERAGE OF THE INTERNATIONAL PISA TARGET POPULATION

In an international survey in education, the types of exclusion must be defined internationally and the exclusion rates have to be limited. Indeed, if a significant proportion of students were excluded, this would mean that survey results would not be deemed representative of the entire national school system. Thus, efforts were made to ensure that exclusions, if they were necessary, were minimised.

Exclusion can take place at the school level (the whole school is excluded) or at the within-school level. In PISA, there are several reasons why a school or a student can be excluded.

Exclusions at school level might result from removing a small, remote geographical region due to inaccessibility or size, or from removing a language group, possibly due to political, organisational or operational reasons. Areas deemed by the Board of Participating Countries to be part of a country (for the purpose of PISA), but which were not included for sampling were designated as non-covered areas, and documented as such—although, this occurred infrequently. Care was taken in this regard because, when such situations did occur, the national desired target population differed from the international desired target population.

International within-school exclusion rules for students were specified as follows:

- Educable mentally retarded students are students who are considered in the professional opinion of the school principal, or by other qualified staff members, to be educable mentally retarded or who have been tested psychologically as such. This category includes students who are emotionally or mentally unable to follow even the general instructions of the test. Students were not to be excluded solely because of poor academic performance or normal discipline problems.
- Functionally disabled students are students who are permanently physically disabled in such a way that they cannot perform in the PISA testing situation. Functionally disabled students who could respond were to be included in the testing.
- Non-native language speakers—only students who had received less than one year of instruction in the language(s) of the test were to be excluded.

A school attended only by students who would be excluded for mental, functional or linguistic reasons was considered as a school exclusion.

It was required that the overall exclusion rate within a country be kept below 5 per cent. Restrictions on the level of exclusions of various types were as follows:

- School-level exclusions for inaccessibility, size, feasibility or other reasons were required to cover fewer than 0.5 per cent of the total number of students in the International PISA Target Population.
- School-level exclusions for educable mentally retarded students, functionally retarded students or non-native language speakers were required to cover fewer than 2 per cent of students.

- Within-school exclusions for educable mentally retarded students, functionally retarded students or non-native language speakers were required to cover fewer than 2.5 per cent of students.

ACCURACY AND PRECISION

A minimum of 150 schools (or all schools if there were fewer than 150 schools in a participating jurisdiction) had to be selected in each country. Within each participating school, 35 students were randomly selected with equal probability, or in schools with less than 35 eligible students, all students were selected. In total, a minimum sample size of 4 500 assessed students was to be achieved. It was possible to vary the number of students selected per school, but if fewer than 35 students per school were to be selected, then: (i) the sample size of schools was increased beyond 150, so as to ensure that at least 4 500 students were sampled, and (ii) the number of students selected per school had to be at least 20, so as to ensure adequate accuracy in estimating variance components within and between schools—an analytical objective of PISA.

National Project Managers were strongly encouraged to identify stratification variables to reduce the sampling variance.

SCHOOL RESPONSE RATES

A response rate of 85 per cent was required for initially selected schools. If the initial school response rate fell between 65 and 85 per cent, an acceptable school response rate could still be achieved through the use of replacement schools. To compensate for a sampled school that did not participate, where possible two replacement schools were identified for each sampled school. Furthermore, schools with a student participation rate between 25 and 50 per cent were not considered as a participating school for the purposes of calculating and documenting response rates. However, data from such schools were included in the database and contributed to the estimates included in the initial PISA international report. Data from schools with a student participation rate of less than 25 per cent were not included in the database.

The rationale for this approach was as follows. There was concern that, in an effort to meet the requirements for school response rates, a national centre might accept participation from schools that would not make a concerted effort to have students attend the assessment sessions. To avoid this, a standard for student participation was required for each individual school in order that the school be regarded as a participant. This standard was set at 50 per cent. However, there were a few schools in many countries that conducted the assessment without meeting that standard. Thus a *post-hoc* judgement was needed to decide if the data from students in such schools should be used in the analyses, given that the students had already been assessed. If the students from such schools were retained, non-response bias would be introduced to the extent that the students who were absent were different in achievement from those who attended the testing session, and such a bias is magnified by the relative sizes of these two groups. If one chose to delete all assessment data from such schools, then non-response bias would be introduced to the extent that the school was different from others in the sample, and sampling variance is increased because of sample size attrition.

The judgement was made that, for a school with between 25 and 50 per cent student response, the latter source of bias and variance was likely to introduce more error into the study estimates than the former, but with the converse judgement for those schools with a student response rate below 25 per cent. Clearly the cut-off of 25 per cent is an arbitrary one, as one would need extensive studies to try to establish this cut-off empirically. However, it is clear that, as the student response rate decreases within a school, the bias from using the assessed students in that school will increase, while the loss in sample size from dropping all of the students in the school will rapidly decrease.

Figure 4 provides a summary of the international requirements for school response rates.

These PISA standards applied to weighted school response rates. The procedures for calculating weighted response rates are presented in Chapter 8. Weighted response rates weight each school by the number of students in the population that are represented by the students sampled from within that school. The weight consists primarily of the enrolment size of

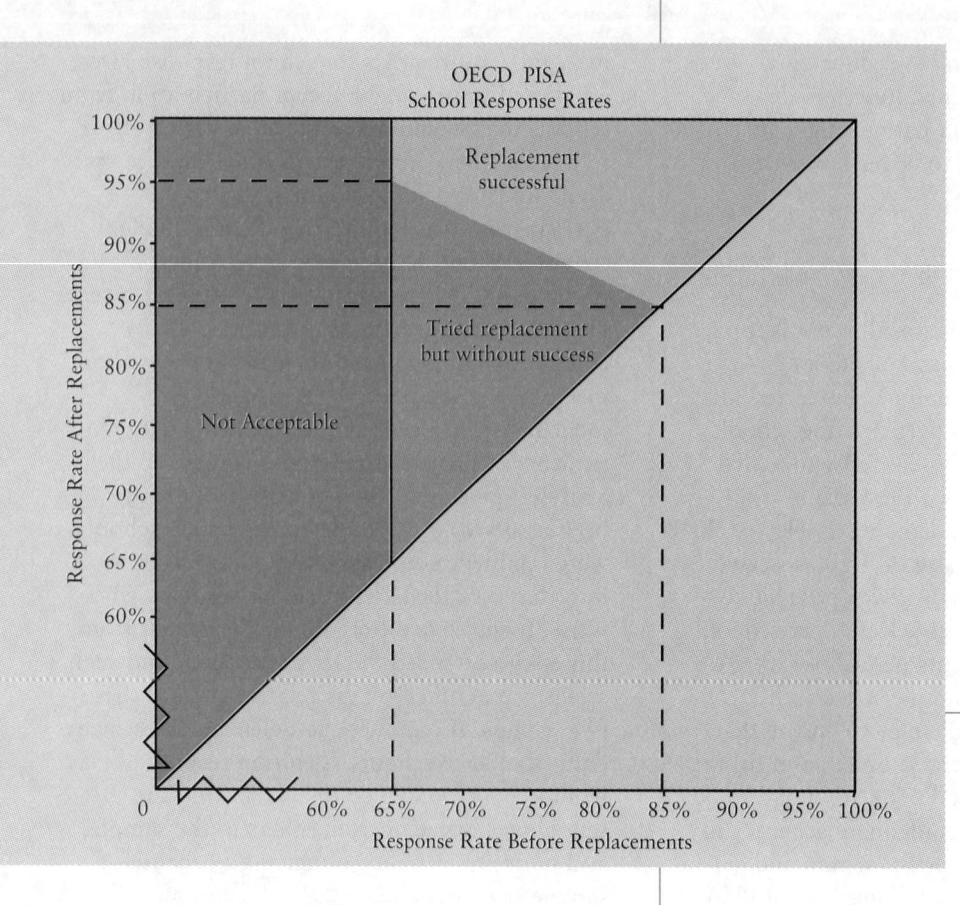

Figure 4: School Response Rate Standards - Criteria for Acceptability

15-year-old students in the school, divided by the selection probability of the school. Because the school samples were in general selected with probability proportional to size, in most countries most schools contributed equal weights, so that weighted and unweighted school response rates were very similar. Exceptions could occur in countries that had explicit strata that were sampled at very different rates. However, in no case did a country differ substantially with regard to the response rate standard when unweighted rates were used, compared to weighted rates.

Details as to how the PISA participants performed relative to these school response rate standards are included in the quality indicators section of Chapter 15.

STUDENT RESPONSE RATES

A response rate of 80 per cent of selected students in participating schools was required. A student who had participated in the first part of the testing session was considered to be a participant. A student response rate of 50 per cent was required for a school to be regarded as participating: the student response rate was computed using only students from schools with at least a 50 per cent response rate. Again, weighted student response rates were used for assessing this standard. Each student was weighted by the reciprocal of his/her sample selection probability. Weighted and unweighted rates differed little within any country.[3]

MAIN STUDY SCHOOL SAMPLE

DEFINITION OF THE NATIONAL TARGET POPULATION

National Project Managers (NPMs) were first required to confirm their dates of testing and age definition with the PISA Consortium. Once these were approved, NPMs were alerted to avoid having the possible drift in the assessment period lead to an unapproved definition of the national target population

Every NPM was required to define and describe his/her country's *national* desired target

---

[3] After students from schools with below 50 per cent student response were removed from the calculations.

population and explain how and why it might deviate from the international target population. Any hardships in accomplishing complete coverage were specified, discussed and approved or not, in advance. Where the national desired target population deviated from full national coverage of all eligible students, the deviations were described and enrolment data provided to measure how much coverage was reduced.

School-level and within-school exclusions from the national desired target population resulted in a *national defined* target population corresponding to the population of students recorded on each country's school sampling frame. Schools were usually excluded for practical reasons such as increased survey costs or complexity in the sample design and/or difficult test conditions. They could be excluded, depending on the percentage of 15-year-old students involved, if they were geographically inaccessible (but not part of a region omitted from the national desired target population), or extremely small, or if it was not feasible to administer the PISA assessment. These difficulties were mainly addressed by modifying the sample design to reduce the number of such schools selected rather than to exclude them, and exclusions from the national desired target population were held to a minimum and were almost always below 0.5 per cent. Otherwise, countries were instructed to include the schools but to administer the PISA SE booklet[4], consisting of a subset of the easier PISA assessment items.

Within-school, or student-level, exclusions were generally expected to be less than 2.5 per cent in each country, allowing an overall level of exclusions within a country to be no more than 5 per cent. Because definitions of within-school exclusions could vary from country to country, however, NPMs were asked to adapt the following rules to make them workable in their country but still to code them according to the PISA international coding scheme.

Within participating schools, all eligible students (*i.e.*, born within the defined time period, regardless of grade) were to be listed. From this, either a sample of 35 students was randomly selected or all students were selected if there were fewer than 35 15-year-olds. The lists had to include sampled students deemed to meet one of the categories for exclusion, and a variable maintained to briefly describe the reason for exclusion. This made it possible to estimate the size of the within-school exclusions from the sample data.

It was understood that the exact extent of within-school exclusions would not be known until the within-school sampling data were returned from participating schools, and sampling weights computed. Country participant projections for within-school exclusions provided before school sampling were known to be estimates.

NPMs were made aware of the distinction between within-school exclusions and non-response. Students who could not take the achievement tests because of a permanent condition were to be excluded and those with a temporary impairment at the time of testing, such as a broken arm, were treated as non-respondents along with other *absent* sampled students.

Exclusions by country participant are documented in Chapter 12 in Section 4.

THE SAMPLING FRAME

All NPMs were required to construct a school sampling frame to correspond to their national defined target population. This was defined by the manual as a frame that would provide complete coverage of the national defined target population without being contaminated by incorrect or duplicate entries or entries referring to elements that were not part of the defined target population. Initially, this list was to include any school with 15-year-old students, even those who might later be excluded. The quality of the sampling frame directly effects the survey results through the schools' probabilities of selection and therefore their weights and the final survey estimates. NPMs were therefore advised to be very careful in constructing their frames, while realising that the frame depends largely on the availability of appropriate information about schools and students.

All but three countries used school-level sampling frames as their first stage of sample selection. The *Sampling Manual* indicated that the quality of sampling frames for both two and

---

[4] The SE booklet, also referred to as Booklet 0, was described in the section on test design in Chapter 2.

three-stage designs would largely depend on the accuracy of the approximate enrolment of 15-year-olds available (*ENR*) for each first-stage sampling unit. A suitable *ENR* value was a critical component of the sampling frames since selection probabilities were based on it for both two and three-stage designs. The best *ENR* for PISA would have been the number of currently enrolled 15-year-old students. Current enrolment data, however, were rarely available at the time of sampling, which meant using alternatives. Most countries used the first option from the best alternatives given as follows:

- student enrolment in the target age category (15-year-olds) from the most recent year of data available;
- if 15-year-olds tend to be enrolled in two or more grades, and the proportions of students who are 15 in each grade are approximately known, the 15-year-old enrolment can be estimated by applying these proportions to the corresponding grade-level enrolments;
- the grade enrolment of the modal grade for 15-year-olds; or
- total student enrolment, divided by the number of grades in the school.

The *Sampling Manual* noted that if reasonable estimates of *ENR* did not exist or if the available enrolment data were too out of date, schools might have to be selected with equal probabilities. This situation did not occur for any country.

Besides *ENR* values, NPMs were instructed that each school entry on the frame should include at minimum:

- school identification information, such as a unique numerical national identification, and contact information such as name, address and phone number; and
- coded information about the school, such as region of country, school type and extent of urbanisation, which could be used as stratification variables.[5]

As noted, three-stage designs and area-level sampling frames were used by three countries where a comprehensive national list of schools was not available and could not be constructed without undue burden, or where the procedures for administering the test required that the schools be selected in geographic clusters. As a consequence, area-level sampling frames introduced an additional stage of frame creation and sampling (called the first stage of sampling) before actually sampling schools (the second stage of sampling). Although generalities about three-stage sampling and using an area-level sampling frame were outlined in the *Sampling Manual* (for example that there should be at least 80 first-stage units and about half of them needed to be sampled), NPMs were also instructed in the *Sampling Manual* that the more detailed procedures outlined there for the general two-stage design could easily be adapted to the three-stage design. NPMs using a three-stage design were also asked to notify the Consortium and received additional support in using an area-level sampling frame. The countries that used a three-stage design were Poland, the Russian Federation and the United States. Germany also used a three-stage design but only in two of its explicit data.

STRATIFICATION

Prior to sampling, schools were to be ordered, or stratified, in the sampling frame. Stratification consists of classifying schools into *like* groups according to some variables—referred to as stratification variables. Stratification in PISA was used for the following reasons:

- to improve the efficiency of the sample design, thereby making the survey estimates more reliable;
- to apply different sample designs, such as disproportionate sample allocations, to specific groups of schools, such as those in states, provinces, or other regions;
- to ensure that all parts of a population were included in the sample; and
- to ensure adequate representation of specific groups of the target population in the sample.

There were two types of stratification possible: explicit and implicit. Explicit stratification consists of building separate school lists, or sampling frames, according to the set of explicit stratification variables under consideration. Implicit stratification consists essentially of sorting the schools within each explicit stratum by a set of implicit stratification variables. This type of stratification is a very simple way of ensuring a strictly proportional sample allocation of schools across all implicit strata. It

---

[5] Variables used for dividing the population into mutually exclusive groups so as to improve the precision of sample-based estimates.

can also lead to improved reliability of survey estimates, provided that the implicit stratification variables being considered are correlated with PISA achievement (at the school level). Guidelines were provided on how to go about choosing stratification variables.

Table 15 provides the explicit stratification variables used by each country, as well as the number of explicit strata, and the variables and their number of levels used for implicit stratification.[6]

---

[6] As countries were requested to sort the sampling frame by school size, school size was also an implicit stratification variable, though it is not listed in Table 15. A variable used for stratification purposes is not necessarily included in the PISA data files.

Table 15: Stratification Variables

Country	Explicit Stratification Variables	Number of Explicit Strata	Implicit Stratification Variables
Australia	State/Territory (8); Sector (3)	24	Metropolitan/Country (2)
Austria	School Type (20)	19	School Identification Number (State, district, school)
Belgium (Fl.)	School Type (5)	5	Within strata 1-3: Combinations of School Track (8); Organised by: Private/Province/State/Local Authority/Other
Belgium (Fr.)	School Size (3); Special Education	4	Proportion of Over-Age Students
Brazil	School Grade (grades 5-10, 5-6 only, 7-10) and Urbanisation	3	Public/Private (2); Region (5); Score Range (5)
Canada	Province (10); Language(3); School Size (5)	49	Public/Private (2); Urban/Rural (2)
Czech Republic	School Type (6); School Size (4)	24	None
Denmark	School Size (3)	3	School Type (4); County (15)
England	School Size (2)	2	Very small schools: School type (2); Region (4) Other schools: School Type (3); Exam results: LEA schools (6), Grant Maintained schools (3) or Coeducational status in Independent schools (3); Region (4)
Finland	Region (6); Urban/Rural (2)	11	None
France	Type of school for large schools (4); Very small schools; Moderately small schools	6	None
Germany	Federal State (16); School Type (7)	73	For Special Education and Vocational Schools: Federal State (16)
Greece	Region (10); Public/Private (2)	20	School Type (3)
Hungary	School Type (5)	2	Region (20)
Iceland	Urban/Rural (2); School Size (4)	8	None

Table 15 (cont.)

Country	Explicit Stratification Variables	Number of Explicit Strata	Implicit Stratification Variables
Ireland	School Size (3)	3	School Type (3); School Gender Composition (3)
Italy	School Type (2); School Size (3); School Programme (4)	21	Area (5)
Latvia	School Size (3)	3	Urbanisation (3); School Type (5)
Korea	School Type and Urbanisation	10	Administrative Units (16)
Japan	Public/Private (2); School Programme (2)	4	None
Liechtenstein	Public/Private (2)	2	None
Luxembourg	None	1	None
Mexico	School Size (3)	3	School Type for Lower Secondary (4); School Type for Upper Secondary (3)
Netherlands	None	1	School Track (5)
New Zealand	School Size (3)	3	Public/Private (2); School Gender Composition (3); Socio-Economic Status (3); Urban/Rural (2)
Northern Ireland	None	1	School Type (3); Exam Results: Secondary (4), Grammar (2); Region (5)
Norway	School Size/School Type (5)	5	None
Poland	Type of School (4)	4	Type of *Gmina* (Region) (4)
Portugal	School Size (2)	2	Public/Private (2); Region (7); Index of Social Development (4)
Russian Federation	Region (45); Small Schools (2)	47	School Programme (2); Urbanisation (6)
Scotland	Public/Private (2)	2	For Public Schools: Average School Achievement (5)
Spain	Community (17); Public/Private (2)	34	Geographic unit in some communities; Population size in others
Sweden	Public (1); Private (3); Community Group for Public Schools (5); Secondary Schools (1)	10	Private schools: Community Group (9); Public schools: Income Quartile (4); Secondary Schools: Geographic Area (22)
Switzerland	Area and Language (11); Public/Private (2); School Programme (4); Has grade 9 or not (2); School Size (3)	27	National Track (9); Canton (26); Cantonal Track
United States	None	1	Public/Private (2); High/Low Minority (2); Private School Type (3); Primary Sampling Unit (52)

Note: The absence of brackets indicates that numerous levels existed for that stratification variable.

Treatment of small schools in stratification

In PISA, small, moderately small and very small schools were identified, and all others were considered large. A small school had an approximate enrolment of 15-year-olds (*ENR*) below the target cluster size (*TCS* = 35 in most countries) of numbers of students to be sampled from schools with large enrolments. A very small school had an *ENR* less than one-half the *TCS*—17 or less in most countries. A moderately small school had an *ENR* in the range of *TCS*/2 to *TCS*. Unless they received special treatment, small schools in the sample could reduce the sample size of students for the national sample to below the desired target because the in-school sample size would fall short of expectations. A sample with many small schools could also be an administrative burden. To minimise these problems, procedures for stratifying and allocating school samples were devised for small schools in the sampling frame.

To determine what was needed—a single stratum of small schools (very small and moderately small combined), a stratum of very small schools only, or two strata, one of very small schools and one of moderately small schools—the *Sampling Manual* stipulated that if the percentage of students in small schools (those schools for which *ENR* < *TCS*) was:

- less than 5 per cent and the percentage in very small schools (those for which (*ENR* < *TCS*/2) was less than 1 per cent, no small school strata were needed.
- less than 5 per cent but the percentage in very small schools was 1 per cent or more, a stratum for very small schools was needed.
- 5 per cent or more, but the percentage in very small schools was less than 1 per cent, a stratum for small schools was needed, but no special stratum for very small schools was required.
- 5 per cent or more, and the percentage in very small schools was 1 per cent or more, a stratum for very small schools was needed, and a stratum for moderately small schools was also needed.

The small school strata could be further divided into additional explicit strata on the basis of other characteristics (*e.g.*, region). Implicit stratification could also be used.

When small schools were explicitly stratified, it was important to ensure that an adequate sample was selected without selecting too many small schools as this would lead to too few students in the assessment. In this case, the entire school sample would have to be increased to meet the target student sample size.

The sample had to be proportional to the number of students and not to the number of schools. Suppose that 10 per cent of students attend moderately small schools, 10 per cent very small schools and the remaining 80 per cent attend large schools. In the sample of 5 250, 4 200 students would be expected to come from large schools (*i.e.*, 120 schools by 35 students), 525 students from moderately small schools and 525 students from very small schools. If moderately small schools had an average of 25 students, then it would be necessary to include 21 moderately small schools in the sample. If the average size of very small schools was 10 students, then 52 very small schools would be needed in the sample and the school sample size would be equal to 193 schools rather than 150.

To balance the two objectives of selecting an adequate sample of explicitly stratified small schools, a procedure was recommended that assumes identifying strata of both very small and moderately small schools. The underlying idea is to under-sample by a factor of two the very small school stratum and to increase proportionally the size of the large school strata. When there was just a single small school stratum, the procedure was modified by ignoring the parts concerning very small schools. The formulae below also assume a school sample size of 150 and a student sample size of 5 250.

- *Step 1:* From the complete sampling frame, find the proportions of total *ENR* that come from very small schools (*P*), moderately small schools (*Q*), and larger schools (those with *ENR* of at least TCS) (*R*). Thus $P + Q + R = 1$.

- *Step 2:* Calculate the figure *L*, where $L = 1 - (P/2)$. Thus *L* is a positive number slightly less than 1.0.

- *Step 3:* The minimum sample size for larger schools is equal to $150 \times (R/L)$, rounded to the nearest integer. It may need to be enlarged because of national considerations, such as the need to achieve minimum sample sizes for geographic regions or certain school types.

- *Step 4:* Calculate the mean value of *ENR* for moderately small schools (*MENR*), and for very small schools (*VENR*). *MENR* is a number in the range of *TCS*/2 to *TCS*, and *VENR* is a number no greater than *TCS*/2.

- *Step 5:* The number of schools that must be sampled from the stratum of moderately small schools is given by: (5 250 x *Q*)/(*L* x *MENR*)

- *Step 6:* The number of schools that must be sampled from the stratum of very small schools is given by: (2 625 x *P*)/(*L* x *VENR*).

To illustrate the steps, suppose that in participant country X, the *TCS* is equal to 35, with 0.1 of the total enrolment of 15-year-olds in moderately small schools and in very small schools. Suppose that the average enrolment in moderately small schools is 25 students, and in very small schools it is 10 students. Thus *P* = 0.1, *Q* = 0.1, *R* = 0.8, *MENR* = 25 and *VENR* = 10.

From *Step 2*, *L* = 0.95, then (*Step 3*) the sample size of larger schools must be at least 150 x (0.80/0.95) = 126.3. That is, at least 126 of the larger schools must be sampled. From *Step 5*, the number of moderately small schools required is (5 250 x 0.1)/(0.95 x 25) = 22.1 —i.e., 22 schools. From *Step 6*, the number of very small schools required is (2 625 x 0.1)/(0.95 x 10) = 27.6— *i.e.*, 28 schools.

This gives a total sample size of 126 + 22 2 28 = 176 schools, rather than just 150, or 193 as calculated above. Before considering school and student non-response, the larger schools will yield a sample of 126 x 35 = 4 410 students. The moderately small schools will give an initial sample of approximately 22 x 25 = 550 students, and very small schools will give an initial sample size of approximately 28 x 10 = 280 students. The total initial sample size of students is therefore 4 410 + 550 + 280 = 5 240.

ASSIGNING A MEASURE OF SIZE TO EACH SCHOOL

For the probability proportional to size sampling method used for PISA, a measure of size (*MOS*) derived from *ENR* was established for each school on the sampling frame. Where no explicit stratification of very small schools was required *or* if small schools (including very small schools) were separately stratified because school size was an explicit stratification variable and they did not account for 5 per cent or more of the target population, NPMs were asked to construct the *MOS* as: *MOS* = max(*ENR*,*TCS*).

The measure of size was therefore equal to the enrolment estimate, unless it was less than the *TCS*, in which case it was set equal to the target cluster size. In most countries, *TCS* = 35 so that the *MOS* was equal to *ENR* or 35, whichever was larger.

When an explicit stratum of very small schools (schools with ENR less than or equal to *TCS*/2) was required, the MOS for each very small school was set equal to *TCS*/2. As sample schools were selected according to their size (PPS), setting the measure of size of small schools to 35 is equivalent to drawing a simple, random sample of small schools.

SCHOOL SAMPLE SELECTION
Sorting the sampling frame

The *Sampling Manual* indicated that, prior to selecting schools from the school sampling frame, schools in each explicit stratum were to be sorted by variables chosen for implicit stratification and finally by the *ENR* value within each implicit stratum. The schools were first to be sorted by the first implicit stratification variable, then by the second implicit stratification variable within the levels of the first sorting variable, and so on, until all implicit stratification variables were exhausted. This gave a cross-classification structure of cells, where each cell represented one implicit stratum on the school sampling frame. NPMs were to alternate the sort order between implicit strata, from high to low and then low to high, etc., through all implicit strata within an explicit stratum.

School sample allocation over explicit strata

The total number of schools to be sampled in each country needed to be allocated among the explicit strata so that the expected proportion of students in the sample from each explicit stratum was approximately the same as the population proportions of eligible students in each corresponding explicit stratum. There were two exceptions. If an explicit stratum of very small schools was required, students in them had smaller percentages in the sample than those in the population. To compensate for the resulting loss of sample, the large school strata had slightly higher percentages in the sample than the corresponding population percentages. The other exception occurred if only one school was allocated to any explicit stratum. In these cases, NPMs were requested to allocate two schools for selection in the stratum.

Determining which schools to sample

The Probability Proportional to Size (PPS) systematic sampling method used in PISA first required the computation of a sampling interval for each explicit stratum. This calculation involved the following steps:
- recording the total measure of size, S, for all schools in the sampling frame for each specified explicit stratum;
- recording the number of schools, D, to be sampled from the specified explicit stratum, which was the number allocated to the explicit stratum;
- calculating the sampling interval, I, as follows: $I = S/D$; and
- recording the sampling interval, I, to four decimal places.

Next, a random number (drawn from a uniform distribution) had to be selected for each explicit stratum. The generated random number (RN) was to be a number between 0 and 1 and was to be recorded to four decimal places.

The next step in the PPS selection method in each explicit stratum was to calculate selection numbers—one for each of the D schools to be selected in the explicit stratum. Selection numbers were obtained using the following method:
- obtaining the first selection number by multiplying the sampling interval, I, by the random number, RN. This first selection number was used to identify the first sampled school in the specified explicit stratum;
- obtaining the second selection number by simply adding the sampling interval, I, to the first selection number. The second selection number was used to identify the second sampled school; and
- continuing to add the sampling interval, I, to the previous selection number to obtain the next selection number. This was done until all specified line numbers (1 through D) had been assigned a selection number.

Thus, the first selection number in an explicit stratum was $RN \times I$, the second selection number was $(RN \times I) + I$, the third selection number was $(RN \times I) + I + I$, and so on.

Selection numbers were generated independently for each explicit stratum, with a new random number selected for each explicit stratum.

Identifying the sampled schools

The next task was to compile a cumulative measure of size in each explicit stratum of the school sampling frame that determined which schools were to be sampled. Sampled schools were identified as follows.

Let Z denote the first selection number for a particular explicit stratum. It was necessary to find the first school in the sampling frame where the cumulative MOS equalled or exceeded Z. This was the first sampled school. In other words, if C_s was the cumulative MOS of a particular school S in the sampling frame and $C_{(s-1)}$ was the cumulative MOS of the school immediately preceding it, then the school in question was selected if: C_s was greater than or equal to Z, and $C_{(s-1)}$ was strictly less than Z. Applying this rule to all selection numbers for a given explicit stratum generated the original sample of schools for that stratum.

Identifying replacement schools

Each sampled school in the main survey was assigned two replacement schools from the sampling frame, identified as follows. For each sampled school, the schools immediately preceding and following it in the explicit stratum were designated as its replacement schools. The school immediately following the sampled school was designated as the first replacement and labelled R_1, while the school immediately preceding the sampled school was designated as the second replacement and labelled R_2. The *Sampling Manual* noted that in small countries, there could be problems when trying to identify two replacement schools for each sampled school. In such cases, a replacement school was allowed to be the potential replacement for two sampled schools (a first replacement for the preceding school, and a second replacement for the following school), but an actual replacement for only one school. Additionally, it may have been difficult to assign replacement schools for some very large sampled schools because the sampled schools appeared very close to each other in the sampling frame. There were times when NPMs were only able to assign a single replacement school, or even none, when two consecutive schools in the sampling frame were sampled.

Exceptions were allowed if a sampled school happened to be the last school listed in an explicit stratum. In this case the two schools immediately preceding it were designated as replacement schools, or the first school listed in an explicit stratum, in which case the two schools immediately following it were designated replacement schools.

Assigning school identifiers

To keep track of sampled and replacement schools in the PISA database, each was assigned a unique, three-digit school code and two-digit stratum code (corresponding to the explicit strata) sequentially numbered starting with one within each explicit stratum. For example, if 150 schools are sampled from a single explicit stratum, they are assigned identifiers from 001 to 150. First replacement schools in the main survey are assigned the school identifier of their corresponding sampled schools, incremented by 200. For example, the first replacement school for sampled school 023 is assigned school identifier 223. Second replacement schools in the main survey are assigned the school identifier of their corresponding sampled schools, but incremented by 400. For example, the second replacement school for sampled school 136 took the school identifier 536.

Tracking sampled schools

NPMs were encouraged to make every effort to confirm the participation of as many sampled schools as possible to minimise the potential for non-response biases. They contacted replacement schools after all contacts with sampled schools were made. Each sampled school that did not participate was replaced if possible. If both an original school and a replacement participated, only the data from the original school were included in the weighted data.

Monitoring the School Sample

All countries had the option of having their school sample selected by the Consortium. Belgium (Fl.), Belgium (Fr.), Latvia, Norway, Portugal and Sweden took this option. They were required to submit sampling forms 1 (time of testing and age definition), 2 (national desired target population), 3 (national defined target population), 4 (sampling frame description), 5 (excluded schools), 7 (stratification), 11 (school sampling frame) and 12 (school tracking form). The Consortium completed and returned the others (forms 6, 8, 9 and 10).

For each country drawing its own sample, the target population definition, the levels of exclusions, the school sampling procedures, and the school participation rates were monitored by 12 sampling forms submitted to the Consortium for review and approval. Table 16 provides a summary of the information required on each form and the timetables (which depended on national assessment periods). (*See Appendix 9 for copies of the sampling forms.*)

Once received from each country, each form was reviewed and feedback was provided to the country. Forms were only approved after all criteria were met. Approval of deviations was only given after discussion and agreement by the Consortium. In cases where approval could not be granted, countries were asked to make revisions to their sample design and sampling forms.

Checks that were performed in the monitoring of each form follow. All entries were observed in their own right but those below are additional matters explicitly examined.

Sampling Form 1: Time of Testing and Age Definition
- Assessment dates had to be appropriate for the selected target population dates.
- Assessment dates could not cover more than a 42-day period.

Sampling Form 2: National Desired Target Population
- Large deviations between the total national number of 15-year-olds and the enrolled number of 15-year-olds were questioned.

Table 16: Schedule of School Sampling Activities

Activity	Sampling Form Submitted to Consortium	Due Date
Specify time of testing and age definition of population to be tested	1 - Time of Testing and Age Definition	At least six months before the beginning of testing and at least two months before planned school sample selection.
Define National Desired Target Population	2 - National Desired Target Population	Two months prior to the date of planned selection of the school sample.
Define National Defined Target Population	3 - National Defined Target Population	Two months prior to the date of planned selection of the school sample.
Create and describe sampling frame	4 - Sampling Frame Description	One month before final approval of the school sample is required, or two months before data collection is to begin, whichever is the earlier.
Decide on schools to be excluded from sampling frame	5 - Excluded Schools	One month before final approval of the school sample is required, or two months before data collection is to begin, whichever is the earlier.
Decide how to treat small schools	6 - Treatment of Small Schools	One month before final approval of the school sample is required, or two months before data collection is to begin, whichever is the earlier.
Decide on explicit and implicit stratification variables	7 - Stratification	One month before final approval of the school sample is required, or two months before data collection is to begin, whichever is the earlier.
Describe population within strata	8 - Population Counts by Strata	One month before final approval of the school sample is required, or two months before data collection is to begin, whichever is the earlier.
Allocate sample over explicit strata	9 - Sample Allocation by Explicit Strata	One month before final approval of the school sample is required, or two months before data collection is to begin, whichever is the earlier.
Select the school sample	10 - School Sample Selection	One month before final approval of the school sample is required, or two months before data collection is to begin, whichever is the earlier.
Identify sampled schools, replacement schools and assign PISA school identification numbers	11 - School Sampling Frame	One month before final approval of the school sample is required, or two months before data collection is to begin, whichever is the earlier.
Create a school tracking form	12 - School Tracking Form	Within one month of the end of the data collection period.

- Any population to be omitted from the international desired population was noted and discussed, especially if the percentage of 15-year-olds to be excluded was more than 2 per cent.
- Calculations were verified.

Sampling Form 3: National Defined Target Population

- The population figure in the first question needed to correspond with the final population figure on Sampling Form 2.
- Reasons for excluding schools were checked for appropriateness.
- The number and percentage of students to be excluded at the school level and whether the percentage was less than the maximum percentage allowed for such exclusions were checked.
- Calculations were verified and the overall coverage figures were assessed.

Sampling Form 4: Sampling Frame Description

- Special attention was paid to countries who reported on this form that a three-stage sampling design was to be implemented and additional information was sought from countries in such cases to ensure that the first-stage sampling was done adequately.
- The type of school-level enrolment estimate and the year of data availability were assessed for reasonableness.

Sampling Form 5: Excluded Schools

- The number of schools and the total enrolment figures, as well as the reasons for exclusion, were checked to ensure correspondence with figures reported on Sampling Form 3 about school-level exclusions.

Sampling Form 6: Treatment of Small Schools

- Calculations were verified, as was the decision about whether or not a moderately small schools stratum and/or a very small schools stratum were needed.

Sampling Form 7: Stratification

- Since explicit strata are formed to group *like* schools together to reduce sampling variance and to ensure appropriate representativeness of students in various school types, using variables that might have an effect on outcomes, each country's choice of explicit stratification variables was assessed. If a country was known to have school tracking, and tracks or school programmes were not among the explicit stratifiers, a suggestion was made to include this type of variable.
- If no implicit stratification variables were noted, suggestions were made about ones that might be used.
- The sampling frame was checked to ensure that the stratification variables were available for all schools. Different explicit strata were allowed to have different implicit stratifiers.

Sampling Form 8: Population Counts by Strata

- Counts on Sampling Form 8 were compared to counts arising from the frame. Any differences were queried and almost always corrected.

Sampling Form 9: Sample Allocation by Explicit Strata

- All explicit strata had to be accounted for on Sampling Form 9.
- All explicit strata population entries were compared to those determined from the sampling frame.
- The calculations for school allocation were checked to ensure that schools were allocated to explicit strata based on explicit stratum student percentages and not explicit stratum school percentages.
- The percentage of students in the sample for each explicit stratum had to be close to the percentage in the population for each stratum (very small schools strata were an exception since under-sampling was allowed).
- The overall number of schools to be sampled was checked to ensure that at least 150 schools would be sampled.
- The overall number of students to be sampled was checked to ensure that at least 5 250 students would be sampled.

Sampling Form 10: School Sample Selection

- All calculations were verified.
- Particular attention was paid to the four decimal places that were required for both the sampling interval and the random number.

Sampling Form 11: School Sampling Frame

- The frame was checked for proper sorting according to the implicit stratification scheme and enrolment values, and the proper assignment of the measure of size value, especially for moderately small and very small schools. The accumulation of the measure of size values was also checked for each explicit stratum. This final cumulated measure of size value for each stratum had to correspond to the 'Total Measure of Size' value on Sampling Form 10 for each explicit stratum. Additionally, each line selection number was checked against the frame cumulative measure of size figures to ensure that the correct schools were sampled. Finally, the assignment of replacement schools and PISA identification numbers were checked to ensure that all rules laid out in the *Sampling Manual* were adhered to. Any deviations were discussed with each country and either corrected or the deviations accepted.

Sampling Form 12: School Tracking Form

- Sampling Form 12 was checked to see that the PISA identification numbers on this form matched those on the sampling frame.
- Checks were made to ensure that all sampled and replacement schools were accounted for.
- Checks were also made to ensure that status entries were in the requested format.

STUDENT SAMPLES

Student selection procedures in the main study were the same as those used in the field trial. Student sampling was generally undertaken at the national centres from lists of all eligible students in each school that had agreed to participate. These lists could have been prepared at national, regional, or local levels as data files, computer-generated listings, or by hand, depending on who had the most accurate information. Since it was very important that the student sample be selected from accurate, complete lists, the lists needed to be prepared not too far in advance of the testing and had to list all eligible students. It was suggested that the lists be received one to two months before testing so that the NPM would have the time to select the student samples.

Some countries chose student samples that included students aged 15 and/or enrolled in a specific grade (*e.g.*, grade 10). Thus, a larger overall sample, including 15-year-old students and students in the designated grade (who may or may not have been aged 15) were selected. The necessary steps in selecting larger samples are highlighted where appropriate in the following steps. Only Iceland, Japan, Hungary and Switzerland selected grade samples and none used the standard method described here. For Iceland and Japan, the sample was called a grade sample because over 99.5 per cent of the PISA eligible 15-year-olds were in the grade sampled. Switzerland supplemented the standard method with additional schools where only a sample of grade-eligible students (15-year-olds plus others) was selected. Hungary selected a grade 10 classroom from each PISA school, independent of the PISA student sample.

Preparing a list of age-eligible students

Appendix 10 shows an example *Student Listing Form* as well as school instructions about how to prepare the lists. Each school drawing an additional grade sample was to prepare a list of *age* and *grade-eligible* students that included all students in the designated grade (*e.g.*, grade 10); and all other 15-year-old students (using the appropriate 12-month age span agreed upon for each country) currently enrolled in other grades.

NPMs were to use the Student Listing Form as shown in the Appendix 10 example but could develop their own instructions. The following were considered important:

- Age-eligible students were all students born in 1984 (or the appropriate 12-month age span agreed upon for the country).
- The list was to include students who might not be tested due to a disability or limited language proficiency.
- Students who could not be tested were to be excluded from the assessment after the student sample was selected.
- It was suggested that schools retain a copy of the list in case the NPM had to call the school with questions.
- A computer list was to be up-to-date at the time of sampling rather than prepared at the beginning of the school year.

Students were identified by their unique student identification numbers.

Selecting the student sample

Once NPMs received the list of eligible students from a school, the student sample was to be selected and the list of selected students (*i.e.*, the

Student Tracking Form) returned to the school. NPMs were encouraged to use KeyQuest®, the PISA sampling software, to select the student samples. Alternatively, they were to undertake the steps that follow.

Verifying student lists

Student lists were checked to confirm a 1984 (or within the agreed-upon time span) year of birth or grade specified by the NPM (if grade sampling took place) and when this was not the case, the students name was crossed out. The schools were contacted regarding any questions or discrepancies. Students not born in 1984 (or within the agreed-upon time span, or grade if grade sampling was to be done) were to be deleted from the list (after confirming with the school). Duplicates were deleted from the list before sampling.

Numbering students on the list

Using the line number column on the Student Listing Form (or the margin if using another list), eligible students on the list were numbered consecutively for each school. The numbering was checked for repetition or ellipses, and corrected before the student sample was selected.

Computing the sampling interval and random start

After verifying the list, the total number of 15-year-old students (born in 1984 or the agreed-upon time span) was recorded in Box A on the Student Tracking Form (*see Appendix 11*). This would be the same number as the last line number on the list, if no grade sampling were being done. The total number of listed students was entered in Box B. The desired sample size (usually 35) was generally the same for each school and was entered in Box C on the Student Tracking Form. A random number was chosen from the *RN* table and recorded as a four-digit decimal (*e.g.*, 3 279 = 0.3279) in Box D.

Whether or not grade sampling was being done, the sampling interval was computed by dividing the total number of students aged 15 (Box A) by the number in Box C, the planned student sample size for each school, and recorded in Box E. If the number was less than 1.0000, a 1 was recorded. If grade sampling was being done, this interval was applied to the larger list (grade and age-eligible students) to generate a larger sample.

A random start point was computed by multiplying the *RN* decimal by the sampling interval plus one, and the result was recorded in Box F. The integer portion of this value was the line number of the first student to be selected.

Determining line numbers and selecting students

The sampling interval (Box E) was added to the value in Box F to determine the line numbers of the students to be sampled until the largest line number was equal to or larger than the total number of students listed (Box B). Each line number selected was to be recorded in whole integers. Column (2) on the Student Tracking Form was used to record selected line numbers in sequence. NPMs were instructed to write an *S* in front of the line number on the original student list for each student selected. If a grade sample was being selected, the total student sample was at least as large as (probably somewhat larger than) the number in Box C, and included some age-eligible (about equal to the number in Box C) and grade-eligible students.

Preparing the Student Tracking Form

Once the student sample was selected, the Student Tracking Form for each school could be completed by the NPM. The Student Tracking Form was the central administration document for the study. When a Student Tracking Form was sent to a school, it served as the complete list of the student sample. Once booklets were assigned to students, the Student Tracking Form became the link between the students, the test booklets, and background questionnaires that they received. After the testing, the results of the session (in terms of presence, absence, exclusion, etc.) were entered on the Student Tracking Form and summarised. The Student Tracking Form was sent back to the national centre with the test instruments and was used to make sure that all materials were accounted for correctly.

The Student Tracking Form was completed as follows:
- The header of the Tracking Form was prepared with the country name, the school name and the school identifier.
- Boxes A to F were checked for completion. These boxes provided the documentation for the student sampling process.
- The names of the selected students were listed

in column (3) of the Student Tracking Form. The line number for each selected student, from the Listing Form, had already been entered in column (2). The pre-printed student number in column (1) was the student's new 'ID' number which became part of a unique number used to identify the student throughout the assessment process.

The Student Tracking Form, which consisted of two sides, was designed to accommodate student samples of up to 35 students, which was the standard PISA design. If the student sample was larger than 35, NPMs were instructed to use more than one Student Tracking Form, and on the additional forms, to renumber the pre-printed identification numbers in column (1) to correspond to the additional students. For example, column (1) of the second form would begin with 36, 37, 38, etc.

- For each sampled student, the student's grade, date of birth and sex were entered on the Student Tracking Form. It was possible for NPMs to modify the form to include other demographic variables.
- The 'Excluded' column was to be left blank by the NPM. This column was to be used by the school to designate any students who could not be tested due to a disability or limited language proficiency.
- If booklet numbers were to be assigned to students at the national centre, the booklet number assigned to each student was entered in column (8). Participation status on the Student Tracking Form was to be left blank at the time of student sampling. This information would only be entered at the school when the assessment was administered.

Preparing instructions for excluding students

PISA was a timed assessment administered in the instructional language(s) of each country and designed to be as inclusive as possible. For students with limited language proficiency or with physical, mental, or emotional disabilities who could not participate, PISA developed instructions in cases of doubt about whether a selected student should be assessed.

NPMs used the guidelines in Figure 5 to develop instructions; School Co-ordinators and Test Administrators[7] needed precise instructions for exclusions. The national operational definitions for within-school exclusions were to be well documented and submitted to the Consortium for review before testing.

Sending the Student Tracking Form to the School Co-ordinator and Test Administrator

The School Co-ordinator needed to know which students were sampled in order to notify them and their teachers (and parents), to update information and to identify the students to be excluded. The Student Tracking Form and Guidelines for Excluding Students were therefore sent about two weeks before the assessment session. It was recommended that a copy of the Tracking Form be made and kept at the national centre. Another recommendation was to have the NPM send a copy of the form to the Test Administrator with the assessment booklets and questionnaires in case the school copy was misplaced before the assessment day. The Test Administrator and School Co-ordinator manuals (see Chapter 6) both assumed that each would have a copy.

---

[7] The roles of School Co-ordinators and Test Administrators are described in detail in Chapter 6.

INSTRUCTIONS FOR EXCLUDING STUDENTS

The following guidelines define general categories for the exclusion of students within schools. These guidelines need to be carefully implemented within the context of each educational system. The numbers to the left are codes to be entered in column (7) of the Student Tracking Form to identify excluded students.

1 = Functionally disabled students. These are students who are permanently physically disabled in such a way that they cannot perform in the PISA testing situation. Functionally disabled students who can respond to the test should be included in the testing.

2 = Educable mentally retarded students. These are students who are considered in the professional opinion of the school principal or by other qualified staff member to be educable mentally retarded or who have been psychologically tested as such. This includes students who are emotionally or mentally unable to follow even the general instructions of the test. However, students should not be excluded solely because of poor academic performance or disciplinary problems.

3 = Students with limited proficiency in the test language. These are students who are unable to read or speak the language of the test and would be unable to overcome the language barrier in the test situation. Typically, a student who has received less than one year of instruction in the language of the test should be excluded, but this definition may need to be adapted in different countries.

4 = Other.

It is important that these criteria be followed strictly for the study to be comparable within and across countries. When in doubt, the student was included.

Figure 5: Student Exclusion Criteria as Conveyed to National Project Managers

CHAPTER 5

TRANSLATION AND CULTURAL APPROPRIATENESS OF THE TEST AND SURVEY MATERIAL

Aletta Grisay

INTRODUCTION

Translation errors are known to be a major cause for items to function poorly in international tests. They are much more frequent than other problems, such as clearly identified discrepancies due to cultural biases or curricular differences.

If a survey is done merely to rank countries or students, this problem can be avoided somewhat since once the most unstable items have been identified and dropped, the few remaining problematic items are unlikely to affect the overall estimate of a country's mean in any significant way.

The aim of PISA, however, is to develop descriptive scales, and in this case translation errors are of greater concern. Their interpretation can be severely biased by unstable item characteristics from one country to another. PISA has therefore implemented stricter verification procedures for translation equivalence than those used in many prior surveys. This chapter describes these procedures and their implementation and outcomes.

A number of quality assurance procedures were implemented in the PISA 2000 assessment to ensure equivalent national test and questionnaire materials. These included:
- providing two parallel source versions (in English and French), and recommending that each country develop two independent versions in their instruction language (one from each source language), then reconcile them into one national version;
- systematically adding information to the test and questionnaire materials to be translated about Question Intent, to clarify the scope and characteristics, and appending frequent Translation Notes for possible translation or adaptation problems;
- developing detailed translation/adaptation guidelines for the test material, and for revising it after the field trial, as an important part of the PISA *National Project Manager Manual*;
- training key staff from each national team on recommended translation procedures; and
- appointing and training a group of international verifiers (professional translators proficient in English and French, with native command of each target language), to verify the national versions against the source versions.

DOUBLE TRANSLATION FROM TWO SOURCE LANGUAGES

A *back translation* procedure is the most frequently used to ensure linguistic equivalence of test instruments in international surveys. It requires translating the source version of the test (generally English language) into the national languages, then translating them back to and comparing them with the source language to identify possible discrepancies.

This technique is relatively effective for detecting mistranslation or major interpretation problems (Hambleton *et al.*, in press). For example, in the original English version of one of the PISA reading texts proposed for the field trial, no lexical or grammatical clue enabled the reader to identify the main character's gender.

Many languages imposed a choice in almost every sentence in which the character occurs. The comparison of several back translations almost inevitably brings out this type of problem.

Back translation has a serious deficiency, however, which has often been pointed out. In many cases, the translation is *incorrect because it is too literally transposed*, but there is a fairly high risk that the back translation would merely recover the original text without revealing the error.

Somerset Maugham's short story *The Ant and the Grasshopper* was initially proposed as a reading text for the PISA 2000 field trial. Both translators who worked on the French source version translated the content of the underlined sentence in the following passage word for word:

> 'In this admirable fable (<u>I apologise for telling something which everyone is politely, but inexactly, supposed to know</u>) the ant spends a laborious summer gathering its winter store, while the grasshopper sits on a blade of grass singing to the sun.'

Translation 1:
> «Dans cette fable remarquable (<u>que le lecteur me pardonne si je raconte quelque chose que chacun est courtoisement censé savoir, mais pas exactement</u>), la fourmi consacre un été industrieux à rassembler des provisions pour l'hiver, tandis que la cigale le passe sur quelque brin d'herbe, à chanter au soleil. »

Translation 2:
> «Dans cette fable admirable (<u>veuillez m'excuser de rappeler quelque chose que chacun est supposé connaître par politesse mais pas précisément</u>), la fourmi passe un été laborieux à constituer des réserves pour l'hiver, tandis que la cigale s'installe sur l'herbe et chante au soleil. »

Both translations are literally correct, and would back-translate into an English sentence quite parallel to the original sentence. However, both are semantically unacceptable, since neither reflects the irony of '*politely, but inexactly supposed to know*'. The versions were reconciled and eventually translated into:

> « Dans cette fable remarquable (<u>que l'on me pardonne si je raconte quelque chose que chacun est supposé connaître – supposition qui relève de la courtoisie plus que de l'exactitude</u>), la fourmi consacre un été industrieux à rassembler des provisions pour l'hiver, tandis que la cigale le passe sur quelque brindille, à chanter au soleil. »

Both translations 1 and 2 would probably appear to be correct when back-translated, whereas the reconciled version would appear further from the original.

It is also interesting to note that both French translators and the French reconciler preferred (rightly so, for a French-speaking audience) to revert to the *cigale* [*i.e.*, *cicada*] of La Fontaine's original text, while Somerset Maugham adapted the fable to his English-speaking audience by referring to a *grasshopper* [which would have been *sauterelle* in French]. However, both translators neglected to draw the entomological consequences from their return to the original: they were too faithful to the English text and allowed a strictly arboreal insect [the cicada] to live on a *brin d'herbe* [*i.e.*, *a blade of grass*], that the reconciler replaced by a *brindille* [*i.e.*, *a twig*]. In such a case, the back translation procedure would consider *cigale* and *brindille* as deviations or errors.

A *double translation* procedure (*i.e.*, two independent translations from the source language, and reconciliation by a third person) offers significant advantages in comparison with the back translation procedure:

- Equivalence of the source and target languages is obtained by using three different people (two translators and a reconciler) who all work on the source and the target versions. In the back translation procedure, by contrast, the first translator is the only one to focus simultaneously on the source and target versions.
- Discrepancies are recorded directly in the target language instead of in the source language, as would be the case in a back translation procedure.

These examples are deliberately borderline cases, where both translators happened to make a common error (that could theoretically have been overlooked, had the reconciliation have been less accurate). But the probability of detecting errors is obviously considerably higher when three people rather than one compare the source language with the target language.

A double translation procedure was used in the Third International Mathematics and Science Study-Repeat (TIMSS-R) instead of the back translation procedure used in earlier studies by the International Association for the Evaluation of Educational Achievement (IEA).

PISA used double translation *from two different languages* because both back translation and double translation procedures fall short in that the equivalence of the various national versions depends exclusively on their consistency with a single source version (in general, English). This leads to implicitly giving more weight than would be desirable on those cultural forms related to the reference language.

Furthermore, one would wish for as purely a *semantic* equivalence as possible (since the principle is to measure access that students from different countries would have to a same meaning, through written material presented in different languages). However, using a single reference language is likely to give more importance than would be desirable to the *formal* characteristics of that language. If a single source language is used, its lexical and syntactic features, stylistic conventions and typical organisational patterns of ideas within the sentence will have more impact than desirable on the target language versions.

Other expected advantages from using two source languages included:
- The verification of the equivalence between the source and the target versions was performed by four different people who all worked directly on the texts in the relevant national languages (*i.e.*, two translators, one national reconciler and the Consortium's verifier).
- The degree of freedom to take with respect to a source text often causes translation problems. A translation that is too faithful may appear awkward; if it is too free or too literary it is very likely to fail to be equivalent. Having two source versions in different languages (for which the translation fidelity/freedom has been carefully calibrated and approved by Consortium experts) provides benchmarks for a national reconciler that are far more accurate in this respect, that neither back translation nor double translation from a single language could provide.
- Many translation problems are due to idiosyncrasies: words, idioms, or syntactic structures in one language appear untranslatable into a target language. In many cases, the opportunity to consult the other source version will provide hints at solutions.
- Similarly, resorting to two different languages will, to a certain extent, tone down problems linked to the impact of cultural characteristics of a single source language. Admittedly, both languages used here share an Indo-European origin, which may be regrettable in this particular case. However, they do represent sets of relatively different cultural traditions, and are both spoken in several countries with different geographic locations, traditions, social structures and cultures.

Nevertheless, as all major international surveys prior to PISA always used English as their source language, empirical evidence to inform on the consequences of using an alternative reference language was lacking. As far as we know, the only interesting findings in this respect were reported in the IEA/Reading Comprehension survey (Thorndike, 1973), which showed a better item coherence (factorial structure of the tests, distribution of the discrimination coefficients) between English-speaking countries than across other participating countries. In this perspective, the *double source* procedure used in PISA was quite innovative.

DEVELOPMENT OF SOURCE VERSIONS

Participating countries contributed most of the text passages used as stimuli in the PISA field trial and some of the items: the material retained in the field trial contained submissions from 18 countries.[1] An alternative source version was

---

[1] Other than material sourced from IALS, 45 units were included in the field trial, each with its own set of stimulus materials. Of these, 27 sets of stimuli were from five different English-speaking countries while 18 came from countries with 12 other languages (French 4, Finnish 3, German 2, Danish 1, Greek 1, Italian 1, Japanese 1, Korean 1, Norwegian 1, Russian 1, Spanish 1 and Swedish 1) and were translated into English to prepare the English source version, which was then used to prepare the French version.

developed mainly through double translating an essentially English *first* source version of the material and reconciling it into French.

A group of French domain experts, chaired by Mrs. Martine Rémond (one of the PISA Reading Functional Expert Group members), was appointed to review the French source version for equivalence with the English version, for linguistic correctness and for the appropriateness of the terminology used (particularly for mathematics and science material).

Time constraints led to starting the process before the English version was finalised. This put some pressure on the French translators, who had to carefully follow all changes made to the English originals. It did however make it possible for them to detect a few residual errors overlooked by the test developers, and to anticipate potential translation problems. In particular, a number of ambiguities or *pitfall expressions* could be spotted and avoided from the beginning by slightly modifying the source versions, and the list of aspects requiring national adaptations could be refined, and further translation notes could be added when a need was identified. In this respect, the development of the French source version served as a translation trial, and probably helped provide National Project Managers (NPMs) with source material that was somewhat easier to translate or contained fewer potential translation traps than it would have had if a single source had been developed.

Two additional features were embedded in both source versions to help translators. *Translation notes* were added wherever the test developers thought it necessary to draw the translator's attention to some important aspect, *e.g.*:
- Imitate as closely as possible some stylistic characteristic of the source version.
- Indicate particular cases where the wording of a question must be the same (or NOT the same) as in a specific sentence in the stimulus;
- Alert to potential difficulties or translation traps.
- Point out aspects for which a translator is expressly asked to use national adaptations.
- A short description of the Question Intent was provided for each item, to help translators and test markers to better understand the cognitive process that the test developers wished to assess. This proved to be particularly useful for the reading material, where the Question Intent descriptions often contained important information such as whether a question:
  - required a literal match between the question stem and the corresponding passage in the text, or whether a synonym or paraphrase should be provided in the question stem;
  - required the student to make some inference or to find some implicit link between the information given in various places in the text. In such cases, for example, the PISA *Translation Guidelines* (see next section) instructed the translators that they should never add connectors likely to facilitate the student's task, such as *however, because, on the other hand, by comparison*, etc., where the author did not put any (or the converse: never forget to use a connector if one had been used by the author); or
  - was intended to assess the student's perception of textual form or style. In such cases, it was important that the translation convey accurately such subtleties of the source text as irony, word colour and nuances in character motives.

PISA TRANSLATION GUIDELINES

NPMs also received a document with detailed information on:
- *PISA requirements in terms of necessary national version(s)*. PISA takes as a general principle that students should be tested in the language of instruction used in their school. Therefore, the NPMs of multilingual countries were requested to develop as many versions of the test instruments as there were languages of instruction used in the schools included in their national sample. Cases of minority languages used in only a very limited number of schools could be discussed with the sampling referee to decide whether such schools could be excluded from the target population without affecting the overall quality of the data collection.
- *Which parts of the materials had to be double translated, or could be single translated*. Double-translation was required for the

cognitive tests, questionnaires and for the optional Computer Familiarity or Information Technology (IT) and Cross-Curriculum Competency (CCC) instruments, but not for the manuals and other logistic material.
- *Instructions related to the recruitment of translators and reconcilers, their training, and the scientific and technical support to be provided to the translation team.* It was suggested, in particular, that translated material and national adaptations deemed necessary for inclusion be submitted for review and approval to a national expert panel composed of domain specialists.
- *Description of the PISA translation procedures.* It was required that national version(s) be developed by double translation and reconciliation with the source material. It was recommended that one independent translator use the English source version and that the second use the French version. In countries where the NPM had difficulty appointing competent French translators, double translation from English only was considered acceptable according the PISA standards.

Other sections of the *PISA Translation Guidelines* were more directly intended for use by the national translators and reconciler(s):
- Recommendations to prevent common translation traps—a rather extensive section giving detailed examples on problems frequently encountered when translating survey materials, and advice on how to avoid them;
- Instructions on how to use translation notes and descriptions of Question Intents included in the material;
- Instructions on how to adapt the material to the national context, listing a variety of rules identifying acceptable/unacceptable national adaptations;
- Special notes on translating mathematics and science material;
- Special notes on translating questionnaires and manuals; and
- a National Adaptation Form, to document national adaptations included in the material.

An additional section of the *Guidelines* was circulated to NPMs after the field trial, together with the revised materials to be used in the main study, to help them and their translation team revise their national version(s).

TRANSLATION TRAINING SESSION

NPMs received sample material to use for recruiting national translators and training them at the national level. The NPM meeting held in November 1998, prior to the field trial translation activities, included a training session for members of the national translation teams (or the person responsible for translation activities) from the participating countries. A detailed presentation was made of the material, of recommended translation procedures, of the *Translation Guidelines*, and verification process.

INTERNATIONAL VERIFICATION OF THE NATIONAL VERSIONS

One of the most productive quality control procedures implemented in PISA to ensure high quality standards in the translated assessment materials consisted in having a team of independent translators, appointed and trained by the Consortium, verify each national version against the English and French source versions.

Two Verification Co-ordination centres were established. One was at the Australian Concil for Educational Research (ACER) in Melbourne (for national adaptations used in the English-speaking countries and national versions developed by participating Asian countries). The second one was at cApStAn, a translation firm in Brussels (for all other national versions, including the national adaptations used in the French-speaking countries). cApStAn had been involved in preparing the French source version of the PISA material, and was retained both because of its familiarity with the study material and because of its large network of international translators.

The Consortium undertook international verifications of all national versions in languages used in schools attended by more than 5 per cent of the country's target population. For languages used in schools attended by 5 per cent or less minorities, international-level verification was deemed unnecessary since the impact on the country results would be negligible, and verification of very low frequency languages was more feasible at national level. In Spain, for instance, the Consortium took up the verification of the Castilian and Catalan test material (respectively 72 and 16 per cent of the target population), while the Spanish National Centre was responsible for verifying their Galician, Valencian and Basque test material at national level (respectively 3, 4 and 5 per cent of the target population).

For a few minority languages, national versions were only developed (and verified) in the main study phase. This was considered acceptable when a national centre had arranged with another PISA country to borrow its field trial national version for their minority (adapting the Swedish version for the Swedish schools in Finland, the Russian version for Russian schools in Latvia), and when the minority language was considered to be a dialect that differed only slightly from the main national language (Nynorsk in Norway).

A few English or French-speaking countries or communities (Canada (Fr.), Ireland, Switzerland (Fr.) and United Kingdom) were constrained by early testing windows, and submitted only National Adaptation Forms for verification. This was also considered acceptable, since these countries used national versions that were identical to the source version except for the national adaptations.

The main criteria used to recruit translators to lead the verification of the various national versions were that they were (or had):
- native speakers of the target language;
- experienced translators from either English or French into their target language;
- sufficient command of the second source language (either English or French) to be able to use it for cross-checks in the verification of the material; and
- experience as teachers and/or have higher education degrees in psychology, sociology or education, as far as possible.

All appointed verifiers met the first two requirements; fewer than 10 per cent of them did not have sufficient command of the French language to fully meet the third requirement; and two-thirds of the verifiers met the last requirement. The remaining one-third had higher degrees in other fields, such as philosophy or political and social sciences.

As a general rule, the same verifiers were used for homo-lingual versions (*i.e.*, the various national versions from English, French, German, Italian and Dutch-speaking countries or communities). However, the Portuguese language differs significantly from Brazil to Portugal, and the Spanish language is not the same in Spain and in Mexico, so independent native translators had to be appointed for those four countries.

In a few cases, both in the field trial and the main study verification exercises, the time constraints were too tight for a single person to meet the deadlines, and additional translators had to be appointed and trained.

Verifier training sessions were held in Melbourne and in Brussels, prior to the verification of both the field trial and the main study material. Attendees received copies of the PISA information brochure, *Translation Guidelines*, the English and French source versions of the material and a *Verification Check List* developed by the Consortium. When made available by the countries, a first bundle of target material was also delivered. The training session focused on:
- presenting verifiers with PISA objectives and structure;
- familiarising them with the material to be verified;
- reviewing and extensively discussing the *Translation Guidelines* and the *Verification Check List*;
- checking that all verifiers who would work on electronic files knew how to deal with some important Microsoft Word® commands (track changes, comments, edit captions in graphics, etc.) and (if hard copies only had been provided) that they knew how to use standard international proof-reading abbreviations and conventions;
- arranging for schedules and for dispatch logistics; and
- insisting on security requirements.

Verification for the field trial tests required on average 80 to 100 hours per version. Somewhat less time was required for the main study versions. Most countries submitted their material in several successive shipments, sometimes with a large delay that was inconsistent with the initially negotiated and agreed Verification Schedule. The role of the verification co-ordinators proved to be particularly important in ensuring continued and friendly contact with the national teams, maintaining flexibility in the availability of the verifiers, keeping records of the material being circulated, submitting doubtful cases of too-free national adaptations to the test developers, forwarding all last minute changes and edits introduced in the source versions by the test developers to the verifiers, and archiving the reviewed material and verification reports returned by the verifiers.

The PISA 2000 Field Trial led to the introduction of a few changes in the main study verification procedure:

- Manuals to be used by the School Co-ordinator and the Test Administrator should be included in the material to be internationally verified in order to help prevent possible deviations from the standard data collection procedures.
- Use of electronic files rather than hard copies for verifying the item pool and marking guides was recommended in order to save time and to revise the verified material by the national teams more easily and more effectively.
- NPMs were asked to submit hard copies of their test booklets before sending them to the printer, so that the verifiers could check the final layout and graphic format, and the instructions given to the students. This also allowed them to check the extent to which their suggestions had been implemented.

TRANSLATION AND VERIFICATION PROCEDURE OUTCOMES

In an international study where reading was the major domain, the equivalence of the national versions and the suitability of the procedures employed to obtain it was, predictably, the focus of many discussions both among the Board of Participating Countries (BPC) members and among national research teams. The following questions in particular were raised.

- Is equivalence across languages attainable at all? Many linguistic features differ so fundamentally from language to language that it may be unrealistic to expect equal difficulty of the reading material in all versions.
- In particular, the differences in the length of translated material from one language to another are well known. In a time-limited assessment, won't students from certain countries be at some disadvantage if all stimuli and items are longer in their language than in others, requiring them to use more time to read, and therefore decreasing the time available for answering questions?
- Is double translation really preferable to other well-established methods such as back-translation?
- Is there a risk that using two source languages will result in more rather than fewer translation errors?
- What is the real value of such a costly and time-consuming exercise as international verification? Wouldn't the time and resources be better spent on additional national verifications?
- Will the verifiers appointed by the Consortium be competent enough, when compared to national translators chosen by an NPM and working under his or her supervision?

Concerns about the value of the international verification were usually allayed when the NPMs started receiving their verified material. Although the quality of the national translations was rather high (and, in some cases, outstanding) with only very few exceptions, verifiers still found many flaws in virtually all national versions. The most frequent of them included:

- Late corrections introduced in the source versions of the material had been overlooked.
- New mistakes had been introduced when entering revisions (mainly typographical errors or subject-verb agreement errors).
- Graphics errors (keys, captions, text embedded in graphics). Access to a number of these appeared to be very difficult, partly because English words tend to be rather short, and the size of the text frames often lacked space for longer formulations. The results were sometimes barely legible.
- Layout and presentation (frequent alignment problems and font or font size discrepancies).
- Line numbers (frequent changes in the layout resulted in incorrect references to line numbers).
- Incorrect quotations from the text, mostly due to edits implemented in the stimulus without making them in question stems or scoring instructions.
- Missing words or sentences.
- Cases where a question contained a literal

match in the source versions but a synonymous match in the translated version—often due to the well-known translator's syndrome of avoiding double and triple repetitions in a text.
- Inconsistencies in punctuation, instructions to students, ways of formulating the question, spelling of certain words, and so on.

The verifiers' reports also provided some interesting indications of three types of translation errors that seemed to occur less frequently in national versions developed through double translation from the two source versions rather than through single translation or double translation from a single-source version. These included mistranslations; literal translations of idioms or colloquial expressions (loan translations); incorrect translation of questions with stems such as 'which of the following...' into national expressions meaning 'which *one* of the following...'. A cross-check with the French source version ('Laquelle ou lesquelles des propositions suivantes...') would have alerted the translator to the fact that the student was expected to provide *one or more* answers.

Based on the data collected in the field trial, a few empirical analyses could be made to explore some of the other issues raised by the BPC members and the NPMs focused on two questions. To what extent could the English and French source versions be considered 'equivalent'? Did the recommended procedure actually result in better national versions than other procedures used by some of the participating countries?

To explore these two issues, the following analyses were performed:
- Since reading was the major domain in the PISA 2000 assessment, it was particularly crucial that the stimuli used in the test units be as equivalent as possible in terms of linguistic difficulty. Length, and a few indicators of lexical and syntactic difficulty of the English and French versions of a sample of PISA stimuli, were compared, using readability formulae to assess their relative difficulty in both languages.
- The field trial data from the English and French-speaking countries or communities were used to check whether the psychometric characteristics of the items in the versions adapted from the English source were similar to those in the versions adapted from the French source. In particular, it was important to know whether any items showed flaws in all or most of the French-speaking countries or communities, but none in the English-speaking countries or communities, or *vice versa*.
- Based on the field trial statistics, the national versions developed through the recommended procedure were compared with those obtained through alternative procedures to identify the translation methods that produced fewest flawed items.

LINGUISTIC CHARACTERISTICS OF THE ENGLISH AND FRENCH SOURCE VERSIONS OF THE STIMULI

Differences in length

The length of stimuli was compared using the texts included in 50 reading and seven science or Integrated units.[2] No mathematics units were included, since they had no or very short text stimuli. Some of the reading and science units were also excluded, since the texts were very short or they had only tables.

The French version of the stimuli proved to be significantly longer than the English version. There were, on average, 12 per cent more words in French (410 words in the French stimuli on average compared to 367 in English). In addition, the average length of words is greater in French (5.09 characters per word, versus 4.83 characters per word in English). So the total character count was considerably higher in French (on average, 18.84 per cent more characters in the French than in the English version of the sampled stimuli). This did not affect the relative length of the passages in the two languages, however. The correlation between both the French and English word counts and between the French and English character count was 0.99.

Some variation was observed from text to text in the *increase* in length from English to French. There was some evidence that texts that were originally in French or in languages other than English tended to have fewer words (*Pole Sud*: 2 per cent fewer; *Shining Object*: 4 per cent fewer; *Macondo*: 5 per cent fewer) or to have

---

[2] Integrated units were explored in the field trial, but they were not used in the main study.

only minor differences (*Police*: 2.5 per cent more; *Amanda and the Duchess*: 1.2 per cent more; *Rhinoceros*: 5 per cent more; *Just Judge*: 1.6 per cent more; *Corn*: 4 per cent more).

Differences in text length and item difficulty

Forty-nine prose texts of sufficient length (more than 150 words in the English version) were retained for an analysis on the possible effects on item difficulty of the higher word count associated with translation into French. For ten of them, the French version was shorter than the English version or very similar in length (less than a 5 per cent increase in the word count). Ten others had a 6 to 10 per cent increase in the French word count. Fifteen had an increase from 11 to 20 per cent, and the remaining 14 had an increase of more than 20 per cent.

Eleven PISA countries had English or French as (one of) their instruction language(s). The English source version of the field trial instruments was used, with a few national adaptations, in Australia, Canada (Eng.), Ireland, New Zealand, United Kingdom and United States. The French source version was used, with a few national adaptations, in Belgium (Fr.), Canada (Fr.), France, Luxembourg and Switzerland (Fr.).

The booklets used in Luxembourg, however, contained both French and German material, which made it impossible to use the statistics from Luxembourg for a comparison between the French and English data. Therefore the analysis was done using the item statistics from the remaining 10 countries: six countries in the *Adaptation from English* group, and four in the *Adaptation from French* group.

In the field trial, the students answered a total of 277 questions related to the selected stimuli (five or six questions per text). The overall percentage of correct answers to the subset of questions related to each text was computed for each country in each language group. Table 17 shows the average results by type of stimuli.

In both English and French-speaking countries, the item difficulty appeared to be higher in the group of test units where the French stimuli were only slightly longer than the English version, whereas, when the French stimuli were significantly longer, it proved to be easier.

The mean per cent of correct answers was slightly higher in the English-speaking countries or communities for all groups of test units, but more so for the groups of units containing the stimuli with the largest increase in length in the French version. This group-by-language interaction was significant ($F=3.62$, $p<0.5$), indicating that the longer French units tended to be (proportionally) more difficult for French-speaking students than those with only slightly greater word count.

Table 17: Percentage of Correct Answers in English and French-Speaking Countries or Communities for Groups of Test Units with Small or Large Differences in Length of Stimuli in the Source Languages

Word Count in French versus English	English-Speaking Countries or Communities — Mean Per Cent Correct	English-Speaking Countries or Communities — Standard Deviation	French-Speaking Countries or Communities — Mean Per Cent Correct	French-Speaking Countries or Communities — Standard Deviation
French less than 5 per cent longer than English (10 units)	59.7	11.3	58.1	13.4
French between 6 and 10 percent longer than English (10 units)	63.1	13.4	59.1	15.0
French between 11 and 20 per cent longer than English (15 units)	65.0	13.7	62.1	14.1
French more than 20 per cent longer than English (14 units)	68.2	11.8	63.7	12.6

Note: N=490 (10 countries and 49 texts).

This pattern suggests that the additional burden to the reading tasks in countries using the longer version does not seem to be substantial, but the hypothesis of some effect on the students' performance cannot be discarded.

Linguistic difficulty

Readability indices were computed for the French passages, using Flesch-Delandsheere (De Landsheere, 1973; Flesch, 1949) and Henry (1975) formulae. For some 26 English texts, readability indices were computed using Fry (1977), Dale and Chall (1948) and Spache (1953) formulae.

Most of these formulae use similar indicators to quantify the linguistic density of the texts. The most common indicators, included in both the French and English formulae, are: (i) average length of words (lexical difficulty); (ii) percentage of low-frequency words (abstractness); and (iii) average length of sentences (syntactical complexity).

Metrics vary across languages, and a number of other factors—sometimes language-specific—are used in each of the formulae, which prevents true direct comparison of the indices obtained for the English and French versions of a same text. Therefore, the means in Table 18 below must be considered with caution, whereas the correlations between the English and French indices are more reliable.

The correlations were all reasonably high or very high, indicating that the stimuli with higher indices of linguistic difficulty in English tended to also have higher difficulty indices than other passages in French. That is, English texts with more abstract or more technical vocabulary, or with longer and more complex sentences, tended to show the same characteristics when translated into French.

PSYCHOMETRIC QUALITY OF THE FRENCH AND ENGLISH VERSIONS

Using the statistics from the field trial item analyses, all items presenting one or more of the following flaws were identified in each national version of the instruments:
- a DIF (*i.e.*, the item proved to be significantly easier (or harder) than in most other versions);
- fit index was too high (> 1.20); or
- discrimination index was too low (< 0.15).

Some 30 items (of the 561 reading, mathematics, and science items included in the field trial material) appeared to have problems in all or most of the 32 participating countries. Since, in these cases, one can be rather confident that the flaw had to do with the item content rather than with the quality of the translation, all related observations were discarded from the comparisons. A few items with no statistics in some of the countries (items with 0 per cent or 100 per cent correct answers) also had to be discarded. Table 19 shows the distribution of flawed items in the English-speaking and French-speaking countries or communities.

Table 19 clearly shows a very similar pattern

Table 18: Correlation of Linguistic Difficulty Indicators in 26 English and French Texts

	English Mean	English Standard Deviation	French Mean	French Standard Deviation	Correlation
Average Word Length	4.83 char.	0.36	5.09 char.	0.30	0.60
Percentage of Low-Frequency Words	18.7%	8.6	21.5%	5.4	0.61
Average Sentence Length	18 words	6.7	21 words	7.1	0.92
Average Readability Index	Dale-Chall: 32.84	Dale-Chall: 9.76	Henry: 0.496 Flesch-DL: 38.62	Henry: 0.054 Flesch-DL: 4.18	0.72 / 0.83

Table 19: Percentage of Flawed Items in the English and French National Versions

	Number of Items	Too Easy (%)	Too Hard (%)	Large Fit (%)	Low Discrimination (%)	Total Percentage of Potentially Flawed Items
Australia	532	0.4	0.0	5.6	3.0	7.7
Canada (Eng.)	532	0.0	0.6	3.4	3.6	6.6
Ireland	527	0.0	0.4	5.9	3.6	7.8
New Zealand	532	0.2	0.0	6.8	1.9	7.5
United Kingdom	530	0.0	0.0	8.9	1.5	9.4
United States	532	0.4	0.6	4.1	1.7	5.8
English-Speaking Countries or Communities	3 185	0.1	0.3	5.8	2.5	7.5
Belgium (Fr.)	531	0.0	0.6	5.6	3.8	7.9
Canada (Fr.)	531	0.0	0.2	5.6	5.6	8.9
France	532	0.2	0.9	2.8	2.4	5.3
Switzerland (Fr.)	530	0.0	0.2	3.6	6.2	8.7
French-Speaking Countries or Communities	2 124	0.4	0.4	4.4	4.5	7.7

in the two groups of countries. The percentage of flawed items in the field trial material varied from 5.8 to 9.4 per cent in the English-speaking countries or communities and from 5.3 to 8.9 per cent in the French-speaking countries or communities, and had almost identical means (English: 7.5 per cent, French 7.7 per cent; $F=0.05$, $p>0.83$).

The details by item show that only one item ($R228Q03$) was flawed in all four French-speaking countries or communities, but in none of the English-speaking countries or communities. Three other items ($R069Q03A$, $R069Q05$ and $R247Q01$) were flawed in three of four French-speaking countries or communities, but in none of the English-speaking countries or communities. Conversely, only four items had flaws in all six English-speaking countries or communities or in four or five of them, but only in one French-speaking country or community ($R070Q06$, $R085Q06$, $R088Q03$, $R119Q10$). None of the science or mathematics items showed the same kind of imbalance.

PSYCHOMETRIC QUALITY OF THE NATIONAL VERSIONS

In the countries with instruction languages other than English and French, the national versions of the PISA field trial instruments were developed either through the recommended procedures, or through the following alternative methods.[3]

- *Double translation from English, with cross-checks against French*—done in Denmark, Finland, Poland and in the German-speaking countries or communities (Austria, Germany, Switzerland (Ger.)).
- *Double translation from English, without cross-checks against French*—done in the Spanish and Portuguese-speaking countries or communities (Mexico and Spain, Brazil and Portugal).
- *Single translation from English or from French*—done in Greece, Korea, Latvia and the Russian Federation. Most of the material was single-translated from English in these countries. In Greece and in Latvia, a small

[3] Not all of these were approved.

part of the material was single-translated from French and the remainder from English.
- *Mixed methods*—e.g., Luxembourg had bilingual booklets, the French material was adapted from French, and the German material was adapted from the 'common' German version. Japan had reading stimuli double translated from English and French and the reading items and the mathematics and science material double translated from English. Italy and Switzerland (Ital.) single translated the material, one from English, the other from French to reconcile the two versions, but they ran out of time and were able to reconcile only part of the reading material. Therefore they both kept the remaining units single translated, with some checks against the version derived from the other source language.

In each country, potentially flawed items were identified using the same procedure as for the English and French-speaking countries or communities (explained above). Table 20 shows the percentage of flawed items observed by method and by country.

The results show between-country variation in

Table 20: Percentage of Flawed Items by Translation Method

Method	Mean Percentage of Flawed Items per Translation Method	Country	Total Number of Items	Percentage of Potentially Flawed Items
Adaptation from Source Version	7.6	Adapted from English	3 185	7.5
		Adapted from French	2 124	7.7
Double Translation from English and French	8.0	Belgium (Fl.)	532	9.0
		Hungary	532	7.5
		Iceland	532	7.3
		Netherlands	532	10.3
		Norway	532	7.0
		Sweden	532	7.0
Double Translation from English (with cross-checks against French)	8.8	Austria	532	5.6
		Germany	532	7.9
		Switzerland (Ger.)	532	10.5
		Denmark	532	7.5
		Finland	532	8.5
		Poland	532	12.8
Double Translation from English (without use of French)	12.1	Brazil	532	13.9
		Portugal	532	10.3
		Mexico	532	16.0
		Spain	532	8.3
Single Translation	11.1	Greece	532	9.4
		Korea	532	16.0
		Latvia	532	9.2
		Russian Fed.	532	9.8
Other (Mixed Methods)	10.3	Czech Republic	532	9.4
		Italy	532	9.2
		Switzerland (Ital.)	532	13.9
		Japan	532	13.2
		Luxembourg	532	5.6

Table 21: Differences Between Translation Methods

	B. Double Translation English and French	C. Double Translation and Checks	D. Other Methods	E. Single Translation	F. Double Translation with No Checks
A. Adapted from Sources	A>B $F=0.45$ $p=0.51$	A>C $F=1.73$ $p=0.21$	A>D $F=5.23$ $p=0.04$	A>E $F=4.24$ $p=0.06$	A>F $F=13.79$ $p=0.02$
B. Double Translation English and French		B>C $F=0.45$ $p=0.52$	B>D $F=2.27$ $p=0.17$	B>E $F=4.37$ $p=0.07$	B>F $F=7.12$ $p=0.03$
C. Double Translation and Checks			C>D $F=0.69$ $p=0.43$	C>E $F=1.58$ $p=0.24$	C>F $F=3.14$ $p=0.11$
D. Other Methods				D>E $F=0.14$ $p=0.72$	D>F $F=0.66$ $p=0.44$
E. Single Translation					E>F $F=0.19$ $p=0.68$

the number of flawed items within each group of countries using the same translation method, this indicates that the method used was not the only determinant of the psychometric quality achieved in developing the instruments. Other important factors were probably the accuracy of the national translators and reconcilers, and the quality of the work done by the international verifiers.

Significance tests of the differences between methods are shown in Table 21. These results seem to confirm the hypothesis that the recommended procedure (Method B: double translation from English and French) produced national versions that did not differ significantly in terms of the number of flaws from the versions derived through adaptation from one of the source languages. Double translation from a single language also appeared to be effective, but only when accompanied by extensive cross-checks against the other source (Method C).

The average number of flaws was higher in all other groups of countries than in those that used *both* sources (either double translating from the two languages or using one source for double translation and the other for cross-checks). Methods E (single translation) and F (double translation from one language, with no cross-checks) proved to be the least trustworthy methods.

DISCUSSION

The analyses discussed in this chapter show that the relative linguistic complexity of the reading stimuli in English and French field trial versions of the PISA assessment materials (as measured using readability formulae) was reasonably comparable. However, the absolute differences in word and character counts between the two versions were significant, and had a (modest) effect on the difficulty of the items associated with those stimuli that were much longer in the French version than in the English version.

The average length of words and sentences differs across languages and obviously cannot be entirely controlled by translators when they adapt test instruments. In this respect, it is probably impossible to develop 'true' equivalent versions of tests involving large amounts of written material. However, longer languages often have slightly more redundant morphological or syntactical characteristics, which may help compensate part of the additional burden on reading tasks, especially in test situations like PISA, with no strong requirements for speed.

No significant differences were observed between the two source versions in the overall number and distribution of flawed items.

With a few exceptions, the number of translation errors in the field trial national versions translated from the source materials remained acceptable. Only nine participants had more than 10 per cent of flawed items—compared to the average of 7.6 per cent observed in countries that used one source version with only small national adaptations.

The data seem to support the hypothesis that double translation from *both* (rather than one) source versions resulted in better translations, with a lower incidence of flaws. Double translation from one source with extensive cross-checks against the other source was an effective alternative procedure.

CHAPTER 6 { FIELD OPERATIONS

Nancy Caldwell and Jan Lokan

OVERVIEW OF ROLES AND RESPONSIBILITIES

The study was implemented in each country by a National Project Manager (NPM) who implemented the procedures prepared by the Consortium. To implement the assessment in schools the NPMs were assisted by School Co-ordinators and Test Administrators. Each NPM typically had several assistants, working from a base location that is referred to throughout this report as a 'national centre'.

NATIONAL PROJECT MANAGERS

National Project Managers (NPMs) were responsible for implementing the project within their own country. They selected the school sample, ensured that schools co-operated and then selected the student sample from a list of eligible students provided by each school (the Student Listing Form). NPMs could follow strictly defined international procedures for selecting the school sample and then submit complete reports on the process to the Consortium, or provide complete lists of schools with age-eligible students and have the Consortium carry out the sampling.

NPMs were also given a choice of two methods for selecting the student sample (*see Chapter 4*). These two methods were: (i) using the PISA student sampling software prepared by the Consortium and (ii) selecting a random start number and then calculating the sampling interval following the instructions in the *Sampling Manual*. A complete list was prepared for each school using the Student Tracking Form that served as the central administration document for the study and linked students, test booklets and student questionnaires.

NPMs had additional operational responsibilities both before and after the assessment. These included:
- hiring and training Test Administrators to administer tests in individual schools;
- scheduling test sessions and deploying external Test Administrators (the recommended model);
- translating and adapting test instruments, manuals, and other materials into the testing language(s);
- submitting translated documents to the Consortium for review and approval;
- sending instructions for preparing lists of eligible students to the selected schools;
- assembling test booklets according to the design and layout specified by the Consortium;
- overseeing printing of test booklets and questionnaires;
- maintaining ties with the School Quality Monitors appointed by the Consortium (monitoring activities are described in Chapter 7);
- co-ordinating the activities of Test Administrators and School Quality Monitors;
- overseeing the packing and shipping of all materials;
- overseeing the receipt of test and other materials from the schools, and marking and data entry;
- sending completed materials to the Consortium; and

- preparing the NPM report of activities and submitting it to the Consortium.

SCHOOL CO-ORDINATORS

School Co-ordinators (SCs) co-ordinated school-related activities with the national centre and the Test Administrators. Their first task was to prepare the Student Listing Form with the names of all eligible students in the school and to send it to the NPM so that the NPM could select the student sample.

Prior to the test, the SC was to:
- establish the testing date and time in consultation with the NPM;
- receive the list of sampled students on the Student Tracking Form from the NPM and update it if necessary, plus identify students with disabilities or limited test language proficiency who could not take the test according to criteria established by the Consortium;
- receive, distribute and collect the School Questionnaire and then deliver it to the Test Administrator;
- inform school staff, students and parents of the nature of the test and the test date, and secure parental permission if required by the school or education system;
- inform the NPM and Test Administrator of any test date or time changes; and
- assist the Test Administrator with room arrangements for the test day.

On the test day, the SC was expected to ensure that the sampled students attended the test session(s). If necessary, the SC also made arrangements for a make-up session and ensured that absent students attended the make-up session.

TEST ADMINISTRATORS

The Test Administrators (TAs) were primarily responsible for administering the PISA test fairly, impartially and uniformly, in accordance with international standards and PISA procedures. To maintain fairness, a TA could not be the reading, mathematics or science teacher of the students being assessed and it was preferred that they not be a staff member at any participating school.

Prior to the test date, TAs were trained by national centres. Training included a thorough review of the *Test Administrator Manual* (*see next section*) and the script to be followed during the administration of the test and questionnaire. Additional responsibilities included:
- ensuring receipt of the testing materials from the NPM and maintaining their security;
- co-operating fully with the SC;
- contacting the SC one to two weeks prior to the test to confirm plans;
- completing final arrangements on the test day;
- conducting a make-up session, if needed, in consultation with the SC;
- completing the Student Tracking Form and the Assessment Session Report Form (a form designed to summarise session times, student attendance, any disturbance to the session, etc.);
- ensuring that the number of tests and questionnaires collected from students tallied with the number sent to the school;
- obtaining the School Questionnaire from the SC; and
- sending the School Questionnaire and all test materials (both completed and not completed) to the NPM after the testing was carried out.

DOCUMENTATION

NPMs were given comprehensive procedural manuals for each major component of the assessment.
- The *National Project Manager's Manual* provided detailed information about duties and responsibilities, including general information about PISA; field operations and roles and responsibilities of the NPM, the SC and the TA; translating the manuals and test instruments; selecting the student sample; assembling and shipping materials; data marking and entry; and documentation to be submitted by the NPM to the Consortium.
- The *School Coodinator's Manual* described, in detail, the activities and responsibilities of the SC. Information was provided regarding all aspects, from selecting a date for the assessment to arranging for a make-up session and storing the copies of the assessment forms.
- The *Test Administrator's Manual* not only provided a comprehensive description of the duties and responsibilities of the TA, from

attending the TA training to conducting a make-up session, but also included the script to be read during the test as well as a Return Shipment Form (a form designed to track materials to and from the school).
- The *Sampling Manual* provided detailed instructions regarding the selection of the school and student samples and the reports that had to be submitted to the Consortium to document each step in the process of selecting these samples.

These manuals also included checklists and timetables for easy reference. NPMs were required to fill in country specific information in addition to adding specific dates in both the *School Co-ordinator's Manual* and the *Test Administrator's Manual*.

KeyQuest®, a sampling software package, was prepared by the Consortium and given to NPMs as one method for selecting the student sample from the Student Listing Form. Although about half did, in fact, use this software, some NPMs used their own sampling software (which had to be approved by the Consortium).

MATERIALS PREPARATION

ASSEMBLING TEST BOOKLETS AND QUESTIONNAIRES

As described in Chapter 2, nine different test booklets had to be assembled with clusters of test items arranged according to the balanced incomplete block design specified by the Consortium. Test items were presented in units (stimulus material and two or more items relating to the stimulus) and each cluster contained several units. Test units and questionnaire items were initially sent to NPMs several months before the testing dates, to enable translation to begin. Units allocated to clusters and clusters allocated to booklets were provided a few weeks later, together with detailed instructions to NPMs about how to assemble their translated or adapted clusters into booklets.

For reference, master hard copies of all booklets were provided to NPMs and master copies in both English and French were also available through a secure website. NPMs were encouraged to use the cover design provided by the OECD (both black and white and coloured versions of the cover design were made available). In formatting translated or adapted test booklets, they had to follow as far as possible the layout in the English master copies, including allocation of items to pages. A slightly smaller or larger font than in the master copy was permitted if it was necessary to ensure the same page set-up as that of the source version.

NPMs were required to submit copies of their assembled test booklets for verification by the Consortium before printing the booklets.

The Student Questionnaire contained one, two, or three modules, according to whether the international options of Cross-Curricular Competency (CCC) and Computer Familiarity or Information Technology (IT) were being added to the core component. About half the countries chose to administer the IT component and just over three-quarters used the CCC component. The core component had to be presented first in the questionnaire booklet. If both international options were used, the IT module was to be placed ahead of the CCC module.

NPMs were permitted to add questions of national interest as 'national options' to the questionnaires. Proposals and text for these had to be submitted to the Consortium for approval. It was recommended that, if more than two pages of additional questions were proposed and the tests and questionnaires were being administered in a single session, the additional material should be placed at the end of the questionnaire. The Student Questionnaire was modified more often than the School Questionnaire.

NPMs were required to submit copies of their assembled questionnaires for verification by the Consortium prior to printing.

PRINTING TEST BOOKLETS AND QUESTIONNAIRES

Printing had to be done such that the content of the instruments was constantly secure. Given that the test booklet was administered in two parts to give students a brief rest after the first hour, the second half of the booklet had to be distinguishable from the first half so that TAs could see if a student was working in the wrong part. It was recommended that this be done either by having a shaded strip printed across the top (or down the outside edge) of pages in the second half of the booklet, or by having the second half of the booklet sealed with a sticker.

If the Student Questionnaire was to be included in the same booklet as the test items, then the questionnaire section had to be indicated in a different way from the two parts of the test booklet. Although this complicated the distribution of materials, it was simpler to print the questionnaire in a separate booklet and most countries did so.

PACKAGING AND SHIPPING MATERIALS

Regardless of how materials were packaged and shipped, the following needed to be sent either to the TA or to the school:

- test booklets and Student Questionnaires for the number of students sampled;
- Student Tracking Form;
- two copies of the Assessment Session Report Form;
- Packing Form;
- Return Shipment Form;
- additional materials, *e.g.*, rulers and calculators, as per local circumstances; and
- additional School and Student Questionnaires and a bundle of extra test booklets.

Of the nine separate test booklets, one could be pre-allocated to each student by the KeyQuest® software from a random starting point in each school. KeyQuest® could then be used to generate the school's Student Tracking Form, which contained the number of the allocated booklet alongside each sampled student's name. Instructions were also provided for carrying out this step manually, starting with Booklet 1 for the first student in the first school, and assigning booklets in order up to the 35th student for the designated number of students in the sample. With 35 students (the recommended number of students to sample per school), the last student in the first school would be assigned Booklet 8. At the second school, the first student would be assigned Booklet 9, the second, Booklet 1, and so on. In this way, the booklets would be rotated so that each would be used more or less equally, as they also would be if allocated from a random starting point.

It was recommended that labels be printed, each with a student identification number and test booklet number allocated to that identification, plus the student's name if this was an acceptable procedure within the country. Two or three copies of each student's label could be printed, and used to identify the test booklet, the questionnaire, and a packing envelope if used.

NPMs were allowed some flexibility in how the materials were packaged and distributed, depending on national circumstances. It was specified however that the test booklets for a school be packaged so that they remained secure, possibly by wrapping them in clear plastic and then heat sealing the package, or by sealing each booklet in a labelled envelope.

Three scenarios, summarised here, were described as illustrative of acceptable approaches to packaging and shipping the assessment materials:

- *Country A* – all assessment materials shipped directly to the schools (with fax-back forms provided for SCs to acknowledge receipt of materials); school staff (not teachers of the students in the assessment) used to conduct the testing sessions; test booklets and Student Questionnaires printed separately; materials assigned to students before packaging for shipment; each test booklet and questionnaire labelled, and then sealed in an identically labelled envelope for shipping to the school.
- *Country B* – all assessment materials shipped directly to the schools (with fax-back forms provided for SCs to acknowledge receipt of materials); test sessions conducted by TAs employed by the national centre; test booklets and Student Questionnaires printed separately, and labelled and packaged in separately bound bundles assembled in Student Tracking Form order; on completion of the assessment, each student places and seals his/her test booklet and questionnaire in a labelled envelope provided to protect student confidentiality within the school.
- *Country C* – test sessions conducted by TAs employed by the national centre, with assessment materials for the scheduled schools shipped directly to the TAs; test and Student Questionnaires printed in the one booklet, with a black bar across the top of each page in the second part of the test; bundles of 35 booklets loosely sealed in plastic, so that their number can be checked without opening the packages; school packages opened immediately prior to the session by the TA and identification number and name labels

affixed according to the assignment of booklets pre-recorded on the Student Tracking Form at the national centre.

RECEIPT OF MATERIALS AT THE NATIONAL CENTRE AFTER TESTING

It was recommended that the national centre establish a database of schools before testing began with fields for recording shipment of materials to and from schools, tallies of materials sent and tallies of completed and unused booklets returned, and for various steps in processing booklets after the testing. KeyQuest® could be used for this purpose if desired. TAs recorded the student's participation status (present/absent) on the Student Tracking Form for each of the two test parts and for the Student Questionnaire. This information was to be checked at the national centre during the unpacking step.

PROCESSING TESTS AND QUESTIONNAIRES AFTER TESTING

This section describes PISA's marking procedures, including multiple marking, and also makes brief reference to pre-coding of responses to a few items in the Student Questionnaire. Because about one-third of the mathematics and science items and more than 40 per cent of the reading items required students to write in their answers, the answers had to be evaluated and marked (scored). This was a complex operation, as booklets had to be randomly assigned to markers and, for the minimum recommended sample size per country of 4 500 students, more than 120 000 responses had to be evaluated. Each of the nine booklets had between 20 and 31 items requiring marking.

It is crucial for comparability of results in a study such as PISA that students' responses be scored uniformly from marker to marker and from country to country. Comprehensive criteria for marking, including many examples of acceptable and not acceptable responses, were prepared by the Consortium and provided to NPMs in *Marking Guides* for each of reading, mathematics and science.

STEPS IN THE MARKING PROCESS

In setting up the marking of students' responses to open-ended items, NPMs had to carry out or oversee several steps:
- adapt or translate the *Marking Guides* as needed;
- recruit and train markers;
- locate suitable local examples of responses to use in training and practice;
- organise booklets as they were returned from schools;
- select booklets for multiple marking;
- single mark booklets according to the international design;
- multiple mark a selected sub-sample of booklets once the single marking was completed;
- submit a sub-sample of booklets for the Inter-Country Rater Reliability Study (*see Chapter 10*).

Detailed instructions for each step were provided in the *NPM Manual*. Key aspects of the process are included here.

International training

Representatives from each national centre were required to attend two international marker training sessions—one immediately prior to the field trial and one immediately prior to the main study. At the training sessions, Consortium staff familiarised national centre staff with the marking guides and their interpretation.

Staffing

NPMs were responsible for recruiting appropriately qualified people to carry out the single and multiple marking of the test booklets. In some countries, pools of experienced markers from other projects could be called on. It was not necessary for markers to have high-level academic qualifications, but they needed to have a good understanding of either mid-secondary level mathematics and science or the language of the test, and to be familiar with ways in which secondary-level students express themselves. Teachers on leave, recently retired teachers and senior teacher trainees were all considered to be potentially suitable markers. An important factor in recruiting markers was that they could commit their time to the project for the duration of the marking, which was expected to take up to two months.

The Consortium provided a *Marker Recruitment Kit* to assist NPMs in screening applicants. These materials were similar in nature to the *Marking Guides*, but were much briefer. They were designed so that applicants who were considered to be potentially suitable could be given a brief training session, after which they marked some student responses. Guidelines for assessing the results of this exercise were supplied. The materials also provided applicants with the opportunity to assess their own suitability for the task.

The number of markers required was governed by the design for multiple marking (described in a later section). For the main study, markers were required in multiples of eight, with 16 as the recommended number for reading, and eight—who could mark both mathematics and science—recommended for those areas. These numbers of markers were considered to be adequate for countries testing between 4 500 (the minimum number required) and 6 000 students to meet the timeline of submitting their data within three months of testing.

For larger numbers of students or in cases where reading markers could not be obtained in multiples of eight, NPMs could prepare their own design for reading marking and submit it to the Consortium for approval—only a handful of countries did this. For NPMs who were unable to recruit people who could mark both mathematics and science, an alternative design involving four mathematics markers and four science markers was provided (but this design had the drawback that it yielded less comprehensive information from the multiple marking). Given that several weeks were required to complete the marking, it was recommended that at least two back-up reading markers and one back-up mathematics/science marker be trained and included in at least some of the marking sessions.

The marking process was complex enough to require a full-time overall supervisor of activities who was familiar with logistical aspects of the marking design, the procedures for checking marker reliability, the marking schedules and also the content of the tests and *Marking Guides*.

NPMs were also required to designate persons with subject-matter expertise, familiarity with the PISA tests and, if possible, experience in marking student responses to open-ended items, in order to act as 'table leaders' during the marking. Good table leaders were essential to the quality of the marking, as their main role was to monitor markers' consistency in applying the marking criteria. They also assisted with the flow of booklets, and fielded and resolved queries about the *Marking Guide* and about particular student responses in relation to the guide, consulting the supervisor as necessary when queries could not be resolved. The supervisor was then responsible for checking such queries with the Consortium.

Depending on their level of experience and on the design followed for mathematics/science, between two and four table leaders were recommended for reading and either one or two for mathematics/science. Table leaders were expected to participate in the actual marking and spend extra time monitoring consistency.

Several persons were needed to unpack, check, and assemble booklets into labelled bundles so that markers could respect the specified design for randomly allocating sets of booklets to markers.

Confidentiality forms

Before seeing or receiving any copies of PISA test materials, prospective markers were required to sign a Confidentiality Form, obligating them not to disclose the content of the PISA tests beyond the groups of markers and trainers with whom they would be working.

National training

Anyone who marked the PISA main survey test booklets had to participate in specific training sessions, regardless of whether they had had related experience or had been involved in the PISA field trial marking. To assist NPMs in carrying out the training, the Consortium prepared training materials in addition to the detailed *Marking Guides*. Training within a country could be carried out by the NPM or by one or more knowledgeable persons appointed by the NPM. Subject matter knowledge was important for the trainer as was understanding the procedures, which usually meant that more than one person was involved in leading the training.

Training sessions were organised as a function of how marking was done. The recommendation was to mark by cluster, completing the marking of each item separately within a cluster before moving to the next item, and completing one cluster before moving to the next. The recommended allocation of booklets to markers assumed marking by cluster, though an alternative design involving marking by booklet was also provided.

If marking was done by cluster, then markers were trained by cluster for the nine reading clusters and four clusters for each of mathematics and science. If prospective markers had done as recommended and worked through the test booklets and read through the *Marking Guides* in advance, training for each cluster took about half a day. During a training session, the trainer reviewed the *Marking Guide* for a cluster of units with the markers, then had the markers assign marks to some sample items for which the appropriate marks had been supplied by the Consortium. The trainer reviewed the results with the group, allowing time for discussion, querying and clarification of reasons for the pre-assigned marks. Trainees then proceeded to mark independently some local examples that had been carefully selected by the supervisor of marking in conjunction with national centre staff.

Training was more difficult if marking was done by booklet. Each booklet contained either two or three 30-minute reading clusters and from two to four 15-minute mathematics/science clusters (except Booklet 7, which had four reading clusters). Thus, markers had to be trained in several clusters before they could begin marking a booklet.

It was recommended that prospective markers be informed at the beginning of training that they would be expected to apply the *Marking Guides* with a high level of consistency, and that reliability checks would be made frequently by table leaders and the overall supervisor as part of the marking process.

Ideally, table leaders were trained before the larger groups of markers since they needed to be thoroughly familiar with both the test items and the *Marking Guides*. The marking supervisor explained these to the point where the table leaders could mark and reach a consensus on the selected local examples to be used later with the larger group of trainees. They also participated in the training sessions with the rest of the markers, partly to strengthen their own knowledge of the *Marking Guides* and partly to assist the supervisor in discussions with the trainees of their pre-agreed marks to the sample items.

Table leaders received additional training in the procedures for monitoring the consistency with which markers applied the criteria.

Length of marking sessions

Marking responses to open-ended items is mentally demanding, requiring a level of concentration that cannot be maintained for long periods of time. It was therefore recommended that markers work for no more than six hours per day on actual marking, and take two or three breaks for coffee and lunch. Table leaders needed to work longer on most days so that they had adequate time for their monitoring activities.

LOGISTICS PRIOR TO MARKING
Sorting booklets

When booklets arrived back at the national centre, they were first tallied and checked against the session participation codes on the Student Tracking Form. Unused and used booklets were separated; used booklets were sorted by student identification number if they had not been sent back in that order and then were separated by booklet number; and school bundles were kept in school identification order, filling in sequence gaps as packages arrived. Student Tracking Forms were carefully filed in ring binders in school identification order. If the school identification number order did not correspond with the alphabetical order of school names, it was recommended that an index of school name against school identification be prepared and kept with the binders.

Because of the time frame within which countries had to have all their marking done and data submitted to the Consortium, it was usually impossible to wait for all materials to reach the national centre before beginning to mark. In order to manage the design for allocating booklets to markers, however, it was recommended to start marking only when at least half of the booklets had been returned.

Selection of booklets for multiple marking

The Technical Advisory Group decided to set aside in each country 48 each of Booklets 1 to 7 and 72 each of Booklets 8 and 9 for multiple marking. The mathematics and science clusters were more thinly spread in Booklets 1 to 7 than in Booklets 8 and 9. The larger number of Booklets 8 and 9 was specified to have sufficient data on which to base the marker reliability analyses for mathematics and science.

The main principle in setting aside the booklets for multiple marking was that the selection needed to ensure a wide spread of schools and students across the whole sample and to be random as far as possible. The simplest method for carrying out the selection was to use a ratio approach based on the expected total number of completed booklets, combined with a random starting point.

In the minimum recommended student sample of 4 500 students per country, approximately every tenth booklet of Booklets 1 to 7 and every seventh booklet of Booklets 8 and 9 needed to be set aside. Random numbers between 1 and 10 and between 1 and 7 needed to be drawn as the starting points for selection. Depending on the actual numbers of completed booklets received, the selection ratios needed to be adjusted so that the correct numbers of each booklet were selected from the full range of participating schools.

Booklets for single marking

Only one marker was required to mark all booklets remaining after those for multiple marking had been set aside. For the minimum required sample size of 4 500, there would have been approximately 450 of each of Booklets 1 to 7 and 430 of each of Booklets 8 and 9 in this category.

Some items requiring marking did not need to be included in the multiple marking. The last marker in the multiple-marking process marked items in the booklets set aside for multiple marking.

HOW MARKS WERE SHOWN

A string of small code numbers corresponding to the possible codes for the item as delineated in the relevant *Marking Guide* (including the code for '*not applicable*' to allow for a misprinted item) appeared in the upper right-hand side of each item in the test booklets requiring judgement. For booklets being processed by a single marker, the mark assigned was indicated directly in the booklet by circling the appropriate code number alongside the item.

Tailored marking record sheets were prepared for each booklet for the multiple marking and used by all but the last marker so that each marker undertaking multiple marking did not know which marks other markers had assigned.

For the reading tests, item codes were often just 0, 1, 9 and 'n', indicating incorrect, correct, missing and 'not applicable', respectively. Provision was made for some of the open-ended items to be marked as partially correct, usually with '2' as fully correct and '1' as partially correct, but occasionally with three degrees of correctness indicated by codes of '1', '2' and '3'.

For the mathematics and science tests, a two-digit coding scheme was adopted for the items requiring constructed responses. The first digit represented the 'degree of correctness' mark, as in reading; the second indicated the content of the response or the type of solution method used by the student. Two-digit codes were originally proposed by Norway for the Third International Mathematics and Science Study (TIMSS) and were adopted in PISA because of their potential for use in studies of student learning and thinking.

MARKER IDENTIFICATION NUMBERS

Marker identification numbers were assigned according to a standard three-digit format specified by the Consortium. The first digit had to show if the marker was a reading, mathematics or science marker (or mathematics/science), and the second and third digits had to uniquely identify the markers within their set. Marker identification numbers were used for two purposes: implementing the design for allocating booklets to markers; and in monitoring marker consistency in the multiple-marking exercises.

DESIGN FOR ALLOCATING BOOKLETS TO MARKERS

Reading

If marking was done by cluster, each reading marker needed to handle three of the nine booklet types at a time because the clusters were featured in three booklets, except for the ninth cluster, which appeared in only two of the booklets. For example, reading Cluster 1 occurred in Booklets 1, 5 and 7, which therefore had to be marked before any other items in another cluster. Moreover, since marking was done item by item, the item was marked across three booklets before the next item was marked.

A design to ensure the random allocation of booklets to reading markers was prepared based on the recommended number of 16 markers and the minimum sample size of 4 500 students from 150 schools.[1] Booklets were to be sorted by student indentification within schools. With 150 schools and 16 markers, each marker had to mark a cluster within a booklet from eight or nine schools (150 ÷ 16 ≅ 9). Figure 6 shows how booklets needed to be assigned to markers for the reading single marking. Further explanation of the information in this table is presented below.

According to this design, Cluster 1 in subset 1 (schools 1 to 9) was to be marked by Reading Marker 1 (M1 in Figure 6), Cluster 1 in subset 2 (schools 10 to 18) was to be marked by Reading Marker 2 (M2 in Figure 6), and so on. For Cluster 2, Reading Marker 1 was to mark all from subset 2 (schools 10 to 18) and Reading Marker 2 was to mark all from subset 3 (schools 19 to 27). Subset 1 of Cluster 2 (schools 1 to 9) was to be marked by Reading Marker 16.

If booklets from all participating schools were available before the marking began, the following steps would be involved in implementing the design:

---

[1] Countries with more or fewer than 150 schools or a different number of markers had to adjust the size of the school subsets accordingly.

Step 1: Set aside booklets for multiple marking and then divide the remaining booklets into school subsets as above; (subset 1: schools 1 to 9; subset 2: schools 10 to 18, etc., to achieve 16 subsets of schools).

Step 2: Assuming that marking begins with Cluster 1:
Marker 1 takes Booklets 1, 5 and 7 for School Subset 1;
Marker 2 takes Booklets 1, 5 and 7 for School Subset 2; etc.; until
Marker 16 takes Booklets 1, 5 and 7 for School Subset 16.

Step 3: Markers mark all of the first Cluster 1 item requiring marking in the booklets that they have—1, 5 and 7.

Step 4: The second Cluster 1 item is marked in all three booklet types, followed by the third Cluster 1 item, etc., until all Cluster 1 items are marked.

Step 5: For Cluster 2, as per the row of the table in Figure 6 corresponding to R2 in the left-most column, each marker is allocated a subset of schools different from their subset for Cluster 1. Marking proceeds item by item within the cluster.

Step 6: For the remaining clusters, the rows corresponding to R3, R4, etc., in the table are followed in succession.

		Subsets of Schools															
Cl	Bklt	1	2	3	4	5	6	7	8	9	10	11	12	13	14	15	16
R1	1,5,7	M1	M2	M3	M4	M5	M6	M7	M8	M9	M10	M11	M12	M13	M14	M15	M16
R2	1,2,6	M16	M1	M2	M3	M4	M5	M6	M7	M8	M9	M10	M11	M12	M13	M14	M15
R3	2,3,7	M15	M16	M1	M2	M3	M4	M5	M6	M7	M8	M9	M10	M11	M12	M13	M14
R4	1,3,4	M14	M15	M16	M1	M2	M3	M4	M5	M6	M7	M8	M9	M10	M11	M12	M13
R5	2,4,5	M13	M14	M15	M16	M1	M2	M3	M4	M5	M6	M7	M8	M9	M10	M11	M12
R6	3,5,6	M12	M13	M14	M15	M16	M1	M2	M3	M4	M5	M6	M7	M8	M9	M10	M11
R7	4,6,7	M11	M12	M13	M14	M15	M16	M1	M2	M3	M4	M5	M6	M7	M8	M9	M10
R8	7,8,9	M10	M11	M12	M13	M14	M15	M16	M1	M2	M3	M4	M5	M6	M7	M8	M9
R9	8,9	M9	M10	M11	M12	M13	M14	M15	M16	M1	M2	M3	M4	M5	M6	M7	M8

Figure 6: Allocation of the Booklets for Single Marking of Reading by Cluster

As a result of this procedure, the booklets from each subset of schools are processed by nine different reading markers and each student's booklet is marked by three different reading markers (except Booklet 7, which has four reading clusters, and Booklets 8 and 9, which have only two reading clusters). Spreading booklets among markers in this way minimises the effects of any systematic leniency or harshness in marking.

In practice, most countries would not have had completed test booklets back from all their sampled schools before marking needed to begin. NPMs were encouraged to organise the marking in two waves, so that it could begin after materials were received back from one-half of their schools. Schools would not have been able to be assigned to school sets for marking exactly in their school identification order, but rather by identification order combined with when their materials were received and processed at the national centre.

Mathematics and science

With eight mathematics/science markers who could mark in both areas, the booklets needed to be assigned to markers according to Figure 7 for marking by cluster. Here, the subsets of schools would contain twice the number of schools as for the reading marking, because schools were shared among eight and not 16 markers. This could be done by combining subsets 1 and 2 from reading into subset 1 for mathematics/science, and so on—unless the mathematics/science marking was done before the reading, in which case the reading subsets could be formed by halving the mathematics/science subsets. (Logistics were complex because all of the booklets that contained mathematics or science items also contained reading items, and had to be shared with the reading markers.)

It was recommended that the marking in one stage be completed before marking in the other began. Stage 2 could be undertaken before Stage 1, if this helped with the flow of booklets.

If separate markers were needed for mathematics and science, the single marking could be accomplished with the design shown in Figure 8, in which case schools needed to be divided into only four subsets.

			\multicolumn{8}{c}{Subsets of Schools}
Stage	Cluster	Booklet	1	2	3	4	5	6	7	8
1: Mathematics	M1	1,9	M1	M2	M3	M4	M5	M6	M7	M8
	M2	1,5,8	M7	M8	M1	M2	M3	M4	M5	M6
	M3	3,5,9	M5	M6	M7	M8	M1	M2	M3	M4
	M4	3,8	M3	M4	M5	M6	M7	M8	M1	M2
2: Science	S1	2,8	M1	M2	M3	M4	M5	M6	M7	M8
	S2	2,6,9	M7	M8	M1	M2	M3	M4	M5	M6
	S3	4,6,8	M5	M6	M7	M8	M1	M2	M3	M4
	S4	4,9	M3	M4	M5	M6	M7	M8	M1	M2

Figure 7: Booklet Allocation for Single Marking of Mathematics and Science by Cluster, Common Markers

Mathematics		Science		\multicolumn{4}{c}{Subsets of Schools}
Cluster	Booklet	Cluster	Booklet	1	2	3	4
M1	1,9	S1	2,8	M1	M2	M3	M4
M2	1,5,8	S2	2,6,9	M2	M3	M4	M1
M3	3,5,9	S3	4,6,8	M3	M4	M1	M2
M4	3,8	S4	4,9	M4	M1	M2	M3

Figure 8: Booklet Allocation for Single Marking of Mathematics and Science by Cluster, Separate Markers

SE booklet (Booklet 0)

Countries using the shorter, special purpose SE booklet (numbered as Booklet 0) were advised to process this separately from the remaining booklets. Small numbers of students used this booklet, only a few items required marking, and they were not arranged in clusters. NPMs were cautioned that booklets needed to be allocated to several markers to ensure uniform application of marking criteria for the SE booklet, as for the main marking.

MANAGING THE ACTUAL MARKING

Booklet flow

To facilitate the flow of booklets, it was important to have ample table surfaces on which to place and arrange them by type and school subset. The bundles needed to be clearly labelled. For this purpose, it was recommended that each bundle of booklets be identified by a *batch header* for each booklet type (Booklets 1 to 9), with spaces for the number of booklets and school identifications represented in the bundle to be written in. In addition, each header sheet was to be pre-printed with a list of the clusters in the booklet, with columns alongside which the date and time, marker's name and identification and table leader's initials could be entered as the bundle was marked and checked.

Separating the reading and mathematics/science marking

It was recommended that reading and mathematics/science marking be done at least partly at different times (for example, mathematics/science marking could start a week or two ahead of the reading marking). Eight of the nine booklets contained material in reading together with material in mathematics and/or science. Except for Booklet 7, which contained only reading, it could have been difficult to maintain an efficient flow of booklets through the marking process if all marking in all three domains were done simultaneously.

Familiarising markers with the marking design

The relevant design for allocating booklets to markers was explained either during the marker training session or at the beginning of the first marking session (or both). The marking supervisor was responsible for ensuring that markers adhered to the design, and used clerical assistants if needed. Markers could better understand the process if each was provided with a card indicating the bundles of booklets to be taken and in which order.

Consulting table leaders

During the initial training, practice, and review, it was expected that coding issues would be discussed openly until markers understood the rationale for the marking criteria (or reached consensus where the *Marking Guide* was incomplete). Markers were advised to work quietly, referring queries to their table leader rather than to their neighbours. If a particular query arose often, the table leader was advised to discuss it with the rest of the group.

Markers were not permitted to consult other markers or table leaders during the additional practice exercises (*see next subsection*) to gauge whether all or some markers needed more training and practice, or during the multiple marking.

Monitoring single marking

The steps described here represent the minimum level of monitoring activities required. Countries wishing to implement more extensive monitoring procedures during single marking were encouraged to do so.

The supervisor, assisted by table leaders, was advised to collect markers' practice papers after each cluster practice session and to tabulate the marks assigned. These were then to be compared with the pre-agreed marks: each matching mark was considered a hit and each discrepant mark was considered a miss. To reflect an adequate standard of reliability, the ratio of hits to the total of hits plus misses needed to be 0.85 or more. In mathematics and science, this reliability was to be assessed on the first digit of the two-digit codes. A ratio of less than 0.85, especially if lower than 0.80, was to be taken as indicating that more practice was needed, and possibly also more training.

Table leaders played a key role during each marking session and at the end of each day, by spot-checking a sample of booklets or items that had already been marked to identify problems for discussion with individual markers or with the wider group, as appropriate. All booklets that had not been set aside for multiple marking were candidates for this spot-checking. It was recommended that, if there were indications from the practice sessions that one or more particular markers might be experiencing problems in using the *Marking Guide* consistently, then more of those markers' booklets should be included in the checking.

Table leaders were advised to review the results of the spot-checking with the markers at the beginning of the next day's marking. This was regarded primarily as a mentoring activity, but NPMs were advised to keep in contact with table leaders and the marking supervisor if there were individual markers who did not meet criteria of adequate reliability and would need to be removed from the pool.

Table leaders were to initial and date the header sheet of each batch of booklets for which they had carried out spot-checking. Some items/booklets from each batch and each marker had to be checked.

MULTIPLE MARKING

For PISA 2000, multiple marking meant that four separate markers marked all short response and open constructed-response items in 48 of each of Booklets 1 to 7 and 72 of each of Booklets 8 and 9. Multiple marking was done at or towards the end of the marking period, after markers had familiarised themselves with and were confident in using the *Marking Guides*.

As noted earlier, the first three markers of the selected booklets circled codes on separate record sheets, tailored to booklet type and subject area (reading, mathematics or science), using one page per student. The marking supervisor checked that markers correctly entered student identification numbers and their own identification number on the sheets, which was crucial to data quality. Also as noted earlier, the SE booklet was not included in the multiple marking.

In a country where booklets were provided in more than one language, multiple marking was required only in the language used for the majority of the PISA booklets, though encouraged in more than one language if possible. If two languages were used equally, the NPM could choose either language.

While markers would have been thoroughly familiar with the *Marking Guides* by this time, they may have most recently marked a different booklet from those allocated to them for multiple marking. For this reason, they needed to have time to re-read the relevant *Marking Guide* before beginning the marking. It was recommended that at least half a day be used for markers to refresh their familiarity with the guides and to look again at the additional practice material before proceeding with the multiple marking.

As in the single marking, marking was to be done item by item. For manageability, all items within a booklet were to be marked before moving to the next booklet. Rather than marking by cluster across several booklet types, it was considered that markers would be experienced enough in applying the marking criteria by this time that marking by booklet would be unlikely to detract from the quality of the data.

Booklet allocation design

The specified multiple marking design for reading, shown in Figure 9, assumed 16 markers with identification numbers 201 to 216. The importance of following the design exactly as specified was stressed, as it provides for balanced links between clusters and markers.

Step	Booklet Groups	Marker	Marker Identification
1	1	❶ and ❷	201, 202, 203, 204
	2	❸ and ❹	205, 206, 207, 208
	3	❺ and ❻	209, 210, 211, 212
	4	❼ and ❽	213, 214, 215, 216
2	7	❷ and ❸	203, 204, 205, 206
	5/6	❹ and ❺	207, 208, 209, 210
	8	❻ and ❼	211, 212, 213, 214
	9	❽ and ❶	215, 216, 201, 202

Figure 9: Booklet Allocation to Markers for Multiple Marking Reading

Figure 8 shows 16 markers grouped into eight pairs of two, with Group 1 comprising the first two markers (201 and 202), Group 2 the next two (203 and 204), etc. The design involved two steps, with the booklets divided into two sets. Booklets 1 to 4 made up one set, and Booklets 5 to 9 the second set. The four markings were to be carried out by allocating booklets to the four markers shown in the right-hand column of the table for each booklet.

In this scenario, with all 16 markers working, Booklets 1 to 4 were to be marked at the same time in the first step. The 48 Booklet 1's, for example, were to be divided into four bundles of 12, and rotated among markers 201, 202, 203 and 204, so that each marker eventually would have marked all 48 of this booklet. The same pattern was to be followed for Booklets 2, 3 and 4. Each booklet had approximately the same number of items requiring marking and the same number of booklets (48) to be marked.

After Booklets 1 to 4 had been put through the multiple-marking process, the pairs of markers were to regroup (but remain in their pairs) and follow the allocation in the second half of Figure 9. That is, markers 203, 204, 205 and 206 were to mark Booklet 7, markers 207, 208, 209 and 210 were to mark Booklets 5 and 6, and so on for the remaining booklets. Booklets 5 and 6 contained fewer items requiring marking than Booklet 7, and there were more Booklets 8 and 9 to process. The closest to a balanced workload was achieved by regarding Booklets 5 and 6 as equivalent to one booklet for this exercise.

If only eight markers were available, the design could be applied by using the group designations in Figure 9 to indicate marker identification numbers. However, four steps, not two, were needed to achieve four markings per booklet. The third and fourth steps could be achieved by starting the third step with Booklet 1 marked by markers 3 and 4 and continuing the pattern in a similar way as in the figure, and by starting the fourth step with Booklet 7 marked by markers 4 and 5.

Allocating booklets to markers for multiple marking was quite complex and the marking supervisor had to monitor the flow of booklets throughout the process.

The multiple-marking design for mathematics and science shown in Figure 10 assumed eight markers, with identification numbers 401 to 408, who each marked both mathematics and science. This design also provided for balanced links between clusters and markers. The design required four stages, which could be carried out in a different order from that shown if this helped with booklet flow, but the allocation of booklets to markers had to be retained. Since there were more items to process in stage 4, it was important for all markers to undertake this stage together.

Stage	Booklet	Domain	Marker Identifications
1	1	Mathematics	401, 402, 403, 404
	2	Science	405, 406, 407, 408
2	3	Mathematics	402, 403, 404, 405
	4	Science	406, 407, 408, 401
3	5	Mathematics	403, 404, 405, 406
	6	Science	407, 408, 401, 402
4	8	Maths and Science	404, 405, 406, 407
	9	Maths and Science	408, 401, 402, 403

Figure 10: Booklet Allocation for Multiple Marking of Mathematics and Science, Common Markers

If different markers were used for mathematics and science, a different multiple-marking design was necessary. Assuming four markers for each of mathematics and science, then each booklet had to be marked by each marker. According to the scheme for assigning marker identification numbers, the markers would have had identification numbers: 101, 102, 103 and 104 for mathematics; and 301, 302, 303 and 304 for science.

Five booklets contained mathematics items (Booklets 1, 3, 5, 8 and 9), and five contained science items (Booklets 2, 4, 6, 8 and 9). Because there were different numbers of booklets and very large differences in numbers of items requiring multiple marking within them, it was important for all markers to work on the same booklet at the same time.

The design in Figure 11 was suggested, with an analogous one for science. The rotation numbers are marker identification numbers. If it helped the overall workflow, booklets could be marked in a different order from that shown in the figure.

Booklet	First Rotation	Second Rotation	Third Rotation	Fourth Rotation
1	101	102	103	104
3	102	103	104	101
5	103	104	101	102
8	104	101	102	103
9	101	102	103	104

Figure 11: Booklet Allocation for Multiple Marking of Mathematics

CROSS-NATIONAL MARKING

Cross-national comparability in assigning marks was explored through an inter-country rater reliability study (*see Chapter 10* and *Chapter 14*).

QUESTIONNAIRE CODING

The main coding required for the Student Questionnaire internationally was the mother's and father's occupation and student's occupational expectation. Four-digit International Standard Classification of Occupations (ISCO88) codes (International Labour Organisation, 1988) were assigned to these three variables. In several countries, this could be done in many ways. NPMs could use a national coding scheme with more than 100 occupational title categories, provided that this national classification could be recoded to ISCO. A national classification was preferred because relationships between occupational status and achievement could then be compared within a country using both international and national measures of occupational status.

The PISA website gave a short, clear summary of ISCO codes and occupational titles for countries to translate if they had neither a national occupational classification scheme nor access to a full translation of ISCO.

In their national options, countries may also have needed to pre-code responses to some items before data from the questionnaire were entered into the software.

DATA ENTRY, DATA CHECKING AND FILE SUBMISSION

DATA ENTRY

The Consortium provided participating countries with data entry software (KeyQuest®) that ran under Windows 95® or later, and Windows NT 4.0® or later. KeyQuest® contained the database structures for all the booklets and questionnaires used in the main survey. Variables could be added or deleted as needed for national options. Data were to be entered directly from the test booklets and questionnaires, except for the multiple-marking study, where the marks from the first three markers had been written on separate sheets.

KeyQuest® performed validation checks as data were entered. Importing facilities were also available if data had already been entered into text files, but it was strongly recommended that data be entered directly into KeyQuest® to take advantage of its many PISA-specific features.

A separate *Data Entry Manual* provided full details of the functionality of the KeyQuest® software and complete instructions on data entry, data management and how to carry out validity checks.

DATA CHECKING

NPMs were responsible for ensuring that many checks of the quality of their country's data were made before the data files were submitted to the Consortium. The checking procedures required that the List of Sampled Schools and the Student Tracking Form for each school were already accurately completed and entered into KeyQuest®. Any errors had to be corrected before the data were submitted. Copies of the cleaning reports were to be submitted together with the data files. More details on the cleaning steps are provided in Chapter 11.

DATA SUBMISSION

Files to be submitted included:
- data for the test booklets and context questionnaires;
- data for the international option instrument(s) if used;
- data for the multiple-marking study;
- List of Sampled Schools; and
- Student Tracking Forms.

Hard or electronic copies of the last two items were also required.

AFTER DATA WERE SUBMITTED

NPMs were required to designate a data manager who would work actively with the Consortium's data processing centre at ACER during the international data cleaning process. Responses to requests for information by the processing centre were required within three working days of the request.

CHAPTER 7 { QUALITY MONITORING

Adrian Harvey-Beavis and Nancy Caldwell

It is essential that a high profile and expensive project such as PISA be undertaken with high standards. This requires not only that procedures be carefully developed, but that they be carefully monitored to ensure that they are in fact fully and completely implemented. Should it happen that they were not implemented fully, it is necessary to understand to what extent they were not, and the likely implications of this for data quality. This is the task of quality monitoring.

Quality Monitoring in PISA is, therefore, about observing the extent to which data are collected, retrieved, and stored according to the procedures described by the field operations manuals. Quality control is embedded in the field operations procedures. For PISA 2000, Quality Monitors were appointed to do this observing, but the responsibility for quality control resided with the National Project Managers (NPMs) who were to implement the field operation guidelines and thus establish quality control.

A program of national centre and school visits was central to ensuring full, valid implementation of PISA procedures. The main aims of the site visit program were to forestall operational problems and to ensure that the data collected in different countries were comparable and of the highest quality.

There were two levels of quality monitoring in the PISA project:
- *National Centre Quality Monitors* (NCQMs)—To observe how PISA field operations were being implemented at the national level, Consortium representatives monitored the national centres by visiting NPMs in each country just prior to the field trial and just prior to the main study.
- *School Quality Monitors* (SQMs)—Employed by the Consortium, but located in participating countries, SQMs visited a sample of schools to record how well the field operations guidelines were followed. They visited a small number of schools for the field trial (typically around five in each country) and around 30 to 40 schools for the main study.

PREPARATION OF QUALITY MONITORING PROCEDURES

National Centre Quality Monitors (NCQMs) were members of the Consortium. They met prior to the field trial to develop the instruments needed to collect data for reporting purposes. A standardised interview schedule was developed for use in discussions with the NPM. This instrument addressed key aspects of procedures described in the *NPM Manual* and other topics relevant to considering data quality, for example, relations between participating schools and the national centre.

A *School Quality Monitor Manual* was prepared for the field trial and later revised for the main study. This manual outlined the duties of SQMs, including con-fidentiality requirements. It contained the Data Collection Sheet to be used by the SQM when visiting a school. An interview schedule to be used with the School Co-ordinator was also included. Additionally, for the field trial, a short interview to get student feedback on questionnaires was included.

IMPLEMENTING QUALITY MONITORING PROCEDURES

TRAINING NATIONAL CENTRE QUALITY MONITORS AND SCHOOL QUALITY MONITORS

The Consortium organised training sessions for the National Centre Quality Monitors (NCQMs), who trained the School Quality Monitors (SQMs).

As part of their training, NCQMs received an overview of the design and purpose of the project, which gave special attention to the responsibilities of NPMs in conducting the study in their country.

The Manual for National Centre Quality Monitors was used for the training session, and NCQMs were trained to use a schedule for interviewing NPMs.

School Quality Monitors were trained to conduct on-site quality monitoring in schools and to prepare a report on the school visits. The *School Quality Monitor Manual* was used for their training sessions.

National Project Managers were asked to:
- nominate individuals who could fulfil the role of SQM, who were then approved by the Consortium. Where nominations were not approved, new nominations were solicited; and
- provide the SQMs with the schedule for testing dates and times and other details such as name of school, location, contact details, name of School Co-ordinator and Test Administrator (if the two were different).

NATIONAL CENTRE QUALITY MONITORING

For both the field trial and the main study, NCQMs visited all national centres, including national centres where a Consortium member was based.[1]

The visits to the NPMs took place about a month before testing started. This meant that procedures could be reviewed when possible to make minor adjustments. It also meant that the NCQMs could train SQMs not too long before the testing. National Centre Quality Monitors asked NPMs about (i) implementing procedures at the national centre and (ii) any difficulties suggesting that changes may be needed to the field operations.

Questions on procedures were focused on:
- how sampling procedures were implemented;
- communication between national centres and participating schools;
- translating, printing and distribution of materials to schools;
- management procedures for materials at the national centre;
- planning for data preparation, data checking and analysis;
- data collection quality control procedures, particularly documentation of data collection and data entry; and
- data management procedures.

While visiting NPMs, the NCQMs collected copies of manuals and tracking forms used in each country, that were subsequently reviewed and evaluated.

SCHOOL QUALITY MONITORING

National Project Managers (NPMs) were asked to nominate SQMs and advised to consider that persons nominated:
- should be knowledgeable, or might reasonably be expected to easily learn about, the procedures and materials of PISA;
- must speak fluently the language of the country and either English or French;
- should have an education or assessment background;
- may be Consortium staff or individuals specifically selected to undertake school monitoring;
- need to be approved by the Consortium and work independently of NPMs;
- need to be available to attend a training session; and
- may undertake monitoring in their own country or exchange with another country through a reciprocal agreement.

For the main study, NPMs were also advised that it was preferable that an SQM trained for the field trial should also undertake school visits during the main study in 2000.

The Consortium paid SQMs' expenses and fees.

---

[1] To ensure independence of the Quality Monitors from the centres they visited it was decided, for the field trial, that nationals should not visit their own centre. For the main study, this was relaxed, as there was no evidence in the field trial of problems among these national centres.

For school visits, the field trial provided the opportunity to observe and judge:
- the quality of the *Test Administrator's Manual*;
- the clarity of instructions used by the Test Administrators; and
- whether any of the procedures or documentation used in the main study should be modified.

For the main study, school visits focused explicitly on observing the implementation of procedures, and the impact of the testing environment on data. During their visits, SQMs:
- reviewed the activities preliminary to the test administration, such as distribution of booklets;
- observed test administration;
- verified the school Test Administrator's record keeping—for example, whether assessed students match sampled students;
- asked for comments on procedures and materials; and
- completed a report on each school visited, which was returned to the Consortium.

The original plan was to have SQMs visit schools selected at random, but this procedure proved too costly to implement. In all countries, at least one school was randomly selected, and the remainder were selected with consideration given to proximity to the residence of the SQM to contain travel and accommodation costs. In many countries, the school selection procedure was to divide the country into regions with one SQM responsible for each region. One school was randomly selected in each region, and the remainder selected also with consideration given to proximity to the SQM's residence. In practice, SQMs often still had to travel large distances because many schools had testing on the same day.

The majority of school visits were unannounced. Three countries would not permit this because national policy and other circumstances (especially, for example, remote schools) required making prior arrangements with the schools so they could assist with transportation and accommodation.

SITE VISIT DATA

Reports on the results of the national centre and school site visits were prepared by the Consortium and distributed to national centres after both the field trial and the main study.

For the main study, the national Quality Monitoring reports were used as part of the data adjudication process (*see Chapter 4*). An aggregated report on quality monitoring is also included as Appendix 5.

SECTION THREE: DATA PROCESSING

CHAPTER 8
SURVEY WEIGHTING AND THE CALCULATION OF SAMPLING VARIANCE

Keith Rust and Sheila Krawchuk

Survey weights were required to analyse PISA data, to calculate appropriate estimates of sampling error, and to make valid estimates and inferences. The Consortium calculated survey weights for all assessed and excluded students, and provided variables in the data that permit users to make approximately unbiased estimates of standard errors, to conduct significance tests and to create confidence intervals appropriately, given the sample design for PISA in each individual country.

SURVEY WEIGHTING

Students included in the final PISA sample for a given country are not all equally representative of the entire student population, despite random sampling of schools and students for selecting the sample. Survey weights must therefore be incorporated into the analysis.

There are several reasons why the survey weights are not the same for all students in a given country:

- A school sample design may intentionally over or under-sample certain sectors of the school population: in the former case, so that they could be effectively analysed separately for national purposes, such as a relatively small but politically important province or region, or a sub-population using a particular language of instruction; and in the latter case, for reasons of cost, or other practical considerations,[1] such as very small or geographically remote schools.

- Information about school size available at the time of sampling may not have been completely accurate. If a school was expected to be very large, the selection probability was based on the assumption that only a sample of its students would be selected for PISA. But if the school turned out to be quite small, all students would have to be included and would have, overall, a higher probability of selection in the sample than planned, making these inclusion probabilities higher than those of most other students in the sample. Conversely, if a school thought to be small turned out to be large, the students included in the sample would have had smaller selection probabilities than others.

- School non-response, where no replacement school participated, may have occurred, leading to the under-representation of students from that kind of school, unless weighting adjustments were made. It is also possible that only part of the eligible population in a school (such as those 15-year-olds in a single grade) were represented by its student sample, which also requires weighting to compensate for the missing data from the omitted grades.

- Student non-response, within participating schools, occurred to varying extents. Students of the kind that could not be given achievement test scores (but were not excluded for linguistic or disability reasons)

---

[1] Note that this is not the same as excluding certain portions of the school population. This also happened in some cases, but cannot be addressed adequately through the use of survey weights.

will be under-represented in the data unless weighting adjustments are made.
- Trimming weights to prevent undue influence of a relatively small subset of the school or student sample might have been necessary if a small group of students would otherwise have much larger weights than the remaining students in the country. This can lead to unstable estimates—large sampling errors—but cannot be well estimated. Trimming weights introduces a small bias into estimates but greatly reduces standard errors.
- Weights need adjustment for analysing mathematics and science data to reflect the fact that not all students were assessed in each subject.

The procedures used to derive the survey weights for PISA reflect the standards of best practice for analysing complex survey data, and the procedures used by the world's major statistical agencies. The same procedures were used in other international studies of educational achievement: the Third International Mathematics and Science Study (TIMSS), the Third International Mathematics and Science Study-Repeat (TIMSS-R), the Civic Education Study (CIVED), the Progress in International Reading Literacy Study 2001 (PIRLS), which were all implemented by the International Association for the Evaluation of Educational Achievement (IEA); and the International Assessment of Educational Progress (IAEP, 1991). (See Cochran, 1977 and Särndal, Swensson and Wretman, 1992 for the underlying statistical theory on survey sampling texts.)

The weight, W_{ij}, for student j in school i consists of two base weights—the school and the within-school—and five adjustment factors, and can be expressed as:

$$W_{ij} = t_{2ij} f_{1i} f_{2i} f_{1ij}^{A} t_{1i} w_{2ij} w_{1i}$$

where:

w_{1i}, the school base weight, is given as the reciprocal of the probability of inclusion of school i into the sample;

w_{2ij}, the within-school base weight, is given as the reciprocal of the probability of selection of student j from within the selected school i;

f_{1i} is an adjustment factor to compensate for non-participation by other schools that are somewhat similar in nature to school i (not already compensated for by the participation of replacement schools);

f_{1ij}^{A} is an adjustment factor to compensate for the fact that, in some countries, in some schools only 15-year-old students who were enrolled in the modal grade for 15-year-olds were included in the assessment;

f_{2i} is an adjustment factor to compensate for the absence of achievement scale scores from some sampled students within school i (who were not excluded);

t_{1i} is a school trimming factor, used to reduce unexpectedly large values of w_{1i}; and

t_{2ij} is a student trimming factor, used to reduce the weights of students with exceptionally large values for the product of all the preceding weight components.

THE SCHOOL BASE WEIGHT

The term w_{1i} is referred to as the school base weight. For the systematic probability-proportional-to-size school sampling method used in PISA, this is given as:

$$w_{1i} = \begin{cases} int(g/i) / mos(i) & \text{if } mos(i) < int(g/i) \\ 1 & \text{otherwise} \end{cases} .(1)$$

The term $mos(i)$ denotes the measure of size given to each school on the sampling frame. Despite country variations, $mos(i)$ was usually equal to the (estimated) number of 15-year-olds in the school, if it was greater than the predetermined target cluster size (35 in most countries). If the enrolment of 15-year-olds was less than the Target Cluster Size (TCS), then $mos(i) = TCS$. In addition in countries where a stratum of very small schools was used, if the number of 15-year-olds in a school was below $TCS/2$, then $mos(i) = TCS/2$.

The term $int(g/i)$ denotes the sampling interval used within the explicit sampling stratum g that contains school I and is calculated as the total of $mos(i)$ values for all schools in stratum g, divided by the school sample size for that stratum.

Thus, if school i was estimated to have 100 15-year-olds at the time of sample selection, $mos(i) = 100$. If the country had a single explicit stratum ($g=1$) and the total of the $mos(i)$ values over all schools was 150 000, with a school sample size of 150, then $int(1/i) = 150\,00/150 = 1\,000$, for school i (and others in the sample), giving $w_{1i} = 1\,000/100 = 10.0$. Roughly speaking, the school can be thought of as representing about 10 schools from the population. In this example, any school with 1 000 or more 15-year-old students would be included in the sample with certainty, with a base weight of $w_{1i} = 1$.

THE SCHOOL WEIGHT TRIMMING FACTOR

Once school base weights were established for each sampled school in the country, verifications were made separately within each explicit sampling stratum to see if the school weights required trimming. The school trimming factor t_{1i}, is the ratio of the trimmed to the untrimmed school base weight, and is equal to 1.0000 for most schools and therefore most students, and never exceeds this value. (*See Table 23* for the number of school records in each country that received some kind of base weight trimming.)

The first check was for schools that had been assigned very small selection probabilities because of very small enrolments, although the school sampling procedure described in the *Sampling Manual* and in Chapter 4 of this report was designed to prevent this. Cases did arise where schools had very small probabilities of selection relative to others in the same stratum because they were assigned a value of $mos(i)$ that was much smaller than $TCS/2$, usually because the actual enrolment was used as the value of $mos(i)$, even when it was much smaller than $TCS/2$. Where the value for TCS was 35, as in most jurisdictions, if a school with one 15-year-old enrolled student was given $mos(i)$ of 1 rather than 17.5 (or 35, depending on whether or not a small school stratum was used), the school base weight was very large. The sampled students in that school would have received a weight 35 times greater than that of a student in the sample from a school with 35 15-year-old students.

These schools were given a compromise weight neither excessively large nor introducing a bias by under-representing students from very small schools (that often constituted a sizeable fraction of the PISA student population). This was done by essentially replacing the inappropriate $mos(i)$ with $TCS/6$, giving them and their students weights six times as great as that of most students in the country and three times as great as they would have had if the small school sampling option been implemented correctly. Permitting these schools to have weights three times as great as they would have had, had they been sampled correctly, was also consistent with the other trimming procedures, described below.

The second school-level trimming adjustment was applied to schools that turned out to be much larger than was believed at the time of sampling—where 15-year-old enrolment exceeded $3 \times \max(TCS, mos(i))$. For example, if $TCS = 35$, then a school flagged for trimming had more than 105 PISA-eligible students, and more than three times as many students as was indicated on the school sampling frame. Because the student sample size was set at TCS regardless of the actual enrolment, the student sampling rate was much lower than anticipated during the school sampling. This meant that the weights for the sampled students in these schools would have been more than three times greater than anticipated when the school sample was selected. These schools had their school base weights trimmed by having $mos(i)$ replaced by $3 \times \max(TCS, mos(i))$ in the school base weight formula.

THE STUDENT BASE WEIGHT

The term w_{2ij} is referred to as the student base weight. With the PISA procedure for sampling students, w_{2ij} did not vary across students (j) within a particular school i. Thus w_{2ij} is given as:

$$w_{2ij} = \frac{enr(i)}{sam(i)}, \qquad (2)$$

where $enr(i)$ is the actual enrolment of 15-year-olds in the school (and so, in general, is somewhat different from the estimated $mos(i)$), and $sam(i)$ is the sample size within school i. It follows that if all students from the school were selected, then $w_{2ij} = 1$ for all eligible students in the school. For all other cases $w_{2ij} > 1$.

SCHOOL NON-RESPONSE ADJUSTMENT

In order to adjust for the fact that those schools that declined to participate, and were not replaced by a replacement school, were not in general typical of the schools in the sample as a whole, school-level non-response adjustments were made. Several groups of somewhat similar schools were formed within a country, and within each group the weights of the responding schools were adjusted to compensate for the missing schools and their students. The compositions of the non-response groups varied from country to country, but were based on cross-classifying the explicit and implicit stratification variables used at the time of school sample selection. Usually, about 10 to 15 such groups were formed within a given country depending upon school distribution with respect to stratification variables. If a country provided no implicit stratification variables, schools were divided into three roughly equal groups, within each stratum, based on their size (small, medium or large). It was desirable to ensure that each group had at least six participating schools, as small groups can lead to unstable weight adjustments, which in turn would inflate the sampling variances. However, it was not necessary to collapse cells where all schools participated, as the school non-response adjustment factor was 1.0 regardless of whether cells were collapsed or not. Adjustments greater than 2.0 were flagged for review, as they can cause increased variability in the weights, and lead to an increase in sampling variances. In either of these situations, cells were generally collapsed over the last implicit stratification variable(s) until the violations no longer existed. In countries with very high overall levels of school non-response after school replacement, the requirement for school non-response adjustment factors all to be below 2.0 was waived.

Within the school non-response adjustment group containing school i, the non-response adjustment factor was calculated as:

$$f_{1i} = \frac{\sum_{k \in \Omega(i)} w_{1k} enr(k)}{\sum_{k \in \Gamma(i)} w_{1k} enr(k)}, \qquad (3)$$

where the sum in the denominator is over $\Gamma(i)$, the schools within the group (originals and replacements) that participated, while the sum in the numerator is over $\Omega(i)$, those same schools, plus the original sample schools that refused and were not replaced. The numerator estimates the population of 15-year-olds in the group, while the denominator gives the size of the population of 15-year-olds directly represented by participating schools. The school non-response adjustment factor ensures that participating schools are weighted to represent all students in the group. If a school did not participate because it had no eligible students enrolled, no adjustment was necessary since this was neither non-response nor under-coverage.

Table 22 shows the number of school non-response classes that were formed for each country, and the variables that were used to create the cells.

Table 22: Non-Response Classes

Country	Variables Used to Create Non-Response Classes	Original Number of Cells	Final Number of Cells After Collapsing Small Cells
Australia	Metropolitan/Country	42	24
Austria	No school non-response adjustments		
Belgium (Fl.)	For strata 1-3, School Type and Organisation	27	8
Belgium (Fr.)	5 categories of the school proportion of overage students	14	4
Brazil	Public/Private, Region, Score Range	104	50
Canada	Public/Private, Urban/Rural	134	64
Czech Republic	3 School Sizes	65	65
Denmark	First 2 digits of concatenated School Type and County	78	24

Table 22 (cont.)

Country	Variables Used to Create Non-Response Classes	Original Number of Cells	Final Number of Cells After Collapsing Small Cells
England	For very small schools: School Type, Region; For other schools: School Type, Exam Results (LEA or Grant Maintained schools) or Co-educational Status (Independent Schools), Region	50	17
Finland	No school non-response adjustments		
France	3 School Sizes	18	10
Germany	For strata 66 and 67, State was used. For all others, the explicit stratum was used.	60	29
Greece	School Type	30	14
Hungary	Combinations of School Type, Region, and Location (75 values)	100	31
Iceland	3 School Sizes	21	14
Ireland	School Type, Gender Composition	16	9
Italy	No school non-response adjustments		
Japan	3 School Sizes	12	10
Korea	No school non-response adjustments		
Latvia	Urbanisation, School Type	29	10
Liechtenstein	No school non-response adjustments		
Luxembourg	3 School Sizes	6	4
Mexico	No school non-response adjustments		
Netherlands	3 School Sizes	15	7
New Zealand	Public/Private, School Gender composition, Socio-Economic Status, Urban/Rural	15	9
Northern Ireland	School Type, Examination Results, Region	30	14
Norway	3 School Sizes	15	9
Poland	3 School Sizes	9	9
Portugal	First 2 digits of Public/Private, 3 digits of Region and the Index of Social Development for 3 regions.	22	11
Russian Federation	School Program, Urbanisation	47	46
Scotland	For strata 1, Average School Achievement and the first 2 digits of the National ID; for strata 2, the first 2 digits of the National ID.	49	11
Spain	No school non-response adjustments		
Sweden	Combinations of the implicit stratification variables	15	11
Switzerland	Pseudo Sampling Strata and 3 School Sizes	49	37
United States	Public/Private, High/Low Minority and Private School Type, PSU	101	18

GRADE NON-RESPONSE ADJUSTMENT

In a few countries, several schools agreed to participate in PISA but required that participation be restricted to 15-year-olds in the modal grade for 15-year-olds, rather than all 15-year-olds, because of perceived administrative inconvenience. Since the modal grade generally included the majority of the population to be covered, some of these schools were accepted as participants. For the part of the 15-year-old population in the modal grade, these schools were respondents, while for the rest of the grades in the school with 15-year-olds, this school was a refusal. This situation occasionally arose for a grade other than the modal grade because of other reasons, such as other testing being carried out for certain grades at the same time as the PISA assessment. To account for this, a special non-response adjustment was calculated at the school level for students not in the modal grade (and was automatically 1.0 for all students in the modal grade).

Within the same non-response adjustment groups used for creating school non-response adjustment factors, the grade non-response adjustment factor for all students in school i, f_{1ij}^A, is given as:

$$f_{1ij}^A = \begin{cases} \dfrac{\sum_{k \in C(i)} w_{1k} enra(k)}{\sum_{k \in B(i)} w_{1k} enra(k)} & \text{for students not in the modal grade} \\ 1 & \text{otherwise} \end{cases} \quad (4)$$

The variable $enra(k)$ is the approximate number of 15-year-old students in school k but not in the modal grade. The set $B(i)$ is all schools that participated for all eligible grades (from within the non-response adjustment group with school (i)), while the set $C(i)$ includes these schools and those that only participated for the modal responding grade.

This procedure gave a single grade non-response adjustment factor for each school, which depended upon its non-response adjustment class. Each individual student received this factor value if they did not belong to the modal grade, and 1.0000 if they belonged to the modal grade. In general, this factor is not the same for all students within the same school.

STUDENT NON-RESPONSE ADJUSTMENT

Within each participating school, the student non-response adjustment f_{2i} was calculated as:

$$f_{2i} = \frac{\sum_{k \in X(i)} f_{1i} w_{1i} w_{2ik}}{\sum_{k \in \Delta(i)} f_{1i} w_{1i} w_{2ik}}, \quad (5)$$

where the set $\Delta(i)$ is all assessed students in the school and the set $X(i)$ is all assessed students in the school plus all others who should have been assessed (*i.e.*, who were absent, not excluded or ineligible).

In most cases, this student non-response factor reduces to the ratio of the number of students who should have been assessed to the number who were assessed. In some cases of small schools (fewer than 15 respondents), it was necessary to collapse schools together, and then the more complex formula above applied.

Additionally, an adjustment factor greater than 2.0 was not allowed for the same reasons noted under school non-response adjustments. If this occurred, the school with the large adjustment was collapsed with the next school in the same school non-response cell.

Some schools in some countries had very low student response levels. In these cases it was determined that the small sample of assessed students was potentially too biased as a representation of the school to be included in the PISA data. For any school where the student response rate was below 25 per cent, the school was therefore treated as a non-respondent, and its student data were removed. In schools with between 25 and 50 per cent student response, the student non-response adjustment described above would have resulted in an adjustment factor of between 2.0000 and 4.0000, and so these schools were collapsed with others to create student non-response adjustments.

(Chapter 12 describes these schools as being treated as non-respondents for the purpose of response rate calculation, even though their student data were used in the analyses.)

TRIMMING STUDENT WEIGHTS

This final trimming check was used to detect student records that were unusually large compared to those of other students within the same explicit stratum. The sample design was intended to give all students from within the same explicit stratum an equal probability of selection and therefore equal weight, in the absence of school and student non-response. As already noted, inappropriate school sampling procedures and poor prior information about the number of eligible students in each school could lead to substantial violations of this principle. Moreover, school, grade, and student non-response adjustments, and, occasionally, inappropriate student sampling could, in a few cases, accumulate to give a few students in the data relatively very large weights, which adds considerably to sampling variance. The weights of individual students were therefore reviewed, and where the weight was more than four times the median weight of students from the same explicit sampling stratum, it was trimmed to be equal to four times the median weight for that explicit stratum.

The student trimming factor t_{2ij} is equal to the ratio of the final student weight to the student weight adjusted for student non-response, and therefore equal to 1.0000 for the great majority of students. The final weight variable on the data file was called *w_fstuwt*, which is the final student weight that incorporates any student-level trimming. Table 23 shows the number of students with weights trimmed at this point in the process (*i.e.*, $t_{2ij} < 1.0000$) for each country and the number of schools for which the school base weight was trimmed (*i.e.*, $t_{1i} < 1.0000$).

Table 23: School and Student Trimming

Country	Schools Trimmed	Students Trimmed
Australia	1	0
Austria	45	0
Belgium (Fl.)	0	0
Belgium (Fr.)	0	0
Brazil	2	0
Canada	2	0
Czech Republic	1	0
Denmark	1	0
England	0	0
Finland	0	0
France	0	0
Germany	0	0
Greece	1	0
Hungary	2	0
Iceland	0	0
Ireland	0	0
Italy	1	0
Japan	0	37
Korea	1	4
Latvia	1	0
Liechtenstein	0	0
Luxembourg	0	0
Mexico	1	23
Netherlands	0	0
New Zealand	0	0
Northern Ireland	0	0
Norway	0	0
Poland	1	0
Portugal	0	0
Russian Federation	3	39
Scotland	0	0
Spain	5	11
Sweden	0	0
Switzerland	2	0
United States	0	0

SUBJECT-SPECIFIC FACTORS FOR MATHEMATICS AND SCIENCE

The weights described above are appropriate for analysing data collected from all assessed students—*i.e.*, questionnaire and reading achievement data. Because a special booklet (SE or Booklet 0) was used in some countries for certain kinds of students and not at random, additional weighting factors are required to analyse data obtained from only a subset of the 10 PISA test booklets, particularly for analysing mathematics and science scale scores. These additional weighting factors were calculated and included with the data.

The mathematics weight factor was given as: 1.0 for each student assigned Booklet 0; 1.8 for each student assigned Booklet 1, 3, 5, 8, or 9; and 0.0 for each student assigned Booklet 2, 4, 6, or 7, which contained no mathematics items.

The science weight factor was given as: 1.0 for each student assigned Booklet 0; 1.8 for each student assigned Booklet 2, 4, 6, 8, or 9; and 0.0 for each student assigned Booklet 1, 3, 5, or 7, which contained no science items.

CALCULATING SAMPLING VARIANCE

To estimate the sampling variances of PISA estimates, a replication methodology was employed. This reflected the variance in estimates due to the sampling of schools and students. Additional variance due to the use of plausible values from the posterior distributions of scaled scores was captured separately, although computationally the two components can be carried out in a single program, such as WesVar 4 (Westat, 2000).

THE BALANCED REPEATED REPLICATION VARIANCE ESTIMATOR

The approach used for calculating sampling variances for PISA is known as Balanced Repeated Replication (BRR), or Balanced Half-Samples; the particular variant known as Fay's method was used. This method is very similar in nature to the jackknife method used in previous international studies of educational achievement, such as TIMSS. It is well documented in the survey sampling literature (see Rust, 1985; Rust and Rao, 1996; Shao, 1996; Wolter, 1985). The major advantage of BRR over the jackknife is that the jackknife method is not fully appropriate for use with non-differentiable functions of the survey data, most noticeably quantiles. It provides unbiased estimates, but not consistent ones. This means that, depending upon the sample design, the variance estimator can be very unstable, and despite empirical evidence that it can behave well in a PISA-like design, theory is lacking. In contrast BRR does not have this theoretical flaw. The standard BRR procedure can become unstable when used to analyse sparse population subgroups, but Fay's modification overcomes this difficulty, and is well justified in the literature (Judkins, 1990).

The BRR approach was implemented as follows, for a country where the student sample was selected from a sample of rather than all schools:

- Schools were paired on the basis of the explicit and implicit stratification and frame ordering used in sampling. The pairs were originally sampled schools, or pairs that included a participating replacement if an original refused. For an odd number of schools within a stratum, a triple was formed consisting of the last school and the pair preceding it.
- Pairs were numbered sequentially, 1 to H, with pair number denoted by the subscript h. Other studies and the literature refer to such pairs as variance strata or zones, or pseudo-strata.
- Within each variance stratum, one school (the Primary Sampling Unit, PSU) was randomly numbered as 1, the other as 2 (and the third as 3, in a triple), which defined the variance unit of the school. Subscript j refers to this numbering.
- These variance strata and variance units (1, 2, 3) assigned at school level are attached to the data for the sampled students within the corresponding school.
- Let the estimate of a given statistic from the full student sample be denoted as X^*. This is calculated using the full sample weights.
- A set of 80 replicate estimates, X_t^* (where t runs from 1 to 80), was created. Each of these replicate estimates was formed by multiplying the sampling weights from one of the two primary sampling units (PSUs) in each stratum by 1.5, and the weights from the remaining

PSUs by 0.5. The determination as to which PSUs received inflated weights, and which received deflated weights, was carried out in a systematic fashion, based on the entries in a Hadamard matrix of order 80. A Hadamard matrix contains entries that are +1 and −1 in value, and has the property that the matrix, multiplied by its transpose, gives the identity matrix of order 80, multiplied by a factor of 80. Examples of Hadamard matrices are given in Wolter (1985).

- In cases where there were three units in a triple, either one of the schools (designated at random) received a factor of 1.7071 for a given replicate, with the other two schools receiving factors of 0.6464, or else the one school received a factor of 0.2929 and the other two schools received factors of 1.3536. The explanation of how these particular factors came to be used is explained in Appendix 12.
- To use a Hadamard matrix of order 80 requires that there be no more than 80 variance strata within a country, or else that some combining of variance strata be carried out prior to assigning the replication factors via the Hadamard matrix. The combining of variance strata does not cause any bias in variance estimation, provided that it is carried out in such a way that the assignment of variance units is independent from one stratum to another within strata that are combined. That is, the assignment of variance units must be completed before the combining of variance strata takes place, and this approach was used for PISA.
- The reliability of variance estimates for important population subgroups is enhanced if any combining of variance strata that is required is conducted by combining variance strata from different subgroups. Thus in PISA, variance strata that were combined were selected from different explicit sampling strata and, to the extent possible, from different implicit sampling strata also.
- In some countries, it was not the case that the entire sample was a two-stage design, of first sampling schools and then sampling students. In some countries for part of the sample (and for the entire samples for Iceland, Liechtenstein and Luxembourg), schools were included with certainty into the sampling, so that only a single stage of student sampling was carried out for this part of the sample. In these cases instead of pairing schools, pairs of individual students were formed from within the same school (and if the school had an odd number of sampled students, a triple of students was formed also). The procedure of assigning variance units and replicate weight factors was then conducted at the student level, rather than at the school level.
- In contrast, in a few countries there was a stage of sampling that preceded the selection of schools, for at least part of the sample. This was done in a major way in the Russian Federation and the United States, and in a more minor way in Germany and Poland. In these cases there was a stage of sampling that took place before the schools were selected. Then the procedure for assigning variance strata, variance units and replicate factors was applied at this higher level of sampling. The schools and students then inherited the assignment from the higher-level unit in which they were located.
- The variance estimator is then:

$$V_{BRR}(X^*) = 0.05 \sum_{t=1}^{80} \left\{ \left(X_t^* - X^* \right)^2 \right\}. \qquad (6)$$

The properties of BRR have been established by demonstrating that it is unbiased and consistent for simple linear estimators (*i.e.*, means from straightforward sample designs), and that it has desirable asymptotic consistency for a wide variety of estimators under complex designs, and through empirical simulation studies.

REFLECTING WEIGHTING ADJUSTMENTS

This description glosses over one aspect of the implementation of the BRR method. Weights for a given replicate are obtained by applying the adjustment to the weight components that reflect selection probabilities (the school base weight in most cases), and then re-computing the non-response adjustment replicate by replicate.

Implementing this approach required that the Consortium produce a set of replicate weights in addition to the full sample weight. Eighty such replicate weights were needed for each student in the data file. The school and student non-response adjustments had to be repeated for each set of replicate weights.

To estimate sampling errors correctly, the analyst must use the variance estimation formula above, by deriving estimates X_t^* using the t-th set of replicate weights instead of the full sample weight. Because of the weight adjustments (and the presence of occasional triples), this does not mean merely increasing the final full sample weights for half the schools by a factor of 1.5 and decreasing the weights from the remaining schools by a factor of 0.5. Many replicate weights will also be slightly disturbed, beyond these adjustments, as a result of repeating the non-response adjustments separately by replicate.

FORMATION OF VARIANCE STRATA

With the approach described above, all original sampled schools were sorted in stratum order (including refusals and ineligibles) and paired, by contrast to other international education assessments such TIMSS and TIMSS-R that have paired participating schools only. However, these studies did not use an approach reflecting the impact of non-response adjustments on sampling variance. This is unlikely to be a big component of variance in any PISA country, but the procedure gives a more accurate estimate of sampling variance.

COUNTRIES WHERE ALL STUDENTS WERE SELECTED FOR PISA

In Iceland, Liechtenstein and Luxembourg, all eligible students were selected for PISA. It might be considered surprising that the PISA data should reflect any sampling variance in these countries, but students have been assigned to variance strata and variance units, and the BRR formula does give a positive estimate of sampling variance for three reasons. First, in each country there was some student non-response, and, in the case of Luxembourg, some school non-response. Not all eligible students were assessed, giving sampling variance. Second, only 55 per cent of the students were assessed in mathematics and science. Third, the issue is to make inference about educational systems and not particular groups of individual students, so it is appropriate that a part of the sampling variance reflect random variation between student populations, even if they were to be subjected to identical educational experiences. This is consistent with the approach that is generally used whenever survey data are used to try to make direct or indirect inference about some underlying system.

CHAPTER 9 { SCALING PISA COGNITIVE DATA

Ray Adams

The mixed coefficients multinomial logit model as described by Adams, Wilson and Wang (1997) was used to scale the PISA data, and implemented by ConQuest software (Wu, Adams and Wilson, 1997).

THE MIXED COEFFICIENTS MULTINOMIAL LOGIT MODEL

The model applied to PISA is a generalised form of the Rasch model. The model is a mixed coefficients model where items are described by a fixed set of unknown parameters ξ, while the student outcome levels (the latent variable), θ, is a random effect.

Assume that I items are indexed $i = 1,...,I$ with each item admitting $K_i + 1$ response categories indexed $k = 0,1,...,K_i$. Use the vector valued random variable,
$\mathbf{X}_i = \left(X_{i1}, X_{i2},..., X_{iK_i}\right)^T$, where

$$X_{ij} = \begin{cases} 1 & \text{if response to item } i \text{ is in category } j \\ 0 & \text{otherwise} \end{cases}, \quad (7)$$

to indicate the $K_i + 1$ possible responses to item i.

A vector of zeroes denotes a response in category zero, making the zero category a reference category, which is necessary for model identification. Using this as the reference category is arbitrary, and does not affect the generality of the model. The $\mathbf{X}_i$ can also be collected together into the single vector $\mathbf{X}^T = \left(\mathbf{X}_1^T, \mathbf{X}_2^T,..., \mathbf{X}_I^T\right)$, called the response vector (or pattern). Particular instances of each of these random variables are indicated by their lower case equivalents; $\mathbf{x}$, $\mathbf{x}_i$ and x_{ik}.

Items are described through a vector $\boldsymbol{\xi}^T = \left(\xi_1, \xi_2,..., \xi_p\right)$, of p parameters. Linear combinations of these are used in the response probability model to describe the empirical characteristics of the response categories of each item. Design vectors $\mathbf{a}_{ij}$, $\left(i = 1,...,I; j = 1,...K_i\right)$, each of length p, which can be collected to form a design matrix

$\mathbf{A}^T = \left(\mathbf{a}_{11}, \mathbf{a}_{12},..., \mathbf{a}_{1K_1}, \mathbf{a}_{21},..., \mathbf{a}_{2K_2},..., \mathbf{a}_{IK_I}\right)$

define these linear combinations.

The multi-dimensional form of the model assumes that a set of D traits underlies the individuals' responses. The D latent traits define a D-dimensional latent space. The vector $\boldsymbol{\theta} = \left(\theta_1, \theta_2,..., \theta_D\right)'$, represents an individual's position in the D-dimensional latent space.

The model also introduces a scoring function that allows the specification of the score or performance level assigned to each possible response category to each item. To do so, the notion of a response score b_{ijd} is introduced, which gives the performance level of an observed response in category j, item i, dimension d. The scores across D dimensions can be collected into a column vector $\mathbf{b}_{ik} = \left(b_{ik1}, b_{ik2},..., b_{ikD}\right)^T$ and again collected into the scoring sub-matrix for item i, $\mathbf{B}_i = \left(\mathbf{b}_{i1}, \mathbf{b}_{i2},..., \mathbf{b}_{iD}\right)^T$ and then into a scoring

matrix $\mathbf{B} = \left(\mathbf{B}_1^T, \mathbf{B}_2^T,..., \mathbf{B}_I^T\right)^T$ for the entire test. (The score for a response in the zero category is zero, but other responses may also be scored zero).

The probability of a response in category j of item i is modelled as:

$$\Pr(\mathbf{X}_{ij} = 1; \mathbf{A}, \mathbf{B}, \boldsymbol{\xi} | \boldsymbol{\theta}) = \frac{\exp(\mathbf{b}_{ij}\boldsymbol{\theta} + \mathbf{a}'_{ij}\boldsymbol{\xi})}{\sum_{k=1}^{K_i} \exp(\mathbf{b}_{ik}\boldsymbol{\theta} + \mathbf{a}'_{ik}\boldsymbol{\xi})}. \tag{8}$$

For a response vector

$$f(\mathbf{x}; \boldsymbol{\xi} | \boldsymbol{\theta}) = \Psi(\boldsymbol{\theta}, \boldsymbol{\xi}) \exp[\mathbf{x}'(\mathbf{B}\boldsymbol{\theta} + \mathbf{A}\boldsymbol{\xi})], \tag{9}$$

with

$$\Psi(\boldsymbol{\theta}, \boldsymbol{\xi}) = \left\{ \sum_{\mathbf{z} \in \Omega} \exp[\mathbf{z}^T (\mathbf{B}\boldsymbol{\theta} + \mathbf{A}\boldsymbol{\xi})] \right\}^{-1}, \tag{10}$$

where Ω is the set of all possible response vectors.

THE POPULATION MODEL

The item response model is a conditional model, in the sense that it describes the process of generating item responses conditional on the latent variable, θ. The complete definition of the model, therefore, requires the specification of a density, $f_\theta(\boldsymbol{\theta}; \boldsymbol{\alpha})$, for the latent variable, θ. Let α symbolise a set of parameters that characterise the distribution of θ. The most common practice, when specifying uni-dimensional marginal item response models, is to assume that students have been sampled from a normal population with mean μ and variance σ^2. That is:

$$f_\theta(\boldsymbol{\theta}; \boldsymbol{\alpha}) \equiv f_\theta(\theta; \mu, \sigma^2) = (2\pi\sigma^2)^{-\frac{1}{2}} \exp\left[-\frac{(\theta - \mu)^2}{2\sigma^2}\right], \tag{11}$$

or equivalently

$$\theta = \mu + E, \tag{12}$$

where $E \sim N(0, \sigma^2)$.

Adams, Wilson and Wu (1997) discuss how a natural extension of (11) is to replace the mean, μ, with the regression model, $\mathbf{Y}_n^T \boldsymbol{\beta}$, where $\mathbf{Y}_n$ is a vector of u, fixed and known values for student n, and β is the corresponding vector of regression coefficients. For example, $\mathbf{Y}_n$ could be constituted of student variables such as gender or socio-economic status. Then the population model for student n becomes:

$$\theta_n = \mathbf{Y}_n^T \boldsymbol{\beta} + E_n, \tag{13}$$

where it is assumed that the E_n are independently and identically normally distributed with mean zero and variance σ^2 so that (13) is equivalent to:

$$f_\theta(\theta_n; \mathbf{Y}_n, b, \sigma^2) = (2\pi\sigma^2)^{-1/2} \exp\left[-\frac{1}{2\sigma^2}(\theta_n - \mathbf{Y}_n^T \boldsymbol{\beta})^T (\theta_n - \mathbf{Y}_n^T \boldsymbol{\beta})\right], \tag{14}$$

a normal distribution with mean $\mathbf{Y}_n^T \boldsymbol{\beta}$ and variance σ^2. If (14) is used as the population model then the parameters to be estimated are β, σ^2 and ξ.

The generalisation needs to be taken one step further to apply it to the vector valued $\boldsymbol{\theta}$ rather than the scalar valued θ. The extension results in the multivariate population model:

$$f_\theta(\boldsymbol{\theta}_n; \mathbf{W}_n, \boldsymbol{\gamma}, \boldsymbol{\Sigma}) = (2\pi)^{-d/2} |\boldsymbol{\Sigma}|^{-\frac{1}{2}} \exp\left[-\frac{1}{2}(\boldsymbol{\theta}_n - \boldsymbol{\gamma}\mathbf{W}_n)^T \boldsymbol{\Sigma}^{-1} (\boldsymbol{\theta}_n - \boldsymbol{\gamma}\mathbf{W}_n)\right], \tag{15}$$

where γ is a $u \times d$ matrix of regression coefficients, Σ is a $d \times d$ variance-covariance matrix and W_n is a $u \times 1$ vector of fixed variables.

In PISA, the W_n variables are referred to as conditioning variables.

COMBINED MODEL

In (16), the conditional item response model (12) and the population model (15) are combined to obtain the unconditional, or marginal, item response model:

$$f_x(\mathbf{x}; \xi, \gamma, \Sigma) = \int_{\theta} f_x(\mathbf{x}; \xi | \theta) f_\theta(\theta; \gamma, \Sigma) \, d\theta. \tag{16}$$

It is important to recognise that under this model, the locations of individuals on the latent variables are not estimated. The parameters of the model are γ, Σ and ξ.

The procedures used to estimate model parameters are described in Adams, Wilson and Wu (1997), Adams, Wilson and Wang (1997), and Wu, Adams and Wilson (1997).

For each individual it is possible however to specify a posterior distribution for the latent variable, given by:

$$h_\theta(\theta_n; \mathbf{W}_n, \xi, \gamma, \Sigma | \mathbf{x}_n) = \frac{f_x(\mathbf{x}_n; \xi | \theta_n) f_\theta(\theta_n; \mathbf{W}_n, \gamma, \Sigma)}{f_x(\mathbf{x}_n; \mathbf{W}_n, \xi, \gamma, \Sigma)}$$

$$= \frac{f_x(\mathbf{x}_n; \xi | \theta_n) f_\theta(\theta_n; \mathbf{W}_n, \gamma, \Sigma)}{\int_{\theta_n} f_x(\mathbf{x}_n; \xi | \theta_n) f_\theta(\theta_n; \mathbf{W}_n, \gamma, \Sigma)}. \tag{17}$$

APPLICATION TO PISA

In PISA, this model was used in three steps: national calibrations; international scaling; and student score generation.

For both the national calibrations and the international scaling, the conditional item response model (9) is used in conjunction with the population model (15), but conditioning variables are not used. That is, it is assumed that students have been sampled from a multivariate normal distribution.

The PISA model is five-dimensional, made up of three reading, one science and one mathematics dimension. The design matrix was chosen so that the partial credit model was used for items with multiple score categories and the simple logistic model was fit to the dichotomously scored items.

NATIONAL CALIBRATIONS

National calibrations were performed separately country-by-country using unweighted data. The results of these analyses, which were used to monitor the quality of the data and to make decisions regarding national item treatment, are given in Chapter 13.

The outcomes of the national calibrations were used to make a decision about how to treat each item in each country. This means that: an item may be deleted from PISA altogether if it has poor psychometric characteristics in more than eight countries (a *dodgy item*); it may be regarded as not-administered in particular countries if it has poor psychometric characteristics in those countries but functions well in the vast majority of others; or an item with sound characteristics in each country but which shows substantial item-by-country interactions may be regarded as a different item (for scaling purposes) in each country (or in some subset of countries)—that is, the difficulty parameter will be free to vary across countries.

Both the second and third options have the same impact on comparisons between countries. That is, if an item is identified as behaving differently in different countries, choosing either the second or third option will have the same impact on inter-country comparisons. The choice between them could, however, influence within-country comparisons.

When reviewing the national calibrations, particular attention was paid to the fit of the items to the scaling model, item discrimination and item-by-country interactions.

ITEM RESPONSE MODEL FIT (INFIT MEAN SQUARE)

For each item parameter, the ConQuest fit mean square statistic index (Wu, 1997) was used to provide an indication of the compatibility of the model and the data. For each student, the model describes the probability of obtaining the different item scores. It is therefore possible to compare the model prediction and what has been observed for one item across students. Accumulating comparisons across cases gives us an item-fit statistic.

As the fit statistics compare an observed value with a predicted value, the fit is an analysis of residuals. In the case of the item infit mean square, values near one are desirable. An infit mean square greater than one is often associated with a low discrimination index, and an infit mean square less than one is often associated with a high discrimination index.

DISCRIMINATION COEFFICIENTS

For each item, the correlation between the students' scores on that item and their aggregate scores on the set for the same domain and booklet as the item of interest was used as an index of discrimination. If p_{ij} ($= x_{ij}/m_I$) is the proportion of score levels that student i achieved on item j, and $p_I = \sum_j p_{ij}$, (where the summation is of the items from the same booklet and domain as item j) is the sum of the proportions of the maximum score achieved by student i, then the discrimination is calculated as the product-moment correlation between p_{ij} and p_i for all students. For multiple-choice and short-answer items, this index will be the usual point-biserial index of discrimination.

The point-biserial index of discrimination for a particular category of an item is a comparison of the aggregate score between students selecting that category and all other students. If the category is the correct answer, the point-biserial index of discrimination should be higher than 0.25. Non-key categories should have a negative point-biserial index of discrimination. The point-biserial index of discrimination for a partial credit item should be ordered, *i.e.*, categories scored 0 should be lower than the point-biserial correlation of categories scored 1, and so on.

ITEM-BY-COUNTRY INTERACTION

The national scaling provides nationally specific item parameter estimates. The consistency of item parameter estimates across countries was of particular interest. If the test measured the same latent trait per domain in all countries, then items should have the same relative difficulty, or, more precisely, would fall within the interval defined by the standard error on the item parameter estimate.

NATIONAL REPORTS

After national scaling, five reports were returned to each participating country to assist in reviewing their data with the Consortium:[1]

- *Report 1* presented the results of a basic item analysis in tabular form. For each item, the number of students, the percentage of students and the point-biserial correlation were provided for each valid category.
- *Report 2* provided, for each item and for each valid category, the point-biserial correlation and the student-centred Item Response Theory (IRT) ability average in graphical form.
- *Report 3* provided a graphical comparison of the Item Infit Mean Square coefficients and the item discrimination coefficients computed at national and international levels.
- *Report 4* provided a graphical comparison of both the item difficulty parameter and the item thresholds,[2] computed at national and international levels.
- *Report 5* listed the items that National Project Managers (NPMs) needed to check for mistranslation and/or misprinting, referred to as *dodgy items*.

Report 1: Descriptive Statistics on Individual Items in Tabular Form

A detailed item-by-item report was provided in tabular form showing the basic item analysis statistics at the national level (see Figure 12 for an example).

The table shows each possible response category for each item. The second column indicates the *score* assigned to the different categories. For each category, the number and percentage of students responding is shown, along with the point-biserial correlation and the associated *t* statistic. Note that for the item in the example the correct answer is '4', indicated by the '1' in the score column; thus the point-biserial for a response of '4' is the item's discrimination index, also shown along the top.

---

[1] In addition, two reports showing results from the Student and School Questionnaires were also returned to participants.

[2] A threshold for an item score is the point on the scale at which the probability of a response at that score or higher becomes greater than 50 per cent.

```
Item 1
------
item:1 (M033Q01)
Cases for this item   1372   Discrimination is   0.39
-----------------------------------------------------------------
   Label     Score     Count    % of total   Pt Bis        t
-----------------------------------------------------------------
     0                    0       0.00        NA          NA
     1       0.00        17       1.28       -0.08       -3.14
     2       0.00       127       9.57       -0.19       -7.15
     3       0.00       102       7.69       -0.12       -4.57
     4       1.00      1053      79.35        0.39       16.34
     5                    0       0.00        NA          NA
     6                    0       0.00        NA          NA
     7                    0       0.00        NA          NA
     8       0.00         2       0.15        0.02        0.61
     9       0.00        57       4.30       -0.22       -8.47
     r       0.00        14       1.06       -0.24       -9.15
=================================================================
```

Figure 12: Example of Item Statistics Shown in Report 1

The report shows two kinds of missing data: row 9 indicates students who omitted the item but responded validly to at least one subsequent item; row r shows students who did not reach this item.

Report 2: Descriptive Statistics on Individual Items in Graphical Form

Report 2 (*see Figure 13*) graphs the ability average and the point-biserial correlation by category. Average Ability by Category is calculated by domain and centred for each item. This makes it easy to identify positive and negative ability categories, so that checks can be made to ensure that, for multiple-choice items, the key category has the highest average ability estimate, and for constructed-response items, the mean abilities are ordered consistently with the score levels. The displayed graphs also facilitate the process of identifying the following anomalies:

- a non-key category with a positive point-biserial or a point-biserial higher than the key category;
- a key category with a negative point-biserial; and
- for partial-credit items, average abilities (and point-biserials) not increasing with the score points.

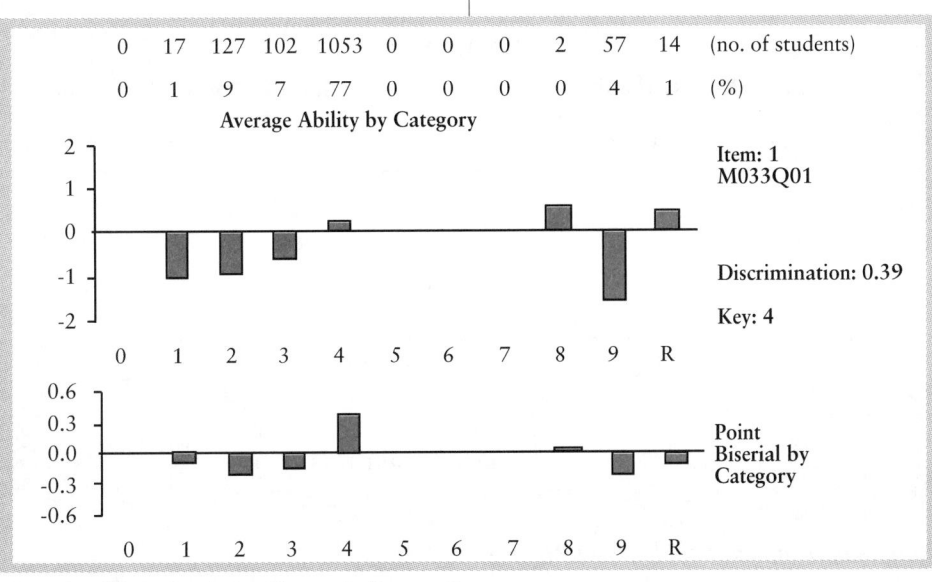

Figure 13: Example of Item Statistics Shown in Report 2

Report 3: Comparison of National and International Infit Mean Square and Discrimination Coefficients

The national scaling provided the infit mean square, the point-biserial correlation, the item parameter estimate (or difficulty estimate) and the thresholds for each item in each country. Reports 3 (*see Figure 14*) and 4 (*see Figure 15*) compare the value computed for one country with those computed for all other countries and with the value computed at international level for each item.

The black crosses present the values of the coefficients computed from the international database. Shaded boxes represent the mean plus or minus one standard deviation of these national values. Shaded crosses represent the values for the national data set of the country to which the report was returned.

Substantial differences between the national and international value on one or both of these indices show that the item is behaving differently in that country. This might reflect a mistranslation or another problem specific to the national version, but if the item was misbehaving in all or nearly all countries, it might reflect a specific problem in the source item and not with the national versions.

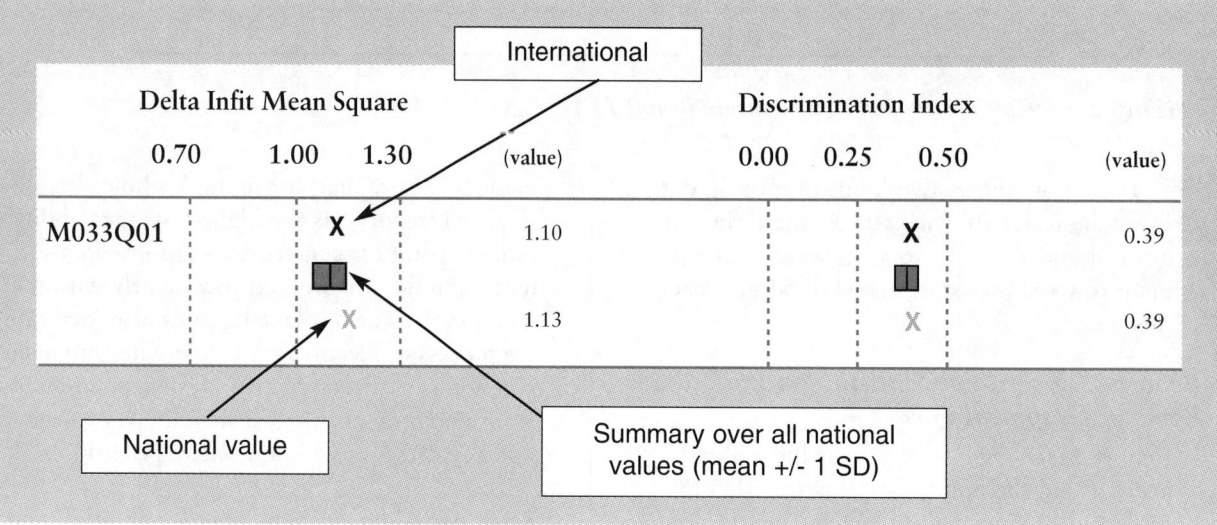

Figure 14: Example of Item Statistics Shown in Report 3

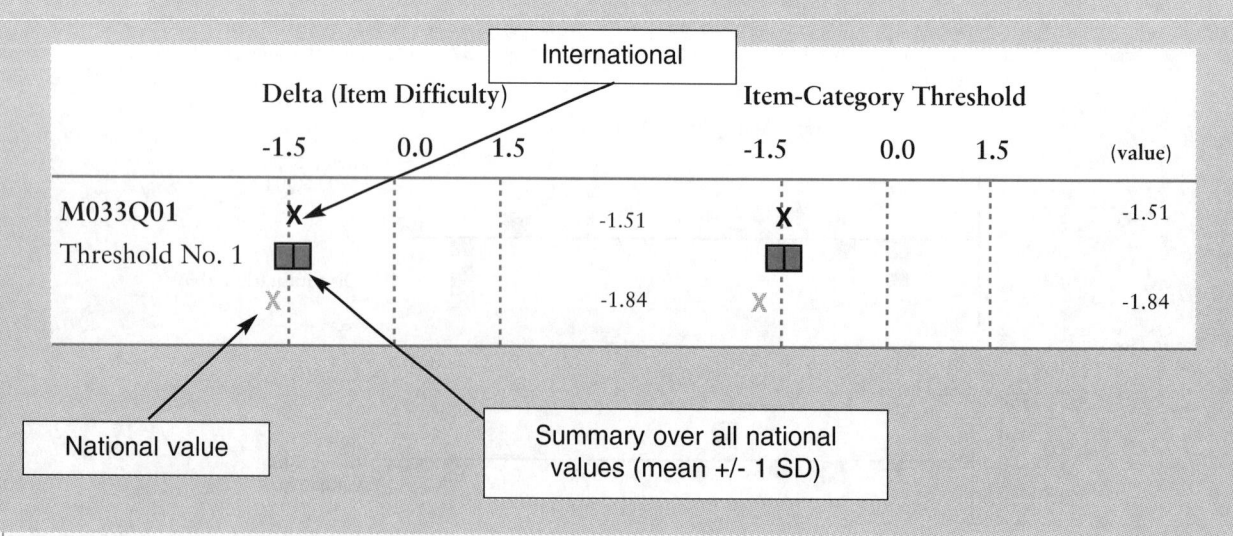

Figure 15: Example of Item Statistics Shown in Report 4

Report 4: Comparison of National and International Item Difficulty Parameters and Thresholds

Report 4 presents the item difficulty parameters and the thresholds, in the same graphic form as Report 3. Substantial differences between the national value and the international value (*i.e.*, the national value mean) might be interpreted like an item-by-country interaction. Nevertheless, appropriate estimates of the item-by-country interaction are provided in Report 5.

Report 5: National Dodgy Item Report

For each country's *dodgy* items, Report 5 lists where the items were flagged for one or more of the following reasons: difficulty is significantly easier or harder than average; a non-key category has a point-biserial correlation higher than 0.05 if at least 10 students selected it; the key category point-biserial correlation is lower than 0.25; the categories abilities for partial credit items are not ordered; and/or the infit mean square is higher than 1.20 or lower than 0.8. An example extract is shown in Figure 16.

INTERNATIONAL CALIBRATION

International item parameters were set by applying the conditional item response model (9) in conjunction with the multivariate population model (15), without using conditioning variables, to a sub-sample of students. This sub-sample of students, referred to as the international calibration sample, consisted of 13 500 students comprising 500 students drawn at random from each of the 27 participating OECD countries that met the PISA 2000 response rate standards (*see Chapter 13*). This excluded any SE booklet students and was stratified by linguistic community within the country.

The allocation of each PISA item to one of the five PISA 2000 scales is given in Appendix 1 (for reading), Appendix 2 (for mathematics) and Appendix 3 (for science).

STUDENT SCORE GENERATION

As with all item response scaling models, student *proficiencies* (or measures) are not observed; they are missing data that must be inferred from the observed item responses. There are several possible alternative approaches for making this inference. PISA used two approaches: maximum likelihood, using Warm's (1985) Weighted Likelihood Estimator (WLE), and plausible values (PVs). The WLE proficiency makes the actual score that the student attained the most likely. PVs are a selection of likely proficiencies for students that attained each score.

COMPUTING MAXIMUM LIKELIHOOD ESTIMATES IN PISA

Six weighted likelihood estimates were provided for each student, one each for mathematical literacy, reading literacy and scientific literacy and one for each of the three reading literacy,

	Item by Country Interactions		Discrimination			Fit	
	Easier than Expected	Harder than Expected	Non-key Point-Biserial Correlation is Positive	Key Point-Biserial Correlation is Negative	Ability not Ordered	Small high discr. item	Large low discr. item
M033Q01	☑	☐	■	■	■	☐	☐
M037Q02T	☐	☑	■	■	■	☐	☐
M124Q01	☐	☑	■	■	■	☐	☐

Figure 16: Example of Item Statistics Shown in Report 5

sub-scales. These can be treated as (essentially) unbiased estimates of student *abilities*, and analysed using standard methods.

Weighted maximum likelihood ability estimates (Warm, 1985) are produced by maximising (9) with respect to θ_n, that is, solving the likelihood equations:

$$\sum_{d \in D} \left(\sum_{i \in \Omega} \left(b_{ix_{ni}} - \sum_{j=1}^{K_i} \frac{b_{ij} \exp\left(b_{ij} s_{nd} \theta_{nd} + a'_{ij} \hat{\xi}\right)}{\sum_{k=1}^{K_i} \exp\left(b_{ik} s_{nd} \theta_{nd} + a'_{ik} \hat{\xi}\right)} + \frac{J_{nd}}{2I_{nd}} \right) \right) = 0, \quad (18)$$

for each case, where $\hat{\xi}$ are the item parameter estimates obtained from the international calibration and d indicates the latent dimensions. I_{nd} is the test information for student n on dimension d, and J_{nd} is the first derivative with respect to θ. These equations are solved using a routine based on the Newton-Raphson method.

PLAUSIBLE VALUES

Using item parameters anchored at their estimated values from the international calibration, the plausible values are random draws from the marginal posterior of the latent distribution, (15), for each student. For details on the uses of plausible values, see Mislevy (1991) and Mislevy *et al.* (1992).

In PISA, the random draws from the marginal posterior distribution (17) are taken as follows.

M vector-valued random deviates, $\{\varphi_{mn}\}_{m=1}^{M}$, from the multivariate normal distribution, $f_\theta(\theta_n; W_n, \gamma, \Sigma)$, for each case n.[3] These vectors are used to approximate the integral in the denominator of (17), using the Monte-Carlo integration:

$$\int_\theta f_x(x; \xi | \theta) f_\theta(\theta, \gamma, \Sigma) d\theta \approx \frac{1}{M} \sum_{m=1}^{M} f_x(x; \xi | \varphi_{mn}) \equiv \Im. \quad (19)$$

At the same time, the values:

$$p_{mn} = f_x(x_n; \xi | \varphi_{mn}) f_\theta(\varphi_{mn}; W_n, \gamma, \Sigma) \quad (20)$$

are calculated, yielding the set of pairs $\left(\varphi_{mn}, p_{mn}/\Im\right)_{m=1}^{M}$, which can be used as an approximation of the posterior density (17); and the probability that φ_{nj} could be drawn from this density is given by:

$$q_{nj} = \frac{p_{mn}}{\sum_{m=1}^{M} p_{mn}}. \quad (21)$$

At this point, L uniformly distributed random numbers $\{\eta_i\}_{i=1}^{L}$ are generated; and for each random draw, the vector, φ_{ni_0}, that satisfies the condition:

$$\sum_{s=1}^{i_0-1} q_{sn} < \eta_i \leq \sum_{s=1}^{i_0} q_{sn} \quad (22)$$

is selected as a plausible vector.

---

[3] The value M should be large. In PISA, $M = 2000$ was used.

CONSTRUCTING CONDITIONING VARIABLES

The PISA conditioning variables are prepared using procedures based on those used in the United States National Assessment of Educational Progress (Beaton, 1987) and in TIMSS (Macaskill, Adams and Wu, 1998). The steps involved in this process are as follows:

- *Step 1.* Each variable in the Student Questionnaire was dummy coded according to the coding presented in Appendix 8.[4]
- *Step 2.* For each country, a principal components analysis of the dummy-coded variables was performed, and component scores were produced for each student (a sufficient number of components to account for 90 per cent of the variance in the original variables).
- *Step 3.* Using item parameters anchored at their international location and conditioning variables derived from the national principal components analysis, the item-response model was fit to each national data set and the national population parameters γ and Σ were estimated.[5]
- *Step 4.* Five vectors of plausible values were drawn using the method described above.

ANALYSIS OF DATA WITH PLAUSIBLE VALUES

It is very important to recognise that plausible values are *not* test scores and should not be treated as such. They are random numbers drawn from the distribution of scores that could be reasonably assigned to each individual—that is, the marginal posterior distribution (17). As such, plausible values contain random error variance components and are not optimal as scores for individuals.[6] Plausible values as a set are better suited to describing the performance of the population. This approach, developed by Mislevy and Sheehan (1987, 1989) and based on the imputation theory of Rubin (1987), produces consistent estimators of population parameters.

Plausible values are intermediate values provided to obtain consistent estimates of population parameters using standard statistical analysis software such as SPSS® and SAS®. As an alternative, analyses can be completed using ConQuest (Wu, Adams and Wilson, 1997).

The PISA student file contains 30 plausible values, five for each of the five PISA 2000 cognitive scales and five for the combined reading scale. *PV1MATH* to *PV5MATH* are five for mathematical literacy; *PV1SCIE* to *PV5SCIE* for scientific literacy, and *PV1READ* to *PV5READ* for combined reading literacy. For the three reading literacy sub-scales, *retrieving information, interpreting texts* and *reflection and evaluation*, the plausible values variables are *PV1READ1* to *PV5READ1*, *PV1READ2* to *PV5READ2* and *PV1READ3* to *PV5READ3*, respectively.

If an analysis were to be undertaken with one of these five cognitive scales or for the combined reading scale, then it would ideally be undertaken five times, once with each relevant plausible values variable. The results would be averaged, and then significance tests adjusting for variation between the five sets of results computed.

More formally, suppose that $r(\boldsymbol{\theta}, \mathbf{Y})$ is a statistic that depends upon the latent variable and some other observed characteristic of each student. That is: $(\boldsymbol{\theta}, \mathbf{Y}) = (\theta_1, y_1, \theta_2, y_2, ..., \theta_N, y_N)$ where (θ_n, y_n) are the values of the latent variable and the other observed characteristic for student *n*. Unfortunately θ_n is not observed. However, the item responses, x_n, from which the marginal posterior $h_\theta(\theta_n; y_n, \xi, \gamma, \Sigma | \mathbf{x}_n)$ can be constructed for each student *n*, are observed. If $h_\theta(\boldsymbol{\theta}; \mathbf{Y}, \xi, \gamma, \Sigma | \mathbf{X})$ is the joint marginal posterior for *n*=1,...,*N* then:

$$r^*(\mathbf{X}, \mathbf{Y}) = E\left[r^*(\boldsymbol{\theta}, \mathbf{Y}) | \mathbf{X}, \mathbf{Y}\right]$$
$$= \int_\theta r(\boldsymbol{\theta}, \mathbf{Y}) h_\theta(\boldsymbol{\theta}; \mathbf{Y}, \xi, \gamma, \Sigma | \mathbf{X}) d\boldsymbol{\theta} \quad (23)$$

can be computed.

The integral in (23) can be computed using the Monte-Carlo method. If *M* random vectors $(\Theta_1, \Theta_2, ..., \Theta_M)$ are drawn from $h_\theta(\boldsymbol{\theta}; \mathbf{Y}, \xi, \gamma, \Sigma | \mathbf{X})$ (23) is approximated by:

$$r^*(\mathbf{X}, \mathbf{Y}) \approx \frac{1}{M} \sum_{m=1}^{M} r(\theta_m, \mathbf{Y})$$
$$= \frac{1}{M} \sum_{m=1}^{M} \hat{r}_m \quad , \quad (24)$$

---

[4] With the exception of gender and *ISEI*.

[5] In addition to the principal components, gender, *ISEI* and school mean performance were added as conditioning variables.

[6] Where optimal might be defined, for example, as either unbiased or minimising the mean squared error at the student level.

where $\hat{r}_m$ is the estimate of r computed using the m-th set of plausible values.

From (23) we can see that the final estimate of r is the average of the estimates computed using each plausible value in turn. If U_m is the sampling variance for $\hat{r}_m$ then the sampling variance of r^* is:

$$V = U^* + \left(1 + M^{-1}\right) B_M, \quad (25)$$

where $U^* = \dfrac{1}{M} \sum_{m=1}^{M} U_m$ and

$$B_M = \frac{1}{M-1} \sum_{m=1}^{M} \left(\hat{r}_m - r^*\right)^2.$$

An α-% confidence interval for r^* is: $r^* \pm t_\upsilon\left(\dfrac{(1-\alpha)}{2}\right) V^{\frac{1}{2}}$ where $t_\upsilon(s)$ is the s percentile of the t-distribution with υ degrees of freedom. $\upsilon = \dfrac{1}{\dfrac{f_M^2}{M-1} + \dfrac{(1-f_M)^2}{d}}$,

$f_M = \left(1 + M^{-1}\right) B_M / V$ and d is the degrees of freedom that would have applied had θ_n been observed. In PISA, d will vary by country and have a maximum possible value of 80.

CHAPTER 10: CODING AND MARKER RELIABILITY STUDIES

As explained in the first section of this report, on Test Design (*see Chapter 2*), a substantial proportion of the PISA 2000 items were open-ended and required marking by trained markers (or coders). It was important therefore that PISA implemented procedures that maximised the validity and consistency (both within and between countries) of this marking.

Each country coded items on the basis of *Marking Guides* prepared by the Consortium (*see Chapter 2*) using the marking design described in Chapter 6. Training sessions to train countries in the use of the *Marking Guides* were held prior to both the field trial and the main study.

This chapter describes three aspects of the coding and marking reliability studies undertaken in conjunction with the field trial and the main study. These are the homogeneity analyses undertaken with the field trial data to assist the test developers in constructing valid, reliable scoring rubrics; the variance component analyses undertaken with the main study data to examine within-country rater reliability; and an Inter-country Reliability Study undertaken to examine the between-country consistency in applying the *Marking Guides*.

EXAMINING WITHIN-COUNTRY VARIABILITY IN MARKING

Norman Verhelst

To obtain an estimate of the between-marker variability within each country, multiple marking was required for at least some student answers. Therefore, it was decided that multiple markings would be collected for all open-ended items in both the field trial and the main study for a moderate number of students. In the main study, either 48 or 72 students' booklets were multiply marked, depending on the country. The requirement was that the same four expert markers per domain (reading, mathematics and science) should mark all items appearing together in a test booklet. A booklet containing, for example, 15 reading items, would give a three-dimensional table for reading (48 or 72 students by 15 items by 4 markers), where each cell contains a single category. For each domain and each booklet, such a table was produced and processed in several analyses, which are described later. These data sets were required from each participating country.

The field trial problems were quite different from those in the main study. In the field trial, many more items were tried than were used in the main study. One important purpose of the field trial was to select a subset of items to be used in the main study. One obvious concern was to ensure that markers agreed to a reasonable degree in their categorisation of the answers. More subtle problems can arise, however. In the final administration of a test, a student answer is scored numerically. But in the construction phase of an item, more than two response categories may be provided, say *A*, *B* and *C*, and it may not always be clear how these should be converted to numerical scores. The technique used to analyse the field trial data can provide at least a partial answer, and also give an indication of the agreement between markers for each item separately. The technique is called *homogeneity analysis*. It is important to note that the data set for this analysis is treated as a collection of nominal or qualitative variables.

In the main study, the problem was different. The field trial concluded with a selection of a definite subset of items and a scoring rule for each. The main problem in the main study was to determine how much of the total variance of the numerical test scores could be attributed to variability across markers. The basic data set to be analysed therefore consisted of a three-dimensional table of numerical scores. The technique used is referred to as *variance component analysis*.

Some items in the field trial appeared to function poorly because of well-identified defects (*e.g.*, poor translation). To get an impression of the differences in marker variability between field trial and main study, most field trial data analyses were repeated using the main study data. Some comparisons are reported below.

This chapter uses a consistent notational system, summarised in Figure 17.

Nested data structures are occasionally referred to, as every student and every marker belong to a single country. In such cases, the indices m and v take the subscript c.

HOMOGENEITY ANALYSIS

In the analysis, the basic observation is the category into which marker m places the response of student v on item i, denoted O_{ivm}. Basic in the approach of homogeneity analysis is to consider observations as qualitative or nominal variables. (For a more mathematical treatment of homogeneity analysis, see Nishisato, 1980; Gifi, 1990; or Greenacre, 1984.) Although observations may be coded as digits, these digits are considered as labels, not numbers. To have a consistent notational system, it is assumed in the sequel that the response categories of item i are labelled $1,\ldots,\ell,\ldots,L_i$. The main purpose of the analysis is to convert these qualitative observations into (quantitative) data which are in some sense optimal.

The basic loss function

The first step in the analysis is to define a set of (binary) indicator variables that contain all the information of the original observations, defined by:

$$O_{ivm} = \ell \Leftrightarrow g_{vim\ell} = 1, \qquad (26)$$

where it is to be understood that $g_{ivm\ell}$ can take only the values 0 and 1.

The basic principle of homogeneity analysis is to assign a number x_{iv} to each student (the student score on item i), and a number $y_{im\ell}$ to each observation O_{ivm}, called the category quantification, such that student scores are in some way the best summary of all category quantifications that apply to them. To understand this in more detail, consider the following loss function:

$$F_i = \sum_v \sum_m \sum_\ell g_{ivm\ell}(x_{iv} - y_{im\ell})^2. \qquad (27)$$

Symbol	Range	Meaning
i	$1,\ldots,I$	item
c	$1,\ldots,C$	country
V_c		Number of students from country c
v	$1,\ldots,V_c$	student
M_c		Number of markers from country c
m	$1,\ldots,M=\sum M_c$	marker
ℓ	$1,\ldots,L_i$	category of item i

Figure 17: Notational System

The data are represented by indicator variables $g_{ivm\ell}$. If marker m has a good idea of the potential of student v, and thinks it appropriate to assign him/her to category ℓ, then, ideally, one would expect that $x_{iv} = y_{im\ell}$, yielding a zero loss for that case. But the same marker can have used the same category for student v', who has a different potential ($x_{iv'}$), and since the quantification $y_{im\ell}$ is unique, there cannot be a zero loss in both cases. Thus, some kind of compromise is required, which is made by minimising the loss function F_i.

Four observations have to be made in connection with this minimisation:

- The loss function (27) certainly has no unique minimum, because adding an arbitrary constant to all x_{iv} and all $y_{im\ell}$ leaves F_i unaltered. This means that in some way an origin of the scale must be chosen. Although this origin is arbitrary, there are some theoretical advantages in defining it through the equality:

$$\sum_v x_{iv} = 0. \qquad (28)$$

- If for all v and all m and ℓ one chooses $x_{iv} = y_{im\ell} = 0$ then $F_i = 0$ (and (28) is fulfilled), which is certainly a minimum. Such a solution, where all variability in the student scores and in the category quantifications is suppressed, is called a degenerate solution. To avoid such degeneracy, and at the same time to choose a unit of the scale, requires the restriction:

$$\frac{1}{V} \sum_v^V x_{iv}^2 = 1. \qquad (29)$$

Restrictions (28) and (29) jointly guarantee that a unique minimum of F_i exists and corresponds to a non-degenerate solution except in some special cases, as discussed below.

- Notice that in the loss function, missing observations are taken into account in an appropriate way. From definition (26) it follows that if O_{ivm} is missing, $g_{ivm\ell} = 0$ for all ℓ, such that a missing observation never contributes to a positive loss.

- A distinct loss function is minimised for each item. Although other approaches to homogeneity analysis are possible, the present one serves the purpose of item analysis well. The data pertaining to a single item are analysed separately, requiring no assumptions on their relationships. A later subsection shows how to combine these separate analyses to compare markers and countries.

Another way to look at homogeneity analysis is to arrange the basic observations (for a single item i) in a table with rows corresponding to students and columns corresponding to markers, as in the left panel of Figure 18. The results can be considered as a transformation of the observations into numbers, as shown in the right panel of the figure. At the minimum of the loss function, the quantified observations $y_{im\ell}$ have the following interesting properties. The total variance can be partitioned into three parts: one part attributable to the columns (the markers), another part attributable to the rows (the students), and a residual variance. At the solution point it holds that:

$$\begin{aligned} Var(students) &\text{ is maximised}, \\ Var(markers) &= 0, \\ Var(residuals) &\text{ is minimised}. \end{aligned} \qquad (30)$$

If the markers agree well among themselves, *Var(residuals)* will be a small proportion of the total variance, meaning that the markers are very homogeneous. The index of homogeneity is defined therefore as:

$$H_{ic} = \frac{Var(students)}{Var(students) + Var(residuals)}, \qquad (31)$$

at the point where F_i attains its minimum. The subscript c has been added to indicate that this index of homogeneity can only be meaningfully computed within a single country, as explained in the next sub-section.

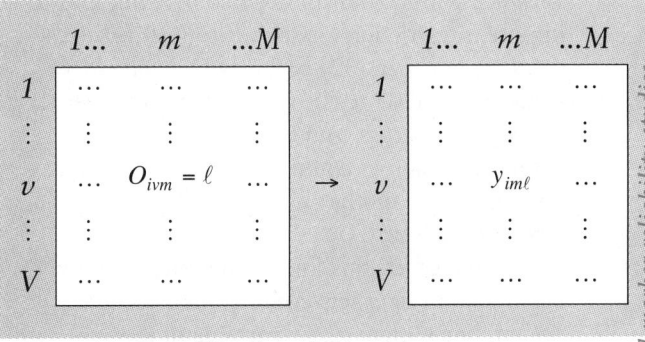

Figure 18: Quantification of Categories

The indices H_{ic} can be compared meaningfully with each other, and across countries and items, because they are all proportions of variance attributable to the same source (students), compared to the total variance attributable to students and markers. The differences between the H_{ic}-indices, therefore, must be attributed to the items, and can therefore be used as an instrument for item analysis. Items with a high H_{ic}-index are less susceptible to marker variation, and therefore the scores obtained on them are more easily generalisable across markers.

Degenerate and quasi-degenerate solutions

Although restriction (29) was introduced to avoid degenerate solutions, it is not always sufficient, and the data collection design or some peculiarities in the collected data can lead to other kinds of degeneration. First, degeneracy due to the design is discussed.

Using the notational conventions explained in the introduction, the loss function (27) can, in the case of the data of all countries analysed jointly, be written as:

$$F_i = \sum_c^C \sum_{v_c}^{V_c} \sum_{m_c}^{M_c} \sum_\ell^{L_i} g_{iv_c m_c \ell}(x_{iv_c} - y_{im_c \ell})^2 . \quad (32)$$

To see the degeneracy clearly, suppose $C = 2$, $V_1 = V_2$ and there are no missing responses. The value $F_i = 0$ (and thus H_i) can be reached as follows: $x_{iv_c} = 1$ if $c = 1$, $x_{iv_c} = -1$ if $c = 2$ and $y_{im_c \ell} = x_{iv_c}$ (all ℓ). This solution complies with (28) and (29), but it can easily be seen that it does nothing else than maximise the variance of the x's between countries and minimise the variance within countries. Of course, one could impose a restriction analogous to (29) for each country, but then (32) becomes C independent sums, and the scores (x-values) are no longer comparable across countries. A meaningful comparison across countries requires imposing restrictions of another kind, described in the next subsection.

In some cases, this kind of degeneracy may occur also in data sets collected in a complete design, but with extreme patterns of missing observations. Suppose some student has got a code from only one marker and assume, moreover, that this marker used this code only once. A degenerate solution may then occur where this student is contrasted with all others (collapsed into a single point), much in the same way as in the example above.

Similar cases may occur when a certain code ℓ, say, is used a very few times. Assume this code is used only once, by marker m. By choosing a very extreme value for $y_{im_c \ell}$, a situation may occur where the student given code ℓ by marker m tends to contrast with all the others, although fully collapsing them may be avoided (because this student's score is 'pulled' towards the others by the codes received from the other markers). But the general result will be one where the solution is dominated by this very infrequent coding by one marker. Such cases may be called quasi-degenerate and are examples of chance capitalisation. They are prone to occur in small samples of students, especially in cases where there are many different categories—as in the field trial, especially with items with multiple-answer categories. Cases of quasi-degeneracy give a spuriously high H_i-index, and one should be very careful not to cherish such an item too much, because it might show very poor performance in a cross-validation.

Quasi-degeneracy is an intuitive notion that is not rigorously defined, and will continue to be a major source of concern, although adequate restrictions on the model parameters usually address the problem.

To develop good guidelines for selecting a *good* test from the many items used in the field trial, one should realise that a low homogeneity index points to items that will introduce considerable variability into the test score because of rater variance, and may therefore best be excluded from the definitive test. But an item with a high index is not necessarily a good item. Quasi-degeneracy will tend to occur in cases where one or more response categories are used very infrequently. It might therefore be useful to develop a device that can simultaneously judge homogeneity and the risk of quasi-degeneracy.

HOMOGENEITY ANALYSIS WITH RESTRICTIONS

Apart from cases of quasi-degeneracy, there is another reason for imposing restrictions on the model parameters in homogeneity analysis. The specific value of H_i obtained from the minimisation of (27) can only be attained if the quantification issued from the homogeneity analysis is indeed used in applications, *i.e.*, when the score obtained by student v on item i when categorised by marker m in category ℓ is equal to the category quantification $y_{im\ell}$. But this means that the *number of points* to be earned from receiving category ℓ may differ across markers. An extra difficulty arises when new markers are used in future applications. This would imply that in every application a new homogeneity analysis has to be completed. And this is not very attractive for a project like PISA, where the field trial is meant to determine a (more or less) definite scoring rule, whereby the same scoring applies across all raters and countries.

Restrictions within countries

As a first restriction, one might wish for no variation across markers within the same country so that for each country c the restriction:

$$y_{im_c\ell} = y_{ic\ell}, \ (m = 1,\ldots,M_c, \ \ell = 1,\ldots,L_i) \quad (33)$$

is imposed. But since students and markers are nested within countries, this amounts to minimising the loss function for each country:

$$F^*_{ic} = \sum_{v_c}^{V_c} \sum_{m_c}^{M_c} \sum_{\ell}^{L_i} g_{iv_c m_c \ell}(x^*_{iv_c} - y_{ic\ell})^2, \quad (34)$$

such that the overall loss function is minimised automatically to:

$$F^*_i = \sum_c F^*_{ic}. \quad (35)$$

To minimise (34), technical restrictions similar to (28) and (29) must hold per country.

As in the case without restrictions, homogeneity indices can be computed in this case also (*see equation (31)*), and will be denoted H^*_{ic}. It is easy to understand that for all items and all countries the inequality:

$$H^*_{ic} \leq H_{ic} \quad (36)$$

must hold.

In contrast to some indices to be discussed further, H^*_{ic}-indices are not systematically influenced by the numbers of students or raters. If students and raters within a country can be considered to be a random sample of some populations of students and markers, the computed indices are a consistent (and unbiased) estimate of their population counterparts. The number of students and markers influence only the standard error.

The H^*_{ic}-indices can be used for a double purpose:

- Comparing H^*_{ic} with H_{ic} within countries: if for some item, H^*_{ic} is much lower than H_{ic}, this may point to systematic differences in interpretation of the *Marking Guides* among markers. Suppose, as an example, a binary item with categories A and B, and all markers in a country except one agree perfectly among themselves in their assignment of students to these categories; one marker, however, disagrees perfectly with the others in assigning to category A where the others choose B, and *vice versa*. Since each marker partitions all students in the same two subsets, the index of homogeneity H_{ic} for this item will be one, but the category quantifications of the outlying marker will be different from those of the other markers. Requiring that the category quantifications be the same for all markers will force some compromise, and the resulting H^*_{ic} will be lower than one.

- Differences between H^*_{ic} and H_{ic} can also be used to compare different countries among each other (per item). Differences, especially if they are persistent across items, make it possible to detect countries where the marking process reveals systematic disagreement among the markers.

Restrictions within and across countries

Of course, different scoring rules for different countries are not acceptable for the main study. More restrictions are therefore needed to ascertain that the same category should correspond to the same item score (quantification) in each country. This amounts to a further restriction on (33), namely:

$$y_{ic\ell} = y_{i\ell}, \ (c = 1,\ldots,C; \ \ell = 1,\ldots,L_i), \quad (37)$$

leading to the loss function:

$$F^{**}_i = \sum_c^C \sum_{v_c}^{V_c} \sum_{m_c}^{M_c} \sum_{\ell}^{L_i} g_{iv_c m_c \ell}(x^{**}_{iv_c} - y_{i\ell})^2, \quad (38)$$

and a corresponding index of homogeneity, denoted as H^{**}_i.

To provide an impression of the use of these indices, a summary plot for the open-ended items in science is displayed in Figure 19. The line shown in the chart connects the H_i^{**}-indices for all items (sorted in decreasing order). An interval is plotted, for each item, based on the H_{ic}^*-indices of 24 countries. For these countries, the H_{ic}^*-indices were sorted in ascending order and the endpoints of the intervals correspond to the 6th and 18th values. This figure may be a useful guide for selecting items for the main study since it allows a selection based on the value of H_i^{**}, but also shows clear differences in the variability of the H_{ic}^*-indices. The first three items, for example, have almost equal H_i^{**}-indices, but the second one shows more variability across countries than the other two, and therefore may be less suitable for the main study. But perhaps the clearest example is the last one, with the lowest H_i^{**}-index and showing large variations across countries.

AN ADDITIONAL CRITERION FOR SELECTING ITEMS

An ideal situation (from the viewpoint of statistical stability of the estimates) occurs when each of the L_i response categories of an item has been used an equal number of times: for each marker separately when one does the analysis without restrictions; across markers within a country when an analysis is done with restrictions within a country (restriction (33)); or across markers and countries when restriction (38) applies. If the distribution of the categories departs strongly from uniformity, cases of quasi-degeneracy may occur: the contrast between a single category with very small frequency and all the other categories may tend to dominate the solution. Very small frequencies are more likely to occur in small samples than in large samples, hence the greater possibility of being influenced by chance. The most extreme case occurs when the whole distribution is concentrated in a single

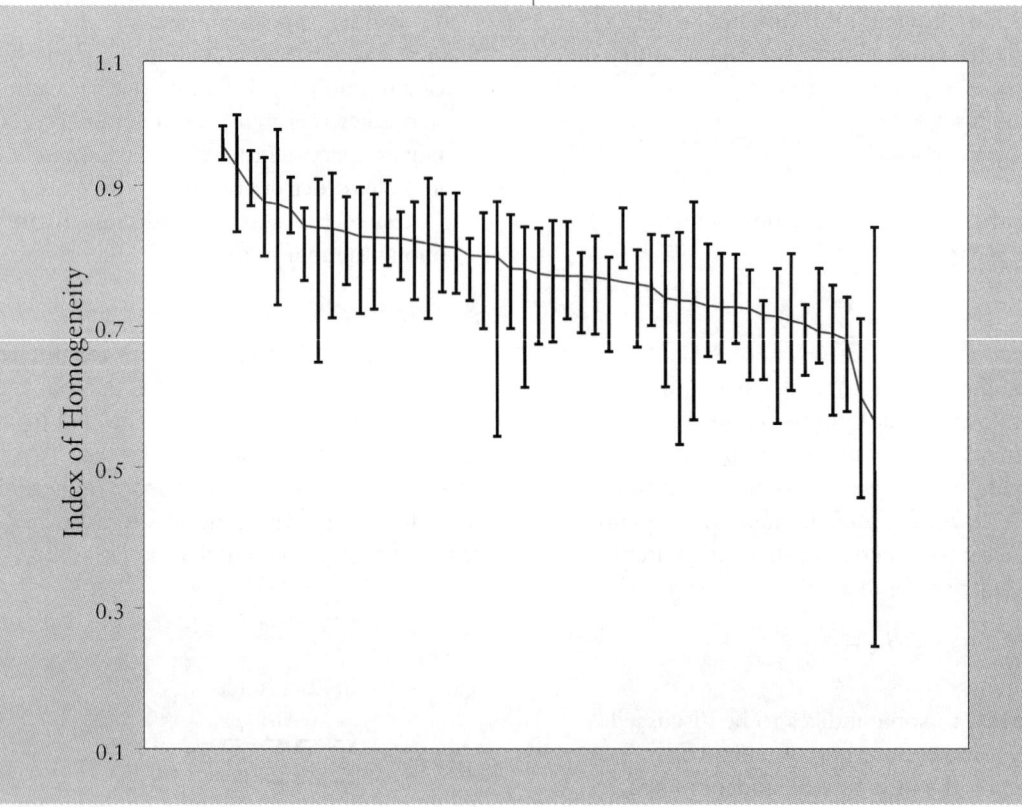

Figure 19: H^* *and* H^{**} *for Science Items*

category; a homogeneity analysis thus has no meaning (and technically cannot be carried out because normalisation is not defined).

From a practical point of view, an item with a distribution very close to the extreme case of no variability is of little use in testing, but may have a very acceptable index of homogeneity. Therefore it seems wise to judge the quality of an item by considering simultaneously the homogeneity index and the form of distribution.

To measure the departure from a uniform distribution in the case of nominal variables, the index to be developed must be invariant under permutation of the categories. For a binary item, for example, the index for an item with p-value p must be equal to that of an item with p-value $1-p$.

Pearson's well known X^2 statistic, computed with all expected frequencies equal to each other, fulfils this requirement, and can be written in formula form as:

$$X^2 = \sum_\ell^L \frac{(f_\ell - \bar{f})^2}{\bar{f}} = n \sum_\ell^L \frac{(p_\ell - \bar{p})^2}{\bar{p}}, \quad (39)$$

where, in the middle expression, f_ℓ is the frequency of category ℓ, $\bar{f}$ is the average frequency and L is the number of categories, and, in the right-hand expression, p_ℓ and $\bar{p}$ ($=1/L$) are observed and average proportion, and n is the sample size. This index, however, changes with changing sample size, and comparison across items (even with constant sample size) is difficult because the maximum value increases with the number of categories. It can be shown that:

$$X^2 \leq n(L-1), \quad (40)$$

where equality is reached only where $L-1$ categories have frequency zero, i.e., the case of no variability. The index:

$$\Delta = \frac{X^2}{n(L-1)} \quad (41)$$

is proposed as an index of departure from uniformity. Its minimum is zero (uniform distribution), its maximum is one (no variability). It is invariant under permutation of the categories and is independent of the sample size. This means that it does not change when all frequencies are multiplied by a positive constant. Using proportions p_ℓ instead of frequencies f_ℓ, (41) can be written as:

$$\Delta = \frac{L}{L-1} \sum_\ell (p_\ell - \tfrac{1}{L})^2. \quad (42)$$

Table 24 gives some distributions and their associated values for $L = 2$ and $L = 3$. (Row frequencies always sum to 100.)

Table 24: Some Examples of Δ

L = 2			L = 3			
Frequency		Δ	Frequency			Δ
50	50	0.00	50	50	0	0.25
60	40	0.04	40	30	30	0.01
70	30	0.16	50	25	25	0.06
75	25	0.25	50	48	2	0.22
80	20	0.36	70	15	15	0.30
90	10	0.64	70	28	2	0.35
95	5	0.81	80	10	10	0.49
99	1	0.96	80	18	2	0.51

As an example, the H_{ic}^*-indices are plotted in Figure 20 against the Δ-values for the 22 open-ended reading items in Booklet 9 of the field trial, using the Australian data. The binary (b) items are distinguished from the items with more than two categories (p). One can see that most of the items are situated in the lower right-hand corner of the figure, combining high homogeneity with a response distribution that does not deviate too far from a uniform distribution. But some items have high homogeneity indices and a very skewed distribution, which may make them less suitable for inclusion in the main study.

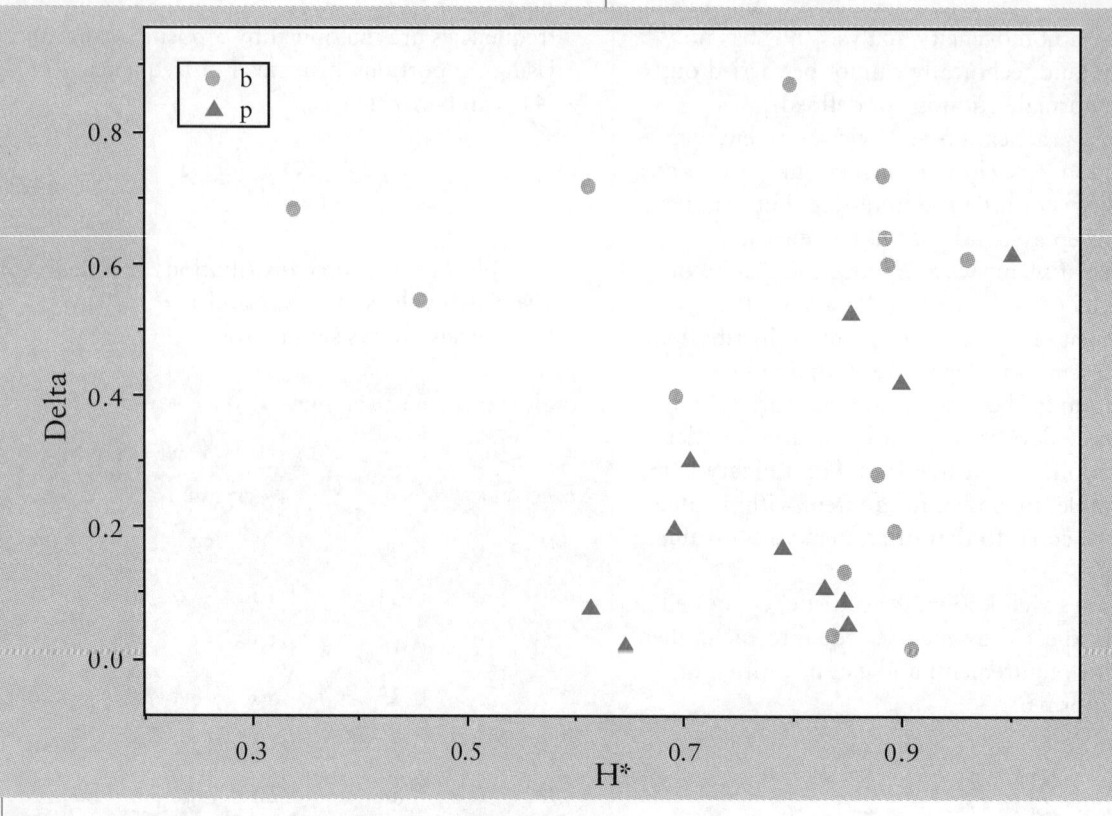

Figure 20: Homogeneity and Departure from Uniformity

A COMPARISON BETWEEN FIELD TRIAL AND MAIN STUDY

The main study used a selection of items from the field trial, but the wording in the item text of the *Marking Guides* was changed in some cases (mainly due to incorrect translations). The changed items were not tested in an independent field trial, however. If they did really represent an improvement, their homogeneity indices should rise in comparison with the field trial.

Another reason for repeating the homogeneity analysis in the main study is the relative numbers of students and markers used for the reliability study in the field trial and in the main study. Small numbers easily give rise to chance capitalisation, and therefore repeating the homogeneity analyses in the main study serves as a cross-validation.

Figure 21 shows a scatter-plot of the H^*_{ic}-indices of the reading items in the Australian field trial and main study samples, where items are distinguished by the reading subscale to which they belong: 1 = *retrieving information*, 2 = *interpreting texts* and
3 = *reflection and evaluation*.

As the dashed line in the figure indicates equality, it is immediately clear that the H^*_{ic}-indices for the great majority of items have increased in the main study. Another interesting feature is that the reflection items systematically show the least homogeneity among markers.

VARIANCE COMPONENT ANALYSIS

The general approach to estimating the variability in the scores due to markers is generalisability theory. Introductions to the approach can be found in Cronbach, Gleser, Nanda and Rajaratnam (1972), and in Brennan (1992). In the present section, a short introduction is given of the general theory and the common estimation methods. A generalisability coefficient is then derived, as a special correlation coefficient, and its interpretation is discussed. Finally some special PISA-related estimation problems are discussed.

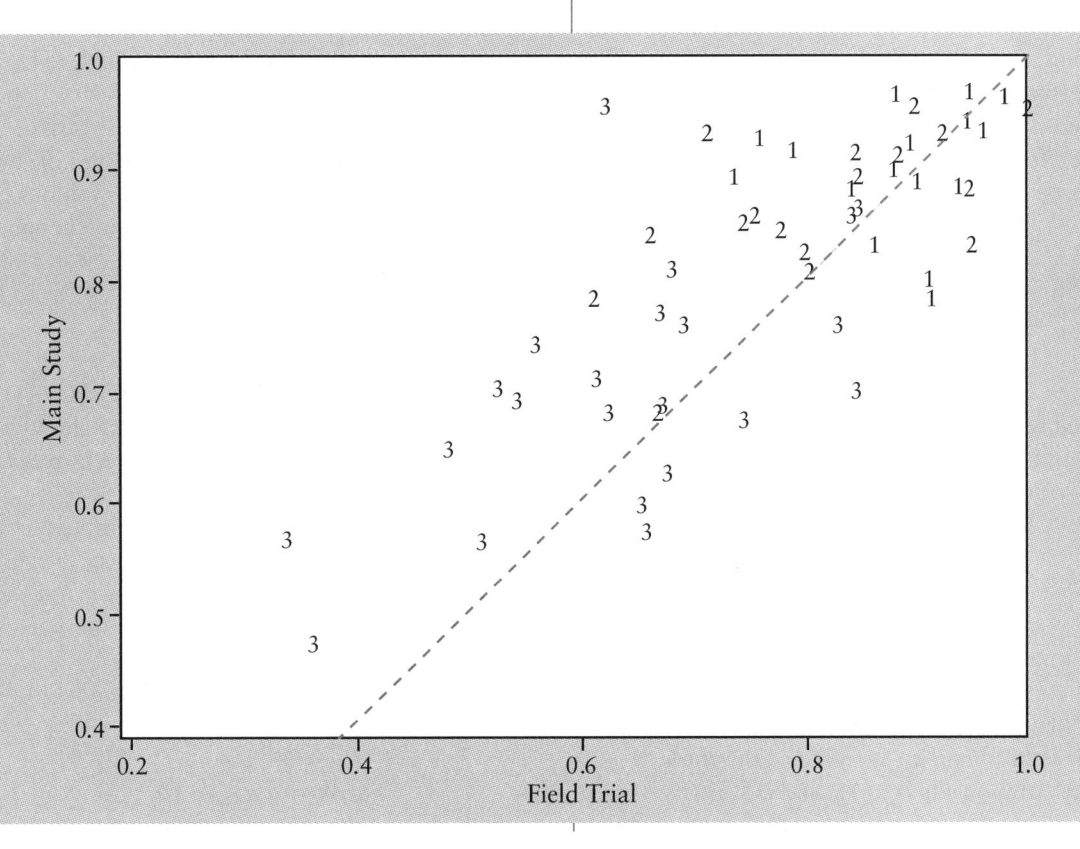

Figure 21: Comparison of Homogeneity Indices for Reading Items in the Main Study and the Field Trial in Australia

Analysis of two-way tables

To make the notion of generalisability theory clear, a simple case where a number of students answer a number of items, and for each answer they get a numerical score which will be denoted as Y_{vi}, the subscript v referring to the student, and the subscript i referring to the item, is described first. These observations can be arranged in a $V \times I$ rectangular table or matrix, and the main purpose of the analysis is to explain the variability in the table.

Conceptually, the model used to explain the variability in the table is the following:

$$Y_{vi} = \mu + \alpha_v + \beta_i + (\alpha\beta)_{vi} + \varepsilon^*_{vi}, \qquad (43)$$

where μ is an unknown constant, α_v is the student effect, β_i is the item effect, $(\alpha\beta)_{vi}$ (to be read as a single symbol, not as a product) is the student-item interaction effect and ε^*_{vi} is the measurement error. The general approach in generalisability theory is to assume that the students in the sample are randomly drawn from some population, but also that the items are randomly drawn from a population, usually called a universe. This means that the specific value α_v can be considered as a realisation of a random variable, α for example, and similarly for the item effect: β_i is a realisation of the random variable β. Also the interaction effect $(\alpha\beta)_{vi}$ and the measurement error ε^*_{vi} are considered as realisations of random variables. So, the model says that the observed score is a sum of an unknown constant μ and four random variables.

The model as given in (43), however is not sufficient to work with, for several reasons. First, since each student in the sample gives only a single response to each item in the test, the interaction effects and the measurement error are confounded. This means that there is no possibility to disentangle interaction and measurement error. Therefore, they will be taken together as a single random variable, ε for example, which is called the residual (and which is definitely not the same as the measurement error). This is defined as:

$$\varepsilon_{vi} = (\alpha\beta)_{vi} + \varepsilon^*_{vi}, \qquad (44)$$

and (43) can be rewritten as:

$$Y_{vi} = \mu + \alpha_v + \beta_i + \varepsilon_{vi}. \qquad (45)$$

Second, since the right-hand side of (45) is a sum of four terms, and only this sum is observed, the terms themselves are not identified, and therefore three identification restrictions have to be imposed. Suitable restrictions are:

$$E(\alpha) = E(\beta) = E(\varepsilon) = 0. \quad (46)$$

Third, apart from the preceding restriction, which is of a technical nature, there is one important theoretical assumption: all the non-observed random variables (student effects, item effects and residuals) are mutually independent. This assumption leads directly to a rather simple variance decomposition:

$$\sigma_Y^2 = \sigma_\alpha^2 + \sigma_\beta^2 + \sigma_\varepsilon^2. \quad (47)$$

The total variance σ_Y^2 can easily be estimated from the observed data, as well as the constant μ. The first purpose of variance component analysis is to obtain an estimate of the three variance components $\sigma_\alpha^2, \sigma_\beta^2$ and σ_ε^2. If the data matrix is complete, good estimators are given by the traditional techniques of variance analysis, using the decomposition of the total sum of squares SS_{tot} as:

$$SS_{tot} = SS_{row} + SS_{col} + SS_{res}, \quad (48)$$

where *row* refers to the students and *col* refers to the items. Dividing each SS by their respective number of degrees of freedom yields the corresponding so-called mean squares, from which unbiased estimates of the three unknown variance components can be derived:

$$\hat{\sigma}_\varepsilon^2 = MS_{res}, \quad (49)$$

$$\hat{\sigma}_\alpha^2 = \frac{MS_{row} - MS_{res}}{I}, \quad (50)$$

and

$$\hat{\sigma}_\beta^2 = \frac{MS_{col} - MS_{res}}{V}. \quad (51)$$

Usually the exact value of the three variance components will be of little use, but their relative contribution to the total variance is. Therefore the variance components will be expressed as a percentage of the total variance (the sum of the components) in what follows.

The estimators given by (49) through (51) have the attractive property that they are unbiased, but they also have an unattractive property: the results of the formulae in (50) and (51) can be negative. In practice, this seldom occurs, and if it does, it is common to change the negative estimates to zero.

Analysis of three-way tables

The approach for three-way tables is a straightforward generalisation of the case of two-way tables. The observed data are now represented by Y_{vim}, the score student v gets for his/her answer on item i when marked by marker m. The observed data are arranged in a three-dimensional array (a box), where the student dimension will be denoted as *rows*, the item dimensions as *columns* and the marker dimensions as *layers*.

The model is a generalisation of model (45):

$$Y_{vim} = \mu + \alpha_v + \beta_i + \gamma_m \\ + (\alpha\beta)_{vi} + (\alpha\gamma)_{vm} + (\beta\gamma)_{im} + \varepsilon_{vim}. \quad (52)$$

The observed variable Y_{vim} is the sum of a constant, three main effects, three first-order interactions and a residual. The residual in this case is the sum of the second-order interaction $(\alpha\beta\gamma)_{vim}$ and the measurement error ε_{vim}^*. Both effects are confounded because there is only one observation in each cell of the three-dimensional data array. The same restrictions as in the case of a two-way table apply: zero mean of the effects and mutual independence. Therefore the total variance decomposes into seven components:

$$\sigma_Y^2 = \sigma_\alpha^2 + \sigma_\beta^2 + \sigma_\gamma^2 \\ + \sigma_{\alpha\beta}^2 + \sigma_{\alpha\gamma}^2 + \sigma_{\beta\gamma}^2 + \sigma_\varepsilon^2 \quad (53)$$

and each component can be estimated with techniques similar to those demonstrated in the case of a two-way table. (The formulae are not displayed.)

The risk of ending up with negative estimates is usually greater for a three-dimensional table than for a two-way table. This will be illustrated by one case. The main effect γ_m reflects the relative leniency of marker m: marker m is relatively mild if the effect is positive; relatively strict if it is negative. It is not too unrealistic to assume that markers differ systematically in mildness, meaning that the variance component

σ_γ^2 will differ markedly from zero, and consequently that its estimator will have a very small probability of yielding a negative estimate. A positive interaction effect γ_{vm} means that marker m is especially mild for student v (more than on average towards the other students), reflecting in some way a positive or negative bias to some students. But if the marking procedure has been seriously implemented—students not being known to the markers—it is to be expected that these effects will be very small if they do exist at all. And this means that the corresponding variance component will be close to zero, making a negative estimate quite likely.

Correlations

If one wants to determine the reliability of a test, one of the standard procedures is to administer the test a second time (under identical circumstances), and compute the correlation between the two sets of test scores. This correlation is the reliability of the test (by definition). But if all variance components are known, this correlation can be computed from them. This is illustrated here for the case of a two-way table. To make derivations easy, the relative test scores $Y_{v.}$ are used, defined as:

$$Y_{v.} = \frac{1}{I} \sum_i Y_{vi} . \quad (54)$$

Using model (43) and substituting in (54):

$$Y_{v.} = \mu + \alpha_v + \frac{1}{I}\sum_i \beta_i + \frac{1}{I}\sum_i (\alpha\beta)_{vi} + \frac{1}{I}\sum_i \varepsilon^*_{vi} . \quad (55)$$

If the test is administered a second time using the same students and the same items, the relative scores on the repeated test will of course have the same structure as the right-hand side of (55), and, moreover, all terms will be identical with the exception of the last one, because the test replication is assumed to be independent.

To compute the covariance between the two sets of test scores, observe that the mean item effects in both cases are the same for all students, meaning that this average item effect does not contribute to the covariance or to the variance. And because the measurement error is independent in the two administrations, it does not contribute to the covariance. So the covariance between the two series of test scores is:

$$Cov(Y_{v.}, Y'_{v.}) = \sigma_\alpha^2 + \frac{\sigma_{\alpha\beta}^2}{I} . \quad (56)$$

The variance of the test scores is equal in the two administrations:

$$Var(Y_{v.}) = Var(Y'_{v.}) = \sigma_\alpha^2 + \frac{\sigma_{\alpha\beta}^2 + \sigma_{\varepsilon^*}^2}{I} . \quad (57)$$

Dividing the right-hand sides of (56) and (57) gives the correlation:

$$\rho_1(Y_{v.}, Y'_{v.}) = \frac{\sigma_\alpha^2 + \dfrac{\sigma_{\alpha\beta}^2}{I}}{\sigma_\alpha^2 + \dfrac{\sigma_{\alpha\beta}^2 + \sigma_{\varepsilon^*}^2}{I}} . \quad (58)$$

But this correlation cannot be computed from a two-way table, because the interaction component $\sigma_{\alpha\beta}^2$ cannot be estimated. It is common to drop this term from the numerators in (58), giving as a result Cronbach's alpha coefficient (Sirotnik, 1970):

$$\begin{aligned} \text{alpha} &= \frac{\sigma_\alpha^2}{\sigma_\alpha^2 + \dfrac{\sigma_{\alpha\beta}^2 + \sigma_{\varepsilon^*}^2}{I}} \\ &= \frac{\sigma_\alpha^2}{\sigma_\alpha^2 + \dfrac{\sigma_\varepsilon^2}{I}} \quad (59) \\ &\leq \rho_1(Y_{v.}, Y'_{v.}) . \end{aligned}$$

where the equality holds if and only if the interaction component $\sigma_{\alpha\beta}^2$ is zero.

Another interesting question concerns the correlation one would find if on the two test occasions an independent set of I items (both randomly drawn from the same universe) were presented to the same students. In this case, the mean item effect will contribute to variance of the test scores, but not to the covariance, and the correlation will be given by:

$$\rho_2(Y_{v.}, Y'_{v.}) = \frac{\sigma_\alpha^2 + \dfrac{\sigma_{\alpha\beta}^2}{I}}{\sigma_\alpha^2 + \dfrac{\sigma_\beta^2 + \sigma_{\alpha\beta}^2 + \sigma_{\varepsilon^*}^2}{I}}, \quad (60)$$

which of course cannot be computed either because interaction and measurement error are confounded. Dropping the interaction component from the numerators gives:

$$\rho_2(Y_{v.}, Y'_{v.}) \geq \frac{\sigma_\alpha^2}{\sigma_\alpha^2 + \dfrac{\sigma_\beta^2 + \sigma_\varepsilon^2}{I}} . \quad (61)$$

In generalisability theory, Cronbach's alpha is also called a generalisability coefficient for relative decisions, while the right-hand side of (61) is called the generalisability coefficient for absolute decisions.

Now the more interesting question of constructing a sensible correlation coefficient for the problem in the PISA study, where there are different sources of variation—three main effects, three first-order interactions and a residual effect—is addressed. The basic problem is to determine the effects associated with the markers, or in other words what would be the correlation between two series of test scores, observed with the same students and the same items but at each replication marked by an independent set of M markers, randomly drawn from the universe of markers. The relative test score is now defined as:

$$Y_{v..} = \frac{1}{I \times M} \sum_i \sum_m Y_{vim} . \qquad (62)$$

Of the eight terms on the right-hand side of (52), some are to be treated as constant, some contribute to the score variance and some to the covariance and the variance, as displayed in Table 25.

Table 25: Contribution of Model Terms to (Co)Variance

constant	μ, β
variance and covariance	$\alpha, (\alpha\beta)$
variance	$\gamma, (\alpha\gamma), (\beta\gamma), \varepsilon$

Using this table, and taking the definition of the relative score (62) into account, it is not too difficult to derive the correlation between the two series of test scores:

$$\rho_3(Y_{v..}, Y'_{v..}) = \frac{\sigma_\alpha^2 + \dfrac{\sigma_{\alpha\beta}^2}{I}}{\sigma_\alpha^2 + \dfrac{\sigma_{\alpha\beta}^2}{I} + \dfrac{\sigma_\gamma^2 + \sigma_{\alpha\gamma}^2}{M} + \dfrac{\sigma_{\beta\gamma}^2 + \sigma_\varepsilon^2}{I \times M}}. \qquad (63)$$

The expression on the right-hand side can be used as a generic formula for computing the correlation with an arbitrary number of items, and an arbitrary number of markers.

Estimation with missing data and incomplete designs

The estimation of the variance components with complete data arrays is an easy task to carry out. With incomplete designs and missing data, however, the estimation procedure becomes rather complicated, and good software to carry out the estimations is scarce. The only commercial package known to the author that can handle such problems is BMDP (1992), but the number of cases it can handle is very limited, and it was found to be inadequate for the PISA analyses.

The next section proceeds in three steps. First, the precise structure of the data that were available for analysis is discussed; second, parameter estimation in cases where some observations are missing at random is addressed; and finally, the estimation procedure in incomplete designs is described.

The structure of the data

In the data collection of the main study, items were included in three domains of performance: mathematics, science and reading. For reporting purposes, however, it was decided that three sub-domains in reading would be distinguished: retrieving information, interpreting texts and reflection and evaluation. In the present section these three sub-domains are treated separately, yielding five domains in total.

Data were collected in an incomplete design, using nine different test booklets. One booklet contained only reading items, while the others had a mixed content (*see Chapter 2*). The multiple marking scheme was designed to have four markers per booklet–domain combination. For example, four markers did the multiple marking on all open-ended reading items in Booklet 1, and four markers completed the same for Booklet 2, but there were no restrictions on the set of markers for different booklets. Therefore, it could happen that in some countries the set of reading markers was the same for all booklets, while in other countries different sets, with some or no overlapping, were used for the marking in the three domains. During the marking process no distinction was made as to the three sub-domains of reading: a marker processed all open-ended reading items appearing in a booklet.[1]

---

[1] See Chapter 6 for a full description of the design.

This marking scheme is not optimal for a variance component analysis, but on top of that there were two other complications:
- If the marking instructions were followed, we would have a three-dimensional array per booklet–domain combination, completely filled with scores, and such an array was the first unit of analysis in estimating the variance components. In many instances, however, scores were not available in some cells of these arrays, causing serious estimation problems. The way these problems were tackled is explained in the discussion of the second step: estimation with missing observations.
- In some countries, the instruction to use four markers per booklet, thus guaranteeing a complete data array per booklet–domain combination, was not followed rigorously. In some instances more markers were used, each of them doing part of the work in a rather uncontrolled way. This caused serious problems in the estimation procedure of the variance components, as explained in the discussion of the third step: estimation in incomplete designs.

Estimation with missing observations

To demonstrate the problems in the estimation of variance components, the analysis of a two-way table is used as an example, starting with the definition of an indicator variable u_{vi}:

$$u_{vi} = \begin{cases} 1 \text{ if } Y_{vi} \text{ is observed} \\ 0 \text{ otherwise} \end{cases}, \quad (64)$$

and defining the number of observations per student v and per item i as:

$$t_v = \sum_i u_{vi} \quad (65)$$

$$n_i = \sum_v u_{vi}, \quad (66)$$

and the total number of observations as:

$$N = \sum_v t_v = \sum_i n_i. \quad (67)$$

For averages, the dot notation will be used:

$$Y_{v.} = \frac{1}{t_v} \sum_i u_{vi} Y_{vi}, \quad (68)$$

$$Y_{.i} = \frac{1}{n_i} \sum_v u_{vi} Y_{vi} \quad (69)$$

and

$$\begin{aligned} Y_{..} &= \frac{1}{N} \sum_v \sum_i u_{vi} Y_{vi} \\ &= \frac{1}{N} \sum_v t_v Y_{v.} \\ &= \frac{1}{N} \sum_i n_i Y_{.i} \end{aligned} \quad (70)$$

All averages are weighted averages, and since the weights at the single observation level are either one or zero, the value of Y_{vi} is arbitrary if u_{vi} is zero.

Of course the following can always be written:

$$\begin{aligned} Y_{vi} - Y_{..} &= (Y_{v.} - Y_{..}) + (Y_{.i} - Y_{..}) \\ &+ (Y_{vi} - Y_{v.} - Y_{.i} + Y_{..}), \end{aligned} \quad (71)$$

and for the left-hand expression and each of the expressions between parentheses on the right-hand side of (71), one can define the weighted sum of squares as:

$$SS_{tot} = \sum_v \sum_i u_{vi} (Y_{vi} - Y_{..})^2, \quad (72)$$

$$SS_{row} = \sum_v t_v (Y_{v.} - Y_{..})^2, \quad (73)$$

$$SS_{col} = \sum_i n_i (Y_{.i} - Y_{..})^2, \quad (74)$$

and

$$SS_{res} = \sum_v \sum_i u_{vi} (Y_{vi} - Y_{v.} - Y_{.i} + Y_{..})^2. \quad (75)$$

But a very nice property, which holds in the case of complete data, is lost in general. It does not hold in general that:

$$SS_{tot} = SS_{row} + SS_{col} + SS_{res}.$$

The estimation procedure in common analysis of variance proceeds by equating the observed sum of squares (or mean squares) to their expected value; so the estimation procedure is a moment estimation. Denote with p one of the elements $\{tot, row, col, res\}$. With complete data, it turns out that:

$$E(SS_p) = A_p \sigma_\alpha^2 + B_p \sigma_\beta^2 + R_p \sigma_\varepsilon^2, \quad (76)$$

where the coefficients A_p, B_p and R_p are very simple functions of the number of students and the number of items. The expected value operator also has a straightforward meaning, since the sampled students and items are considered as a random sample from their respective universes.

With missing data, the situation is more complicated. The indicator variables u_{vi} are to be considered as random variables, and in order to define expected values of sums of squares, difficult problems have to be solved, as can easily be seen from equation (72), where products of u and Y-variables appear, so that assumptions about the joint distribution of both kinds of variables have to be made. But the assumptions in classical variance component theory about the Y-variables are very weak. In fact, the only assumption is that row effects, column effects and residuals have a finite variance. Without adding very specific assumptions about the Y-variables, the only workable assumption about the joint distribution of Y and u is that they are independent, or that the missing observations are missing completely at random. All analyses carried out on the multiple-marking data of the main study of PISA make this assumption. The consequences of the violation of these assumptions are outlined below.

With this assumption, the expected value operator in (76) is well defined and the general form of (76) is also valid with missing data, although the coefficients A_p, B_p and R_p are more complicated than in the complete case. The case of a two-way analysis is given in Table 26.

In the complete case, it holds that $t_v = I$ and $n_i = V$ such that the coefficients reduce to a much simpler form, as displayed in Table 27.

In Table 27, it is easily checked that the sum of the last three rows yields the coefficients for $E(SS_{tot})$. This means that any three of the four observed sums of squares can be used to solve the three unknown variance components, and each system will lead to the same solution. With missing data, however, this feature is lost, and each system of three equations using the coefficients in Table 26 will lead to a different solution, showing that moment estimators are not unique. If the model assumptions are fulfilled, however, the differences between the solutions are reasonably small. (See Verhelst (2000) for more details.)

Table 26: Coefficients of the Three Variance Components (General Case)

	Student Component (σ_α^2)	Item Component (σ_β^2)	Measurement Error Component (σ_ε^2)
$E(SS_{tot})$	$N - \dfrac{\sum_v t_v^2}{N}$	$N - \dfrac{\sum_i n_i^2}{N}$	$N - 1$
$E(SS_{row})$	$N - \dfrac{\sum_v t_v^2}{N}$	$V - \dfrac{\sum_i n_i^2}{N}$	$V - 1$
$E(SS_{col})$	$I - \dfrac{\sum_v t_v^2}{N}$	$N - \dfrac{\sum_i n_i^2}{N}$	$I - 1$
$E(SS_{res})$	$I - \dfrac{\sum_v t_v^2}{N}$	$V - \dfrac{\sum_i n_i^2}{N}$	$N - V - I - 1 + 2\sum_v \sum_i \dfrac{u_{vi}}{t_v n_i}$

Table 27: Coefficients of the Three Variance Components (Complete Case)

	Student Component (σ_α^2)	Item Component (σ_β^2)	Measurement Error Component (σ_ε^2)
$E(SS_{tot})$	$N-1$	$N-V$	$N-1$
$E(SS_{row})$	$N-I$	0	$V-1$
$E(SS_{col})$	0	$N-V$	$I-1$
$E(SS_{res})$	0	0	$N-V-I+1$

For three-way tables, a similar reasoning can be followed, yielding coefficients for the expected sums of squares for the total, the three main effects, the three first-order interactions and the residual; and any subset of seven equations can be used for a moment estimator of the seven variance components. The expressions for the components, however, are all more complicated than in the case of two-way tables and are not presented here. For details, see Longford (1995) and Verhelst (2000).

An extensive simulation study (Verhelst, 2000) has shown that the variance components can be consistently estimated if indeed the missing values are missing completely at random, but if they are not, the estimation method may produce totally unacceptable estimates. As an example, the marking procedure for the reading items in Booklet 1 in the United States was examined. This booklet contains 22 open-ended reading items, and multiple markings were collected for 48 students. Following the marking instructions, four markers had to mark all 22 answers for all 48 students, yielding 48 × 22 = 1 056 markings per marker. In the data set, however, nine different marker identifications were found, with the number of markings per marker ranging from 129 to 618. The design with which the markings were collected is unknown, and can only be partially reconstructed from the data. In Table 28, the variance component estimates for the five 'retrieving information' open-ended items in Booklet 1 arising from the above method analysis are reported. The large negative estimate for the student–marker interaction component is totally unacceptable, and the use of the estimation method in a case such as this is dubious.

Table 28: Estimates of Variance Components (× 100) in the United States

Student Component ($\hat\sigma_\alpha^2$)	9.8
Item Component ($\hat\sigma_\beta^2$)	5.1
Marker Component ($\hat\sigma_\gamma^2$)	0.4
Student-Item Interaction Component ($\hat\sigma_{\alpha\beta}^2$)	10.0
Student-Marker Interaction Component ($\hat\sigma_{\alpha\gamma}^2$)	-12.0
Item-Marker Interaction Component ($\hat\sigma_{\beta\gamma}^2$)	-0.3
Measurement Error Component ($\hat\sigma_\varepsilon^2$)	13.7

The third step in the procedure is the combination of the variance component estimates for a sub-domain. The analysis per booklet yields estimates per booklet, but the booklet is not interesting as a reporting unit; and so the estimates must be combined in some way across booklets. In the case of a two-way table, the estimation equations are (see equation (76)):

$$SS_{bp} = A_{bp}\sigma_\alpha^2 + B_{bp}\sigma_\beta^2 + R_{bp}\sigma_\varepsilon^2, \qquad (77)$$

where b indexes the booklet and p is any element from $\{tot, row, col, res\}$. If it can be assumed that students, items and markers are randomly assigned to booklets, the summation of (77) across booklets will yield estimation equations for the variance components which yield consistent estimates. Therefore, the following equations can be used:

$$\sum_b SS_{bp} = \sigma_\alpha^2 \sum_b A_{bp} + \sigma_\beta^2 \sum_b B_{bp} + \sigma_\varepsilon^2 \sum_b R_{bp}. \quad (78)$$

For the three-way tables used in the present study, similar estimation equations were used, with the right-hand side of (78) having seven

Table 29: Variance Components (%) for Mathematics in the Netherlands

Booklet	Number of Items	Student Component ($\hat{\sigma}_\alpha^2$)	Item Component ($\hat{\sigma}_\beta^2$)	Marker Component ($\hat{\sigma}_\gamma^2$)	Student-Item Interaction Component ($\hat{\sigma}_{\alpha\beta}^2$)	Student-Marker Interaction Component ($\hat{\sigma}_{\alpha\gamma}^2$)	Item-Marker Interaction Component ($\hat{\sigma}_{\beta\gamma}^2$)	Measurement Error Component ($\hat{\sigma}_\varepsilon^2$)
1	7	37.0	15.6	0.0	41.9	0.0	0.0	5.5
3	3	6.9	43.2	0.1	40.5	0.6	0.0	8.8
5	7	19.3	34.3	0.2	38.3	-0.2	0.2	8.0
8	6	19.3	27.8	0.1	41.8	-0.1	0.4	10.7
9	4	19.3	27.8	0.1	47.8	-0.1	0.1	5.4
All	27	23.6	26.4	0.1	42.1	0.1	0.2	7.5

unknown variance components instead of three. The variance components for the mathematics domain are displayed in Table 29 for the Netherlands.

A number of comments are required with respect to this table.

- The table is exemplary for all analyses in the five domains for countries where the marking instructions were rigorously followed. A more complete set of results is given in Chapter 14.
- The most comforting finding is that all variance components where markers are involved (the three columns containing the symbol γ as a subscript of the variance component) are negligibly small, meaning that there are no systematic marker effects.
- The results of Booklet 3 are slightly outlying, yielding a much smaller student effect and a much larger item effect than the other booklets. This could be attributed to sampling error (the standard errors of the variance component estimates for main effects are notoriously high; Searle, 1971) but it could also point to a systematic error in the composition of the booklets. Since it concerns three items only, this effect has not been investigated further.
- The most important variance component is the interaction between students and items. If the marker effects all vanish, the remaining components show that the scores are not additive in student effect and item effect. At first sight, this is contradictory to the use of the Rasch model as the measurement model, but a closer look reveals an essential difference between the Rasch model and the present approach. In IRT models, a transformation to an unbounded latent scale is used, whereas in the present approach the scores themselves are modelled, and since the scores are bounded (and highly discrete), differences in difficulty of the items will automatically lead to interaction effects.
- Using the bottom row of Table 29, the generalisability coefficient ρ_3 (63) can be computed for different values of I and M. These estimates are displayed, using data from the Netherlands, in Table 30. Extensive tables for all participating countries are given in Chapter 14. Here also, the result is exemplary for all countries, although the indices for reading are generally slightly lower than for mathematics. But the main conclusion is that the correlations are quite high, even with one marker, such that the decision to use a single marker for the open-ended items in the main study seems justified *post hoc*.

Table 30: Estimates of ρ_3 for the Mathematics Scale in the Netherlands

I = 8		I = 16		I = 24	
M = 1	M = 2	M = 1	M = 2	M = 1	M = 2
0.963	0.981	0.977	0.988	0.982	0.997

INTER-COUNTRY RATER RELIABILITY STUDY-DESIGN
Aletta Grisay

The PISA 2000 quality control procedures included a limited Inter-Country Rater Reliability (ICR) study, conducted in October-November 2000, to investigate the possibility of systematic bias in marking open-ended reading items. The within-country multiple-marking exercise explored the reliability of the coding completed by the national markers in each country. The objective of the ICR study was to check on whether, globally, or for particular items, marks given by the different national staffs could be considered equivalent.

A subset of 48 Booklet 7s—that is, the sample included in the multiple-marking exercise for reading within each country—was used for the ICR study. Booklet 7 was chosen because it contained only reading material, and therefore a large number of reading items (26) requiring double marking. All participating countries were requested to submit these 48 student booklets to the Consortium, after obliterating any score given by the national markers.

Staff specially trained by the Consortium for the study and proficient in the various PISA languages then marked the booklets. Their marks were compared to the four marks given by the national markers to the same students' answers.

All cases of clear discrepancy (between the marks given by the independent marker and by all or most of the national markers) were submitted for adjudication to Consortium researchers involved in developing the reading material, along with the actual student's answer (translated for countries using languages other than English or French).

RECRUITMENT OF INTERNATIONAL MARKERS

The international scoring of booklets from the seven English-speaking PISA countries (with England and Scotland considered as separate countries for this exercise) was done by three experienced Australian markers and one Canadian marker, all selected by the Consortium. The 48 booklets from Australian students were sent to Canada, to be scored by the trainer for PISA reading in English-speaking Canada. The remaining six English-speaking groups (from English-speaking Canada, Ireland, New Zealand, Scotland, the United Kingdom and the United States) were re-scored at ACER by a group of three verifiers selected from the Australian PISA administration. One of these was the trainer for PISA reading in Australia. The other two had demonstrated a high level of reliability during the Australian national operational marking. Each one had sole responsibility for scoring booklets from two countries.

To cover instruction languages used in all other PISA countries, the Consortium appointed 15 of the 25 translators who had already served in the verification of the national translations of PISA material, and were therefore very familiar with it. The selection criteria retained were (i) perfect command of the language(s) of the country (or countries) whose material had to be scored (as far as possible, the responsible persons were chosen from among those verifiers who mastered more than one PISA language, so that each could mark for two or more countries); (ii) perfect command of English and/or French, so that each could score on the basis of either source version of the reading *Marking Guide* (while checking, when needed, the national version); and (iii) as far as possible, previous experience teaching either the national language or foreign languages at the secondary school level.

INTER-COUNTRY RATER RELIABILITY STUDY TRAINING SESSIONS

A three-day training session was conducted in Brussels to train the 15 verifiers to use the PISA reading *Marking Guide*. Consortium experts led the training session. For the three Australian verifiers who had worked on the Australian marking recently (in September-October) and were very familiar with the items, a shorter refresher session was conducted in Melbourne, Australia. No special training or refresher session was deemed necessary for the Canadian verifier.

The session materials included the source English (and French) versions of reading marking instructions for Booklet 7 items (and a copy of the national marking guide for each language other than English, when available), answers to marking queries on Booklet 7 received at ACER, the Reading Workshop material (*see Chapter 2*), and copies of a benchmark set of English student scripts to be scored independently by all participants to verify their own marking consistency.

This English set of benchmark responses was prepared at ACER as a specific training aid. Most were selected from material sent for the purpose by Ireland, Scotland, the United Kingdom and the United States. Australian booklets and the query records provided other sources. For each item, about 15 responses were chosen to present typical and borderline cases and to illustrate all likely response categories. A score was provided for each response, accompanied in most cases by an explanation or comment. Scores and explanations were in hidden text format.

During the session, the verifiers worked through the material, item by item. Scoring instructions for each item were presented, then the workshop examples were marked and discussed, then the verifiers worked independently on the related benchmark scripts and checked their scores against the recommended scores. Problem responses were discussed with Consortium staff conducting the training session before proceeding to the next item.

At the Brussels session, the verifiers also had the opportunity to start marking part of the material for one of the countries for which they were responsible, under the supervision of the Consortium staff. They were instructed on how to enter their marks in the ICR study software prepared at ACER to help compare their marks with those given by the national markers. Most finished marking at least one of the Booklet 7 clusters for one of their countries. They then received an Excel spreadsheet with the cases where their scores differed from those given by the national markers. They discussed the first few problem cases with the Consortium staff, and received instructions on how to enter their comments and the translation of the student's answer in a column next to the flagged case, so that the Consortium staff could adjudicate the case.

A total of about 15 hours was needed to finish scoring the booklets for each country.

FLAG FILES

For each country, the ICR study software produced a flag file with about 1 248 cases (48 students × 26 items)—numbers varied slightly, since a few countries submitted one or two additional booklets, or could not retrieve some of the booklets requested, or submitted booklets with a missing page.

In the file, an asterisk indicated cases where the verifier's score differed significantly from the four scores given by the national markers (*e.g.*, 0 v. 1, respectively, or *vice versa*; or all national markers giving various partial scores while the verifier gave full or no credit).

Cases with minor discrepancies only (*e.g.*, where the verifier agreed with three out of four of the national markers) were not flagged, nor were cases with national scores too inconsistent to be compared to the verifier's score (*e.g.*, where national marks were 0011 and the verifier's mark was 1, or where national marks were 0123 and the verifier's mark was 2). It was considered that these cases would be identified in the within-country reliability analysis but would be of less interest for the ICR study than cases with a more clear orientation towards leniency or harshness. In each file, a blank column was left for Consortium staff to adjudicate flagged cases.

ADJUDICATION

In the adjudication stage, Consortium staff checked all flagged cases to verify if marks were correct, and if both national markers and the verifier had used wrong codes in these problematic cases.

For the English-speaking countries, the Consortium's adjudicators checked the flagged cases by referring directly to students' answers in the booklets. Responses flagged for adjudication were marked blind by Consortium experts (*i.e.*, the adjudicator saw none of the previous five marks). Subsequently, that mark was checked against the original four national marks and the verifier's mark. If the adjudicator's mark was different from more than two of the original four national marks, the response was submitted for a further blind marking by the other adjudicator.

For the non English-speaking countries, the procedure was different, since the flagged students' answers usually had to be translated by the verifier before they could be adjudicated. To reduce the costs of the exercise, verifiers were instructed (i) to simply copy but not translate the student's answer next to the flagged case for those languages known by the adjudicators (*i.e.*, French, German, Italian, Dutch and Spanish), and (ii) to simply add a brief comment, without translating the answer, for cases when they clearly recognised that they had entered an incorrect code. All other flagged cases were translated into English or French. Almost all files for the non English-speaking countries were adjudicated twice. No blind procedure could be used. Each adjudicator entered comments in the file to explain the rationale for their decision, so that a final consensus could be reached.

The results of this analysis are given in Chapter 14.

CHAPTER 11: DATA CLEANING PROCEDURES

Christian Monseur

This chapter presents the data cleaning steps implemented during the main survey of PISA 2000.

DATA CLEANING AT THE NATIONAL CENTRE

National Project Managers (NPMs) were required to submit their national data in KeyQuest® 2000, the generic data entry package developed by Consortium staff and pre-configured to include the data entry forms, referred to later as *instruments*: the achievement test booklets one to nine (together making up the cognitive data); the SE booklet (also cognitive, known as booklet 0); multiple-marking sheets; School Questionnaire and Student Questionnaire instruments with and without the two international options (*Computer Familiarity* or *Information Tech-nology (IT)* questionnaire and *Cross-Curriculum Competency (CCC)* questionnaire); the List of Schools; and the Student Tracking Forms.

The data were verified at several points (integrity check) from the time of data entry. Validation rules (or range checks) were specified for each variable defined in KeyQuest®, and a variable datum was only accepted if it satisfied pre-specified validation rules.[1] To prevent duplicate records, a set of variables assigned to an instrument were identified as *primary keys*. For the student test booklets, stratum, school and student identifications were the primary keys.

Countries were requested to enter data into the Student Tracking Form module before starting to enter data for cognitive tests or context questionnaires. This module, or instrument, contained complete student identification as it should have appeared on the booklet and questionnaire that the student received at the testing session. When configured, KeyQuest® instruments designed for student data were linked with the Student Tracking Form so that warning messages appeared when data operators tried to enter invalid student identifiers or student identifiers that did not match a record in the form.

After the data entry process was completed, NPMs were required to implement some checking procedures using KeyQuest® before submitting data to the Consortium, and to rectify any integrity errors. These included inconsistencies between: the List of Schools and the School Questionnaire; the Student Tracking Form and achievement test booklets; the Student Tracking Form and the Student Questionnaire; the achievement test booklets and the Student Questionnaire; and, in the multiple-marking, reliability data according to the international design in order to detect other than four duplicate students per booklet.

NPMs were also required to submit an *Adaptation and Modification Form* with their data, describing all changes they had made to variables on the questionnaire, including the addition or deletion of variables or response categories for variables, and changes to the meaning of response categories. NPMs were also required to propose recoding rules where the national data did not match the international data.

---

[1] National centres could modify the configuration of the variables, giving a range of values that was sometimes reduced or extended compared to Consortium expectations.

DATA CLEANING AT THE INTERNATIONAL CENTRE

DATA CLEANING ORGANISATION

Data cleaning was a major component of the PISA 2000 Quality Control and Assurance Program. It was of prime importance that the Consortium detected all anomalies and inconsistencies in submitted data and that no errors were introduced during the cleaning and analysis phases. To reach these high quality requirements, the Consortium implemented dual independent processing.

Two data analysts developed the PISA 2000 data cleaning procedures independently. At each step, the procedures were considered complete only when their application to a fictitious database and to the first two PISA databases received from countries produced identical results and files.

The data files submitted by national centres often needed specific data cleaning or recoding procedures, or at least adaptation of standard data cleaning procedures. Two analysts therefore independently cleaned all submitted data files; the cleaning and analysis procedures were run with both SAS® and SPSS®.

Three teams of data analysts produced the national databases. A team leader was nominated within each team and was the only individual to communicate with the national centres. Each team used SAS® and SPSS®.

DATA CLEANING PROCEDURES

Because of the potential impact of PISA results and the scrutiny to which the data were likely to be put, it was essential that no dubious records remained in the data files. During cleaning as many dubious records as possible were identified, and through a process of extensive discussion between each national centre and the Consortium's data processing centre at the Australian Council for Educational Research (ACER), an effort was made to correct and resolve all data issues. When no adequate solution was found, the offending data records were deleted.[2]

Unresolved inconsistencies in student and school identifications also led to the deletion of records in the database. Unsolved systematic errors for a particular item were replaced by *not applicable* codes. For instance, if countries reported a mistranslation or misprint in the national version of a cognitive booklet, data for the variables were recoded as *not applicable* and were not used in the analyses. Finally, errors or inconsistencies for particular students and particular variables were replaced by *not applicable* codes.

NATIONAL ADAPTATIONS TO THE DATABASE

When data arrived at the Consortium, the first step was to check the consistency of the database structure with the international database structure. An automated procedure was developed for this purpose. For each instrument it reported deleted variables, added variables and variables for which the validation rules (range checks) had been changed. This report was then compared with the information provided by the NPM in the *Adaptation and Modification Form*.

Once all inconsistencies were resolved, the submitted data were recoded where necessary to fit the international structure. All additional or modified variables were set aside in a separate file so that countries could use these data for their own purposes but they were not included in the international database and have not been used in international data processing.

VERIFYING THE STUDENT TRACKING FORM AND THE LIST OF SCHOOLS

The Student Tracking Form and the List of Schools were central instruments, because they contained the information used in computing weight, exclusion, and participation rates. The Student Tracking Form contained all student identifiers, exclusion and participation codes, the booklet number assigned and some demographic data.[3] The List of Schools contained, among other variables, the PISA population size, the grade population size and the sample size. These forms had to be submitted electronically.

The data quality in these two forms and their consistency with the booklets and Student

---

[2] Record deletion was strenuously avoided as it decreased the participation rate.

[3] See Appendix 11 for an example.

Questionnaire data were verified for:
- consistency of exclusion codes and participation codes (for each session) with the data in the test booklets and questionnaires;
- consistency of the sampling information in the List of Schools (*i.e.*, target population size and the sample size) with the Student Tracking Form;
- within-school student samples selected in accordance with required international procedures; and
- consistency of demographic information in the Student Tracking Form (grade, date of birth and gender) with that in the booklets or questionnaires.

VERIFYING THE RELIABILITY DATA

Some 100 checking procedures were implemented to check the following components of the multiple-marking design (*see Chapter 6*):
- number of records in the reliability files;
- number of records in the reliability files and the corresponding booklets;
- marker identification consistency;
- marker design;
- selection of the booklets for multiple marking; and
- extreme inconsistencies in the marks given by different markers (*see Chapter 14*).[4]

VERIFYING THE CONTEXT QUESTIONNAIRE DATA

The Student and School Questionnaire data underwent further checks after recoding for national adaptations. Invalid or suspicious student and school data were reported to and discussed with countries. Four types of consistency checks were run:
- *Non-valid sums:* For example, two questions in the School Questionnaire (*SCQ04* and *SCQ08*) each requested the school principal to provide information as a percentage. The sum of the values had to be 100.
- *Implausible values:* Consistency checks across variables within instruments combined with the information of two or more questions to detect suspicious data, like the number of students and the number of teachers. Outlying ratios were identified and countries were requested to check the correctness of the numbers. These checks included:
  - Identifying numbers of students (*SCQ02*) and numbers of teachers (*SCQ14*). Ratios outside ±2 standard deviations were considered outliers;
  - Identifying numbers of computers (*SCQ13*) and numbers of students (*SCQ02*). Ratios outside ±2 standard deviations were considered outliers;
  - Comparing the mother's completed education level in terms of the International Standard Classification of Education (ISCED, OECD, 1999*b*) categories for ISCED 3A (*STQ12*) and ISCED 5A or higher (*STQ14*). If the mother did not complete ISCED 3A, she could not have completed 5A; and
  - Comparing the father's completed education level similarly.
- *Outliers:* Numerical answers from the School Questionnaire were standardised and outlier values (± 3 standard deviations) were returned to national centres for checking.[5]
- *Missing data confusion:* Possible confusions between valid codes 9, 99, 999, 90, 900 and missing values were encountered during the field trial. Therefore, for all numerical variables, values close to the missing codes were returned to countries for verification.

PREPARING FILES FOR ANALYSIS

For each PISA participating country, several files were prepared for use in analysis:
- a *processed cognitive file* with all student responses to all items for the three domains *after coding*;
- a *raw cognitive file* with all student responses to all items for the three domains *before coding*;

---

[4] For example, some markers reported a missing value while others reported non-zero scores.

[5] The questions checked in this manner were school size (*SCQ02*), instructional time (*SCQ06*), number of computers (*SCQ13*), number of teachers (*SCQ14*), teacher professional development (*SCQ15*), number of hours per week in each of test language, mathematics and science classes (*STQ27*), class size (*STQ28*) and school marks (*STQ41*).

- a *student file* with all data from the Student Questionnaire and the two international options (CCC and IT);
- a *school file* with data from the School Questionnaire (one set of responses per school);
- a *weighting file* with information from the Student Tracking Form and the List of Schools necessary to compute the weights; and
- *reliability files*—19 files with recoded student answers and 19 files with scores, pertaining to two domains from each of six booklets, three domains from each of two booklets and one domain from the remaining booklet, were prepared to facilitate the reliability analyses.

PROCESSED COGNITIVE FILE

For a number of items in the PISA test booklets, a student *score* on the item was determined by combining multiple student responses. Most recoding required combining two answers into one and summarising the information from the complex multiple-choice items.

In the PISA material, some of the open-ended mathematics and science items were coded in two digits while all other items were coded with a one-digit mark. ConQuest, the software used to scale the cognitive data, requires items of the same length. To minimise the size of the data file, the double-digit items were recoded into one-digit variables using the first digit. All data produced through scoring, combining or recoding have *T* added to their item's variable label.

For items omitted by students, embedded missing and non-reached missing items were differentiated. All consecutive missing values starting from the end of each cognitive session (that is, from the end of the first hour and from the end of the second hour separately) were replaced by a non-reached code (*r*), except for the first value of the missing series. Embedded and non-reached missing items were treated differently in the scaling.

Non-reached items for students who were reported to have left the session earlier than expected or arrived later than expected (part participants) were considered *not applicable* in all analyses.

THE STUDENT QUESTIONNAIRE

The Student Questionnaire file includes the data collected from the main questionnaire, the computer familiarity international option and the cross-curriculum competency international option. If a country did not participate in the international options, *not applicable* codes were used for all variables from them.

Six derived variables were computed during the data cleaning process:
- Father's occupation, mother's occupation and the student's expected occupation at age 30, which were each originally coded using ISCO, were transformed into the Ganzeboom, de Graaf and Treiman (1992) International Socio-Economic Index.
- Question *STQ41* regarding school marks is provided in three formats: nominal, ordinal and numerical. The nominal option is used if the country provided data collected with question 41b—that is, *above the pass mark*, *at the pass mark* and *below the pass mark*. Data collected through question 41a were coded according to the reporting policy in the countries. Some countries submitted data in a range of 1-5, or 1-7 etc., while others reported student marks on a scale with maximum score of 20, or 100. These data were recoded in categorical format if fewer than eight categories were provided (1-7) or in percentages if more than seven categories were provided.

The selection of students included in the questionnaire file was based on the same rules as for the cognitive file.

THE SCHOOL QUESTIONNAIRE

No modifications other than the correction of data errors and the addition of the country four-digit codes were made to the School Questionnaire file. All participating schools, *i.e.*, any school for which at least one PISA-eligible student was assessed, have a record in the international database, regardless of whether or not they returned the School Questionnaire.

THE WEIGHTING FILES

The weighting files contained the information from the Student Tracking Form and from the List of Schools. In addition, the following variables were computed and included in the weighting files.

- For each of the three domains and for each student, a *scalability* variable was computed. If all items for one domain were missing, then the student was considered not scalable. These three variables were useful for selecting the sample of students who would contribute to the international item calibration.
- For each student, a participation indicator was computed. A student who participated in the first hour of the testing session[6] (and did not arrive late) was considered a participant. A student who only attended the second cognitive session and/or Student Questionnaire session was not considered a participant. This variable was used to compute the student participation rate.
- For each student, a *scorable* variable was computed. All students who attended at least one cognitive session (that is, either or both hours of the session) were considered *scorable*. Further, if a student only attended the Student Questionnaire session and provided data for the father's or mother's occupation questions, then the student was also considered *scorable*. Therefore, an indicator was also computed to determine whether the student answered the father's or mother's occupation questions.

A few countries submitted data with a grade national option. Therefore, two eligibility variables—*PISA-eligible* and *grade-eligible*—were also included in the Student Tracking Form. These new variables were also used to select the records that were included in the international database and therefore in the cognitive file and Student Questionnaire file. To be included in the international database, the student had to be both PISA-eligible and scorable. In other words, all PISA students who attended one of the cognitive sessions were included in the international database. Those who attended only the questionnaire session were included if they provided an answer for the father's or the mother's occupation questions.

PISA students reported in the Student Tracking Form as not eligible, no longer at school, excluded for physical, mental, or linguistic reasons, or absent were not included in the international database. Students who refused to participate in the assessment were also not included in the international database.

All non-PISA students, *i.e.*, students assessed in a few countries for a national or international grade sample option, were excluded from the international database. Countries submitting such data to the Consortium received them separately.

THE RELIABILITY FILES

One file was created for each domain and test booklet. The data from the reliability booklets were merged with those in the test booklets so that each student selected for the multiple-marking process appears four times in these files.

---

[6] Of either the original session or a make-up session.

SECTION FOUR: QUALITY INDICATORS AND OUTCOMES

CHAPTER 12 { SAMPLING OUTCOMES

Christian Monseur, Keith Rust and Sheila Krawchuk

This chapter reports on PISA sampling outcomes. Details of the sample design are given in Chapter 4.

Table 31 shows the various quality indicators for population coverage and the various pieces of information used to derive them. The following notes explain the meaning of each coverage index and how the data in each column of the table were used.

Indices 1, 2 and 3 are intended to measure PISA population coverage. Indices 4 and 5 are intended to be diagnostic in cases where indices 1, 2 or 3 have unexpected values. Many references are made in this chapter to the various Sampling Forms on which NPMs documented statistics and other information needed in undertaking the sampling. The forms themselves are included in Appendix 9.

Index 1: Coverage of the National Desired Population, calculated by $P/(P+E) \times 3[c]/3[a]$.

- The National Desired Population (NDP), defined by Sampling Form 3 response box [a] and denoted here as 3[a], is the population that includes all enrolled 15-year-olds in each country (with the possibility of small levels of exclusions), based on national statistics. However, the final NDP reflected on each country's school sampling frame might have had some school-level exclusions. The value that represents the population of enrolled 15-year-olds minus those in excluded schools is represented by response box [c] on Sampling Form 3 and denoted here as 3[c]. Thus, the term $3[c]/3[a]$ provides the proportion of the NDP covered in each country based on national statistics.

- The value $(P+E)$ provides the weighted estimate from the student sample of all eligible 15-year-olds in each country, where P is the weighted estimate of eligible non-excluded 15-year-olds and E is the weighted estimate of eligible 15-year-olds that were excluded within schools. Therefore, the term $P/(P+E)$ provides an estimate based on the student sample of the proportion of the eligible 15-year-old population represented by the non-excluded eligible 15-year-olds.

- Thus the result of multiplying these two proportions together ($3[c]/3[a]$ and $P/(P+E)$) indicates the overall proportion of the NDP covered by the non-excluded portion of the student sample.

Index 2: Coverage of the National Enrolled Population, calculated by $P/(P+E) \times 3[c]/2[b]$.

- The National Enrolled Population (NEP), defined by Sampling Form 2 response box [b] and denoted here as 2[b], is the population that includes all enrolled 15-year-olds in each country, based on national statistics. The final NDP, denoted here as 3[c], reflects the 15-year-old population from each country's school sampling frame. This value represents the population of enrolled 15-year-olds less those in excluded schools.

- The value $(P+E)$ provides the weighted estimate from the student sample of all eligible 15-year-olds in each country, where P is the weighted estimate of eligible non-excluded 15-year-olds and E is the weighted estimate of eligible 15-year-olds that were excluded within schools. Therefore, the term

$P/(P+E)$ provides an estimate based on the student sample of the proportion of the eligible 15-year-old population that is represented by the non-excluded eligible 15-year-olds.

- Multiplying these two proportions together (3[c]/2[b] and $P/(P+E)$) gives the overall proportion of the NEP that is covered by the non-excluded portion of the student sample.

Index 3: Coverage of the National 15-Year-Old Population, calculated by $P/2[a]$.

- The National Population of 15-year-olds, defined by Sampling Form 2 response box [a] and denoted here as 2[a], is the entire population of 15-year-olds in each country (enrolled and not enrolled), based on national statistics. The value P is the weighted estimate of eligible non-excluded 15-year-olds from the student sample. Thus $P/2[a]$ indicates the proportion of the National Population of 15-year-olds covered by the non-excluded portion of the student sample.

Index 4: Coverage of the Estimated School Population, calculated by $(P+E)/S$.

- The value $(P+E)$ provides the weighted estimate from the student sample of all eligible 15-year-olds in each country, where P is the weighted estimate of eligible non-excluded 15-year-olds and E is the weighted estimate of eligible 15-year-olds who were excluded within schools.
- The value S is an estimate of the 15-year-old school population in each country. This is based on the actual or (more often) approximate number of 15-year-olds enrolled in each school in the sample, prior to contacting the school to conduct the assessment. The S value is calculated as the sum over all sampled schools of the product of each school's sampling weight and its number of 15-year-olds (ENR) as recorded on the school sampling frame. In the infrequent case where the ENR value was not available, the number of 15-year-olds from the Student Tracking Form was used.
- Thus, $(P+E)/S$ is the proportion of the estimated school 15-year-old population that is represented by the weighted estimate from the student sample of all eligible 15-year-olds. Its purpose is to check whether the student sampling has been carried out correctly, and to assess whether the value of S is a reliable measure of the number of enrolled 15-year-olds. This is important for interpreting Index 5.

Index 5: Coverage of the School Sampling Frame Population, calculated by $S/3[c]$.

- The value $S/3[c]$ is the ratio of the enrolled 15-year-old population, as estimated from data on the school sampling frame, to the size of the enrolled student population, as reported on Sampling Form 3. In some cases, this provides a check as to whether the data on the sampling frame give a reliable estimate of the number of 15-year-olds in each school. In other cases, however, it is evident that 3[c] has been derived using data from the sampling frame by the National Project Manager, so that this ratio may be close to 1.0 even if enrolment data on the school sampling frame are poor. Under such circumstances, Index 4 will differ noticeably from 1.0, and the figure for 3[c] will also be inaccurate.

Tables 32, 33 and 34 present school and student-level response rates. Table 32 indicates the rates calculated by using only original schools and no replacement schools. Table 33 indicates the improved response rates when first and second replacement schools were accounted for in the rates. Table 34 indicates the student response rates among the full set of participating schools.

For calculating school response rates *before* replacement, the numerator consisted of all original sample schools with enrolled age-eligible students who participated (*i.e.*, assessed a sample of eligible students, and obtained a student response rate of at least 50 per cent). The denominator consisted of all the schools in the numerator, plus those original sample schools with enrolled age-eligible students that either did not participate or failed to assess at least 50 per cent of eligible sample students. Schools that were included in the sampling frame, but were found to have no age-eligible students, were omitted from the calculation of response rates. Replacement schools do not figure in these calculations.

Table 31: Sampling and Coverage Rates

	Sampling Sheet Information						Sample Information											Coverage Indices				
	All 15-year-olds	Enrolled 15-year-olds	National Target	School Level Excl'ns	National Target Minus School Excl'ns	% School-Level Excl'ns	Enrolled Students on School Frame	Participants Actual	Participants W'td	Excluded Actual	Excluded W'td	Ineligible Actual	Ineligible W'td	Eligible Actual	Eligible W'td	Within-School Excl'n Rate (%)	Over-all Excl'n Rate (%)	Ineligible Rate (%)	1	2	3	4	5
	SF 2[a]	SF 2[b]	SF 3[a]	SF 3[b]	SF 3[c]	3[b]/3[a]	S		P		E		I & W		P+E	E/(P+E)							
Australia	266 878	248 908	248 738	2 850	245 888	1.15	244 157	5 176	229 152	63	2 688	233	6 795	5 239	231 840	1.16	2.29	2.93	0.98	0.98	0.98	0.95	0.99
Austria	95 041	90 354	90 354	32	90 322	0.04	86 601	4 745	71 547	41	500	259	3 389	4 786	72 047	0.69	0.73	4.70	0.99	0.99	•*	•*	0.96
Belgium[1]	121 121	119 055	118 972	1 091	117 881	0.92	117 836	6 670	110 095	100	1 596	36	572	6 770	111 691	1.43	2.33	0.51	0.98	0.98	0.98	0.95	1.00
Belgium (Fl.)	71 074	68 995	68 912	897	68 015	1.30	69 110	3 890	61 143	25	428	11	128	3 915	61 571	0.70	1.99	0.21	0.98	0.98	0.98	0.89	1.02
Belgium (Fr.)	49 289	49 289	49 289	194	49 095	0.39	48 726	2 780	48 952	75	1 168	25	443	2 855	50 120	2.33	2.72	0.88	0.97	0.97	0.99	1.03	0.99
Brazil[2]	3 464 330	1 841 843	1 837 236	6 633	1 830 603	0.36	2 490 788	4 893	2 402 280	14	7 842	217	80 666	4 907	2 410 122	0.33	0.69	3.35	0.99	0.99	0.69	0.97	1.36
Canada	403 803	396 423	391 788	2 035	389 990	0.52	381 165	29 687	348 481	1 584	16 197	1 709	19 032	31 271	364 678	4.44	4.94	5.22	0.95	0.94	0.86	0.96	0.98
Czech Republic	134 627	132 508	132 508	2 181	130 327	1.65	129 422	5 365	125 639	13	297	81	1 619	5 378	125 936	0.24	1.88	1.29	0.98	0.98	0.93	0.97	0.99
Denmark	53 693	52 161	52 161	345	51 816	0.66	50 236	4 235	47 786	119	1 195	99	1 068	4 354	48 981	2.44	3.08	2.18	0.97	0.97	0.89	0.98	0.97
Finland	66 571	66 561	66 319	550	65 769	0.83	65 875	4 864	62 826	58	673	22	261	4 922	63 499	1.06	1.88	0.41	0.98	0.98	0.94	0.96	1.00
France	788 387	788 387	750 460	17 728	732 732	2.36	744 754	4 673	730 494	59	8 208	41	6 077	4 732	738 702	1.11	3.45	0.82	0.97	0.92	0.93	0.99	1.02
Germany	927 473	924 549	924 549	5 423	919 126	0.59	935 223	5 073	826 816	60	9 163	8	1 053	5 133	835 979	1.10	1.68	0.13	0.98	0.98	0.89	0.89	1.02
Greece	128 175	124 656	124 187	200	123 987	0.16	110 622	3 644	111 363	21	682	35	1 039	3 665	112 045	0.61	0.77	0.93	0.99	0.99	0.87	1.01	0.89
Hungary[3]	120 759	115 325	115 325	0	115 325	0.00	131 291	4 887	107 460	34	765	79	1 762	4 921	108 224	0.71	1.63	0.89	0.99	0.99	0.89	0.82	1.14
Iceland	4 062	4 044	4 044	18	4 026	0.45	4 020	3 372	3 869	79	79	15	15	3 451	3 949	2.01	2.44	0.38	0.98	0.98	0.95	0.98	1.00
Ireland	65 339	64 370	63 572	1 021	62 551	1.61	62 138	3 854	56 209	134	1 734	120	1 501	3 988	57 942	2.99	4.55	2.59	0.95	0.94	0.86	0.93	0.99
Italy	584 417	574 864	574 864	775	574 089	0.13	562 763	4 984	510 792	117	12 247	0	0	5 101	523 039	2.34	2.47	0.00	0.98	0.98	0.87	0.93	0.98
Japan	1 490 000	1 485 269	1 459 296	34 124	1 425 172	2.34	1 420 533	5 256	1 446 596	0	0	0	0	5 256	1 446 596	0.00	2.34	0.00	0.98	0.96	0.97	1.02	1.00
Korea	712 812	602 605	602 605	1 820	600 785	0.30	589 018	4 982	579 109	6	826	81	8 722	4 988	579 936	0.14	0.44	1.50	1.00	1.00	0.81	0.98	0.98
Latvia	38 000	35 981	35 981	886	35 095	2.46	35 629	3 920	30 063	62	402	9	60	3 982	30 465	1.32	3.75	0.20	0.96	0.96	0.79	0.86	1.02
Liechtenstein	415	326	326	0	326	0.00	327	314	325	2	2	9	60	316	327	0.61	0.61	0.00	0.99	0.99	0.78	1.00	1.00
Luxembourg	4 556	4 556	4 556	416	4 140	9.13	4 140	3 528	4 138	0	0	0	0	3 528	4 138	0.00	9.13	0.00	0.91	0.91	0.91	1.00	1.00
Mexico	2 127 504	1 098 605	1 073 317	0	1 073 317	0.00	1 063 524	4 600	960 011	2	564	392	74 897	4 602	960 575	0.06	0.06	7.80	1.00	0.98	0.45	0.90	0.99

Sampling outcomes

Table 31 (cont.)

Sampling Sheet Information

	All 15-year-olds	Enrolled 15-year-olds	National Target	School-Level Excl'ns	National Target Minus School Excl'ns	% School-Level Excl'ns	Enrolled Students on School Frame	Participants Actual	Participants W'td	Excluded Actual	Excluded W'td	Ineligible Actual	Ineligible W'td	Eligible Actual	Eligible W'td	Within-School Excl'n Rate (%)	Overall Excl'n Rate (%)	Ineligible E/(P+E) (%)	Cov 1	Cov 2	Cov 3	Cov 4	Cov 5
	SF 2[a]	SF 2[b]	SF 3[a]	SF 3[b]	SF 3[c]	3[b]/3[a]	S		P		E		I & W		P+E								
Netherlands	178 924	178 924	178 924	7 800	171 124	4.36	180 697	2 503	157 327	1	23	34	2 606	2 504	157 350	0.01	4.37	1.66	0.96	0.96	0.88	0.87	1.06
New Zealand	54 220	51 464	51 464	976	50 488	1.90	50 645	3 667	46 757	137	1 590	245	2 712	3 804	48 347	3.29	5.12	5.61	0.95	0.95	0.86	0.95	1.00
Norway	52 165	51 587	51 474	420	51 054	0.82	50 271	4 147	49 579	93	944	29	278	4 240	50 523	1.87	2.67	0.55	0.97	0.97	0.95	1.01	0.98
Poland[4]	665 500	643 528	643 528	56 524	587 004	8.78	546 842	3 654	542 005	53	5 484	26	3 399	3 707	547 489	1.00	9.70	0.62	0.90	0.90	0.81	1.00	0.93
Portugal	132 325	127 165	127 165	0	127 165	0.00	126 505	4 585	99 998	122	2 777	265	5 284	4 707	102 775	2.70	2.70	5.14	0.97	0.97	0.76	0.81	0.99
Russian Federation	2 268 566	2 259 985	2 259 985	10 867	2 249 118	0.48	2 249 118	6 701	1 968 131	22	4 960	137	−0 166	6 723	1 973 091	0.25	0.73	2.04	0.99	0.99	0.87	0.88	1.00
Spain	462 082	451 685	451 685	2 180	449 505	0.48	444 288	6 214	399 055	153	8 998	180	10 973	6 367	408 053	2.21	2.68	2.69	0.97	0.97	0.86	0.92	0.99
Sweden	100 940	100 940	100 940	1 360	99 580	1.35	100 578	4 416	94 338	174	3 349	32	671	4 590	97 687	3.43	4.73	0.69	0.95	0.95	0.93	0.97	1.01
Switzerland	81 350	79 232	79 232	954	78 278	1.20	97 162	6 100	72 010	62	822	150	1 998	6 162	72 833	1.13	2.32	2.74	0.98	0.98	0.89	0.75	1.24
United Kingdom[5]	731 743	705 875	669 875	17 674	652 201	2.64	654 095	9 340	643 041	219	15 990	261	13 413	9 559	659 030	2.43	5.00	2.04	0.95	0.90	0.88	1.01	1.00
England[6]	603 100	580 546	580 546	16 121	564 425	2.78	567 204	4 120	560 248	133	15 309	100	10 973	4 253	575 558	2.66	5.36	1.91	0.95	0.95	0.93	1.01	1.00
Northern Ireland	26 043	26 477	26 477	436	26 041	1.65	26 129	2 849	25 757	86	681	58	447	2 935	26 438	2.57	4.18	1.69	0.96	0.96	0.99	1.01	1.00
Scotland	65 200	62 852	62 852	1 117	61 735	1.78	60 762	2 371	57 035	0	0	103	1 993	2 371	57 035	0.00	1.78	3.49	0.98	0.98	0.87	0.94	0.98
United States	3 876 000	3 836 000	3 836 000	0	3 836 000	0.00	3 567 961	3 846	3 121 874	211	132 543	221	148 374	4 057	3 254 417	4.07	4.07	4.56	0.96	0.96	0.81	0.91	0.93

Notes:
1. The sampling form numbers for Belgium exceed the sum of the two parts because the German-speaking community in Belgium is also included in these numbers.
2. Brazil's eligible population consists of 15-year-olds in grades 7 to 10. The last two coverage indices are not available because S is an overestimate of the non-grade 5 and 6 population (it only excludes schools with only grades 5 and 6).
3. Hungary used grade 9 enrolments for primary schools, which was not a good measure of size. Therefore, the value of S has been recalculated as 122 609.74 (sum of school base weights weighted by MOS for the secondary schools) plus 8 681 (sum of student weights from the primary schools stratum[1]=131 290.74
4. Primary schools in Poland were not randomly sampled and therefore these students could not be used. As a result, the 6.7 per cent of the population accounted for by these students are added to the school-level exclusion figure.
5. The Sampling Form 2 numbers for the United Kingdom exceed the sum of the three parts because Wales is also included in these numbers. This also affects Indices 2 and 3 for the United Kingdom.
6. On Sampling Form 3, the within-school exclusion figure for England was 1 258. After sampling, special education schools were also excluded. They account for another 14 863 for a new total school-level exclusion of 16 121.
7. (a) Students in vocational schools are enrolled on a part-time/part-year basis. (b) Since the PISA assessment was conducted only at one point in time, these students are captured only partially. (c) It is not possible to assess how well the students sampled from vocational schools represent the universe of students enrolled in vocational schools, and so those students not attending classes at the time of the PISA assessment are not represented in the PISA results.

For calculating school response rates *after* replacement, the numerator consisted of all sample schools (original plus replacement) with enrolled age-eligible students that participated (*i.e.*, assessed a sample of eligible students and obtained a student response rate of at least 50 per cent). The denominator consisted of all the schools in the numerator that were in the original sample, plus those original sample schools that had age-eligible students enrolled, but that failed to assess at least 50 per cent of eligible sample students and for which no replacement school participated. Schools that were included in the sampling frame, but were found to contain no age-eligible students, were omitted from the calculation of response rates. Replacement schools were included only when they participated, and were replacing a refusing school that had age-eligible students.

In calculating weighted school response rates, each school received a weight equal to the product of its base weight (the reciprocal of its selection probability) and the number of age-eligible students enrolled, as indicated on the sampling frame.

With the use of probability proportional-to-size sampling, in countries with few certainty school selections and no over-sampling or under-sampling of any explicit strata, weighted and unweighted rates are very similar.

Thus, the weighted school response rate before replacement is given by the formula:

$$\text{weighted school response rate before replacement} = \frac{\sum_{i \in Y} W_i E_i}{\sum_{i \in (Y \cup N)} W_i E_i}, \quad (79)$$

where Y denotes the set of responding original sample schools with age-eligible students, N denotes the set of eligible non-responding original sample schools, W_i denotes the base weight for school i, $W_i = 1/P_i$, where P_i denotes the school selection probability for school i, and E_i denotes the enrolment size of age-eligible students, as indicated on the sampling frame.

The weighted school response rate, after replacement, is given by the formula:

$$\text{weighted school response rate after replacement} = \frac{\sum_{i \in (Y \cup R)} W_i E_i}{\sum_{i \in (Y \cup N)} W_i E_i}, \quad (80)$$

where Y denotes the set of responding original sample schools, R denotes the set of responding replacement schools, for which the corresponding original sample school was eligible but was non-responding, N denotes the set of eligible refusing original sample schools, W_i denotes the base weight for school i, $W_i = 1/P_i$, where P_i denotes the school selection probability for school i, and for weighted rates, E_i denotes the enrolment size of age-eligible students, as indicated on the sampling frame.

For unweighted student response rates, the numerator is the number of students for whom assessment data were included in the results. The denominator is the number of sampled students who were age-eligible, and not explicitly excluded as student exclusions. The exception is cases where countries applied different sampling rates across explicit strata. In these cases, unweighted rates were calculated in each stratum, and then weighted together according to the relative population size of 15-year-olds in each stratum.

For weighted student response rates, the same number of students appear in the numerator and denominator as for unweighted rates, but each student was weighted by its student base weight. This is given as the product of the school base weight—for the school in which the student is enrolled—and the reciprocal of the student selection probability within the school.

In countries with no over-sampling of any explicit strata, weighted and unweighted student participation rates are very similar.

Overall response rates are calculated as the product of school and student response rates. Although overall weighted and unweighted rates can be calculated, there is little value in presenting overall unweighted rates. The weighted rates indicate the proportion of the student population represented by the sample prior to making the school and student non-response adjustments.

Table 32: School Response Rates Before Replacements

Country	Weighted School Participation Rate Before Replacement (%)	Number of Responding Schools (Weighted by Enrolment)	Number of Schools Sampled (Responding and Non-Responding) (Weighted by Enrolment)	Number of Responding Schools (Unweighted)	Number of Responding and Non-Responding Schools (Unweighted)
Australia	80.95	197 639	244 157	206	247
Austria	99.38	86 062	86 601	212	213
Belgium	69.12	81 453	117 836	171	252
Belgium (Fl.)	61.51	42 506	69 110	91	150
Belgium (Fr.)	79.93	38 947	48 726	80	102
Brazil	97.38	2 425 608	2 490 788	315	324
Canada	87.91	335 100	381 165	1 069	1 159
Czech Republic	95.30	123 345	129 422	217	229
Denmark	83.66	42 027	50 236	194	235
Finland	96.82	63 783	65 875	150	155
France	94.66	704 971	744 754	173	184
Germany	94.71	885 792	935 222	213	220
Greece	83.91	92 824	110 622	98	141
Hungary	98.67	209 153	211 969	193	195
Iceland	99.88	4 015	4 020	130	131
Ireland	85.56	53 164	62 138	132	154
Italy	97.90	550 932	562 763	167	170
Japan	82.05	1 165 576	1 420 533	123	150
Korea	100.00	589 018	589 018	146	146
Latvia	82.39	29 354	35 628	143	174
Liechtenstein	100.00	327	327	11	11
Luxembourg	93.04	3 852	4 140	23	25
Mexico	92.69	985 745	1 063 524	170	182
Netherlands	27.13	49 019	180 697	49	180
New Zealand	77.65	39 328	50 645	136	178
Norway	85.95	43 207	50 271	164	191
Poland	79.11	432 603	546 842	119	150
Portugal	95.27	120 521	126 505	145	152
Russian Federation	98.84	4 445 841	4 498 235	237	242
Spain	95.41	423 900	444 288	177	185
Sweden	99.96	100 534	100 578	159	160
Switzerland	91.81	89 208	97 162	271	311
United Kingdom	61.27	400 737	654 095	292	430
England	58.83	333 674	567 204	106	180
Northern Ireland	70.90	18 525	26 129	100	142
Scotland	79.88	48 537	60 762	86	108
United States	56.42	2 013 101	3 567 961	116	210

Table 33: School Response Rates After Replacements

Country	Weighted School Participation Rate After Replacement (%)	Number of Responding Schools (Weighted by Enrolment)	Number of Schools Sampled (Responding and Non-Responding) (Weighted by Enrolment)	Number of Responding Schools (Unweighted)	Number of Responding and Non-Responding Schools (Unweighted)
Australia	93.65	228 668	244 175	228	247
Austria	100.00	86 601	86 601	213	213
Belgium	85.52	100 833	117 911	214	252
Belgium (Fl.)	79.75	55 144	69 142	119	150
Belgium (Fr.)	93.68	45 689	48 770	95	102
Brazil	97.96	2 439 152	2 489 942	318	324
Canada	93.31	355 644	381 161	1 098	1 159
Czech Republic	99.01	128 551	129 841	227	229
Denmark	94.86	47 689	50 271	223	235
Finland	100.00	65 875	65 875	155	155
France	95.23	709 454	744 982	174	184
Germany	94.71	885 792	935 222	213	220
Greece	99.77	130 555	130 851	139	141
Hungary	98.67	209 153	211 969	193	195
Iceland	99.88	4 015	4 020	130	131
Ireland	87.53	54 388	62 138	135	154
Italy	100.00	562 755	562 755	170	170
Japan	90.05	1 279 121	1 420 533	135	150
Korea	100.00	589 018	589 018	146	146
Latvia	88.51	31 560	35 656	153	174
Liechtenstein	100.00	327	327	11	11
Luxembourg	93.04	3 852	4 140	23	25
Mexico	100.00	1 063 524	1 063 524	182	182
Netherlands	55.50	100 283	180 697	100	180
New Zealand	86.37	43 744	50 645	152	178
Norway	92.25	46 376	50 271	176	191
Poland	83.21	455 870	547 847	126	150
Portugal	95.27	120 521	126 505	145	152
Russian Federation	99.29	4 466 335	4 498 235	238	242
Spain	100.00	444 288	444 288	185	185
Sweden	99.96	100 534	100 578	159	160
Switzerland	95.84	92 888	96 924	282	311
United Kingdom	82.14	537 219	654 022	349	430
England	82.32	466 896	567 204	148	180
Northern Ireland	79.37	20 755	26 150	113	142
Scotland	81.70	49 568	60 668	88	108
United States	70.33	2 503 666	3 559 661	145	210

Table 34: Student Response Rates After Replacements

Country	Weighted Student Participation Rate After Second Replacement (%)	Number of Students Assessed (Weighted)	Number of Students Sampled (Assessed and Absent) (Weighted)	Number of Students Assessed (Unweighted)	Number of Students Sampled (Assessed and Absent) (Unweighted)
Australia	84.24	161 607	191 850	5 154	6 173
Austria	91.64	65 562	71 547	4 745	5 164
Belgium	93.30	88 816	95 189	6 648	7 103
Belgium (Fl.)	95.49	46 801	49 012	3 874	4 055
Belgium (Fr.)	90.98	42 014	46 177	2 774	3 048
Brazil	87.15	1 463 000	1 678 789	4 885	5 613
Canada	84.89	276 233	325 386	29 461	33 736
Czech Republic	92.76	115 371	124 372	5 343	5 769
Denmark	91.64	37 171	40 564	4 212	4 592
Finland	92.80	58 303	62 826	4 864	5 237
France	91.19	634 276	695 523	4 657	5 115
Germany	85.65	666 794	778 516	4 983	5 788
Greece	96.83	136 919	141 404	4 672	4 819
Hungary	95.31	100 807	105 769	4 883	5 111
Iceland	87.09	3 372	3 872	3 372	3 872
Ireland	85.59	42 088	49 172	3 786	4 424
Italy	93.08	475 446	510 792	4 984	5 369
Japan	96.34	1 267 367	1 315 462	5 256	5 450
Korea	98.84	572 767	579 470	4 982	5 045
Latvia	90.73	24 403	26 895	3 915	4 305
Liechtenstein	96.62	314	325	314	325
Luxembourg	89.19	3 434	3 850	3 434	3 850
Mexico	93.95	903 100	961 283	4 600	4 882
Netherlands	84.03	72 656	86 462	2 503	2 958
New Zealand	88.23	35 616	40 369	3 667	4 163
Norway	89.28	40 908	45 821	4 147	4 665
Poland	87.70	393 675	448 904	3 639	4 169
Portugal	86.28	82 395	95 493	4 517	5 232
Russian Federation	96.21	1 903 348	1 978 266	6 701	6 981
Spain	91.78	366 301	399 100	6 214	6 764
Sweden	87.96	82 956	94 312	4 416	5 017
Switzerland	95.13	65 677	69 037	6 084	6 389
United Kingdom	80.97	419 713	518 358	9 250	11 300
England	81.07	366 277	451 828	4 099	5 047
Northern Ireland	86.01	17 049	19 821	2 825	3 281
Scotland	77.90	36 387	46 708	2 326	2 972
United States	84.99	1 801 229	2 119 392	3 700	4 320

DESIGN EFFECT AND EFFECTIVE SAMPLE SIZE

Surveys in education and especially international surveys rarely sample students by simply selecting a random sample of students (a simple random sample). Schools are first selected and, within each selected school, classes or students are randomly sampled. Sometimes, geographic areas are first selected before sampling schools and students. This sampling design is usually referred to as a cluster sample or a multi-stage sample.

Selected students attending the same school cannot be considered as independent observations as they can be with a simple random sample because they are usually more similar than students attending distinct educational institutions. For instance, they are offered the same school resources, may have the same teachers and therefore are taught a common implemented curriculum, and so on. School differences are also larger if different educational programs are not available in all schools. One expects to observe greater differences between a vocational school and an academic school than between two comprehensive schools.

Furthermore, it is well known that within a country, within sub-national entities and within a city, people tend to live in areas according to their financial resources. As children usually attend schools close to their house, it is likely that students attending the same school come from similar social and economic backgrounds.

A simple random sample of 4 000 students is thus likely to cover the diversity of the population better than a sample of 100 schools with 40 students observed within each school. It follows that the uncertainty associated with any population parameter estimate (*i.e.*, standard error) will be larger for a clustered sample than for a simple random sample of the same size.

To limit this reduction of precision in the population parameter estimate, multi-stage sample designs usually use complementary information to improve coverage of the population diversity. In PISA, and in previous international surveys, the following techniques were implemented to limit the increase in standard errors: (i) explicit and/or implicit stratification of the school sample frame and (ii) selection of the schools with probabilities proportional to their size. Complementary information generally cannot fully compensate for the increase in the standard errors due to the multi-stage design, however.

The reduction in design efficiency is usually reported through the 'design effect' (Kish, 1965) that describes the 'ratio of the variance of the estimate obtained from the (more complex) sample to the variance of the estimate that would have been obtained from a simple random sample of the same number of units. The design effect has two primary uses—in sample size estimation and in appraising the efficiency of more complex plans.' (Cochran, 1977).

In PISA, a design effect has been computed for a statistic *t* using:

$$Deff_3(t) = \frac{Var_{BRR}(t)}{Var_{SRS}(t)}, \qquad (81)$$

where $Var_{BRR}(t)$ is the sampling variance for the statistic *t* computed by the BRR replication method (*see Chapter 8*), and $Var_{SRS}(t)$ is the sampling variance for the same statistic *t* on the same data base but considering the sample as a simple random sample.

Another way to express the lack of precision due to the complex sampling design is through the effective sample size, which expresses the simple random sample size that would give the same standard error as the one obtained from the actual complex sample design. In PISA, the effective sample size for statistic *t* is equal to:

$$Effn_3(t) = \frac{n}{Deff_3(t)} = \frac{n \times Var_{SRS}(t)}{Var_{BRR}(t)}, \qquad (82)$$

where *n* is equal to the actual number of units in the sample.

The notion of design effect as given in (81) is extended and produces five design effects to describe the influence of the sampling and test designs on the standard errors for statistics.

The total errors computed for the international PISA initial report consist of two components: sampling variance and measurement variance. The standard error in PISA is inflated because the students were not sampled according to a simple random sample and also because the measure of the student proficiency estimates includes some amount of random error.

For any statistic t, the population estimate and the sampling variance are computed for each plausible value and then combined as described in Chapter 9.

The five design effects and their respective effective sample sizes that are considered are defined as follows:

$$Deff_1(t) = \frac{Var_{SRS}(t) + MVar(t)}{Var_{SRS}(t)}, \quad (83)$$

where $MVar(t)$ is the measurement variance for the statistic t. This design effect shows the inflation of the total variance that would have occurred due to measurement error if in fact the sample were considered a simple random sample.

$$Deff_2(t) = \frac{Var_{BRR}(t) + MVar(t)}{Var_{SRS}(t) + MVar(t)} \quad (84)$$

shows the inflation of the *total* variance due only to the use of the complex sampling design.

$$Deff_3(t) = \frac{Var_{BRR}(t)}{Var_{SRS}(t)} \quad (85)$$

shows the inflation of the *sampling* variance due to the use of the complex design.

$$Deff_4(t) = \frac{Var_{BRR}(t) + MVar(t)}{Var_{BRR}(t)} \quad (86)$$

shows the inflation of the *total* variance due to the measurement error.

$$Deff_5(t) = \frac{Var_{BRR}(t) + MVar(t)}{Var_{SRS}(t)} \quad (87)$$

shows the inflation of the *total* variance due to the measurement error and due to the complex sampling design.

The product of the first and second design effects is equal to the product of the third and fourth design effects, and both products are equal to the fifth design effect.

Tables 35 to 39 provide the design effects and the effective sample sizes, respectively, for the *means* of the combined reading, mathematical and scientific literacy scales, the *percentage of students at level 3* on the combined reading literacy scale, and the *percentage of students at level 5* on the combined reading literacy scale.

The results show that the design effects depend on the computed statistics. It is well known that the design effects due to multi-stage sample designs are usually high for statistics such as means but much lower for relational statistics such as correlation or regression coefficients.

Because the samples for the mathematics and science scales are drawn from the same schools as that for the combined reading scale, but with much fewer students, it follows that the reading sample is much more clustered than for the science and mathematics samples. Therefore it is not surprising to find that design effects are generally substantially higher for reading than for mathematics and science.

The design effect due to the multi-stage sample is generally quite small for the percentage of students at level 3 but generally higher for the percentage of students at level 5. Recoding the student proficiency estimates into being or not being at level 3 suppresses the distinction between high and low achievers and therefore considerably reduces the school variance. Recoding student proficiency estimates into being or not being at level 5, however, keeps the distinction between high and lower achievers and preserves some of the school variance.

The measurement error for the minor domains is not substantially higher than the measurement error for the major domain because the proficiency estimates were generated with a multi-dimensional model using a large set of variables as conditioning variables. This complementary information has effectively reduced the measurement error for the minor domain proficiency estimates.

Table 35: Design Effects and Effective Sample Sizes for the Mean Performance on the Combined Reading Literacy Scale

	Design Effect 1	Design Effect 2	Design Effect 3	Design Effect 4	Design Effect 5	Effective Sample Size 1	Effective Sample Size 2	Effective Sample Size 3	Effective Sample Size 4	Effective Sample Size 5
Australia	1.30	4.77	5.90	1.05	6.20	3 983	1 085	877	4 926	835
Austria	1.06	2.98	3.10	1.02	3.16	4 483	1 590	1 531	4 657	1 502
Belgium	1.06	6.96	7.31	1.01	7.37	6 302	958	912	6 617	905
Brazil	1.19	5.32	6.14	1.03	6.33	4 112	920	797	4 746	773
Canada	1.09	7.41	7.97	1.01	8.06	27 294	4 009	3 726	29 364	3 686
Czech Republic	1.07	3.04	3.18	1.02	3.25	5 019	1 766	1 688	5 251	1 652
Denmark	1.08	2.26	2.36	1.03	2.44	3 924	1 875	1 796	4 097	1 737
Finland	1.14	3.55	3.90	1.04	4.04	4 270	1 370	1 246	4 697	1 203
France	1.12	3.70	4.02	1.03	4.13	4 189	1 262	1 164	4 542	1 131
Germany	1.13	2.20	2.36	1.06	2.49	4 473	2 309	2 152	4 800	2 036
Greece	1.19	10.29	12.04	1.02	12.23	3 930	454	388	4 600	382
Hungary	1.03	8.41	8.64	1.00	8.67	4 743	581	566	4 870	564
Iceland	1.11	0.75	0.73	1.15	0.84	3 045	4 470	4 633	2 936	4 037
Ireland	1.11	4.16	4.50	1.02	4.61	3 474	927	856	3 762	836
Italy	1.16	4.35	4.90	1.03	5.06	4 280	1 147	1 018	4 822	985
Japan	1.11	17.53	19.28	1.01	19.38	4 753	300	273	5 227	271
Korea	1.13	5.33	5.89	1.02	6.02	4 413	935	846	4 875	828
Latvia	1.20	8.62	10.16	1.02	10.36	3 240	451	383	3 817	376
Liechtenstein	1.10	0.52	0.48	1.20	0.57	286	600	658	261	547
Luxembourg	1.16	0.77	0.73	1.22	0.89	3 043	4 603	4 838	2 893	3 970
Mexico	1.17	5.88	6.69	1.02	6.85	3 945	783	688	4 489	671
Netherlands	1.06	3.39	3.52	1.02	3.58	2 369	739	711	2 463	699
New Zealand	1.03	2.35	2.40	1.01	2.43	3 549	1 560	1 531	3 617	1 510
Norway	1.06	2.85	2.97	1.02	3.03	3 895	1 457	1 398	4 058	1 369
Poland	1.16	6.29	7.12	1.02	7.28	3 158	581	513	3 575	502
Portugal	1.20	8.30	9.72	1.02	9.91	3 836	553	472	4 495	462
Russian Federation	1.16	11.79	13.53	1.01	13.69	5 771	568	495	6 622	490
Spain	1.17	5.44	6.18	1.03	6.35	5 323	1 143	1 005	6 050	979
Sweden	1.20	2.10	2.32	1.09	2.52	3 669	2 106	1 903	4 059	1 749
Switzerland	1.05	10.04	10.52	1.00	10.57	5 798	607	580	6 070	577
United Kingdom	1.09	5.55	5.97	1.02	6.07	8 552	1 682	1 564	9 198	1 540
United States	1.10	15.82	17.29	1.01	17.39	3 500	243	222	3 824	221

Sampling outcomes

Table 36: Design Effects and Effective Sample Sizes for the Mean Performance on the Mathematical Literacy Scale

	Design Effect 1	Design Effect 2	Design Effect 3	Design Effect 4	Design Effect 5	Effective Sample Size 1	Effective Sample Size 2	Effective Sample Size 3	Effective Sample Size 4	Effective Sample Size 5
Australia	1.49	2.89	3.81	1.13	4.29	1 923	991	751	2 534	666
Austria	1.01	1.93	1.93	1.00	1.94	2 620	1 370	1 365	2 630	1 360
Belgium	1.12	4.54	4.98	1.03	5.10	3 366	834	761	3 692	742
Brazil	1.25	3.14	3.68	1.07	3.93	2 175	864	739	2 544	692
Canada	1.12	4.05	4.42	1.03	4.55	14 682	4 072	3 726	16 041	3 626
Czech Republic	1.03	2.46	2.51	1.01	2.55	2 964	1 246	1 221	3 025	1 204
Denmark	1.23	1.53	1.65	1.14	1.88	1 936	1 556	1 440	2 090	1 264
Finland	1.25	1.54	1.68	1.15	1.93	2 163	1 751	1 610	2 352	1 402
France	1.21	1.99	2.19	1.09	2.40	2 153	1 305	1 184	2 373	1 082
Germany	1.06	1.62	1.65	1.03	1.71	2 682	1 747	1 711	2 738	1 656
Greece	1.24	5.60	6.68	1.04	6.91	2 108	466	390	2 516	377
Hungary	1.04	4.53	4.66	1.01	4.69	2 701	618	601	2 777	597
Iceland	1.25	1.06	1.08	1.23	1.33	1 505	1 768	1 741	1 527	1 414
Ireland	1.07	2.09	2.17	1.03	2.25	1 984	1 016	979	2 059	948
Italy	1.32	2.21	2.59	1.12	2.91	2 101	1 250	1 066	2 464	950
Japan	1.10	10.60	11.57	1.01	11.67	2 655	276	253	2 899	250
Korea	1.12	2.65	2.84	1.04	2.97	2 470	1 047	974	2 656	934
Latvia	1.18	3.40	3.83	1.05	4.00	1 826	632	562	2 054	537
Liechtenstein	1.15	0.81	0.78	1.19	0.93	153	216	224	147	189
Luxembourg	1.11	0.81	0.79	1.14	0.90	1 761	2 415	2 480	1 713	2 170
Mexico	1.18	3.60	4.06	1.04	4.23	2 181	714	633	2 460	606
Netherlands	1.08	2.17	2.27	1.04	2.35	1 280	636	610	1 334	589
New Zealand	1.14	1.82	1.93	1.07	2.07	1 793	1 128	1 060	1 908	988
Norway	1.24	1.70	1.87	1.13	2.11	1 857	1 357	1 234	2 042	1 093
Poland	1.08	5.20	5.56	1.02	5.64	1 823	380	356	1 947	350
Portugal	1.10	4.63	4.98	1.02	5.07	2 323	550	511	2 497	502
Russian Federation	1.15	8.90	10.09	1.02	10.24	3 232	418	369	3 664	363
Spain	1.03	3.96	4.04	1.01	4.07	3 330	866	848	3 403	841
Sweden	1.12	1.53	1.59	1.07	1.71	2 207	1 609	1 546	2 295	1 441
Switzerland	1.20	5.49	6.37	1.03	6.57	2 841	618	533	3 295	517
United Kingdom	1.17	3.31	3.70	1.05	3.86	4 450	1 570	1 406	4 968	1 345
United States	1.10	11.77	12.79	1.01	12.89	1 950	181	167	2 119	166

Table 37: Design Effects and Effective Sample Sizes for the Mean Performance on the Scientific Literacy Scale

	Design Effect 1	Design Effect 2	Design Effect 3	Design Effect 4	Design Effect 5	Effective Sample Size 1	Effective Sample Size 2	Effective Sample Size 3	Effective Sample Size 4	Effective Sample Size 5
Australia	1.20	3.22	3.67	1.06	3.88	2 374	889	779	2 709	738
Austria	1.07	1.95	2.01	1.03	2.08	2 500	1 370	1 327	2 582	1 284
Belgium	1.03	5.39	5.53	1.01	5.56	3 613	690	674	3 702	670
Brazil	1.63	2.16	2.90	1.22	3.53	1 660	1 253	935	2 220	768
Canada	1.10	4.70	5.06	1.02	5.15	15 047	3 506	3 260	16 181	3 199
Czech Republic	1.08	1.90	1.97	1.04	2.05	2 841	1 611	1 554	2 946	1 495
Denmark	1.04	1.67	1.70	1.02	1.74	2 256	1 405	1 383	2 292	1 351
Finland	1.24	1.80	1.99	1.12	2.23	2 180	1 510	1 363	2 414	1 214
France	1.25	2.01	2.26	1.11	2.50	2 080	1 290	1 148	2 337	1 036
Germany	1.22	1.33	1.41	1.16	1.63	2 341	2 142	2 031	2 466	1 757
Greece	1.02	6.51	6.60	1.00	6.61	2 553	398	393	2 587	392
Hungary	1.05	4.42	4.58	1.01	4.62	2 678	633	612	2 772	606
Iceland	1.03	1.10	1.11	1.03	1.14	1 804	1 684	1 679	1 809	1 634
Ireland	1.02	2.52	2.55	1.01	2.56	2 097	847	838	2 119	833
Italy	1.05	2.54	2.62	1.02	2.68	2 629	1 087	1 054	2 712	1 033
Japan	1.17	9.12	10.50	1.02	10.67	2 489	320	277	2 867	273
Korea	1.22	2.52	2.85	1.08	3.07	2 264	1 095	968	2 561	899
Latvia	1.05	6.80	7.08	1.01	7.13	2 059	317	305	2 142	303
Liechtenstein	1.04	0.95	0.95	1.04	0.99	170	185	185	169	178
Luxembourg	1.15	0.98	0.98	1.15	1.13	1 698	1 983	1 988	1 691	1 727
Mexico	1.19	3.66	4.15	1.04	4.34	2 149	696	613	2 439	587
Netherlands	1.02	2.32	2.35	1.01	2.38	1 364	601	593	1 382	587
New Zealand	1.03	1.12	1.12	1.02	1.15	1 974	1 811	1 805	1 980	1 762
Norway	1.06	1.81	1.85	1.03	1.91	2 181	1 279	1 246	2 237	1 208
Poland	1.43	3.99	5.28	1.08	5.72	1 425	513	387	1 888	357
Portugal	1.03	4.98	5.11	1.01	5.14	2 471	513	499	2 536	496
Russian Federation	1.14	7.42	8.34	1.02	8.48	3 252	501	446	3 656	438
Spain	1.04	3.19	3.27	1.01	3.31	3 339	1 083	1 057	3 420	1 046
Sweden	1.13	1.57	1.64	1.08	1.77	2 163	1 558	1 488	2 265	1 379
Switzerland	1.29	5.18	6.40	1.05	6.70	2 626	656	531	3 248	507
United Kingdom	1.26	3.07	3.61	1.07	3.88	4 099	1 687	1 433	4 826	1 336
United States	1.12	9.91	11.01	1.01	11.13	1 894	215	193	2 105	191

Table 38: Design Effects and Effective Sample Sizes for the Percentage of Students at Level 3 on the Combined Reading Literacy Scale

	Design Effect 1	Design Effect 2	Design Effect 3	Design Effect 4	Design Effect 5	Effective Sample Size 1	Effective Sample Size 2	Effective Sample Size 3	Effective Sample Size 4	Effective Sample Size 5
Australia	1.97	1.60	2.19	1.47	3.16	2 626	3 228	2 366	3 522	1 639
Austria	2.22	1.41	1.92	1.64	3.13	2 141	3 356	2 476	2 897	1 515
Belgium	1.57	1.70	2.09	1.27	2.65	4 259	3 935	3 193	5 237	2 512
Brazil	2.27	2.10	3.50	1.37	4.77	2 156	2 327	1 398	3 584	1 026
Canada	1.77	1.83	2.46	1.32	3.23	16 796	16 249	12 061	22 516	9 194
Czech Republic	2.91	1.12	1.36	2.41	3.27	1 847	4 770	3 938	2 222	1 642
Denmark	1.78	1.14	1.25	1.63	2.03	2 383	3 715	3 392	2 598	2 091
Finland	1.42	1.08	1.11	1.38	1.53	3 426	4 523	4 394	3 518	3 186
France	1.15	1.81	1.93	1.08	2.07	4 076	2 584	2 425	4 340	2 254
Germany	1.79	1.42	1.75	1.47	2.54	2 831	3 583	2 906	3 462	1 999
Greece	3.37	1.98	4.31	1.55	6.67	1 388	2 355	1 084	3 007	700
Hungary	1.57	2.62	3.54	1.16	4.11	3 110	1 868	1 380	4 206	1 188
Iceland	1.09	1.14	1.15	1.08	1.24	3 101	2 961	2 929	3 132	2 723
Ireland	1.94	1.18	1.34	1.73	2.28	1 983	3 280	2 877	2 231	1 688
Italy	1.31	1.78	2.02	1.16	2.34	3 795	2 802	2 464	4 290	2 134
Japan	1.47	2.66	3.43	1.14	3.90	3 582	1 977	1 530	4 626	1 347
Korea	1.12	2.10	2.23	1.05	2.35	4 452	2 376	2 236	4 728	2 123
Latvia	2.37	1.47	2.12	1.68	3.49	1 644	2 644	1 836	2 318	1 116
Liechtenstein	1.80	0.96	0.93	1.89	1.73	174	327	339	167	181
Luxembourg	2.12	1.02	1.04	2.10	2.16	1 663	3 463	3 394	1 677	1 632
Mexico	1.60	2.52	3.42	1.18	4.02	2 877	1 828	1 343	3 901	1 143
Netherlands	1.80	2.10	2.98	1.28	3.79	1 387	1 192	839	1 957	661
New Zealand	2.22	1.08	1.18	2.04	2.40	1 650	3 390	3 105	1 793	1 525
Norway	1.37	1.04	1.06	1.36	1.43	3 028	3 976	3 917	3 056	2 904
Poland	1.44	2.24	2.78	1.16	3.22	2 546	1 630	1 314	3 151	1 136
Portugal	1.51	2.02	2.54	1.20	3.04	3 043	2 269	1 807	3 817	1 506
Russian Federation	1.76	2.15	3.02	1.25	3.78	3 818	3 113	2 217	5 353	1 774
Spain	1.71	1.50	1.85	1.39	2.57	3 624	4 146	3 350	4 456	2 418
Sweden	2.09	1.03	1.07	2.05	2.15	2 114	4 281	4 146	2 150	2 050
Switzerland	1.41	2.30	2.83	1.15	3.24	4 337	2 651	2 155	5 323	1 884
United Kingdom	2.39	1.58	2.39	1.60	3.78	3 909	5 904	3 907	5 854	2 471
United States	1.97	1.60	2.18	1.46	3.15	1 957	2 401	1 763	2 638	1 222

Table 39: Design Effects and Effective Sample Sizes for the Percentage of Students at Level 5 on the Combined Reading Literacy Scale

	Design Effect 1	Design Effect 2	Design Effect 3	Design Effect 4	Design Effect 5	Effective Sample Size 1	Effective Sample Size 2	Effective Sample Size 3	Effective Sample Size 4	Effective Sample Size 5
Australia	1.33	4.05	5.04	1.07	5.37	3 900	1 279	1 026	4 854	964
Austria	1.95	1.73	2.42	1.41	3.37	2 433	2 744	1 960	3 366	1 407
Belgium	1.61	1.69	2.11	1.29	2.71	4 147	3 953	3 168	5 151	2 458
Brazil	4.08	1.23	1.87	2.83	4.95	1 199	3 967	2 623	1 727	989
Canada	1.72	3.12	4.63	1.16	5.35	17 308	9 518	6 407	25 701	5 550
Czech Republic	1.28	1.96	2.22	1.13	2.49	4 206	2 743	2 418	4 765	2 151
Denmark	1.36	1.12	1.16	1.32	1.52	3 112	3 787	3 649	3 214	2 784
Finland	1.86	1.44	1.81	1.47	2.67	2 621	3 382	2 682	3 299	1 822
France	1.50	1.21	1.31	1.38	1.80	3 126	3 876	3 575	3 376	2 593
Germany	1.32	1.25	1.33	1.25	1.65	3 833	4 062	3 816	4 072	3 069
Greece	1.20	3.50	4.00	1.05	4.20	3 892	1 334	1 167	4 445	1 112
Hungary	1.49	3.91	5.33	1.09	5.81	3 290	1 249	918	4 472	841
Iceland	2.09	1.00	1.00	2.10	2.10	1 611	3 368	3 365	1 602	1 609
Ireland	1.25	1.75	1.94	1.13	2.19	3 086	2 200	1 989	3 412	1 762
Italy	1.72	1.45	1.78	1.41	2.51	2 890	3 433	2 798	3 536	1 989
Japan	1.41	5.14	6.85	1.06	7.27	3 718	1 023	767	4 957	723
Korea	1.83	2.01	2.84	1.29	3.67	2 722	2 482	1 752	3 854	1 356
Latvia	1.24	3.00	3.47	1.07	3.71	3 138	1 300	1 121	3 630	1 048
Liechtenstein	1.85	0.89	0.81	2.06	1.66	170	351	390	152	189
Luxembourg	1.71	1.12	1.20	1.60	1.91	2 062	3 161	2 945	2 204	1 848
Mexico	1.66	1.81	2.34	1.29	3.00	2 766	2 539	1 965	3 566	1 531
Netherlands	1.34	1.49	1.65	1.21	1.99	1 875	1 679	1 513	2 075	1 258
New Zealand	1.41	1.64	1.90	1.22	2.31	2 606	2 237	1 930	3 018	1 589
Norway	1.68	1.23	1.38	1.50	2.07	2 465	3 375	2 997	2 770	2 007
Poland	2.12	2.82	4.85	1.23	5.96	1 727	1 297	754	2 963	613
Portugal	1.51	2.20	2.80	1.18	3.31	3 038	2 088	1 636	3 876	1 385
Russian Federation	1.61	2.95	4.14	1.15	4.75	4 164	2 270	1 620	5 833	1 412
Spain	2.92	1.26	1.77	2.11	3.68	2 129	4 928	3 519	2 948	1 686
Sweden	1.55	1.40	1.61	1.34	2.16	2 853	3 163	2 737	3 286	2 043
Switzerland	1.38	5.75	7.57	1.05	7.95	4 409	1 061	806	5 806	767
United Kingdom	1.52	4.20	5.86	1.09	6.38	6 147	2 223	1 593	8 572	1 463
United States	1.60	4.11	5.98	1.10	6.58	2 401	935	643	3 488	584

CHAPTER 13 { SCALING OUTCOMES

Ray Adams and Claus Carstensen

INTERNATIONAL CHARACTERISTICS OF THE ITEM POOL

When main study data were received from each participating country, they were first verified and cleaned using the procedures outlined in Chapter 11. Files containing the achievement data were prepared and national-level Rasch and traditional test analyses were undertaken. The results of these analyses were included in the reports that were returned to each participant.

After processing at the national level, a set of international-level analyses was undertaken. Some involved summarising national analyses, while others required an analysis of the international data set.

The final international cognitive data set (that is, the data set of coded achievement booklet responses) (available as *intcogn.txt*) consisted of 174 896 students from 32 participating countries. Table 40 shows the total number of sampled students, broken down by participating country and test booklet.

TEST TARGETING

Each of the domains was separately scaled to examine the targeting of the tests. Figures 22, 23 and 24 show the match between the international item difficulty distribution and the international distribution of student achievement for each of reading, mathematics and science, respectively.[1] The figures consist of three panels. The first panel, *Students*, shows the distribution of students' Rasch-scaled achievement estimates. Students at the top end of this distribution have higher achievement estimates than students at the lower end of the distribution. The second panel, *Item Difficulties*, shows the distribution of Rasch-estimated item difficulties, and the third panel, *Step Difficulties*, shows the item steps.

The number of steps for an item reported in the right-hand panel is the number of score categories minus 2, the highest step being reported for all items in the middle panel of the figure. That leaves one step to be reported in the right-hand panel for a partial credit item scored 0, 1, 2, and two steps to be reported for a partial credit item scored 0, 1, 2, 3. The item score for each of these items is shown in the right-hand panel in the item label, separated from the item number by a dot point.

In Figure 22, the student achievement distribution, shown by Xs, is located a little higher than the item difficulty distribution. This implies that, on average, the students in the PISA main study had an ability level that was above the level needed to have a 50 per cent chance of solving the average item correctly.

Figure 23 shows a plot of item difficulties and step parameters, together with the student achievement distribution for mathematics. The figure shows that the selected items for the main study, on average, have about a 50 per cent chance of being solved correctly by the average student in the tested population.

---

[1] The results reported here are based on a domain-by-domain unweighted scaling of the full international data set.

Table 40: Number of Sampled Students by Country and Booklet

Country	SE	1	2	3	4	5	6	7	8	9	Total
Australia		566	567	587	593	584	578	581	560	560	5 176
Austria	24	539	525	499	525	511	528	527	532	535	4 745
Belgium	136	735	726	747	720	739	713	727	719	708	6 670
Brazil		545	547	545	539	556	553	537	532	539	4 893
Canada		3 246	3 312	3 326	3 243	3 291	3 307	3 336	3 311	3 315	29 687
Czech Republic	159	571	582	594	584	575	570	563	588	579	5 365
Denmark		474	452	482	478	469	459	464	473	484	4 235
Finland	5	546	548	545	531	527	546	536	545	535	4 864
France		501	506	521	517	531	525	528	520	524	4 673
Germany	47	549	574	573	567	551	556	556	556	544	5 073
Greece		516	509	532	522	517	522	514	526	514	4 672
Hungary	162	520	520	521	522	529	529	517	531	536	4 887
Iceland		379	376	380	377	380	363	374	376	367	3 372
Ireland		420	417	430	441	429	427	441	426	423	3 854
Italy		550	555	555	553	551	549	562	555	554	4 984
Japan		585	582	586	584	590	585	581	578	585	5 256
Korea		558	546	556	555	552	553	559	553	550	4 982
Latvia		427	430	430	435	436	436	443	428	428	3 893
Liechtenstein		34	37	36	34	33	33	35	35	37	314
Luxembourg		377	407	388	383	382	340	507	363	381	3 528
Mexico		524	519	515	516	513	498	500	511	504	4 600
Netherlands	23	280	281	267	280	282	282	278	264	266	2 503
New Zealand		426	408	413	405	395	402	404	416	398	3 667
Norway		459	471	465	458	465	461	450	461	457	4 147
Poland		390	429	407	425	408	418	406	410	361	3 654
Portugal		516	508	499	502	500	512	518	518	512	4 585
Russian Federation		742	744	752	748	745	747	743	740	740	6 701
Spain		685	685	682	710	699	700	691	679	683	6 214
Sweden		484	486	496	498	508	484	484	487	489	4 416
Switzerland		677	654	672	677	663	681	692	692	692	6 100
United Kingdom		1 024	1 049	1 042	1 021	1 051	1 031	1 044	1 040	1 038	9 340
United States		441	418	430	429	421	439	425	435	408	3 846
Total	556	19 286	19 370	19 473	19 372	19 383	19 327	19 523	19 360	19 246	174 896

```
                           +item                        +item*step
   ----------------------------------------------------------------------
              |                                |                         |
            X |                                |                         |
   3          |                                |                         |
           X  | 50                             |                         |
            X |                                |                         |
            X | 19                             |                         |
           XX |                                |                         |
           XX |                                |                         |
          XXX |                                |                         |
   2     XXXX | 68 118                         |                         |
         XXXXX|                                |                         |
        XXXXXX| 38 116                         |                         |
        XXXXXX| 27 129                         |                         |
       XXXXXXX| 62 64 75                       |                         |
       XXXXXXX| 3 43 94                        |                         |
       XXXXXXX| 67 79 80                       |                         |
   1  XXXXXXXX| 63 82 86 90                    |                         |
     XXXXXXXXX| 25 28 32 37 77 92 93 99        | 25.1 77.1               |
       XXXXXXX| 42 59 117 122                  |                         |
       XXXXXXX| 2 7 15 17 22 23 30 123         | 16.1                    |
       XXXXXXX| 13 20 55 60 109 113 120 125    | 84.1 110.1              |
        XXXXXX| 5 16 26 52 83 85 89 97 107     |                         |
        XXXXXX| 51 84 100 101 108 114 127      | 80.1                    |
   0   XXXXXXX| 1 8 10 11 41 45 57 74 87       | 20.1 90.1               |
         XXXXX| 21 31 33 103 110 119 121       | 50.1 82.1               |
        XXXXXX| 12 36 95 112 124               |                         |
          XXXX| 18 24 44 96 104 126            | 15.1 75.1               |
          XXXX| 40 78 88 91                    | 42.1                    |
          XXXX| 49 76 98 106 111 128           |                         |
  -1      XXX | 4 9 29 69 72 73                | 68.1                    |
          XXX | 35 48 53 54 58 71              | 108.1                   |
           XX | 61 66                          |                         |
           XX | 6                              | 43.1                    |
            X | 34 39 65 70 81 102 115         |                         |
            X | 46 47 56                       |                         |
            X | 14                             |                         |
  -2        X | 105                            |                         |
            X |                                |                         |
              |                                |                         |
              |                                |                         |
              |                                |                         |
              |                                |                         |
  -3          |                                |                         |
              |                                |                         |
   =======================================================================
   Each 'X' represents 1125.1 cases
```

Figure 22: Comparison of Reading Item Difficulty and Achievement Distributions

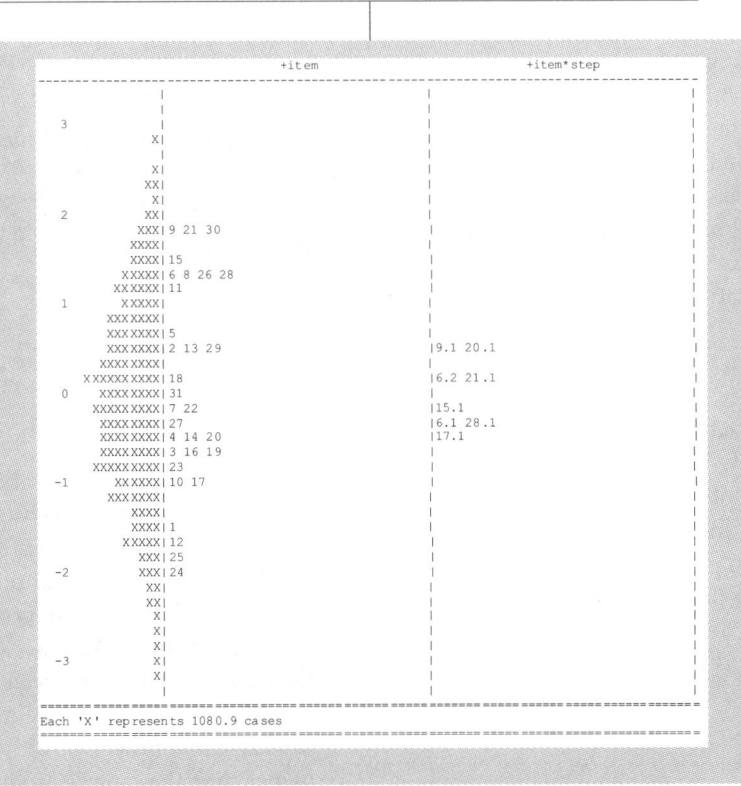

```
                           +item                        +item*step
   ----------------------------------------------------------------------
              |                                |                         |
              |                                |                         |
   3          |                                |                         |
            X |                                |                         |
              |                                |                         |
            X |                                |                         |
           XX |                                |                         |
            X |                                |                         |
   2       XX |                                |                         |
          XXX | 9 21 30                        |                         |
         XXXX |                                |                         |
         XXXX | 15                             |                         |
        XXXXX | 6 8 26 28                      |                         |
       XXXXXX | 11                             |                         |
   1    XXXXX |                                |                         |
      XXXXXXX |                                |                         |
      XXXXXXX | 5                              |                         |
      XXXXXXX | 2 13 29                        | 9.1 20.1                |
      XXXXXXX |                                |                         |
    XXXXXXXXX | 18                             | 6.2 21.1                |
   0 XXXXXXXX | 31                             |                         |
     XXXXXXXX | 7 22                           | 15.1                    |
     XXXXXXXX | 27                             | 6.1 28.1                |
     XXXXXXXX | 4 14 20                        | 17.1                    |
     XXXXXXXX | 3 16 19                        |                         |
     XXXXXXXX | 23                             |                         |
  -1   XXXXXX | 10 17                          |                         |
       XXXXXX |                                |                         |
         XXXX |                                |                         |
         XXXX | 1                              |                         |
        XXXXX | 12                             |                         |
          XXX | 25                             |                         |
  -2      XXX | 24                             |                         |
           XX |                                |                         |
           XX |                                |                         |
            X |                                |                         |
            X |                                |                         |
            X |                                |                         |
  -3        X |                                |                         |
            X |                                |                         |
              |                                |                         |
   =======================================================================
   Each 'X' represents 1080.9 cases
```

Figure 23: Comparison of Mathematics Item Difficulty and Achievement Distributions

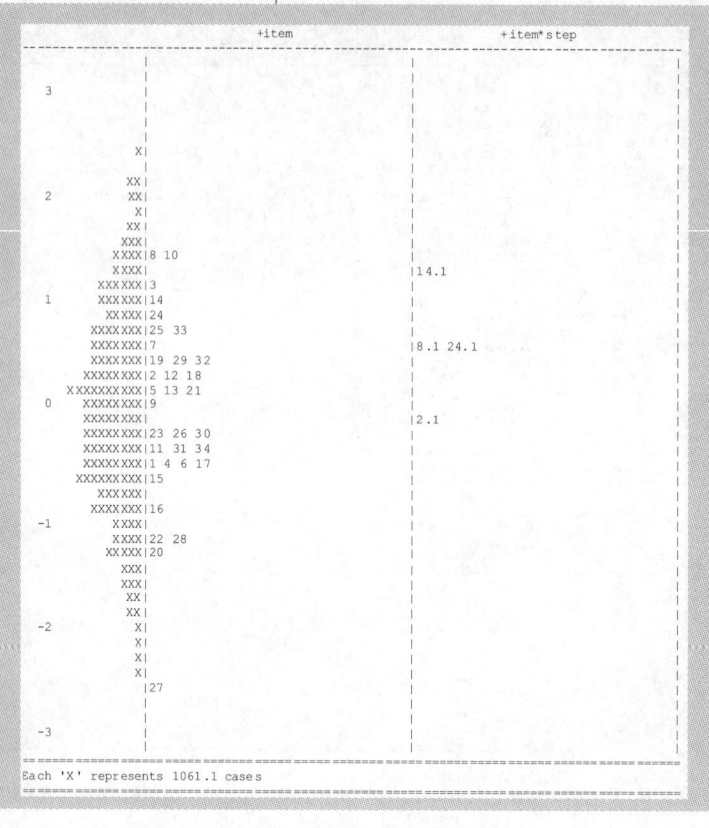

```
                                    +item                    +item*step
          ---------------------------------------------------------------
                       |                         |
       3               |                         |
                       |                         |
                       |                         |
                     X |                         |
                       |                         |
                    XX |                         |
       2            XX |                         |
                     X |                         |
                    XX |                         |
                   XXX |                         |
                  XXXX |8 10                     |
                  XXXX |                         |14.1
                XXXXXX |3                        |
       1        XXXXXX |14                       |
                 XXXXX |24                       |
               XXXXXXX |25 33                    |
               XXXXXXX |7                        |8.1 24.1
              XXXXXXXX |19 29 32                 |
             XXXXXXXXX |2 12 18                  |
           XXXXXXXXXXX |5 13 21                  |
       0     XXXXXXXXX |9                        |
              XXXXXXXX |                         |2.1
             XXXXXXXXX |23 26 30                 |
              XXXXXXXX |11 31 34                 |
              XXXXXXXX |1 4 6 17                 |
             XXXXXXXXX |15                       |
                XXXXXX |                         |
                XXXXXX |16                       |
      -1         XXXXX |                         |
                  XXXX |22 28                    |
                 XXXXX |20                       |
                   XXX |                         |
                   XXX |                         |
                    XX |                         |
                    XX |                         |
      -2             X |                         |
                     X |                         |
                     X |                         |
                     X |                         |
                       |27                       |
                       |                         |
      -3               |                         |
          ================================================================
          Each 'X' represents 1061.1 cases
          ================================================================
```

Figure 24: Comparison of Science Item Difficulty and Achievement Distributions

Figure 24 shows a plot of the item difficulties and item step parameters, and the student achievement distribution for science. The figure shows that the selected items for the main study, on average, have about a 50 per cent chance of being answered correctly by the average student in the tested population.

TEST RELIABILITY

A second test characteristic that is of importance is the test reliability. Table 41 shows the reliability for each of the three overall scales (combined reading literacy, mathematical literacy and scientific literacy) before conditioning and based upon three separate scalings. The reliability for each domain and each country, after conditioning, is reported later.[2]

---

[2] The reliability index is an internal-consistency-like index estimated by the correlation between independent plausible value draws.

Table 41: Reliability of the Three Domains Based Upon Unconditioned Unidimensional Scaling

Scale	Reliability
Mathematics	0.81
Reading	0.89
Science	0.78

DOMAIN INTER-CORRELATIONS

Correlations between the ability estimates for individual students in each of the three domains, the so-called *latent correlations,* as estimated by ConQuest (Wu, Adams and Wilson, 1997) are given in Table 42. It is important to note that these latent correlations are unbiased estimates of the *true* correlation between the underlying latent variables. As such they are not attenuated by the unreliability of the measures and will generally be higher than the typical product moment correlations that have not been disattenuated for unreliability.

Table 42: Latent Correlation Between the Three Domains

Scale	Reading	Science
Mathematics	0.819	0.846
Science	0.890	

READING SUB-SCALES

A five-dimensional scaling was performed on the achievement (cognitive) data, consisting of:
- Scale 1: mathematics items (M)
- Scale 2: reading items—retrieving information (R1)
- Scale 3: reading items—interpreting texts (R2)
- Scale 4: reading items—reflection and evaluation (R3)
- Scale 5: science items (S).

Table 43 shows the latent correlations between each pair of scales.

Table 43: Correlation Between Scales

Scale	R1	R2	R3	S
M	0.854	0.836	0.766	0.846
R1		0.973	0.893	0.889
R2			0.929	0.890
R3				0.840

The correlations between the three reading sub-scales are quite high. The highest is between the *retrieving information* and *interpreting texts* sub-scales, and the lowest is between the *retrieving information* and *reflection and evaluation* sub-scales.

The correlations between the mathematics scale and the other scales are a little above 0.80, except the correlation with the *reflection and evaluation* sub-scale, which is estimated to be about 0.77.

The science scale correlates with the mathematics scale at 0.85. It correlates at about 0.89 with the first two reading sub-scales and at 0.84 with the *reflection and evaluation* sub-scale. It appears that the science scale correlates more highly with the reading sub-scales than with the mathematics scale.

SCALING OUTCOMES

The procedures for the national and international scaling are outlined in Chapter 9 and need not be reiterated here.

Item Name	Countries
R040Q02	Greece, Mexico
R040Q06	Italy
R055Q03	Austria, Germany, Switzerland (Ger.)
R076Q03	England, Switzerland (Ger.)
R076Q04	England
R076Q05	Belgium (Fl.), Netherlands
R091Q05	Russian Federation, Switzerland (Ger.)
R091Q07B	Sweden
R099Q04B	Poland
R100Q05	Belgium (Fl.), Netherlands
R101Q08	Canada (Fr.)
R102Q04A	Korea
R111Q06B	Switzerland (Ger.)
R119Q04	Hungary
R216Q02	Korea
R219Q01T	Italy
R227Q01	Spain
R236Q01	Iceland
R237Q03	Korea
R239Q02	Switzerland (Ger.)
R246Q02	Korea
M033Q01	Brazil
M155Q01	Japan, Switzerland (Ger.)
M155Q03	Austria, Switzerland (Ger.)
M155Q04	Switzerland (Ger.)
S133Q04T	Austria, Germany, Switzerland (Ger.)
S268Q02T	Iceland, Netherlands
S268Q06	Switzerland (Ital.)

Figure 25: Items Deleted for Particular Countries

NATIONAL ITEM DELETIONS

The items were first scaled by country and their fit was considered at the national level, as was the consistency of the item parameter estimates across countries. Consortium staff then adjudicated items, considering the items' functioning both within and across countries in detail. Those items considered to be *dodgy* (see Chapter 9) were then reviewed in consultation with National Project Managers (NPMs). The consultations resulted in the deletion of a few items at the national level. The deleted items, listed in Figure 25, were recoded as *not applicable* and were included in neither the international scaling nor in generating plausible values.

INTERNATIONAL SCALING

The international scaling was performed on the calibration data set of 13 500 students (500 randomly selected students from each of 27 countries). The item parameter estimates from this scaling are reported in Appendices 1, 2 and 3.

GENERATING STUDENT SCALE SCORES

Applying the conditioning approach described in Chapter 9 and anchoring all of the item parameters at the values obtained from the international scaling, weighted likelihood estimates (WLEs) and plausible values were generated for all sampled students.[3] Table 44 gives the reliabilities at the international level for the generated scale scores.

Table 44: Final Reliability of the PISA Scales

Scale	Reliability
Mathematics	0.90
Reading (Combined)	0.93
Reading-R1	0.91
Reading-R2	0.92
Reading-R3	0.90
Science	0.90

DIFFERENTIAL ITEM FUNCTIONING

In Rasch modelling, an item is considered to exhibit differential item functioning (DIF) if the response probabilities for that item cannot be fully explained by the ability of the student and a fixed set of difficulty parameters for that item. In other words, the DIF analysis identifies items that are *unusually* easy or difficult for one group of students relative to another. The key is *unusually*. In DIF analysis, the aim is not to find items with a higher or a lower *p*-value for one group than another—since this may result from genuine differences in the ability levels of the two groups. Rather, the objective is to identify items that appear to be too difficult or too easy, after having controlled for differences in the ability levels of the two groups. The PISA main study uses Rasch methods to explore gender DIF.

When items are scaled with the Rasch model, the origin of the scale is arbitrarily set at zero and student proficiency estimates are then expressed on the scale. A student with a score of 0 has a probability equal to 0.50 of correctly answering an item with a Rasch difficulty estimate of 0. The same student has a probability higher than 0.50 for items with negative difficulty estimates and a probability lower than 0.50 for items with positive difficulty estimates.

If two independent Rasch analyses are run on the same item set, using the responses from a sub-sample consisting of females only and a sub-sample of males only, the first analysis estimates the Rasch item difficulty that best fits for females (independently of males' data), and the second analysis gives the analogous estimate for the males. Two independent difficulty estimates are available. If the males are better achievers than females on average, relative item difficulty will not necessarily be affected.[4]

Figures 26, 27 and 28 show a scatter-plot of the difficulty parameter estimates for male and female students for the three domains respectively. Each item is represented by one point in the plots. The horizontal axis is the item difficulty estimate for females and the vertical axis is the item difficulty estimate for males. All non-biased items are on the diagonal. The further the item is from the diagonal, the bigger the gender DIF.

Most of the items, regardless of the domain, show a statistically significant DIF, which is not surprising, since the standard error of the item parameters is inversely proportional to the sample size. Most of the differences between the estimates of item parameters respectively for males and females are quite small. The graphical displays also show that there are only a small number of outliers.

---

[3] As described later in the chapter, a booklet effect was identified during national scaling. This meant that the planned scaling procedures had to be modified and a booklet correction made. Procedures for the booklet effect correction are described in a later section of this chapter.

[4] The DIF analysis was performed in one run of the multi-facet model of ConQuest. The Item by Gender interaction term was added to the standard model.

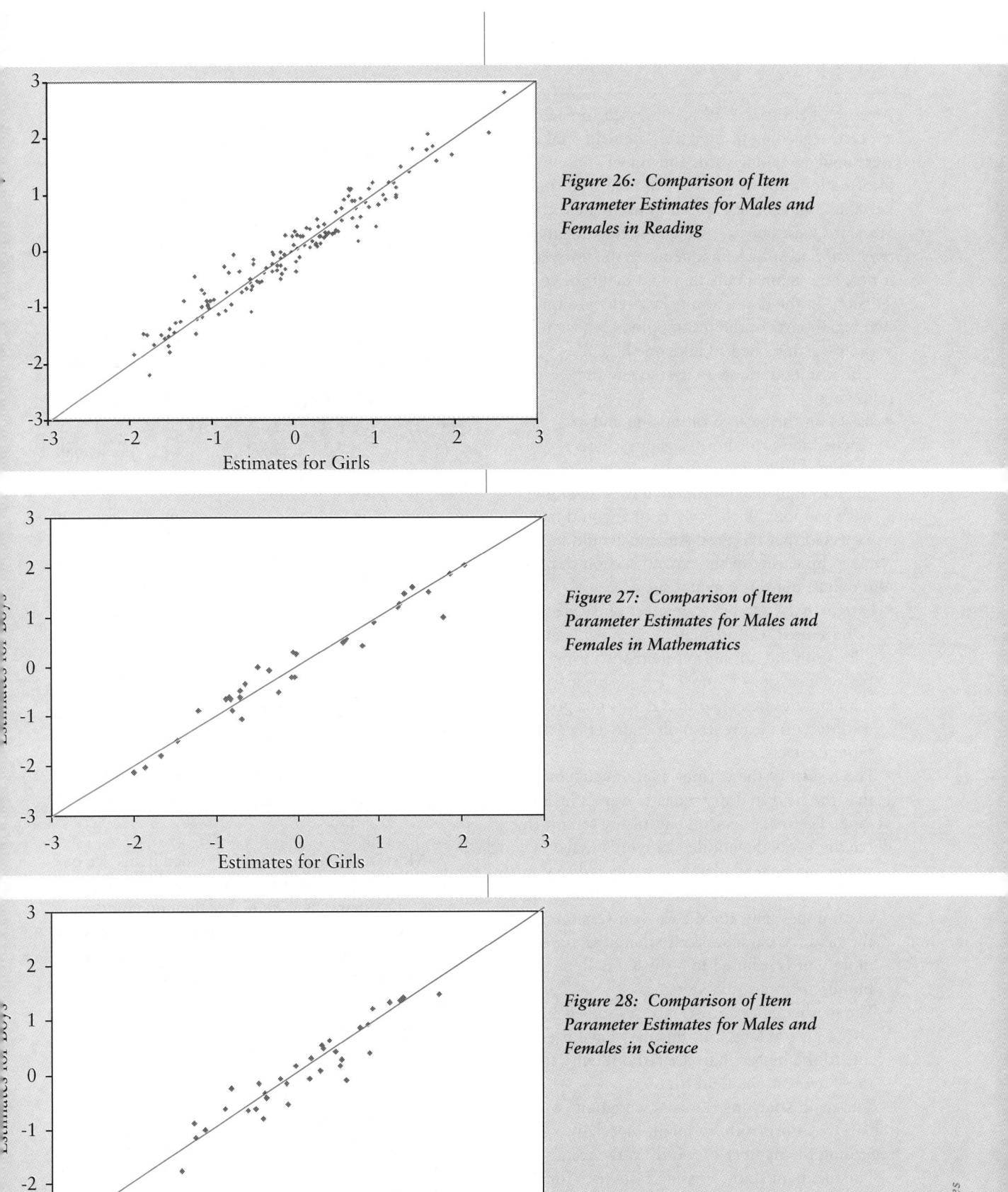

Figure 26: Comparison of Item Parameter Estimates for Males and Females in Reading

Figure 27: Comparison of Item Parameter Estimates for Males and Females in Mathematics

Figure 28: Comparison of Item Parameter Estimates for Males and Females in Science

TEST LENGTH

After the field trial, NPMs expressed some concern regarding test length. The field trial data were analysed using three sources of information: not-reached items; field trial timing variables; and the last question in the field trial Student Questionnaire, which asked students if they had had sufficient time to do the test—and, if not, how many items they had had time to do. 'Session' in the discussion below refers to one of two equal parts of the testing time (*i.e.*, each session was intended to take one hour).

The results of these analyses were the following:

- Based on the pattern of missing and not-reached items for both sessions, there appeared to be no empirical evidence to suggest that two 60-minute testing sessions were too long. If they were, one would have expected that the tired students would have given up earlier in the second session than in the first, but this was not the case.
- Fatigue may also have an effect on student achievement. Unfortunately, the field trial item allocation did not permit item anchoring between sessions 1 and 2 (except for a few mathematics items) so that it was not possible to differentiate any item difficulty effect or fatigue effects.
- The results of the various analyses suggested that the field trial instruments were a little too long. The main determinant of test length (for reading) was the number of words that needed to be read. Analysis suggested that about 3 500 words per session should be set as an upper limit for the English version. In the field trial, test sessions where there were more words resulted in a substantially larger number of not-reached items.
- The mathematics and science sessions were also a bit too long, but this may have been due to the higher than desired difficulty for these items in the field trial.

The main study instruments were built with the above information in mind, especially regarding the number of words in the test.

For the main study, missing responses for the last items in each session were also recoded as not reached. But, if the student was not entirely present for a session, the not-reached items were recoded as not applicable. This means that these missing data are not included in the results presented in this section and that these students' ability estimates were not affected by not responding to these items when proficiency scores were computed.

Table 45 shows the number of missing responses and the number of missing responses recoded as not reached, by booklet, according to these rules. Table 46 shows this information by country.

Table 45: Average Number of Not-Reached Items and Missing Items by Booklet and Testing Session

Booklet	Session 1 Missing	Session 1 Not Reached	Session 2 Missing	Session 2 Not Reached
0	5.68	1.59	NA	NA
1	1.40	0.60	4.70	1.10
2	0.89	0.23	2.44	0.87
3	2.20	0.70	1.97	0.49
4	2.66	1.60	3.11	0.96
5	1.64	1.51	3.95	0.69
6	1.26	0.77	1.77	0.29
7	1.82	0.91	1.75	0.31
8	3.36	1.15	2.91	1.08
9	3.63	0.86	2.49	1.00
Total	2.10	0.93	2.79	0.76

Most of the means of not-reached items are below one in the main study, while more than 50 per cent of these means were higher than one for the field trial. As the aver-ages of not-reached items per session and per booklet are quite similar, it appears that test length was quite similar across booklets for each session.

Like the field trial, the average number of not-reached items differs from one country to another. It is worth noting that countries with higher averages of not-reached items also have higher averages of missing data.

Tables 47 and 48 provide the percentage distribution of not-reached items per booklet and per session. The percentage of students who reached the last item ranges from 70 to 95 per cent for the first session and from 76 to 95 per cent for the second session (*i.e.*, the percentages of students with zero not-reached items).

Table 46: Average Number of Not-Reached Items and Missing Items by Country and Testing Session

Country	Session 1 Missing	Session 1 Not Reached	Session 2 Missing	Session 2 Not Reached
Australia	1.61	0.64	2.23	0.53
Austria	2.09	0.53	2.79	0.41
Belgium	1.85	0.88	2.53	0.95
Brazil	4.16	5.26	5.31	3.98
Canada	1.31	0.54	1.80	0.39
Czech Republic	2.50	1.18	3.19	0.65
Denmark	2.65	1.32	3.57	1.09
Finland	1.39	0.46	1.96	0.41
France	2.44	1.09	2.99	0.91
Germany	2.69	0.98	3.41	0.66
Greece	2.95	1.23	4.75	1.40
Hungary	2.79	1.67	3.59	1.23
Iceland	1.86	0.77	2.58	0.74
Ireland	1.31	0.55	1.86	0.48
Italy	3.12	1.43	4.14	1.21
Japan	2.32	0.80	3.22	0.70
Korea	1.28	0.22	1.88	0.29
Latvia	3.36	1.56	4.42	1.98
Liechtenstein	2.67	0.86	3.50	0.78
Luxembourg	3.01	1.57	4.61	1.07
Mexico	2.37	1.38	3.10	1.13
Netherlands	0.46	0.18	0.70	0.12
New Zealand	1.36	0.49	1.98	0.45
Norway	2.26	0.69	3.23	0.88
Poland	3.16	0.87	4.54	1.00
Portugal	2.60	1.13	3.47	0.66
Russian Federation	3.01	2.43	3.71	1.88
Spain	2.08	1.31	2.93	1.17
Sweden	2.08	0.75	2.81	0.73
Switzerland	2.34	0.82	3.14	0.59
United Kingdom	1.51	0.35	2.25	0.41
United States	1.27	0.77	1.95	0.64

MAGNITUDE OF BOOKLET EFFECTS

After scaling the PISA 2000 data for each country separately, achievement scores for mathematics, reading and science could be compared across countries and across booklets. (In these analyses, some sub-regions within countries were considered as countries.)

Tables 49, 50 and 51 present student scale scores for the three domains, standardised to have a mean of 10 and a standard deviation of 2 for each domain and country combination. The table rows represent countries (or sub-regions within countries) and the columns represent booklets. The purpose of these analyses and tables is to examine the nature of any booklet effects, not to show countries in order—countries are therefore not named.

The variation in the means between booklets is greater than was expected. As the scaling was supposed to *equate* the booklets and because the booklets were systematically rotated within schools, it was expected that the only between-booklet variance would be sampling variance.

The variations observed between booklets are quite stable, however, across countries, leaving a picture of systematically easier and harder booklets. The booklet means over countries, shown in the last row of each table, indicate mean booklet differences up to 0.52 (one-quarter of a student standard deviation).[5]

---

[5] Since the Special Education booklet (Booklet 0) was not randomly assigned to students, the means were expected to be lower than 10.

Table 47: Distribution of Not-Reached Items by Booklet, First Testing Session

No. of Not-Reached Items	0	1	2	3	4	5	6	7	8	9
0	70.1	86.7	95.1	87.4	70.9	79.5	85.9	83.7	81.9	84.1
1	13.4	2.7	0.3	0.7	3.0	1.2	1.0	2.7	3.9	3.4
2	0.7	2.3	0.9	1.6	4.8	1.6	0.8	3.9	1.3	1.0
3	1.3	2.2	0.3	3.9	3.3	4.4	1.7	2.5	0.9	1.8
4	1.3	1.1	0.7	0.2	2.7	1.0	4.7	0.4	1.8	1.4
5	1.7	2.2	0.4	0.9	3.8	0.5	1.6	0.5	0.7	2.3
6	0.7	0.2	1.8	0.4	1.5	1.0	0.6	0.4	0.8	1.5
>6	10.8	2.6	0.5	4.9	10.0	10.8	3.7	5.9	8.7	4.5

Table 48: Distribution of Not-Reached Items by Booklet, Second Testing Session

No. of Not-Reached Items	Booklet 1	2	3	4	5	6	7	8	9
0	76.2	78.7	89.6	85.4	87.3	95.1	91.8	86.9	79.6
1	3.9	12.3	3.1	1.6	3.0	1.4	2.2	1.0	4.2
2	2.9	0.9	2.0	1.9	0.9	0.4	1.1	1.1	2.4
3	6.9	0.6	1.3	2.3	1.5	0.2	0.6	1.0	1.4
4	1.5	1.4	0.5	1.2	1.0	0.5	1.1	1.5	2.8
5	0.7	0.5	0.3	0.7	1.9	0.2	1.0	0.6	3.1
6	3.7	0.4	0.3	0.5	1.3	0.3	0.5	1.4	1.2
> 6	4.2	5.2	2.9	6.4	3.1	1.9	1.7	6.5	5.3

Note: Booklet 0 required only one hour to complete and is therefore not shown in this table.

These differences would affect the ability estimates of the students who worked on *easier* or *harder* booklets, and therefore booklet effects needed to be explained and corrected for in an appropriate way in subsequent scaling.

Exploratory analyses indicated that an order effect that was adversely affecting the between-booklet equating was the most likely explanation for this *booklet effect*. This finding is illustrated in Figure 29, which compares item parameter estimates for cluster 1 obtained from three separate scalings—one for each booklet to which cluster 1 was allocated. For the purposes of this comparison, the item parameters for reading were re-estimated per booklet on the calibration sample of 13 500 students, (about 1 500 students per booklet). To be able to compare the item parameter estimates, they were centred on cases, assuming no differences in ability across booklets in the population level. Figure 29 therefore shows the deviations of each item from the mean parameter for that item over all booklets in which it appeared. Each item of clusters 1 to 8 was administered in three different booklets, and the items in cluster 9 were administered in two different booklets. For each item, the differences between the three (two) estimates and their mean is displayed and grouped into one figure per cluster. The remaining figures are included in Appendix 6.

Except for the first four items, the items in cluster 1 were easier in Booklet 1 than in Booklets 5 and 7. The standard errors, not printed in the figures, ranged from about 0.04 to 0.08 for most items.

The legend indicates the positions of the cluster in the booklets: cluster 1 is the first cluster in the first half of Booklet 1 (Pos. 1.1), the

Table 49: Mathematics Means for Each Booklet and Country

Booklet 0	1	3	5	8	9	Mean
.	9.70	10.19	9.90	10.43	9.78	10.00
.	9.80	10.26	9.60	10.51	9.78	10.00
6.09	9.54	10.36	9.68	10.64	9.80	10.00
.	9.48	10.33	9.88	10.67	9.64	10.00
.	9.62	10.10	9.96	10.57	9.75	10.00
.	9.70	10.20	9.75	10.48	9.86	10.00
.	9.45	10.21	9.80	10.60	9.95	10.00
.	9.60	10.28	9.76	10.59	9.78	10.00
.	9.61	10.24	9.83	10.55	9.77	10.00
6.60	9.83	10.26	9.94	10.47	9.77	10.00
7.74	9.75	10.27	9.99	10.24	9.95	10.00
.	9.73	10.11	9.79	10.56	9.81	10.00
.	9.78	9.98	9.83	10.64	9.75	10.00
.	9.47	10.07	10.25	10.55	9.64	10.00
.	9.85	10.16	9.83	10.39	9.77	10.00
.	9.81	9.98	9.63	10.63	9.93	10.00
.	9.82	10.12	9.82	10.30	9.94	10.00
6.79	9.79	10.38	9.88	10.65	10.01	10.00
.	9.58	10.29	9.87	10.41	9.85	10.00
.	9.74	10.26	9.79	10.30	9.91	10.00
.	9.66	10.13	9.79	10.45	9.98	10.00
.	9.59	10.39	9.74	10.58	9.70	10.00
9.48	10.25	9.85	9.93	11.03	9.80	10.00
7.51	9.90	10.48	9.82	10.61	9.85	10.00
.	9.79	10.35	9.75	10.52	9.60	10.00
.	9.81	9.98	9.85	10.72	9.68	10.00
.	9.72	10.18	9.85	10.30	9.94	10.00
.	9.69	10.32	9.85	10.44	9.62	10.00
.	9.52	10.41	9.93	10.54	9.61	10.00
8.59	9.72	10.39	10.01	10.67	9.63	10.00
.	9.60	10.27	9.75	10.49	9.89	10.00
6.36	9.78	10.20	9.87	10.38	9.95	10.00
7.47	9.72	10.20	10.01	10.59	9.80	10.00
8.73	9.68	10.23	9.85	10.52	9.81	10.00
7.54	9.70	10.20	9.86	10.52	9.78	

Note: Scaled to a mean of 10 and standard deviation of 2. Each row represents a country or a subnational community that was treated independently in the study.

Table 50: Reading Means for Each Booklet and Country

0	1	2	3	4	5	6	7	8	9	Mean
.	10.07	10.43	10.15	9.63	10.04	10.32	9.99	9.64	9.73	10.00
.	10.48	10.18	10.09	9.64	10.02	9.95	9.84	9.68	10.13	10.00
4.00	10.05	10.24	10.13	9.72	10.08	10.11	9.96	9.88	9.87	10.00
.	9.89	10.22	10.22	9.73	10.04	10.14	10.22	9.80	9.74	10.00
.	10.13	10.41	10.12	9.75	10.01	10.17	9.89	9.73	9.78	10.00
.	9.95	10.22	10.01	9.88	9.89	10.15	10.06	9.87	9.97	10.00
.	10.06	10.44	10.11	9.66	9.98	10.27	9.91	9.53	10.03	10.00
.	9.85	10.26	10.21	9.96	10.13	10.11	10.07	9.70	9.71	10.00
.	9.98	10.38	10.14	9.81	10.09	10.05	9.98	9.71	9.88	10.00
4.85	10.18	10.38	10.08	9.82	10.03	10.01	10.14	9.83	9.96	10.00
7.10	10.07	10.07	10.17	9.84	10.11	10.23	9.96	9.81	9.96	10.00
.	10.15	10.31	10.21	9.79	9.99	10.09	10.13	9.52	9.81	10.00
.	10.26	10.36	10.26	9.86	9.90	10.03	9.77	9.75	9.82	10.00
.	9.98	10.44	9.94	9.65	9.98	10.13	10.10	9.90	9.89	10.00
.	10.23	10.21	9.99	9.78	9.89	10.20	9.75	9.92	10.02	10.00
.	10.07	10.39	10.13	9.83	9.86	10.20	9.94	9.84	9.70	10.00
.	10.13	10.23	10.03	9.82	9.92	10.07	10.02	9.80	9.97	10.00
5.94	9.98	10.16	10.00	9.78	10.00	10.25	9.97	10.35	10.42	10.00
.	10.10	10.31	10.10	9.72	9.99	10.07	9.93	9.77	10.00	10.00
.	10.01	10.34	10.14	9.88	10.06	10.00	9.96	9.66	9.93	10.00
.	10.25	10.47	9.87	9.64	9.80	10.18	9.94	9.95	9.91	10.00
.	10.09	10.46	10.08	9.61	9.99	10.08	9.98	9.71	10.00	10.00
8.09	10.35	10.70	10.38	10.07	10.13	10.50	10.39	10.20	10.33	10.00
5.86	10.20	10.45	10.21	9.78	10.10	10.25	10.04	10.00	10.11	10.00
.	10.24	10.58	10.07	9.63	9.94	9.99	9.92	9.51	10.14	10.00
.	10.00	10.50	10.00	9.80	9.99	10.20	9.95	9.84	9.69	10.00
.	10.21	10.51	10.00	9.67	10.01	10.01	10.09	9.71	9.81	10.00
.	10.23	10.42	10.14	9.61	9.98	10.21	10.03	9.56	9.95	10.00
.	9.96	10.29	10.22	9.79	10.00	10.17	10.04	9.68	9.87	10.00
7.95	10.07	10.39	10.24	9.78	10.04	10.28	10.08	9.68	10.09	10.00
.	9.99	10.29	10.12	9.82	9.93	10.15	9.98	9.89	9.82	10.00
5.97	10.12	10.33	10.08	9.92	10.15	10.19	9.85	9.70	9.84	10.00
7.18	10.06	10.42	10.16	9.87	10.05	10.27	10.04	9.82	9.66	10.00
7.48	10.10	10.36	10.11	9.77	10.00	10.14	9.99	9.78	9.94	10.00
6.44	10.11	10.34	10.11	9.78	10.01	10.15	9.99	9.78	9.90	

Note: Scaled to a mean of 10 and standard deviation of 2.

Table 51: Science Means for Each Booklet and Country

Booklet 0	2	4	6	8	9	Mean
.	9.65	9.89	10.29	9.67	10.52	10.00
.	9.66	9.67	10.44	9.39	10.79	10.00
7.72	9.65	9.92	10.43	9.68	10.34	10.00
.	9.68	9.72	10.40	9.58	10.62	10.00
.	9.50	9.85	10.34	9.82	10.50	10.00
.	9.60	9.89	10.32	9.82	10.38	10.00
.	9.50	9.77	10.29	9.93	10.50	10.00
.	9.79	9.86	10.21	9.68	10.47	10.00
.	9.76	9.78	10.28	9.76	10.40	10.00
7.07	9.89	9.95	10.23	9.88	10.31	10.00
8.08	9.64	9.84	10.34	10.07	10.28	10.00
.	9.84	9.76	10.13	9.80	10.46	10.00
.	9.53	9.59	10.08	10.03	10.78	10.00
.	9.44	9.94	10.47	9.68	10.45	10.00
.	9.77	9.83	10.25	9.74	10.41	10.00
.	9.65	9.79	10.08	10.09	10.47	10.00
.	9.85	9.77	10.14	9.94	10.30	10.00
6.87	9.98	9.91	10.43	10.00	10.39	10.00
.	9.69	9.83	10.12	9.80	10.56	10.00
.	9.68	10.00	10.12	9.66	10.54	10.00
.	9.72	9.67	10.22	10.16	10.22	10.00
.	9.93	9.64	10.28	9.77	10.39	10.00
9.55	9.73	10.03	10.35	9.60	11.01	10.00
7.39	9.87	9.95	10.47	9.80	10.64	10.00
.	9.84	9.68	10.22	9.63	10.64	10.00
.	9.57	9.80	10.21	10.03	10.45	10.00
.	9.91	9.82	10.18	9.84	10.25	10.00
.	9.55	9.81	10.41	9.53	10.70	10.00
.	9.64	10.06	10.41	9.45	10.45	10.00
8.54	9.81	9.74	10.42	9.75	10.71	10.00
.	9.57	9.95	10.16	9.92	10.40	10.00
6.54	9.86	9.71	10.36	9.92	10.30	10.00
6.70	9.77	9.91	10.15	10.07	10.54	10.00
8.77	9.72	9.83	10.25	9.81	10.49	10.00
7.72	9.70	9.82	10.26	9.80	10.47	

Note: Scaled to a mean of 10 and standard deviation of 2.

second cluster in the first half in Booklet 5 (Pos 1.2), and the first cluster in the second half of Booklet 7 (Pos 2.1). Items are listed in the order in which they were administered.

The differences in item difficulties over all nine clusters (see Appendix 6) cannot simply be described by a booklet effect, since they vary not only with respect to the booklets but differentially.

Nevertheless, there is evidence of an *order* effect of some kind. The parameters from the first position in the first half are lower than the parameters for other positions for almost every item, although the differences are occasionally negligible. The relation of the other positions (for clusters 1 to 8) is less clear. For clusters 2, 4, 5 and 6, the difficulties of position 1.1 and 2.1 look similar, whereas position 1.2 gives higher item parameter estimates. For clusters 1 and 7, positions 1.2 and 2.1 show a similar difficulty and are both higher than in position 1.1. Strangely, for cluster 3 position 1.2 is similar to position 1.1, and position 2.1 looks much more difficult. The differences in clusters 8 and 9 may well be explained by an order effect. Interestingly, after having some mathematics and science items, position 2.2 looks much harder than after having reading items only (Booklet 8).

CORRECTION OF THE BOOKLET EFFECT
Modelling the effect

Modelling the order effects in terms of item positions in a booklet or at least in terms of cluster positions in a booklet would result in a very complex model. For the sake of handling in the international scaling, the effect was modelled at booklet level.

Booklet effects were included in the measurement model to prevent confounding item difficulties and booklet effects. For the ConQuest model statement, the calibration model was:

item + item*step + booklet.

The booklet parameter, formally defined in the same way as item parameters, reflects *booklet* difficulty.

This measurement model provides item parameter estimates that are not affected by the booklet difficulties and booklet difficulty parameters that can be used to correct student ability scores.

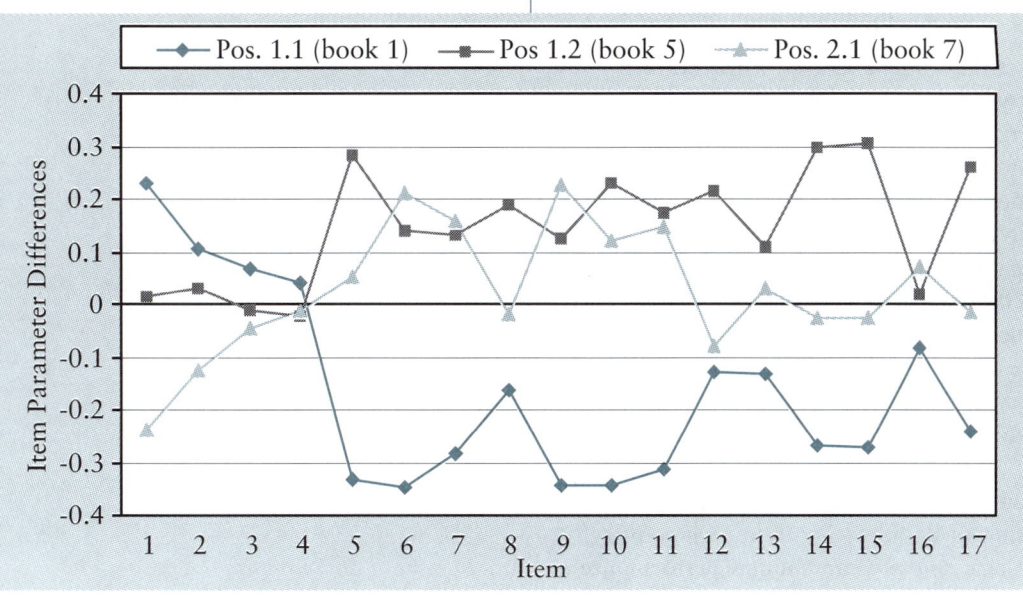

Figure 29: Item Parameter Differences for the Items in Cluster One

Estimating the parameters

The calibration model given above was used to estimate the international item parameters. It was estimated using the international calibration sample of 13 500 students, and not-reached items in the estimation were treated as not administered.

The booklet parameters obtained from this analysis were not used to correct for the booklet effect. Instead, a set of booklet parameters was obtained by scaling the whole international data set using booklet as a conditioning variable and applying a specific weight which gives each OECD country[6] an equal contribution[7]. Further, in this analysis, not-reached items were regarded as incorrect responses, in accordance with the computation of student ability scores reported in Chapter 9. The students who responded to the SE booklet were excluded from the estimation. The booklet parameter estimates obtained are reported in Table 52. Note that the table reports the deviation per booklet from the average within each of the three domains over all booklets and that therefore these parameters add up to zero per domain.

In order to display the magnitude of the effects, the booklet difficulty parameters are presented again in Table 53, after their transformation into the PISA reporting scale which has a mean of 500 and SD of 100.

[6] Due to the decision to omit the Netherlands from reports that focus on variation in achievement scores, the scores were not represented in this sample.
[7] These weights are computed to achieve an equal contribution from each country. They can be based on any weights used in the countries (*e.g.*, to adjust for the sampling design) or unweighted data.

Table 52: Booklet Difficulty Parameters

Booklet	Mathematics	Reading	Science
1	0.23	-0.05	-
2	-	-0.23	0.18
3	-0.14	-0.07	-
4	-	0.12	0.10
5	0.13	-0.01	-
6	-	-0.11	-0.13
7	-	0.01	-
8	-0.35	0.20	0.10
9	0.13	0.13	-0.24

Table 53: Booklet Difficulty Parameters Reported on the PISA Scale

Booklet	Mathematics	Reading	Science
1	17.6	-4.5	-
2	-	-20.9	16.2
3	-10.7	-6.4	-
4	-	10.9	9.0
5	9.9	-0.9	-
6	-	-10.0	-11.7
7	-	0.9	-
8	-26.7	12.8	9.0
9	9.9	11.8	-21.6

Applying the correction

To correct the student scores for the booklet effects, two alternatives were considered:
- to correct all students' scores using one set of the internationally estimated booklet parameters; and
- to correct the students' scores using one set of nationally estimated booklet parameters for each country. These coefficients can be obtained as booklet regression coefficients from estimating the conditioning models, one country at a time.

All available sets of booklet parameters sum to zero. Applying these parameters to every student in a country (having an equal distribution of Booklets 1 to 9 in each country) does not change the mean country performance. Therefore the application of any correction does not change the country ranking.

With the international correction, all countries are treated in exactly the same way, and it is therefore the most desirable option from a theoretical point of view. This is the option that was implemented.

From a statistical point of view, it leaves some slight deviations from equal booklet difficulties in the data. These deviations vary over countries. Using the national correction, these deviations would become negligible.

CHAPTER 14 { OUTCOMES OF MARKER RELIABILITY STUDIES

This chapter reports the result of the various marker reliability studies that were implemented. The methodologies for these studies are described in Chapter 10.

WITHIN-COUNTRY RELIABILITY STUDIES
Norman Verhelst

VARIANCE COMPONENTS ANALYSIS

Tables 54 to 58 show the results of the variance components analysis for the multiply-marked items in mathematics, science and the three reading sub-scales (usually referred to as scales for convenience), respectively. The variance components are each expressed as a percentage of their sum.

The tables show that those variance components associated with markers (those involving γ) are remarkably small relative to the other components. This means that there are no significant systematic within-country marker effects

As discussed in Chapter 10, analyses of the type reported here can result in negative variance estimates. If the amount by which the component is negative is small, then this is a sign that the variance component is negligible (near zero). If the component is large and negative, then it is a sign that the analysis method is inappropriate for the data. In Tables 54 to 58, countries with large inadmissible ρ_3-estimates are listed at the bottom of the tables and are marked with an asterisk. (Some sub-regions within countries were considered as countries for these analyses.) For Poland, some of the estimates were so highly negative that the resulting numbers did not fit in the format of the tables. Therefore Poland has been omitted altogether.

GENERALISABILITY COEFFICIENTS

The generalisability coefficients are computed from the variance components using:

$$\rho_3(Y_{v..},Y'_{v..}) = \frac{\sigma_\alpha^2 + \dfrac{\sigma_{\alpha\beta}^2}{I}}{\sigma_\alpha^2 + \dfrac{\sigma_{\alpha\beta}^2}{I} + \dfrac{\sigma_\gamma^2 + \sigma_{\alpha\gamma}^2}{M} + \dfrac{\sigma_{\beta\gamma}^2 + \sigma_\varepsilon^2}{I \times M}} . (88)$$

They provide an index of *reliability* for the multiple marking in each country.

I denotes the number of items and M the number of markers. By using different values for I and M, one obtains a generalisation of the Spearman-Brown formula for test-lengthening. In Tables 59 to 63, the formula is evaluated for the six combinations of $I = \{8, 16, 24\}$ and $M = \{1, 2\}$, using the variance component estimates from the corresponding tables presented above. For the countries marked with '*' in the above tables, no values are displayed, because they fall outside the acceptable (0,1) range.

Table 54: Variance Components for Mathematics

Country	Student Component $(\hat{\sigma}_\alpha^2)$	Item Component $(\hat{\sigma}_\beta^2)$	Marker Component $(\hat{\sigma}_\gamma^2)$	Student-Item Interaction Component $(\hat{\sigma}_{\alpha\beta}^2)$	Student-Marker Interaction Component $(\hat{\sigma}_{\alpha\gamma}^2)$	Item-Marker Interaction Component $(\hat{\sigma}_{\beta\gamma}^2)$	Measurement Error Component $(\hat{\sigma}_\varepsilon^2)$
Australia	24.99	28.24	0.00	40.54	0.12	0.04	6.07
Austria	15.17	30.81	0.22	45.14	0.17	1.80	6.68
Belgium (Fl.)	23.29	24.86	0.02	46.59	0.06	0.04	5.15
Czech Republic	22.67	27.22	0.01	45.10	-0.02	0.07	4.95
Denmark	19.78	32.69	0.00	42.34	-0.01	0.07	5.14
England	27.49	31.12	0.00	38.10	0.07	0.03	3.20
Finland	15.93	29.44	0.01	51.89	0.00	0.02	2.70
France	18.11	31.27	0.01	43.66	0.08	0.13	6.73
Germany	20.92	26.36	0.00	46.39	-0.01	0.31	6.03
Greece	20.40	23.05	0.02	52.61	0.02	0.04	3.86
Hungary	24.52	23.97	0.01	47.36	-0.30	0.04	4.40
Iceland	22.35	29.47	0.03	43.97	0.10	0.03	4.05
Ireland	22.46	26.31	0.11	41.85	0.18	0.20	8.90
Italy	17.75	24.60	0.01	51.74	0.07	0.14	5.69
Japan	21.35	24.83	0.00	51.90	-0.06	0.02	1.97
Korea	20.32	29.04	-0.01	45.43	0.00	0.14	5.08
Mexico	14.06	19.58	-0.03	54.60	0.70	0.13	10.96
Netherlands	23.66	26.45	0.09	42.09	0.05	0.16	7.49
New Zealand	20.99	29.39	0.03	43.43	0.10	0.16	5.90
Norway	18.66	32.03	0.00	44.55	0.13	0.07	4.56
Portugal	18.56	31.90	-0.01	47.29	0.08	0.05	2.13
Russian Federation	24.39	24.19	0.03	47.17	0.02	0.01	4.18
Spain	19.84	28.64	0.10	44.63	0.19	0.09	6.50
Sweden	21.24	29.35	0.01	44.44	0.08	0.09	4.80
Switzerland (Fr.)	20.80	25.83	0.09	43.71	0.24	0.34	8.99
Switzerland (Ger.)	21.60	28.30	0.00	47.29	0.06	0.01	2.75
Switzerland (Ital.)	19.25	29.62	0.12	41.26	0.82	0.12	8.81
Belgium (Fr.)*	32.85	24.41	0.50	38.04	-29.66	-0.24	34.09
Brazil*	32.59	6.06	0.78	46.99	-32.39	-1.14	47.12
Latvia*	20.29	28.87	0.02	42.83	-1.81	0.26	9.54
Luxembourg*	17.45	23.87	0.03	47.06	-1.79	0.32	13.07
Scotland*	19.66	29.49	0.23	38.00	-3.23	2.10	13.76
United States*	37.21	25.25	1.14	31.21	-42.32	-1.53	49.04

* ρ_3-coefficients were inadmissible (>1) in these countries.

Table 55: Variance Components for Science

Country	Student Component ($\hat{\sigma}^2_\alpha$)	Item Component ($\hat{\sigma}^2_\beta$)	Marker Component ($\hat{\sigma}^2_\gamma$)	Student-Item Interaction Component ($\hat{\sigma}^2_{\alpha\beta}$)	Student-Marker Interaction Component ($\hat{\sigma}^2_{\alpha\gamma}$)	Item-Marker Interaction Component ($\hat{\sigma}^2_{\beta\gamma}$)	Measurement Error Component ($\hat{\sigma}^2_\varepsilon$)
Australia	26.38	11.16	-0.12	46.30	0.06	0.88	15.34
Austria	20.47	9.98	0.47	54.53	0.02	0.58	13.95
Belgium (Fl.)	18.30	17.01	0.05	54.99	-0.14	0.11	9.68
Czech Republic	23.13	10.46	0.01	53.53	0.17	0.35	12.34
Denmark	21.77	10.39	0.01	59.94	-0.02	0.10	7.82
England	19.54	9.03	0.23	55.23	0.29	0.86	14.82
Finland	20.49	13.26	0.04	51.44	0.10	0.27	14.41
France	20.47	13.80	0.00	60.20	0.12	0.04	5.37
Germany	22.23	11.72	0.09	52.88	-0.05	0.24	12.89
Greece	21.29	9.42	0.01	60.84	0.27	0.07	8.11
Hungary	22.42	10.11	0.05	49.84	-0.12	0.78	16.92
Iceland	20.17	8.63	0.15	61.15	0.08	0.06	9.76
Ireland	22.56	14.26	0.06	56.78	0.01	0.05	6.29
Italy	20.82	8.77	0.05	65.03	-0.04	0.04	5.33
Japan	19.11	12.01	0.01	65.77	0.07	0.12	2.91
Korea	25.40	10.13	0.07	52.04	0.06	0.17	12.13
Mexico	19.49	14.20	0.05	57.88	0.19	0.08	8.11
Netherlands	23.04	8.57	0.07	56.11	0.05	0.16	12.00
New Zealand	20.05	10.01	-0.02	59.56	0.12	0.22	10.05
Norway	22.20	8.16	0.00	65.35	-0.02	0.01	4.30
Portugal	22.99	12.26	0.02	57.47	0.10	0.08	7.08
Spain	21.12	8.36	0.01	64.99	0.03	0.05	5.44
Switzerland (Fr.)	24.05	7.11	0.06	48.92	0.14	0.66	19.07
Switzerland (Ger.)	22.93	8.67	0.35	55.60	0.14	0.42	11.90
Switzerland (Ital.)	20.09	7.18	0.00	54.24	0.15	1.02	17.33
Belgium (Fr.)*	24.13	10.15	0.06	57.55	-0.80	0.22	8.68
Brazil*	21.47	7.49	0.06	58.48	-1.18	0.10	13.57
Latvia*	16.74	7.33	0.22	55.63	-1.30	0.58	20.81
Luxembourg*	25.40	9.63	0.17	50.02	-1.55	0.79	15.54
Russian Federation*	31.16	8.83	1.61	47.67	-23.34	0.83	33.24
Scotland*	25.89	9.64	0.14	54.59	-3.48	0.00	13.22
Sweden*	21.12	6.25	0.92	51.20	-28.85	-0.12	49.49
United States*	34.29	6.96	0.73	47.51	-30.26	-1.37	42.13

* ρ_3-coefficients were inadmissible (>1) in these countries.

Table 56: Variance Components for Retrieving Information

Country	Student Component ($\hat{\sigma}_\alpha^2$)	Item Component ($\hat{\sigma}_\beta^2$)	Marker Component ($\hat{\sigma}_\gamma^2$)	Student-Item Interaction Component ($\hat{\sigma}_{\alpha\beta}^2$)	Student-Marker Interaction Component ($\hat{\sigma}_{\alpha\gamma}^2$)	Item-Marker Interaction Component ($\hat{\sigma}_{\beta\gamma}^2$)	Measurement Error Component ($\hat{\sigma}_\varepsilon^2$)
Australia	22.40	19.01	-0.02	50.36	0.01	0.22	8.01
Austria	14.97	23.60	0.00	54.93	-0.12	0.24	6.39
Belgium (Fl.)	11.89	22.59	0.15	50.42	0.10	1.43	13.42
Czech Republic	17.14	19.81	0.03	53.73	-0.23	0.46	9.05
Denmark	13.24	24.56	0.01	54.22	0.16	0.25	7.56
England	14.79	22.14	0.00	59.71	0.01	0.00	3.35
Finland	18.97	18.30	0.02	55.93	-0.11	0.07	6.81
France	19.52	19.37	0.37	52.32	1.01	0.11	7.30
Germany	19.28	21.95	0.00	54.03	-0.09	0.03	4.80
Greece	17.92	15.78	0.04	56.92	-0.26	0.16	9.45
Hungary	16.69	17.65	0.02	58.80	-0.01	0.19	6.65
Iceland	16.42	18.09	0.00	62.69	0.07	0.03	2.71
Ireland	16.62	20.04	0.08	53.30	0.08	0.88	9.01
Italy	9.22	22.47	0.04	60.33	-0.10	0.18	7.86
Japan	17.93	15.22	0.19	51.28	-0.08	0.54	14.92
Korea	11.45	23.50	0.02	55.59	-0.13	0.18	9.39
Mexico	20.34	18.28	0.07	54.53	-0.02	0.04	6.76
Netherlands	17.98	20.14	0.00	52.89	-0.81	0.26	9.54
New Zealand	20.29	19.62	0.04	51.82	0.09	0.19	7.94
Norway	15.66	17.79	0.00	61.43	0.21	0.17	4.74
Portugal	14.03	19.05	0.01	61.34	-0.03	0.12	5.48
Spain	18.43	15.34	0.56	42.02	0.10	2.62	20.93
Switzerland (Fr.)	17.17	20.42	0.12	52.69	0.04	0.30	9.25
Switzerland (Ger.)	16.43	23.52	0.02	50.02	0.00	1.32	8.69
Switzerland (Ital.)	17.46	17.29	0.04	55.23	0.27	0.39	9.32
Belgium (Fr.)*	35.88	21.17	2.94	38.23	-64.09	-1.95	67.83
Brazil*	21.59	19.19	1.16	49.15	-29.54	-0.37	38.82
Latvia*	27.99	9.17	1.12	51.86	-4.05	0.56	13.34
Luxembourg*	30.64	20.92	2.41	45.20	-57.98	-2.14	60.96
Russian Federation*	24.88	19.38	1.22	46.83	-28.09	0.28	35.51
Scotland*	16.70	18.53	0.10	58.15	-1.41	0.06	7.87
Sweden*	14.45	23.71	0.24	53.71	-10.53	0.41	18.00
United States*	29.73	21.35	1.09	42.19	-35.61	-1.23	42.48

* ρ_3-coefficients were inadmissible (>1) in these countries.

Table 57: Variance Components for Interpreting Texts

Country	Student Component ($\hat{\sigma}^2_\alpha$)	Item Component ($\hat{\sigma}^2_\beta$)	Marker Component ($\hat{\sigma}^2_\gamma$)	Student-Item Interaction Component ($\hat{\sigma}^2_{\alpha\beta}$)	Student-Marker Interaction Component ($\hat{\sigma}^2_{\alpha\gamma}$)	Item-Marker Interaction Component ($\hat{\sigma}^2_{\beta\gamma}$)	Measurement Error Component ($\hat{\sigma}^2_\varepsilon$)
Australia	16.46	22.63	0.10	47.56	0.09	0.35	12.80
Austria	15.57	16.43	0.09	52.88	-0.06	1.15	13.94
Belgium (Fl.)	14.90	23.80	0.04	45.18	0.09	0.81	15.18
Czech Republic	16.40	17.76	0.14	49.36	-0.01	1.18	15.16
Denmark	16.88	20.32	-0.02	54.40	0.00	0.28	8.15
England	11.41	27.78	0.02	54.11	-0.08	0.15	6.61
Finland	19.20	18.21	0.04	52.20	0.28	0.43	9.64
France	14.50	20.11	-0.02	53.75	-0.28	0.38	11.55
Germany	15.91	22.73	0.02	50.74	-0.22	0.27	10.55
Greece	13.80	22.63	-0.03	49.56	0.16	0.41	13.47
Hungary	15.62	16.96	0.16	54.81	-0.05	0.73	11.77
Iceland	14.56	22.13	0.05	56.53	-0.14	0.19	6.67
Ireland	12.95	19.45	0.21	50.44	0.07	1.41	15.47
Italy	9.94	22.70	0.07	57.23	-0.12	0.19	9.98
Japan	14.18	9.27	0.48	54.47	0.50	1.03	20.07
Korea	15.03	23.66	0.11	45.35	0.26	0.58	15.01
Mexico	16.29	22.00	0.05	51.38	0.13	0.18	9.97
Netherlands	19.30	15.15	0.02	52.76	-0.42	0.55	12.64
New Zealand	17.61	21.74	0.05	49.03	0.10	0.34	11.13
Norway	13.37	29.90	0.00	47.77	0.04	0.38	8.54
Portugal	13.00	22.16	0.04	56.14	0.23	0.16	8.27
Spain	16.07	16.36	0.83	41.68	0.56	1.42	23.09
Switzerland (Fr.)	15.65	18.91	0.04	50.29	0.22	0.71	14.18
Switzerland (Ger.)	17.49	17.64	0.10	49.75	-0.11	0.68	14.46
Switzerland (Ital.)	16.25	21.70	0.05	45.24	0.29	0.63	15.83
Belgium (Fr.)*	35.47	16.09	2.81	41.04	-62.53	-2.78	69.90
Brazil*	20.03	26.28	0.99	40.64	-29.96	0.26	41.77
Luxembourg*	31.46	17.93	2.84	44.04	-53.26	-1.79	58.78
Latvia*	23.28	14.08	0.46	45.50	-4.65	2.95	18.37
Russian Federation*	24.25	15.18	0.82	46.93	-25.58	0.52	37.89
Scotland*	14.04	17.09	0.12	57.51	-1.24	0.17	12.30
Sweden*	18.03	13.33	0.14	56.29	-10.16	-0.24	22.60
United States*	25.67	19.30	1.29	43.64	-36.52	-1.22	47.84

* ρ_3-coefficients were inadmissible (>1) in these countries.

Table 58: Variance Components for Reflection and Evaluation

Country	Student Component ($\hat{\sigma}_\alpha^2$)	Item Component ($\hat{\sigma}_\beta^2$)	Marker Component ($\hat{\sigma}_\gamma^2$)	Student-Item Interaction Component ($\hat{\sigma}_{\alpha\beta}^2$)	Student-Marker Interaction Component ($\hat{\sigma}_{\alpha\gamma}^2$)	Item-Marker Interaction Component ($\hat{\sigma}_{\beta\gamma}^2$)	Measurement Error Component ($\hat{\sigma}_\varepsilon^2$)
Australia	15.53	25.75	0.41	35.55	0.31	0.75	21.69
Austria	14.90	19.96	0.81	37.20	0.57	1.44	25.13
Belgium (Fl.)	16.26	20.75	0.35	36.20	0.41	1.26	24.77
Czech Republic	15.65	20.78	1.07	32.83	0.69	1.96	27.02
Denmark	14.83	21.54	0.07	49.36	0.05	0.53	13.61
England	13.77	25.57	0.05	47.06	0.02	0.13	13.41
Finland	23.09	15.18	0.21	48.51	0.24	0.27	12.50
France	16.93	21.29	0.40	40.52	0.56	0.52	19.78
Germany	18.32	25.33	0.19	37.09	0.06	0.65	18.35
Greece	13.75	26.20	0.52	32.21	0.41	1.34	25.57
Hungary	15.60	20.52	0.66	39.65	0.16	1.25	22.15
Iceland	16.64	22.44	0.07	49.23	0.01	0.40	11.20
Ireland	14.24	18.67	0.96	41.43	0.34	1.51	22.85
Italy	10.64	26.50	0.50	42.79	0.57	0.99	18.02
Japan	15.13	10.34	1.57	36.68	1.76	1.79	32.73
Korea	11.70	25.36	0.68	29.10	0.78	2.57	29.82
Mexico	18.52	18.75	0.14	40.50	-0.74	0.88	21.95
Netherlands	17.91	24.33	0.37	37.62	0.05	0.45	19.26
New Zealand	14.06	21.79	0.57	43.90	0.50	0.80	18.37
Norway	16.67	21.93	0.28	37.37	-0.23	1.11	22.86
Portugal	18.63	24.58	0.24	34.85	0.50	1.12	20.08
Russian Federation	13.18	25.07	0.07	41.51	0.27	0.59	19.31
Spain	14.97	16.35	1.02	37.29	1.03	1.85	27.50
Switzerland (Fr.)	17.57	19.11	0.77	35.08	0.47	1.86	25.14
Switzerland (Ger.)	17.60	19.74	0.77	37.12	0.61	1.14	23.02
Switzerland (Ital.)	15.49	25.37	0.29	34.01	0.56	1.24	23.04
Belgium (Fr.)*	16.39	17.60	1.03	47.94	-7.09	0.58	23.55
Brazil*	32.02	20.54	2.15	36.32	-45.99	-1.72	56.68
Latvia*	27.95	17.69	2.58	42.76	-40.51	-1.18	50.71
Luxembourg*	21.17	17.66	1.16	34.52	-22.78	0.92	47.35
Scotland*	25.18	14.56	1.02	37.26	-2.91	1.08	23.81
Sweden*	21.58	20.05	1.21	35.26	-18.97	1.14	39.73
United States*	24.39	26.13	0.97	31.25	-28.29	-0.71	46.26

* ρ_3-coefficients were inadmissible (>1) in these countries.

Table 59: ρ_3-Estimates for Mathematics

Country	I = 8 M = 1	I = 8 M = 2	I = 16 M = 1	I = 16 M = 2	I = 24 M = 1	I = 24 M = 2
Australia	0.971	0.986	0.982	0.991	0.986	0.993
Austria	0.935	0.966	0.951	0.975	0.958	0.979
Belgium (Fl.)	0.976	0.988	0.985	0.992	0.988	0.994
Czech Republic	0.978	0.989	0.987	0.994	0.991	0.996
Denmark	0.975	0.987	0.986	0.993	0.990	0.995
England	0.986	0.993	0.991	0.995	0.993	0.996
Finland	0.985	0.992	0.991	0.995	0.993	0.997
France	0.961	0.980	0.976	0.988	0.981	0.991
Germany	0.971	0.985	0.984	0.992	0.989	0.994
Greece	0.981	0.990	0.988	0.994	0.991	0.996
Hungary	0.982	0.991	0.990	0.995	0.993	0.996
Ireland	0.951	0.975	0.967	0.983	0.973	0.986
Iceland	0.978	0.989	0.985	0.992	0.988	0.994
Italy	0.968	0.984	0.979	0.990	0.984	0.992
Japan	0.991	0.996	0.995	0.997	0.996	0.998
Korea	0.976	0.988	0.986	0.993	0.990	0.995
Mexico	0.909	0.952	0.926	0.962	0.934	0.966
Netherlands	0.963	0.981	0.977	0.988	0.982	0.991
New Zealand	0.967	0.983	0.979	0.989	0.984	0.992
Norway	0.972	0.986	0.981	0.990	0.985	0.992
Portugal	0.986	0.993	0.990	0.995	0.992	0.996
Russian Federation	0.981	0.991	0.989	0.994	0.992	0.996
Spain	0.958	0.979	0.970	0.985	0.975	0.987
Sweden	0.974	0.987	0.984	0.992	0.987	0.994
Switzerland (Fr.)	0.946	0.972	0.963	0.981	0.969	0.984
Switzerland (Ger.)	0.985	0.993	0.991	0.995	0.993	0.996
Switzerland (Ital.)	0.922	0.960	0.936	0.967	0.941	0.970

Table 60: ρ_3-Estimates for Science

Country	I = 8 M = 1	I = 8 M = 2	I = 16 M = 1	I = 16 M = 2	I = 24 M = 1	I = 24 M = 2
Australia	0.939	0.969	0.965	0.982	0.975	0.987
Austria	0.922	0.959	0.945	0.972	0.954	0.976
Belgium (Fl.)	0.952	0.975	0.970	0.985	0.978	0.989
Switzerland (Fr.)	0.917	0.957	0.948	0.973	0.961	0.980
Switzerland (Ger.)	0.919	0.958	0.950	0.974	0.962	0.981
Czech Republic	0.936	0.967	0.954	0.977	0.962	0.981
Denmark	0.943	0.971	0.966	0.982	0.975	0.987
England	0.967	0.983	0.981	0.990	0.986	0.993
Finland	0.976	0.988	0.985	0.992	0.989	0.994
France	0.932	0.965	0.957	0.978	0.968	0.984
Germany	0.944	0.971	0.965	0.982	0.973	0.986
Greece	0.972	0.986	0.981	0.991	0.985	0.993
Hungary	0.957	0.978	0.969	0.984	0.975	0.987
Iceland	0.972	0.986	0.982	0.991	0.987	0.993
Ireland	0.927	0.962	0.957	0.978	0.969	0.984
Italy	0.950	0.974	0.966	0.983	0.973	0.986
Japan	0.976	0.988	0.985	0.992	0.988	0.994
Korea	0.983	0.992	0.989	0.994	0.991	0.995
Netherlands	0.950	0.975	0.970	0.985	0.977	0.988
New Zealand	0.948	0.973	0.968	0.984	0.976	0.988
Norway	0.955	0.977	0.968	0.984	0.974	0.987
Portugal	0.983	0.991	0.990	0.995	0.993	0.996
Russian Federation	0.951	0.975	0.969	0.984	0.976	0.988
Spain	0.914	0.955	0.939	0.968	0.949	0.974
Sweden	0.967	0.983	0.979	0.989	0.984	0.992

Table 61: ρ_3-Estimates for Retrieving Information

Country	I = 8 M = 1	I = 8 M = 2	I = 16 M = 1	I = 16 M = 2	I = 24 M = 1	I = 24 M = 2
Australia	0.965	0.982	0.980	0.990	0.986	0.993
Austria	0.963	0.981	0.978	0.989	0.984	0.992
Belgium (Fl.)	0.896	0.945	0.927	0.962	0.942	0.970
Denmark	0.951	0.975	0.970	0.985	0.978	0.989
England	0.977	0.989	0.987	0.993	0.991	0.995
Finland	0.981	0.990	0.988	0.994	0.991	0.996
France	0.868	0.929	0.908	0.952	0.925	0.961
Germany	0.947	0.973	0.968	0.984	0.977	0.988
Greece	0.967	0.983	0.980	0.990	0.986	0.993
Hungary	0.919	0.958	0.925	0.961	0.928	0.963
Iceland	0.965	0.982	0.978	0.989	0.984	0.992
Ireland	0.953	0.976	0.971	0.985	0.979	0.989
Italy	0.943	0.971	0.962	0.981	0.971	0.985
Japan	0.983	0.992	0.988	0.994	0.990	0.995
Korea	0.941	0.970	0.960	0.980	0.969	0.984
Mexico	0.920	0.958	0.948	0.973	0.960	0.980
Netherlands	0.938	0.968	0.960	0.980	0.970	0.985
New Zealand	0.967	0.983	0.980	0.990	0.985	0.992
Russian Federation	0.966	0.983	0.974	0.987	0.978	0.989
Scotland	0.959	0.979	0.974	0.987	0.980	0.990
Spain	0.946	0.972	0.962	0.981	0.969	0.984
Sweden	0.968	0.984	0.980	0.990	0.986	0.993
Switzerland (Fr.)	0.941	0.970	0.958	0.979	0.965	0.982
Switzerland (Ger.)	0.946	0.972	0.964	0.982	0.972	0.986

Outcomes of marker reliability studies

Table 62: ρ_3-Estimates for Interpreting Texts

Country	$I = 8$ $M = 1$	$I = 8$ $M = 2$	$I = 16$ $M = 1$	$I = 16$ $M = 2$	$I = 24$ $M = 1$	$I = 24$ $M = 2$
Australia	0.924	0.961	0.951	0.975	0.962	0.980
Austria	0.918	0.957	0.948	0.973	0.961	0.980
Belgium (Fl.)	0.906	0.951	0.940	0.969	0.955	0.977
Switzerland (Fr.)	0.901	0.948	0.933	0.965	0.946	0.972
Switzerland (Ger.)	0.912	0.954	0.940	0.969	0.953	0.976
Denmark	0.912	0.954	0.944	0.971	0.957	0.978
England	0.942	0.970	0.965	0.982	0.975	0.987
Finland	0.955	0.977	0.971	0.985	0.978	0.989
France	0.827	0.905	0.865	0.927	0.881	0.937
Germany	0.922	0.960	0.952	0.975	0.9640	0.982
Greece	0.942	0.970	0.959	0.979	0.967	0.983
Hungary	0.934	0.966	0.960	0.980	0.971	0.985
Ireland	0.913	0.955	0.943	0.970	0.956	0.977
Iceland	0.929	0.963	0.953	0.976	0.963	0.981
Italy	0.890	0.942	0.923	0.960	0.939	0.968
Japan	0.960	0.979	0.974	0.987	0.981	0.990
Korea	0.927	0.962	0.950	0.975	0.961	0.980
Mexico	0.853	0.921	0.884	0.939	0.898	0.947
Netherlands	0.899	0.947	0.930	0.964	0.943	0.971
New Zealand	0.940	0.969	0.960	0.980	0.968	0.984
Portugal	0.939	0.969	0.964	0.982	0.974	0.987
Russian Federation	0.944	0.971	0.965	0.982	0.974	0.987
Scotland	0.937	0.968	0.960	0.979	0.969	0.984
Spain	0.957	0.978	0.975	0.987	0.982	0.990
Sweden	0.938	0.968	0.954	0.976	0.961	0.980

Table 63: ρ_3-Estimates for Reflection and Evaluation

Country	I = 8 M = 1	I = 8 M = 2	I = 16 M = 1	I = 16 M = 2	I = 24 M = 1	I = 24 M = 2
Australia	0.850	0.919	0.893	0.944	0.911	0.954
Austria	0.806	0.893	0.850	0.919	0.869	0.930
Belgium (Fl.)	0.838	0.912	0.886	0.939	0.906	0.951
Denmark	0.786	0.880	0.832	0.908	0.852	0.920
England	0.897	0.946	0.935	0.966	0.950	0.974
Finland	0.918	0.957	0.948	0.973	0.961	0.980
France	0.774	0.873	0.817	0.899	0.835	0.910
Germany	0.835	0.910	0.873	0.932	0.889	0.941
Greece	0.934	0.966	0.954	0.977	0.962	0.981
Hungary	0.863	0.926	0.897	0.946	0.912	0.954
Iceland	0.846	0.917	0.888	0.941	0.906	0.951
Ireland	0.805	0.892	0.858	0.923	0.880	0.936
Italy	0.817	0.899	0.856	0.923	0.873	0.932
Japan	0.937	0.968	0.961	0.980	0.971	0.985
Korea	0.823	0.903	0.855	0.922	0.870	0.930
Mexico	0.721	0.838	0.760	0.864	0.777	0.875
Netherlands	0.736	0.848	0.795	0.886	0.821	0.902
New Zealand	0.887	0.940	0.925	0.961	0.940	0.969
Norway	0.913	0.954	0.962	0.981	0.983	0.991
Portugal	0.867	0.929	0.914	0.955	0.934	0.966
Russian Federation	0.849	0.919	0.881	0.937	0.895	0.944
Scotland	0.871	0.931	0.910	0.953	0.925	0.961
Spain	0.918	0.957	0.947	0.973	0.960	0.979
Sweden	0.867	0.929	0.909	0.952	0.927	0.962
Switzerland (Fr.)	0.826	0.905	0.871	0.931	0.889	0.942
Switzerland (Ital.)	0.836	0.910	0.882	0.937	0.901	0.948

INTER-COUNTRY RATER RELIABILITY STUDY - OUTCOME
Aletta Grisay

OVERVIEW OF THE MAIN RESULTS

Approximately 1 600 booklets were submitted for the inter-country rater reliability study, in which 41 796 student answers were re-scored by the verifiers. In about 78 per cent of these cases, both the verifier and all four national markers agreed on an identical score, and in another 8.5 per cent of the cases, the verifier agreed with the majority of the national markers.

Of the remaining cases, 5 per cent had national marks considered too inconsistent to allow comparison with the verifier's mark, and 8 per cent were flagged and submitted to Consortium staff for adjudication. In approximately 5 per cent of these cases, the adjudicators found that there was no real problem (marks given by the national markers were correct), while 2.5 per cent of the marks were found to be too lenient and 1 per cent too harsh.

Hence, a very high proportion of the cases (91.5 per cent) showed substantial consistency with the scoring instructions described in the *Marking Guides*. Altogether only 3.5 per cent of cases were identified as either too lenient or too harsh and 5 per cent were identified as inconsistent marks. These percentages are summarised in Table 64.

Table 64: Summary of Inter-Country Rater Reliability Study

Category	Percentage
Agreement	91.5
Inconsistency	5.0
Harshness	1.0
Leniency	2.5

Note: Total cases = 41 796

While relatively infrequent, the inconsistent or biased marks were not uniformly distributed across items or countries, suggesting that scoring instructions may have been insufficiently stringent for some items, and that some national scoring teams may have been less careful than others.

MAIN RESULTS BY ITEM

The *qualitative* analysis of the most frequent cases of marking errors may indicate some problems in the scoring instructions that shed light on the higher rate of inconsistencies observed for these items. For example:

- *Scoring instructions that were too complex.* For many items where a number of criteria had to be taken into account simultaneously when deciding on the code, markers often tended to forget one or more of them. For example, in *R120Q06: Student Opinions*, the response (i) must contain some clear reference to the selected author (Ana, Beatrice, Dieter, or Felix); (ii) must contain details showing that the student understood the author's specific argument(s); (iii) must indicate how these arguments agreed with the student's own opinions about space exploration; and (iv) must be expressed in the student's own words. National markers often gave answers full credit if they commented on Ana's concerns about famine and disease or on Dieter's concerns about environment, but made no explicit or implicit reference to space exploration. They also tended to give full credit to answers that did not sufficiently discriminate among two or more of the five authors, or were not expressed in the student's own words (*i.e.*, they were mere quotations).
- *Lack of precision in the scoring instructions.* For example, in *R119Q05: Gift,* neither the scoring instructions nor the examples sufficiently explained the criteria to be applied to decide on whether the student had actually commented on the *last sentence*, last paragraph, or on the end of the story as a whole. Many answers that did not refer to any specific aspect described in the last sentence were given full or partial credit by the national markers, provided that some reference to the 'ending' was included.
- *Many errors occurred in the marks given to responses where the code depended on the response given to a previous item (e.g., R099Q4B: Plan International).*
- *Cultural differences* could explain why a number of national markers tended to be reluctant to accept the understanding of the text that was sometimes conveyed by the *Marking Guide*. In *R119Q07: Gift*, for example, the idea that the cries of the panther

were mentioned by the author 'to create fear' was often accepted, while this interpretation was considered in the *Marking Guide* to be a clear case of code 0. In *R119Q08: Gift*, the national markers often gave credit to answers suggesting that the woman fed the panther *to get rid of it* or *to avoid being eaten herself*, while the *Marking Guide* specified that pity or empathy were the only motivations to be retained for full credit.

Table 65 presents detailed results by item. Nine of the 26 items which are italicised in Table 65 had total agreement of less than 90 per cent.

Table 66 gives the stem for each of these items.

Table 65: Summary of Item Characteristics for Inter-Country Rater Reliability Study

Item	Frequency	Percentage Agreement	Inconsistency	Harshness	Leniency
R070Q04	1618	89.7	6.5	1.5	2.2
R081Q02	1618	96.4	2.0	0.8	0.8
R081Q05	1618	88.5	6.9	1.5	3.2
R081Q06A	1617	87.8	8.1	1.7	2.5
R081Q06B	1618	87.0	8.6	2.0	2.4
R091Q05	1618	99.4	0.3	0.1	0.2
R091Q07B	1570	90.2	5.7	2.1	2.0
R099Q04B	1618	75.7	13.2	3.3	7.7
R110Q04	1618	98.1	1.2	0.3	0.4
R110Q05	1618	95.1	3.2	0.1	1.7
R119Q05	1617	78.3	13.6	3.2	4.9
R119Q07	1618	79.1	12.9	2.8	5.2
R119Q08	1618	85.2	8.5	1.9	4.4
R119Q09T	1618	90.5	5.1	2.1	2.3
R120Q06	1594	86.4	8.8	1.4	3.5
R219Q01E	1618	94.8	3.3	1.2	0.7
R219Q02	1617	95.7	2.7	0.6	1.1
R220Q01	1618	92.3	4.5	1.6	1.6
R236Q01	1569	92.8	2.1	0.7	4.4
R236Q02	1569	93.0	4.0	0.8	2.2
R237Q01	1618	97.2	1.2	0.4	1.2
R237Q03	1618	92.8	4.3	0.5	2.3
R239Q01	1569	99.0	0.6	0.1	0.3
R239Q02	1569	97.9	1.2	0.2	0.7
R246Q01	1617	98.2	0.9	0.4	0.6
R246Q02	1618	92.8	4.1	0.2	3.0

Note: Items in italics have a total agreement of less than 90 per cent.

Table 66: Items with Less than 90 Per Cent Consistency

Item	Stem
R070Q04: Beach	Does the title of the article give a good summary of the debate presented in the article? Explain your answer.
R081Q05: Graffiti	Why does Sophia refer to advertising?
R081Q06A: Graffiti	Which of the two letter writers do you agree with? Explain your answer by using your own words to refer to what is said in one or both of the letters.
R081Q06B: Graffiti	Which do you think is the better letter? Explain your answer by referring to the way one or both letters are written.
R099Q04B: Plan International	What do you think might explain the level of Plan International's activities in Ethiopia compared with its activities in other countries?
R119Q05: Gift	Do you think the last sentence of "The Gift" is an appropriate ending?
R119Q07: Gift	Why do you think the writer chooses to introduce the panther with these descriptions?
R119Q08: Gift	What does the story suggest was the woman's reason for feeding the panther?
R120Q06: Student Opinions	Which student do you agree with most strongly?

An analysis was conducted to investigate whether the items with major marking problems in a specific country showed particularly poor statistics for that country in the item analysis. Table 67 presents the main inter-country reliability results for the group of items where more than 25 per cent marking inconsistencies were found in at least one country, together with four main study indicators:
- the item fit for that country;
- whether the item difficulty estimate was higher or lower than expected (0: no; 1: yes); and
- whether the item had a problem with score order (cases where ability appeared to be lower for higher scores (0: no; 1: yes)).

Many items for which the inter-country reliability study identified problems in the national marking proved to have large fit indices ($r = 0.40$ between fit and per cent of marking inconsistencies, for $N = 26$ items × 27 national samples = 702 cases). A moderately high correlation was also observed between percentage of inconsistencies and problems in the category order ($r = 0.25$).

One might also expect a significant correlation between the percentage of *too-harsh* or *too-lenient* codes awarded by national markers and possible differential item functioning. Actually the correlations, though significant, were quite low ($r = 0.09$ between FL_HARSH and HIGH_DELTA; and $r = 0.17$ between FL_LENIE and LOW_DELTA). This may be due to the fact that in many countries, when an item showed a high percentage of too-lenient codes, it often also showed non-negligible occurrences of too-harsh codes.

MAIN RESULTS BY COUNTRY

Table 68 presents the detail of the results by country. In most countries (23 of 31), the international verifier or the adjudicator agreed with the national marks in more than 90 per cent of cases. The remaining eight countries—those with less than 90 per cent of the cases in the agreement category—are italicised in the table.

Four of these eight countries had quite a few cases in the 'too inconsistent' category, but showed no specific trend towards harshness or leniency.

Table 67: Inter-Country Reliability Study Items with More than 25 Per Cent Inconsistency Rate in at Least One Country

Country	Item	Inconsistency (%)	Harshness (%)	Leniency (%)	Fit Mean Square	High Fit	Low Fit	Abilities Not Ordered
Austria	R081Q06A	29.2	4.2	0.0	0.99	0	0	0
Canada (Fr.)	R081Q06B	25.5	0.0	2.1	0.94	0	0	0
Canada (Fr.)	R119Q07	29.8	0.0	2.1	1.36	0	0	1
Czech Republic	R099Q04B	33.4	4.2	2.1	1.15	0	1	1
Czech Republic	R119Q05	41.7	4.2	8.3	1.15	0	0	0
Czech Republic	R119Q07	52.1	2.1	4.2	1.28	0	0	1
Denmark	R070Q04	37.5	0.0	8.3	1.02	0	0	0
Denmark	R099Q04B	62.6	0.0	18.8	1.19	0	0	0
Denmark	R119Q05	27.1	0.0	10.4	1.24	0	0	0
Greece	R099Q04B	35.5	2.1	14.6	1.32	0	1	0
Iceland	R236Q01	62.5	0.0	62.5	0.97	0	1	0
Ireland	R119Q05	39.6	0.0	2.1	1.22	0	0	1
Japan	R099Q04B	35.4	4.2	22.9	1.19	0	0	0
Japan	R119Q07	33.3	0.0	12.5	1.20	1	0	0
Korea	R099Q04B	45.9	6.3	31.3	1.20	0	1	0
Korea	R119Q05	37.5	8.3	16.7	1.04	1	0	0
Korea	R119Q07	29.3	4.2	18.8	1.16	1	0	0
Mexico	R091Q07B	39.6	22.9	12.5	1.17	1	0	0
Mexico	R099Q04B	31.2	2.1	20.8	1.21	0	1	0
Netherlands	R119Q08	39.6	0.0	12.5	1.28	0	0	1
Portugal	R119Q05	25.1	2.1	4.2	1.23	0	0	0
Russian Federation	R099Q04B	43.8	4.2	33.3	1.18	0	1	0
Russian Federation	R119Q05	37.5	2.1	27.1	1.25	0	1	0
Russian Federation	R119Q07	31.3	4.2	20.8	1.16	0	1	0
Sweden	R081Q06B	27.2	6.3	4.2	0.96	1	0	0
United States	R119Q07	29.1	8.3	8.3	1.33	0	1	1

However, the rate of 'too lenient' cases was 5 per cent or more in four countries: France (5 per cent), Korea (5 per cent), the Russian Federation (7 per cent) and Latvia (9 per cent). The details provided by the country reports seem to suggest that, in all four countries, scoring instructions were not strictly followed for a number of items. In the Russian Federation, for five of the 26 items in Booklet 7, more than 10 per cent of cases were marked too leniently. In Korea, more than 10 per cent of cases for one item were marked too harshly, while six other items were too leniently marked. In Latvia, four items received very systematic lenient marks (between one-third and one-half of student answers were marked too leniently for these items), while a few others had both high proportions of cases which were either too harshly or too leniently marked.

In both Russia and Latvia, there was some indication that, for a number of partial credit items, the markers may have used codes 0, 1, 2 and 3 in a non-standard way. They gave code 3 to what they thought were the 'best' answers, 2 to answers that seemed 'good, but not perfect', 1 to 'poor, but not totally wrong' answers, and 0 to 'totally wrong' answers, without considering the specific scoring rules for each code provided in the *Marking Guide*. In Latvia, the NPM had decided not to translate the *Marking Guide* into Latvian, on the assumption that all the markers were sufficiently proficient in English to use the English source version.

Ten other countries had leniency problems for just one or two items—sometimes due to residual translation errors. In some of these cases, the proportion of incorrect marks may have been sufficient to affect the item functioning.

In general, harshness problems were very infrequent.

Table 68: Inter-Country Summary by Country

Country	Frequency	Consistent	Inconsistent	Harsh	Lenient
Australia	1 248	92.4	5.6	1.4	0.6
Austria	1 247	91.6	6.4	1.1	0.9
Belgium (Fl.)	*1 078*	85.6	9.6	1.8	3.0
Belgium (Fr.)	1 248	92.2	4.9	1.6	1.3
Brazil	1 248	91.5	4.6	0.6	3.4
Canada (Eng.)	1 248	91.4	6.7	0.7	1.2
Canada (Fr.)	1 222	91.0	6.9	0.6	1.6
Czech Republic	*1 248*	86.9	9.5	0.6	3.0
Denmark	*1 248*	86.8	9.0	0.5	3.8
England	1 248	93.3	5.0	0.4	1.3
Finland	1 248	96.1	2.4	0.6	1.0
France	*1 196*	80.2	12.5	2.3	5.0
Germany	1 224	92.6	5.8	0.7	0.8
Greece	1 247	90.5	3.3	1.7	4.6
Hungary	1 274	92.9	2.3	2.4	2.4
Iceland	1 248	91.7	5.4	0.3	2.6
Ireland	1 248	92.5	5.0	0.6	1.8
Italy	*1 170*	89.8	7.0	1.5	1.7
Japan	1 248	95.0	1.8	0.7	2.5
Korea	*1 248*	89.3	3.9	1.6	5.1
Luxembourg	1 144	95.9	2.1	1.6	0.4
Latvia	*1 066*	80.6	7.5	2.5	9.4
Mexico	1 247	91.1	3.5	2.8	2.6
Netherlands	1 248	91.3	5.8	1.4	1.5
New Zealand	1 222	96.5	2.7	0.1	0.7
Norway	1 248	92.9	4.4	0.6	2.1
Poland	1 248	92.1	3.0	1.0	3.8
Portugal	1 248	92.0	5.4	1.8	0.8
Russian Federation	*1 248*	88.5	3.7	0.9	6.9
Scotland	1 248	94.5	3.8	0.6	1.1
Spain	1 248	94.1	3.4	0.8	1.8
Sweden	1 200	93.2	4.0	1.6	1.3
Switzerland	1 300	93.4	4.0	2.4	0.2
United States	1 247	92.1	5.2	1.4	1.3

Note: Countries with less than 90 per cent of cases in the agreement category are in italics.

CHAPTER 15 } DATA ADJUDICATION

Ray Adams, Keith Rust and Christian Monseur

In January 2001, the PISA Consortium, the Sampling Referee and the OECD Secretariat met to review the implementation of the survey in each participating country and to consider:
- the extent to which the country had met PISA sampling standards;
- the outcomes of the national centre and school quality monitoring visits;
- the quality and completeness of the submitted data;
- the outcomes of the inter-country reliability study; and
- the outcomes of the translation verification process.

The meeting led to a set of recommendations to the OECD Secretariat about the suitability of the data from each country for reporting and use in analyses of various kinds, and a set of follow-up actions with a small number of countries.

This chapter reviews the extent to which each country met the PISA 2000 standards. For each country, a recommendation was made on the use of the data in international analyses and reports. Any follow-up data analyses that needed to be undertaken to allow the Consortium to endorse the data were also noted.

OVERVIEW OF RESPONSE RATE ISSUES

Table 69 presents the results of some simple modelling that was undertaken to consider the impact of non-response on estimates of means. If one assumes a correlation between a school's propensity to participate in PISA and student achievement in that school, the bias in mean scores resulting from various levels of non-response can be computed as a function of the strength of the relationship between the propensity to non-response and proficiency.[1]

The rows of Table 69 correspond to differing response rates, and the columns correspond to differing correlations between propensity and proficiency. The values give the mean scores that would be observed for samples with matching characteristics.

The true mean and standard deviation were assumed to be 500 and 100 respectively. In PISA, the typical standard error for a sample mean is 3.5. This means that any values in the table of approximately 506 or greater have a bias greater than a difference from the true value that would be considered statistically significant. Those values are shaded in Table 69.

While the true magnitude of the correlation between propensity and achievement is not known, standards can be set to guard against potential bias by non-response. The PISA school response rate of 0.85 was chosen to protect against any substantial relationship between propensity and achievement.

---

[1] The values reported in Table 69 were computed using a model that assumes a bivariate normal distribution for propensity to respond and proficiency. The expected means were computed under the assumption that proficiency is only observed for schools whose propensity to non-response is below a value that yields the specified response rate.

Table 69: The Potential Impact of Non-Response on PISA Proficiency Estimates

Response Rate	\multicolumn{11}{c}{Correlation Between Retentivity and Proficiency}
	0.08	0.10	0.20	0.30	0.40	0.50	0.60	0.70	0.80	0.90	1.00
0.05	517	521	541	562	583	603	624	644	665	686	706
0.10	514	518	535	553	570	588	605	623	640	658	675
0.15	512	516	531	547	562	578	593	609	624	640	655
0.20	511	514	528	542	556	570	584	598	612	626	640
0.25	510	513	525	538	551	564	576	589	602	614	627
0.30	509	512	523	535	546	558	570	581	593	604	616
0.35	508	511	521	532	542	553	563	574	585	595	606
0.40	508	510	519	529	539	548	558	568	577	587	597
0.45	507	509	518	526	535	544	553	562	570	579	588
0.50	506	508	516	524	532	540	548	556	564	572	580
0.55	506	507	514	522	529	536	543	550	558	565	572
0.60	505	506	513	519	526	532	539	545	552	558	564
0.65	505	506	511	517	523	528	534	540	546	551	557
0.70	504	505	510	515	520	525	530	535	540	545	550
0.75	503	504	508	513	517	521	525	530	534	538	542
0.80	503	503	507	510	514	517	521	524	528	531	535
0.85	502	503	505	508	511	514	516	519	522	525	527
0.90	502	502	504	506	508	510	512	514	516	518	519
0.95	501	501	502	503	504	505	507	508	509	510	511
0.99	500	500	501	501	501	501	502	502	502	502	503

Figure 30 is a plot of the attained PISA school response rates. It shows a scatter-plot of the school response rates (weighted) that were attained by the PISA participants. Those countries that are plotted in the shaded region were regarded as fully satisfying the PISA school response rate criterion.

As discussed below, each of the six countries (Belgium, the Netherlands, New Zealand, Poland, the United Kingdom and the United States) that did not meet the PISA criterion were asked to provide supplementary evidence that would assist the Consortium in making a balanced judgement about the threat of non-response to the accuracy of inferences which could be made from the PISA data.

The strength of the evidence that the Consortium required to consider a country's sample as sufficiently *representative* is directly related to distance of the achieved response rate from the shaded region in the figure.

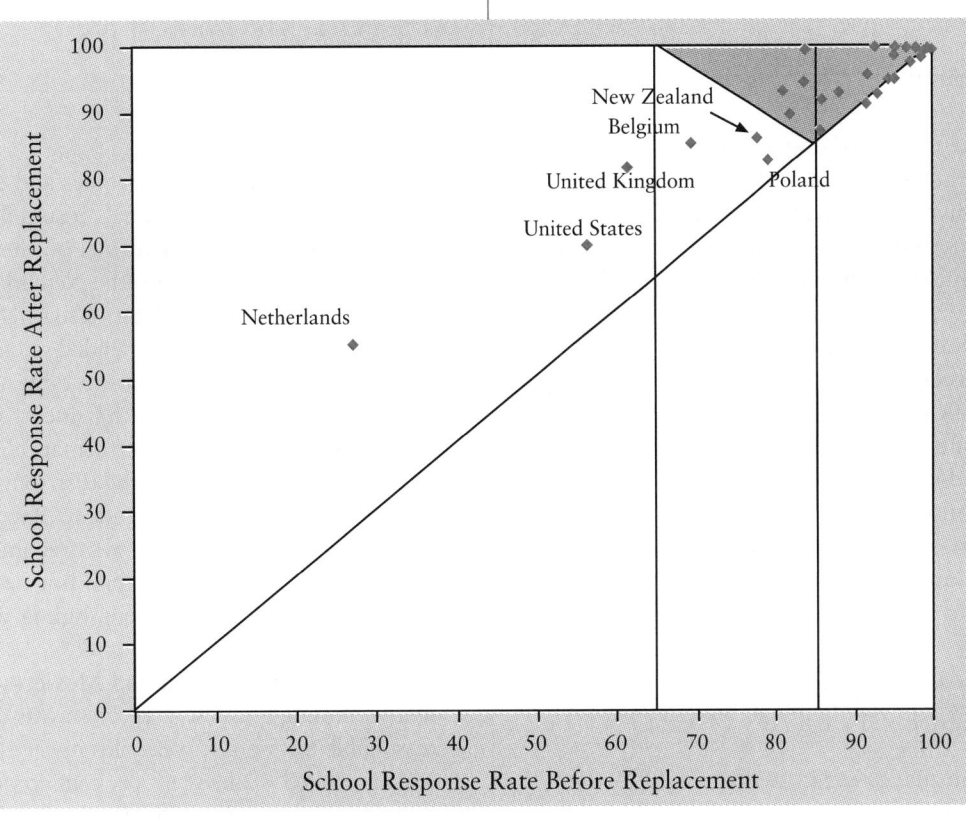

Figure 30: Plot of Attained PISA School Response Rates

FOLLOW-UP DATA ANALYSIS APPROACH

After reviewing the sampling outcomes, the Consortium asked countries falling below the PISA school response rate standards to provide additional data or evidence to determine whether there was a potential bias. Before describing the general statistical approach that the Consortium adopted, it is worth noting that the existence of a potential bias can only be assessed for the variables used in the analyses and does not exclude that the sample is biased with respect to another variable.

In most cases, the Consortium worked with national centres to undertake a range of logistic regression analyses. Logistic regression is widely used for selecting models for variables with only two outcomes. In the analysis recommended by the Consortium, the *dependent* variable is the response or non-response of a particular sampled school. Suppose, for simplicity's sake, that only two characteristics are known for the school—region and urban status. Let Y_{ijk} be the response outcome for the kth school in region i ($i = 1,...,4$) with urban status j ($j = 0,1$). Then define:

Y_{ijk} = 1 if school k participates in the survey,
 = 0 if school k does not participate in the survey.

Under the quasi-randomisation model (see, for example, Oh and Scheuren, 1983), response is modelled as another phase of sampling, assuming that the Y_{ijk} are independent random variables, with probability p_{ijk} for outcome 1 and probability $1 - p_{ijk}$ for outcome 0. p_{ijk} is the school's probability of response, or its response propensity.

The logistic regression model goes a step beyond this to model p_{ijk} and is specified as follows:

$$\ln\left(\frac{p_{ijk}}{1-p_{ijk}}\right) = \mu + \alpha_i + \beta_j,$$

which is algebraically equivalent to:

$$p_{ijk} = \frac{\exp(\mu + \alpha_i + \beta_j)}{1 + \exp(\mu + \alpha_i + \beta_j)}.$$

The quantity $\left(\dfrac{p_{ijk}}{1-p_{ijk}}\right)$ is the odds that the school participates. A logarithm gives a multiplicative rather than an additive model that is almost universally preferred by practitioners (see, for example, McCullagh and Nelder, 1983). The quantities on the right-hand side of the equation define parameters that are then estimated using maximum likelihood methods.

There is concern that non-response bias may be a significant problem if any of the α_i or β_j terms is substantial since this indicates that region and/or urban status are associated with non-response.

Countries occasionally also provided other statistical analyses in addition to or in place of the logistic regression analysis.

REVIEW OF COMPLIANCE WITH OTHER STANDARDS

It is important to recognise that the PISA data adjudication is a late but not necessarily final step in a quality assurance process. By the time each country was adjudicated, quality assurance mechanisms (such as the sampling procedures documentation, translation verification, data cleaning and site visits) had identified a range of issues and ensured that they had been rectified—at least in the majority of cases.

Details on the various quality assurance procedures and their outcomes are documented elsewhere (*see Chapter 7* and *Appendix 5*). Data adjudication focused on residual issues that remained after these quality assurance processes. There were not many such issues and their projected impact on the validity of the PISA results was deemed to be negligible.

Unlike sampling issues, which under most circumstances could directly affect all of a country's data, the residual issues identified in other areas have an impact on only a small proportion of the data. For example, marking leniency or severity for a single item in reading has an effect on between just one-third and one-half of 1 per cent of the reading data—and even for that small fraction, the effect would be minor.

DETAILED COUNTRY COMMENTS

SUMMARY

Concerns with sampling outcomes and compliance problems with PISA standards resulted in recommendations to place constraints on the use of the data for just two countries—the Netherlands and Japan. The Netherlands' response rate was very low. It was therefore recommended to exclude the data from the Netherlands from tables and charts in the international reports that focus on the level or distribution of student performance in one or more PISA domain, or on the distribution of a characteristic of schools or students. Japan sampled intact classes of students. It was recommended, therefore, that data from Japan not be included in analyses that require disentangling variance components.

Two countries—Brazil and Mexico—had noteworthy coverage issues. In Brazil, it was deemed unreasonable to assess 15-year-olds in very low grades, which resulted in about 69 per cent coverage of the 15-year-old population. In Mexico, just 52 per cent of 15-year-olds are enrolled in schools—much lower than all other participating countries.

In two countries—Luxembourg and Poland—higher than desirable exclusions were noted. Luxembourg had a school-level exclusion rate of 9.1 per cent. The majority of these excluded students (6.5 per cent) were instructed in languages other than the PISA test languages. In Poland, primary schools accounting for approximately 7 per cent of the population were excluded.

For all other participants, the problems identified and discussed below were judged to be sufficiently small that their impact on comparability was negligible.

AUSTRALIA

A minor problem occurred in Australia in that six (of 228) schools would not permit a sample to be selected from among all PISA-eligible students, but restricted it in some way, generally by limiting it to those students within the modal grade. Weighting adjustments were made to partially compensate for this. This problem was therefore not regarded as significant and Australia fully met the PISA standards, so that inclusion in the full range of PISA reports was recommended.

AUSTRIA

In Austria, students in vocational schools are enrolled on a part-time/part-year basis. Since the PISA assessment was conducted only at one point in time, these students are captured only partially. Thus, it is not possible to assess how well the students sampled from vocational schools represent the universe of students enrolled in vocational schools, and so those students not attending classes a the time of the PISA assessment are not represented in the PISA results.

Additionally, Austria did not follow the correct procedure for sampling small schools. This led to a need to trim the weights. Consequently, small schools may be slightly under-represented. It was concluded that any effect of this under-representation would be very slight, and the data were therefore suitable for inclusion in the full range of PISA reports.

BELGIUM

The school-weighted participation rate for the Flemish Community of Belgium was quite low: 61.5 per cent before replacement and 79.8 per cent after replacement. However the French Community of Belgium was very close to the international standard before replacement (79.9 per cent) and easily reached the standard after replacement (93.7 per cent). For Belgium as a whole, the weighted school participation rate before replacement was 69.1 per cent and 85.5 per cent after replacement. Belgium did, therefore, not quite meet the school response rate requirements.

The German-speaking community, which accounts for about 1 per cent of the PISA population, did not participate.[2] As the school response rate was below the PISA 2000 standard, additional evidence was sought from the Flemish Community of Belgium with regard to the representativeness of its sample. The Flemish community provided additional data which included a full list of schools (sampling frame) containing the following information on each school:

- whether it had been sampled;
- whether it was a replacement;
- its stratum membership;
- participation status; and
- percentage of over-aged students.

In Belgium, compulsory education starts for all children in the calendar year of the child's sixth birthday. Thus, the student's expected grade can be computed from knowing the birth date.

The Belgian educational systems use grade retention to increase the homogeneity of student abilities within each class. In most cases, a student who does not reach the expected performance level will not graduate to the next grade. Therefore, a comparison of the expected and actual grade provides an indication of student performance.

Table 70 gives the performance on the combined reading literacy scale for the three most frequent grades in the Flemish student sample and the percentage of 15-year-olds attending them.

Table 70: Performance in Reading by Grade in the Flemish Community of Belgium

Grade	Percentage of Students	Reading Performance
8	2.5	363.5
9	22.8	454.7
10	72.2	564.3

The unweighted correlation between school mean performance for the combined reading literacy scale and the percentage of over-aged students is equal to –0.89. The school percentage of over-aged students constitutes a powerful surrogate of the school mean performance, and was therefore used to see if student achievement in responding schools was likely to be systematically different from that in non-responding schools.

Table 71 shows the mean of the school over-aged percentages according to school participation status and sample status (original or replacement). The data used to compute these results are based only on regular schools. Data from special education schools and part-time education schools were not included because all originally sampled students from these strata participated in PISA.

---

[2] In fact, a sample of students from the German-speaking community was tested, but the data were not submitted to the international Consortium.

Table 71: Average of the School Percentage of Over-Aged Students

School Sample and Participation Status	Number of Schools	Mean Percentage
Original sample	145	0.288
All participating schools	119	0.262
Participating schools from the original sample	88	0.255
Non-participating schools from the original sample	57	0.340

The data included in Table 71 show that schools with lower percentages of over-aged students were more likely to participate than schools with higher percentages of over-aged students. It also appears that the addition of replacement schools seems to have reduced the bias introduced by the original schools that refused to participate.

Further, additional analyses showed that the bias was correlated with stratification variables, that is the type of school (academic, technical or vocational) and the school board. The school-level non-response adjustment applied during weighting would thus have reduced the bias.

Given the marginal amount by which Belgium did not meet the sampling criteria, and the success of correcting for potential bias by replacements and non-response adjustments, it was concluded that there was no cause for concern about the potential of significant non-response bias in the PISA sample for Belgium.

It was also noted that the Flemish Community of Belgium did not adhere strictly to the required six-week testing window. All testing sessions were conducted within a three-month testing period and therefore none violated the definition of the target population. Variance analyses were performed according to the testing period and no significant differences were found.

It was concluded that, while Belgium deviated slightly from PISA standards, it could be recommended that the data be used in the full range of PISA analyses and reports.

BRAZIL

In Brazil, 15-year-olds are enrolled in a wide range of grades. It was not deemed appropriate to administer the PISA test to students in grades 1 to 4. This decision was made in consultation with Brazil and the Consortium and resulted in about 69 per cent coverage of the 15-year-old population.

For many secondary schools in Brazil, an additional sampling stage was created between the school and student selection. Many secondary schools operate in three shifts—morning, afternoon and evening. An approved sampling procedure was developed that permitted the selection of one shift (or two if there was a small shift) at random, with 20 students being selected from the selected shifts.

Weighting factors were applied to the student data to reflect this stage of sampling. Thus, if one shift was selected in a school, the student data were assigned a factor of three in addition to the school and student base weight components. After weighting, the weighted total student population was considerably in excess of the PISA population size as measured by official enrolment statistics. It was concluded that, in many cases, either or both of the following occurred: the shift sampling was not carried out according to the procedures; or the data on student numbers within each school reflected the whole school and not just the selected shifts. Since which errors occurred in which schools could not be determined, these problems could not be addressed in weighting. However, there was no evidence of a systematic bias in the sampling procedures.

CANADA

Canada fully met the PISA standards, and inclusion in the full range of PISA reports was recommended.

CZECH REPUBLIC

The Czech Republic fully met the PISA standards, and inclusion in the full range of PISA reports was recommended.

DENMARK

Denmark fully met the PISA standards, and inclusion in the full range of PISA reports was recommended.

FINLAND

Finland fully met the PISA standards, and inclusion in the full range of PISA reports was recommended.

FRANCE

France did not supply data on the actual number of students listed for sampling within each school, as required under PISA procedures for calculating student weights. Rather, France provided the current year enrolment figures for enrolled 15-year-olds as recorded at the Ministry. The data showed that the two quantities were sometimes slightly different, but no major discrepancies were detected. Thus, this problem was not regarded as significant.

Results from the inter-country reliability study indicated an unexpectedly high degree of variation in national ratings of open-ended items. The inter-country reliability study showed that agreement between national markers and international verifiers was 80.2 per cent—the lowest level of agreement among all PISA participants. Of the remaining 19.8 per cent, 12.5 per cent of the ratings were found to be inconsistent, 2.3 per cent too harsh and 5.0 per cent too lenient.

Given that this rater inconsistency was likely to affect only a small proportion of items, and because the disagreement included both harshness and leniency deviations, it was concluded that no systematic bias would exist in scale scores and that the data could be recommended for inclusion in the full range of PISA reports.

GERMANY

Germany fully met the PISA standards, and inclusion in the full range of PISA reports was recommended.

GREECE

The sampling frame for Greece had deficient data on the number of 15-year-olds in each school. This resulted in selecting many schools in the sample with no 15-year-olds enrolled, or that were closed (34 of a sample of 175 schools). Often the replacement school was then included, which was not the correct PISA procedure for such cases. Also quite a few sampled schools (a further 34) had relatively few 15-year-olds. Rather than being assessed or excluded, these schools were also replaced, often by larger schools. This resulted in some degree of over-coverage in the PISA sample, as there were 18 replacement schools in the sample for schools that should not have been replaced, and 32 replacements for small schools where the replacement was generally larger than the school it replaced. It is not possible to evaluate what kinds of students might be over-represented, but since the measures of size were unreliable, this is unlikely to result in any systematic bias. Thus, this problem was not regarded as significant, and inclusion in the full range of PISA reports was recommended.

HUNGARY

Hungary did not strictly follow the correct procedure for the sampling of small schools. However, this had very little negative impact on sample quality and thus inclusion in the full range of PISA reports was recommended.

ICELAND

Iceland fully met the PISA standards, and inclusion in the full range of PISA reports was recommended.

IRELAND

Ireland fully met the PISA standards, and inclusion in the full range of PISA reports was recommended.

ITALY

Italy fully met the PISA standards, and inclusion in the full range of PISA reports was recommended.

JAPAN

The translation of the assessment material in Japan was somewhat deficient. A rather high number of flawed items was observed in both the field trial and main study. However, careful examination of item-by-country interactions and discussion with the Japanese centre resulted in the omission of only one item (*see Figure 25*), where there was a problematic interaction. No remaining potential problem led to detectable item-by-country interactions.

Japan did not follow the PISA 2000 design, which required sampling students rather than classes in each school. This means that the between-class and between-school variance components will be confounded. The Japanese sample is suitable for PISA analyses that do not involve disentangling school and class variance components, but it cannot be used in a range of multilevel analyses.

It was recommended, therefore, not to include data from Japan in analyses that require disentangling variance components, but the data can be included in all other analyses and reports.

KOREA

Korea used non-standard translation procedures, which resulted in a few anomalies. When reviewing items for inclusion or exclusion in the scaling of PISA data (based upon psychometric criteria), the items were carefully reviewed for potential aberrant behaviour because of translation errors. Four reading items were deleted because of potential problems, and the remaining data were recommended for inclusion in the full range of PISA reports.

LATVIA

Latvia did not follow the PISA 2000 translation guidelines, and the international coding study showed many inconsistencies between coding in Latvia and international coding. In the inter-country reliability study, the agreement between national markers and international verifiers was 80.6 per cent. Of the remaining 19.4 per cent, 2.5 per cent of the ratings were found to be too harsh and 9.4 per cent too lenient. These results may be due to the fact that the marking guide was not translated into Latvian on the assumption that all markers were sufficiently proficient in English to use its English version.

Since this rater inconsistency was likely to affect only a small proportion of items, and because the disagreements included both harshness and leniency deviations, it was concluded that the data could be recommended for inclusion in the full range of PISA reports.

LIECHTENSTEIN

Liechtenstein fully met the PISA standards, and inclusion in the full range of PISA reports was recommended.

LUXEMBOURG

The school level exclusion rate of 9.1 per cent in Luxembourg was somewhat higher than the PISA requirements. The majority of excluded students (6.5 per cent) were instructed in languages other than the PISA test languages (French and German) and attended the European School. As this deviation was judged to have no marked effect on the results, it was concluded that Luxembourg could be included in the full range of PISA reports.

MEXICO

Mexico fully met the PISA standards, and inclusion in the full range of PISA reports was recommended. However, the proportion of 15-year-olds enrolled in schools in Mexico was much lower than in all other participating countries (52 per cent).

NETHERLANDS

The international design and methodology were well implemented in the Netherlands. Unfortunately, school participation rates were not acceptable. Though the initial rate of 27.2 per cent was far below the requirement to even consider replacement (65 per cent), the Netherlands was allowed to try to reach an acceptable response rate through replacements. However, the percentage after replacement (55.6 per cent) was still considerably below the standard required.

The Consortium undertook a range of supplementary analyses jointly with the NPM in the Netherlands, which confirmed that the data might be sufficiently reliable to be used in some relational analyses. The very low response rate, however, implied that the results from the PISA data for the Netherlands cannot, with any confidence, be expected to reflect the national population to the level of accuracy and precision required. This concern extends particularly to distribution and sub-group information about achievement.

The upper secondary educational system in the Netherlands consists of five distinct tracks. VWO is the most academic track, and on a continuum through general to vocational education, tracks are HAVO, MAVO, and (I)VBO. Many schools offer more than one track, but few offer all four. Thus, for example, of the 95 schools that participated in PISA which could be matched to the national database of examination results, 38 offered (I)VBO, 76 offered MAVO, 64 offered HAVO and 66 offered VWO. Each part of the analysis therefore applied to only a sub-set of the schools.

Depending upon the track, students take these examinations at the end of grades 10, 11, or 12. The PISA population was mostly enrolled in grades 9 and 10 in 2000 (and thus is neither the same cohort, nor, generally, at the same educational level as the population for which national examination results are available). The school populations for these two groups of students, however, are the same.

To examine the characteristics of the PISA 2000 sample in the Netherlands (at the school level), the NPM was able to access the results of national examinations in 1999. Data from national examinations were combined for the two vocational tracks (IVBO and VBO), but other than this combination, available data were not comparable across tracks, which made it difficult to develop overall summaries of the quality of the PISA school sample. The analyses of data showed two types of outcomes. The first dealt with the percentage of students taking at least three subjects at C or D level[3] in the (I)VBO track. This analysis provided some evidence that, when compared to the original sample, the participating schools had a lower percentage of such students than the non-participants and the rest of the population. However, there were only 18 participants of 69 in the sample, and so the discrepancy was not statistically significant. There is evidence that the inclusion of the replacement schools (20 participated) effectively removed any such imbalance. Since this track covers only about 40 per cent of the schools in the population and sample, little emphasis was placed on this result.

A second analysis was made of the average grade point of the national examinations for each school and for each track, overall and for several subject groupings. The average grade point average across Dutch language, mathematics and science was used. The results are available for each track, but are not comparable across tracks (as evidenced, for example, by the fact that students take the examinations at different grades in different tracks).

For the (I)VBO track, the average grade point across all subjects is 6.17 for PISA participants and 6.29 for the rest of the population, a difference of about 0.375 standard deviations, that is statistically significant ($p = 0.034$). This phenomenon is not reflected in the results for Dutch language, but is seen also in the results for mathematics and science. Here the mean for participants is 5.83, and 6.03 for the rest of the population. This difference is about 0.45 standard deviations, and is statistically significant ($p = 0.009$). These results suggest that PISA data may somewhat under-estimate the overall proficiency of students in the Netherlands, at least for mathematics and science.

In the VWO track, the population variance of the PISA participants is considerably smaller than for the rest of the population, for all subjects combined, for Dutch language, and for mathematics and science. Thus the PISA participants appeared to be a considerably more homogeneous group of schools than the population as a whole, even though their mean achievement is only trivially different. Thus, the variance of the rest of the population is 76 per cent higher than the PISA participants for all subjects combined, 39 per cent higher for Dutch language, and 93 per cent higher for mathematics and science. This is also seen in the HAVO track for all subjects and for Dutch language, and the MAVO track for mathematics and science. These results suggest that the Dutch PISA data might well show a somewhat more homogeneous distribution of student achievement than is true for the whole population, thus leading to biased estimates of population quantiles, percentages above various cut-off points, and sub-group comparisons.

Considering the extent of sample non-response, it was noted that the results of this analysis did show a high degree of similarity between participating schools and the rest of the population on the one hand, and the non-participants on the other. However, since the response rate is so low, even minor differences between these groups are of concern.

An additional factor to consider in judging the quality of the PISA sample for the Netherlands is the actual sample size of students in the PISA data file. PISA targeted a minimum of 4 500 assessed students for each country. Not all countries quite reached this target, primarily because of

---

[3] Difficulty levels in the national examinations.

low levels of school participation, but the sample size for the Netherlands is only 56 per cent of this target (2 503 students). Bias considerations aside, the sample cannot therefore give results to the level of precision envisaged in specifying the PISA design. This is especially serious for mathematics and science, since, by design, only 55.6 per cent of the PISA sample were assessed in each of these subjects.

In summary, it was concluded that the results from the Netherlands PISA sample may not have been grossly distorted by school non-participation. In fact the correspondence in achievement on national examinations between the participants and the population is remarkably high given the high level of non-participation. However, the high level of school non-participation means that even reasonably minor differences between the participants and the intended sample can mean that the non-response bias might significantly affect the results. The findings of follow-up analyses above, together with the low participation rate and the small final sample size, meant that the Consortium could not have confidence that the results from the PISA data for the Netherlands reflected the national population to the level of accuracy and precision called for in PISA, particularly for distribution and sub-group information about achievement.

It was recommended, therefore, to exclude data from the Netherlands from tables and charts in the international reports that focus on the level or distribution of student performance in one or more of the PISA domains, or on the distribution of a characteristic of schools or students. Data from the Netherlands could be included in the international database and the Netherlands could be included in tables or charts that focus primarily on relationships between PISA background variables and student performance.

NEW ZEALAND

The before-replacement response rate in New Zealand was 77.7 per cent, and the after-replacement response rate was 86.4 per cent, slightly short of the PISA 2000 standards.

Non-response bias in New Zealand was examined by looking at national English assessment results for Year 11 students in all schools, where 87.6 per cent of the PISA population can be found.

A logistic regression approach was also adopted by New Zealand to analyse the existence of a potential bias. The dependent variable was the school participation status, and the independent variables in the model were:
- school decile, an aggregate at the school level of the social and economic backgrounds of the students attending the school;
- rural versus urban schools;
- the school sample frame stratification variables, *i.e.*, very small school, certainty[4] or very large schools and other schools;
- Year 11 student marks in English on the national examination; and
- initially, the distinction between public and private schools, but this variable was removed due to the size of the private school population.

Prior to performing the logistic regression, Year 11 student marks were averaged according to school participation status, and (i) school decile, (ii) public versus private school, (iii) rural versus urban school, and (iv) the school size stratification variable from the school sampling frame.

The unweighted logistic regression analyses are summarised in Table 72. There is no evidence that low school response rate introduced bias into the school sample for New Zealand.

Table 72: Results for the New Zealand Logistic Regression

Parameter	Estimate	Chi-Squared	*p*-value
English marks	0.0006	0.0229	0.98
Very small school	-1.3388	1.4861	0.37
Certainty or very large schools	0.5460	0.5351	0.30
Urban	-0.1452	0.4104	0.72

Based on the logistic regression and the sub-group mean achievement, it is possible that students in the responding schools are slightly lower achievers than those in the non-responding schools. But the difference in the average results for responding and non-responding schools was 0.04 standard deviations, which is not

---
[4] Schools with a selection probability of 1.0.

significant. Further, after the effects of the key stratification variables, which were used to make school non-response adjustments, there is no noticeable effect of school mean achievement on PISA participation. Furthermore, there is no evidence that the responding and non-responding schools might differ substantially in their homogeneity (as distinct from the case in the Netherlands).

It was recommended, therefore, that New Zealand data could be included in the full range of PISA reports.

NORWAY

Norway fully met the PISA standards, and inclusion in the full range of PISA reports was recommended.

POLAND

Poland did not follow the international sampling methodology. First, Poland did not follow the guidelines for sampling 15-year-olds in primary schools. Consequently, the small sample of students from these schools, which included approximately 7 per cent of the 15-year-old population, have been excluded from the data. These students were very likely to have been well below the national average in achievement.

Second, Poland extended the testing period, and 14 schools tested outside the three-month testing window that was required to ensure the accurate estimation of student age at testing time. Analysis showed that schools testing outside the window performed better than schools testing inside the window, and the former were dropped from the national database.

Strong evidence was provided that school non-response bias is minimal in the PISA data for Poland, based on the following:
- The majority of school non-response in Poland was not actual school non-response, but the consequence of schools testing too late.
- Schools testing outside the window performed better than those that tested inside the window, which vindicates the decision to omit them from the data, since their higher performance may have been due to the later testing.
- The results with the late schools omitted are about one scale score point lower than they would be had these late schools been included. This indicates that had these schools tested during the window and been included, the results would have been less than one point above the published result. It seems extremely likely that the result would have fallen between the published result and one point higher.
- The bias from the necessary omission of the late assessed schools seems certain to be less than one point, which is insignificant considering the sampling errors involved.
- All non-responding schools (*i.e.*, late-testing schools plus true non-respondents) match the assessed sample well in terms of big city/small city/town/rural representation.

The relatively low level of non-response (*i.e.*, Poland did not fall far below the acceptable standard) indicates that no significant bias has resulted from school non-response.

It was concluded that while the exclusion of the primary schools should be noted, data could be recommended for inclusion in the full range of PISA reports, provided the difference between the target population in Poland and the international target population was clearly noted.

PORTUGAL

Portugal fully met the PISA standards, and inclusion in the full range of PISA reports was recommended.

RUSSIAN FEDERATION

The adjudication noted four concerns about the implementation of PISA 2000 in the Russian Federation. First, material was not translated using the standard procedures recommended in PISA, and the number of flawed items was relatively high in the main study. Second, in the inter-country reliability study, the agreement between national markers and international verifiers was 88.5 per cent, which is just below the 90 per cent required. Of the remaining 11.5 per cent, 0.9 per cent of the ratings were found to be too harsh, 7.0 per cent too lenient and 3.6 per cent inconsistent. The Consortium discussed with the Russian Federation national centre about the possibility of re-scoring the open-ended items but concluded that this would have a negligible effect on country results. In making this assessment, the Consortium carefully examined the psychometric properties of the Russian Federation items and did not identify an unusual number of item-by-country interactions. Third, the Student Tracking Forms did not include students excluded within the school, meaning that it was not possible to estimate the total exclusion rate for the Russian Federation. Fourth, the correct procedure for sampling small schools was not followed which led to a minor requirement to trim the weights, making small schools very slightly under-represented in the weighted data.

It was concluded that while these issues should be noted, the data could be recommended for inclusion in the full range of PISA reports.

SPAIN

Spain did not follow the correct procedure for sampling small schools. This led to a need to trim the weights; small schools consequently may be slightly under-represented. This problem is not regarded as significant, and inclusion in the full range of PISA reports was recommended.

SWEDEN

Sweden fully met the PISA standards, and inclusion in the full range of PISA reports was recommended.

SWITZERLAND

Switzerland included a national option to survey grade 9 students and to over-sample them in some parts of the country. Thus, there were explicit strata containing schools with grade 9, and other strata containing schools with 15-year-olds but no grade 9 students.

From the grade 9 schools, a sample of schools was selected in some strata within which a sample of 50 students was selected from among those in grade 9, plus any other 15-year-olds.

In other strata, where stratum-level estimates for grade 9 students were required from the PISA assessment, a relatively large sample of schools was selected. In a sub-sample of these schools (made via systematic selection), a sample of 50 grade 9 students, plus 15-year-old students, was selected. In the remaining schools, a sample of 35 students was selected from among the grade 9 students only (regardless of their age).

In the strata of schools with no grade 9, a sample of schools was selected, from each of which a sample of 35 15-year-old students was selected.

Thus, the sample contained three groups of students: those in grade 9 aged 15, those in grade 9 not aged 15, and those aged 15 not in grade 9. Within some strata, the students in the third group were sampled at a lower rate (considering the school and student-within-school sampling rates combined) than students in grade 9. The PISA weighting procedure ensured that these differential sampling rates were taken into account when analysing the 15-year-old samples, grade 9 and others combined. This procedure meant that unweighted analyses of PISA data in Switzerland would be very likely to lead to erroneous conclusions, as grade 9 students were over-represented in the sample.

This entire procedure was fully approved and carried out correctly. However, there was a minor problem with school non-response. In one stratum with about 1 per cent of the PISA population in Switzerland, 35 schools in the population had both grade 9 and other 15-year-old students. All 35 schools were included in the grade 9 sample, and a sub-sample of two of the schools was selected to include other 15-year-old students in the sample as well. The school response rate in this stratum was very low. One of the two schools that were to include all 15-year-olds participated, and only three of the other 33 schools participated. This very low response rate (with a big differential between the two parts of the sample) meant that the standard approach to creating school non-response adjustments would not have worked appropriately. Therefore, schools from this explicit stratum had to be combined with those from another stratum to adjust school non-response. The effects on the overall results for Switzerland are very minor, as this stratum is so small.

The translation verifier noted that the Swiss-German version of the material underwent substantial national revisions after the field trial (most of which were not documented), while the changes introduced in the source versions and the corrections suggested by the verifier were often overlooked. As a result, the Swiss-German version differed significantly from the other German versions of the material, and had slightly more flawed items.

It was concluded that none of the deviations from the PISA standards would noticeably affect the results, and inclusion in the full range of PISA reports was recommended.

UNITED KINGDOM

The adjudication revealed three potential problems with data from the United Kingdom. First, schools in Wales were excluded. Second, the school response rate prior to replacement (61.3 per cent) was below the PISA 2000 standard of 65 per cent—the response rate after replacements was 82.1 per cent. Further analyses of the potential for school non-response bias were therefore conducted. Third, test administration procedures in Scotland did not respect the PISA requirements. Test administrators were neither trained nor given an adequate script. This is considered to be a matter of serious concern, but Scotland has only a small percentage of 15-year-olds in the United Kingdom, and this violation did not seriously affect the United Kingdom's results. In addition, student sampling procedures were not correctly implemented in Scotland. The unapproved procedure implemented was dealt with and is very unlikely to have biased the United Kingdom's results, but it did increase the number of absent students in the data.[5]

The potential influence of the exclusion of schools in Wales was considered by comparing the distribution of General Certificate of Secondary Education (GCSE) results for England and Wales. The comparison showed that the distribution of achievement in Wales is essentially the same as in England. Further, since Wales has only 5.1 per cent of the United Kingdom's population, while England has 82.4 per cent, it did not seem credible that the distribution in Wales could be so different as to add a noticeable bias.

The primary source of the problems with school response was in England, where the response rate before replacement was 58.8 per cent. The NPM therefore carried out some regression analyses in order to examine which factors were associated with school non-response (prior to replacement) in England. The possibility of bias in the initial sample of schools, before replacement of refusing schools, was examined by evaluating independent variables as predictors of school non-response. These included educational outcomes of the schools at GCSE level (public examinations taken at age 16); and socio-economic status as measured by the percentage of pupils eligible for free school meals—a widely accepted measure of poverty in education studies in England.

In addition, sample stratification variables were included in the models. Since these were used to make school non-response adjustments, the relevant question is whether GCSE level and the percentage of students eligible for free meals at school are associated with school response when they are also included in the model.

The conclusions were that, in view of the small coefficients for the response status variable and their lack of statistical significance ($p = 0.426$ and 0.150, respectively), there was no substantial evidence of non-response bias in terms of the GCSE average point score (in particular), or of the percentage of students eligible for free school meals. Participating schools were estimated to have a mean GCSE level only 0.734 units higher than those that did not, and a percentage of students eligible for free school meals that was only 0.298 per cent lower.

A further potential problem, in addition to the three discussed above, was that 11 schools (of 349) restricted the sample of PISA-eligible students in some way, generally by limiting it to those students in the lower of the two grades with PISA-eligible students. However, weighting adjustments were able to partially compensate for this.

It was concluded that while these issues should be noted, the data could be recommended for inclusion in the full range of PISA reports.

UNITED STATES

The before-replacement response rate in the Unites States was 56.4 per cent, and the after-replacement response rate was 70.3 per cent, which fell short of the PISA 2000 standards. The NPM explored this matter extensively with the Consortium and provided data as evidence that the achieved sample was representative.

It was not possible to check for systematic differences in the assessment results as the United States had no assessment data from the non-responding schools, but it was possible to

---

[5] Scotland sampled 35 students from each school. The first 30 students were supposed to be tested and the last five students were considered as replacement students if one or more students could not attend the testing session. The Consortium dealt with this deviation by regarding all sampled students who were not tested as absentees/refusals.

check for systematic differences in the school characteristics data available for both the responding and non-responding schools. It is well known from past surveys in the United States that characteristics such as region, urban status, percentage of minorities, public/private status, etc., are correlated with achievement, so that systematic differences in them are likely to indicate the presence of potential bias in assessment estimates.

The potential predictors for school non-participation evaluated in the additional analysis provided by the United States are:
- NAEP region (Northeast, Midwest, South, West);
- urban status (urban or non-urban area);
- public/private status;
- school type (public, Catholic, non-Catholic religious, non-religious private, Department of Defense);
- minority percentage category (less than 4 per cent, 4 to 18 per cent, 18 to 34 per cent, 34 to 69 per cent, higher than 69 per cent);
- percentage eligible for school lunch (less than 13.85 per cent, 13.85 to 37.1 per cent, higher than 37.1 per cent, missing);
- estimated number of 15-year-olds; and
- school grade-span (junior high: low grade, 7th and high grade, 9th; high school: low grade, 9th; middle school: low grade, 4th and high grade, 8th; combined school: all others).

Each characteristic was chosen because it was available for both participating and non-participating schools, and because in past surveys it was found to be linked to response propensity.

The analysis began with a series of logistic regression models that included NAEP region, urban status, and each of the remaining predictors individually in turn. Region and urban status were included in each model because they have historically been correlated with school participation and are generally used to define cells for non-response adjustments. The remaining predictors were then evaluated with region and urban status already included in the model. A model with all predictors was also fitted.

In most models, the South and Northeast region parameters were significant at the 0.05-level. The *p*-value for urban status was significant at the 0.10-level, except in the model containing all predictors.

The other important predictors were percentage of minority students and percentage of students eligible for free lunches. The schools with 34 to 69 per cent minority students were signif-icantly more likely to refuse to participate than schools with more than 69 per cent minority students (*p* = 0.0072). The 18 to 34 per cent minority student category also had a relatively small *p*-value: 0.0857. Two of the categories of percentage of students eligible for free lunches had *p*-values around 0.10. In the final model that included all predictors, the percentage of minority students and percentage of students eligible for free lunches proved to be the most important predictors. These results are confirmed in the model selection analysis presented below.

After fitting a logistic regression model with all potential predictors, three types of model selection were performed to select significant predictors: backward, forward, and stepwise.[6] For this analysis, all three model-selection procedures chose the same four predictors: NAEP region, urban status, percentage of minority students, and percentage of students eligible for free lunches. The parameter estimates, chi-square statistics and *p*-values for this final model are shown in Table 73.

The non-response analyses did find differences in the distribution between respondents and non-respondents on several of the school characteristics.

---

[6] The dependent variable again was the school's participation status. These techniques all select a set of predictor variables from a larger set of candidates. In backward selection, a model is fitted using all the candidate variables. Significance levels are then checked for all predictors. If any level is greater than the cut-off value (0.05 for this analysis), one predictor is dropped from the model—the one with the greatest *p*-value (*i.e.*, the least significant predictor). The procedure then iteratively checks the remaining set of predictors, dropping the least powerful predictor if any are above the cut-off value. NAEP region and urban status were not *allowed* to be dropped. The procedure stops when all remaining predictors have *p*-values smaller than the cut-off value. Forward selection works in a similar fashion, but starts with only the intercept term and any effects forced into the model. It then adds to the model the predictor with the next highest level of significance, as computed by the score chi-squared statistic. The process continues until no effect meets the required level of significance. An effect is never removed once it has entered the model.

Stepwise selection begins like forward selection, but the effects do not necessarily remain in the model once they are entered. A forward selection step may be followed by a backwards elimination step if an effect is no longer significant in the company of a newly-entered effect.

As expected, region and urban status were found to be predictors of response status. In addition, the percentage of minority students and percentage of students eligible for free lunches were also important predictors. Since they are often correlated with achievement, assuming that school non-response is a random occurrence could lead to bias in assessment estimates.

The school non-response adjustment has incorporated these two additional predictors along with region and urban status in defining the adjustment cells. Defining the cells in this way distributes the weight of non-participating schools to 'similar' (in terms of characteristics known for all schools) participating schools, which reduces the potential bias due to lack of assessment in non-participating schools. However, there is no way to completely eliminate all potential non-response bias because assessment information is not available from schools that do not participate.

There is also a strong, but highly non-linear, relationship with minority (black and Hispanic) enrolment. Schools with relatively high and relatively low minority enrolments were considerably more likely to participate than those with intermediate levels of minority enrolment. The implications for the direction of the bias are not clear. Other characteristics examined do not show a discernible relationship.

Many of the 145 participating schools restricted the sample of PISA-eligible students in some way, generally by limiting it to students within the modal grade. Weighting adjustments were made to partially compensate for this. Schools that surveyed the modal grade (10) were treated as respondents in calculating the weighted response rates, while those that did not permit testing of grade 10 students were handled as non-respondents for calculating school response rates, but their student data were included in the database.

It was concluded that while these issues should be noted, the data could be recommended for inclusion in the full range of PISA reports.

Table 73: Results for the United States Logistic Regression

Parameter	Estimate	Chi-Squared	*p*-value
Northeast region	0.4890	2.7623	0.0965
Midwest region	0.3213	1.1957	0.2742
South region	-0.7919	4.7966	0.0285
(West region)	-	-	-
Urban area	-0.3644	2.6241	0.1053
(Non-urban area)	-	-	-
Less than 4% minority	-0.6871	2.7699	0.0960
4-18% minority	-0.2607	0.5384	0.4631
18-34% minority	0.6348	3.8064	0.0511
34-69% minority	1.3001	13.5852	0.0002
(Greater than 69% minority)	-	-	-
Missing free lunch eligibility	0.5443	3.1671	0.0751
≤ 13.85% free lunch eligibility	0.6531	3.6340	0.0566
13.85-37.1% free lunch eligibility	-1.0559	10.329	0.0013

SECTION FIVE: SCALE CONSTRUCTION AND DATA PRODUCTS

CHAPTER 16 { PROFICIENCY SCALES CONSTRUCTION

Ross Turner

INTRODUCTION

PISA seeks to report outcomes in terms of proficiency scales that are based on scientific theory and that are interpretable in policy terms. There are two further considerations for the development of the scales and levels:

- PISA must provide a single score for each country for each of the three domains. It is also recognised that multiple scales might be useful for certain purposes, and the development of these has been considered alongside the need for a single scale.
- The proficiency descriptions must shed light on trends over time. The amount of data available to support the detailed development of proficiency descriptions varies, depending on whether a particular domain is a 'major' or 'minor' domain for any particular survey cycle. Decisions about scale development need to recognise this variation, and must facilitate the description of any changes in proficiency levels achieved by countries from one survey cycle to the next.

Development of a method for describing proficiency in PISA reading, mathematical and scientific literacy took place over more than a year, in order to prepare for the reporting of outcomes of the PISA 2000 surveys. The three Functional Expert Groups (FEGs) (for reading, mathematics and science) worked with the Consortium to develop sets of described proficiency scales for the three PISA 2000 test domains. Consultations of the Board of Participating Countries (BPC), National Project Managers (NPMs) and the PISA Technical Advisory Group (TAG) took place over several stages. The sets of described scales were presented to the BPC for approval in April 2001. This chapter presents the outcomes of this process.

DEVELOPMENT OF THE DESCRIBED SCALES

The development of described proficiency scales for PISA was carried out through a process involving a number of stages. The stages are described here in a linear fashion, but in reality the development process involved some backwards and forwards movement where stages were revisited and descriptions were progressively refined. Essentially the same development process was used in each of the three domains.

STAGE 1: IDENTIFYING POSSIBLE SUB-SCALES

The first stage in the process involved the experts in each domain articulating possible reporting scales (dimensions) for the domain.

For reading, two main options were actively considered. These were scales based on two possible groupings of the five 'aspects' of reading (retrieving information; forming a broad understanding; developing an interpretation; reflecting on content; and reflecting on the form of a text).[1]

In the case of mathematics, a single proficiency scale was proposed, though the

---

[1] While strictly speaking the scales based on aspects of reading are sub-scales of the combined reading literacy scale, for simplicity they are mostly referred to as 'scales' rather than 'sub-scales' in this report.

possibility of reporting according to the 'big ideas' or the 'competency classes' described in the PISA mathematics framework was also considered. This option is likely to be further explored in PISA 2003 when mathematics is the major domain.

For science, a single overall proficiency scale was proposed by the FEG. There was interest in considering two sub-scales, for 'scientific knowledge' and 'scientific processes', but the small number of items in PISA 2000, when science was a minor domain, meant that this was not possible. Instead, these aspects were built into descriptions of a single scale.

Wherever multiple scales were under consideration, they arose clearly from the framework for the domain, they were seen to be meaningful and potentially useful for feedback and reporting purposes, and they needed to be defensible with respect to their measurement properties.

Because of the longitudinal nature of the PISA project, the decision about the number and nature of reporting scales had to take into account the fact that in some test cycles a domain will be treated as 'minor' and in other cycles as 'major'. The amount of data available to support the development of described proficiency scales will vary from cycle to cycle for each domain, but the BPC expects proficiency scales that can be compared across cycles.

STAGE 2: ASSIGNING ITEMS TO SCALES

The second stage in the process was to review the association of each item in the main study with each of the scales under consideration. This was done with the involvement of the subject-matter FEGs, the test developers and Consortium staff, and other selected experts (for example, some NPMs were involved). The statistical analysis of item scores from the field trial was also useful in identifying the degree to which items allocated to each sub-scale fitted within that scale, and in validating the work of the domain experts.

STAGE 3: SKILLS AUDIT

The next stage involved a detailed expert analysis of each item, and in the case of items with partial credit, for each score step within the item, in relation to the definition of the relevant sub-scale from the domain framework. The skills and knowledge required to achieve each score step were identified and described.

This stage involved negotiation and discussion among the interested players, circulation of draft material, and progressive refinement of drafts on the basis of expert input and feedback.

STAGE 4: ANALYSING FIELD TRIAL DATA

For each set of scales being considered, the field trial data for those items that were subsequently selected for the main study were analysed using item response techniques to derive difficulty estimates for each achievement threshold for each item in each sub-scale.

Many items had a single achievement threshold (associated with getting the item right rather than wrong). Where partial credit was available, more than one achievement threshold could be calculated (achieving a score of one or more rather than zero, two or more rather than one, etc.).

Within each sub-scale, achievement thresholds were placed along a difficulty continuum linked directly to student abilities. This analysis gives an indication of the utility of each scale from a measurement perspective (*for examples, see Figures 22, 23 and 24*).

STAGE 5: DEFINING THE DIMENSIONS

The information from the domain-specific expert analysis (Stage 3) and the statistical analysis (Stage 4) was combined. For each set of scales being considered, the item score steps were ordered according to the size of their associated thresholds and then linked with the descriptions of associated knowledge and skills, giving a hierarchy of knowledge and skills that defined the dimension. Natural clusters of skills were found using this approach, which provided a basis for understanding each dimension and describing proficiency levels.

STAGE 6: REVISING AND REFINING MAIN STUDY DATA

When the main study data became available, the information arising from the statistical analysis about the relative difficulty of item thresholds was updated. This enabled a review and revision of Stage 5 by the working groups, FEGs and other interested parties. The preliminary descriptions and levels were then reviewed and revised in the light of further technical information that was provided by the Technical Advisory Group, and an approach to defining levels and associating students with those levels that had arisen from discussion between the Consortium and the OECD Secretariat was implemented.

STAGE 7: VALIDATING

Two major approaches to validation were then considered and used to varying degrees by the three working groups. One method was to provide knowledgeable experts (*e.g.*, teachers, or members of the subject matter expert groups) with material that enabled them to judge PISA items against the described levels, or against a set of indicators that underpinned the described levels. Some use of such a process was made, and further validation exercises of this kind may be used in the future. Second, the described scales were subjected to an extensive consultation process involving all PISA countries through their NPMs This approach to validation rests on the extent to which users of the described scales find them informative.

DEFINING PROFICIENCY LEVELS

Developing described proficiency levels progressed in two broad phases. The first, which came after the development of the described scales, was based on a substantive analysis of PISA items in relation to the aspects of literacy that underpinned each test domain. This produced proficiency levels that reflected observations of student performance and a detailed analysis of the cognitive demands of PISA items. The second phase involved decisions about where to set cut-off points for levels and how to associate students with each level. This is both a technical and very practical matter of interpreting what it means to 'be at a level', and has very significant consequences for reporting national and international results.

Several principles were considered for developing and establishing a useful meaning for 'being at a level', and therefore for determining an approach to locating cut-off points between levels and associating students with them:

- A 'common understanding' of the meaning of levels should be developed and promoted. First, it is important to understand that the literacy skills measured in PISA must be considered as continua: there are no natural breaking points to mark borderlines between stages along these continua. Dividing each of these continua into levels, though useful for communication about students' development, is essentially arbitrary. Like the definition of units on, for example, a scale of length, there is no fundamental difference between 1 metre and 1.5 metres—it is a matter of degree. It is useful, however, to define stages, or levels along the continua, because they enable us to communicate about the proficiency of students in terms other than numbers. The approach adopted for PISA 2000 was that it would only be useful to regard students as having attained a particular level if this would mean that we can have certain expectations about what these students are capable of in general when they are said to be at that level. It was decided that this expectation would have to mean *at a minimum* that students at a particular level would be more likely to solve tasks at that level than to fail them. By implication, it must be expected that they would get at least half of the items correct on a test composed of items uniformly spread across that level, which is useful in helping to interpret the proficiency of students at different points across the proficiency range defined at each level.

- For example, students at the bottom of a level would complete at least 50 per cent of tasks correctly on a test set at the level, while students at the middle and top of each level would be expected to achieve a much higher success rate. At the top end of the bandwidth of a level would be the students who are 'masters' of that level. These students would be likely to solve about 80 per cent of the tasks at that level. But, being at the top border of that level, they would also be at the bottom border of the next level up, where according to the reasoning here they should have a likelihood of at least 50 per cent of solving any tasks defined to be at that higher level.

- Further, the meaning of *being at a level* for a given scale should be more or less consistent for each level. In other words, to the extent possible within the substantively based definition and description of levels, cut-off points should create levels of more or less constant breadth. Some small variation may be appropriate, but in order for interpretation and definition of cut-off points and levels to be consistent, the levels have to be about equally broad. Clearly this would not apply to the highest and lowest proficiency levels, which are unbounded.
- A more or less consistent approach should be taken to defining levels for the different scales. Their breadth may not be exactly the same for each proficiency scale, but the same kind of interpretation should be possible for each scale that is developed.

A way of implementing these principles was developed. This method links the two variables mentioned in the preceding paragraphs, and a third related variable. The three variables can be expressed as follows:

- the expected success of a student at a particular level on a test containing items at that level (proposed to be set at a minimum that is near 50 per cent for the student at the bottom of the level, and higher for other students in the level);
- the width of the levels in that scale (determined largely by substantive considerations of the cognitive demands of items at the level and observations of student performance on the items); and
- the probability that a student in the middle of a level would correctly answer an item of average difficulty for that level (in fact, the probability that a student at any particular level would get an item at the same level correct), sometimes referred to as the 'RP-value' for the scale (where 'RP' indicates 'response probability').

Figure 31 summarises the relationship among these three mathematically linked variables. It shows a vertical line representing a part of the scale being defined, one of the bounded levels on the scale, a student at both the top and the bottom of the level, and reference to an item at the top and an item at the bottom of the level. Dotted lines connecting the students and items are labelled P=? to indicate the probability associated with that student correctly responding to that item.

PISA 2000 implemented the following solution: start with the substantively determined range of abilities for each bounded level in each scale (the desired band breadth); then determine the highest possible RP value that will be common across domains—that would give effect to the broad interpretation of the meaning of 'being at a level' (an expectation of correctly responding to a minimum of 50 per cent of the items in a test at that level).

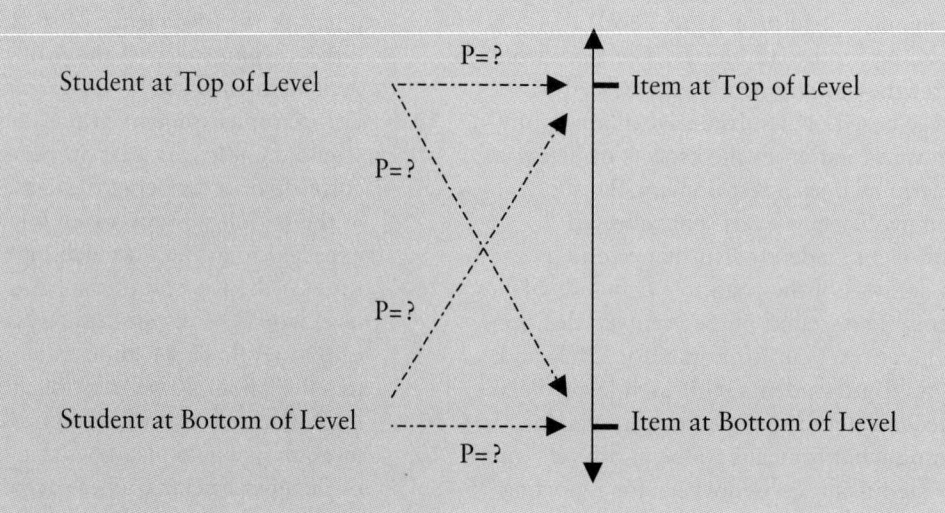

Figure 31: What it Means to be at a Level

After doing this, the exact average percentage of correct answers on a test composed of items at a level could vary slightly among the different domains, but will always be at least 50 per cent at the bottom of the level.

The highest and lowest described levels are unbounded. For a certain high point on the scale and below a certain low point, the proficiency descriptions could, arguably, cease to be applicable. At the high end of the scale, this is not such a problem since extremely proficient students could reasonably be assumed to be capable of at least the achievements described for the highest level. At the other end of the scale, however, the same argument does not hold. A lower limit therefore needs to be determined for the lowest described level, below which no meaningful description of proficiency is possible.

As levels 2, 3 and 4 (within a domain) will be equally broad, it was proposed that the floor of the lowest described level be placed at this *breadth* below the upper boundary of level 1 (that is, the cut-off between levels 1 and 2). Student performance below this level is lower than that which PISA can reliably assess and, more importantly, describe.

READING LITERACY

SCOPE

The purpose of the PISA reading literacy assessment is to monitor and report on the reading proficiency of 15-year-olds as they approach the end of compulsory schooling. Each task in the assessment has been designed to gather a specific piece of evidence about reading proficiency by simulating a reading activity that a reader might experience in or outside school, as an adolescent, or in adult life.

PISA reading tasks range from very straightforward comprehension activities to quite sophisticated activities requiring deep and multiple levels of understanding. Reading proficiency is characterised by organising the tasks into five levels of increasing proficiency, with Level 1 describing what is required to respond successfully to the most basic tasks, and Level 5 describing what is required to respond successfully to the most demanding tasks.

THREE READING PROFICIENCY SCALES

Why aspect scales?

The scales represent three major reading aspects or purposes, which are all essential parts of typical reading in contemporary developed societies: retrieving information from a variety of reading materials; interpreting what is read; and reflecting upon and evaluating what is read.

People often have practical reasons for *retrieving information* from reading material, and the tasks can range from locating details required by an employer from a job advertisement to finding a telephone number with several prefixes.

Interpreting texts involves processing a text to make internal sense of it. This includes a wide variety of cognitive activities, all of which involve some degree of inference. For example, a task may involve connecting two parts of a text, processing the text to summarise the main ideas, or finding a specific instance of something described earlier in general terms. When interpreting, a reader is identifying the underlying assumptions or implications of part or all of a text.

Reflection and evaluation involves drawing on knowledge, ideas, or attitudes that are external to the text in order to relate the new information that it provides to one's own conceptual and experiential frames of reference.

Dividing reading into different aspects is not the only possible way to divide the task of reading. Text types or formats could be used for organising the domain, as earlier large-scale studies, including the International Association for the Evaluation of Educational Achievement (IEA) Reading Literacy Study (narrative, exposition and document) and the International Adult Literacy Survey (IALS, prose and document) did. However, using aspects seems to reflect most closely the policy objectives of PISA, and the hope is that the provision of these scales will offer a different perspective to understanding how reading proficiency develops.

Why three scales rather than five?

The three scales are based on the set of five aspect variables described in the PISA reading literacy framework (OECD, 1999a): retrieving information; forming a broad understanding; developing an interpretation; reflecting on the content of a text; and reflecting on the form of a text. These five aspects were defined primarily to ensure that the PISA framework and the collection of items developed according to this framework would provide an optimal coverage of the domain of reading literacy as it was defined by the experts. For reporting purposes and for communicating the results, a more parsimonious model was thought to be more appropriate. Collapsing the five-aspect framework on to three aspect scales is justified by the high correlations between the sets of items. Consequently 'developing an interpretation' and 'forming a broad understanding' have been grouped together because information provided in the text is processed by the reader in some ways. In the case of 'forming a broad understanding', this occurs in the whole text, and in the case of 'developing an interpretation', this occurs in one part of the text in relation to another. 'Reflecting on the content of a text' and 'reflecting on the form of a text' have been collapsed into a single *reflection and evaluation* sub-scale because the distinction between reflecting on form and reflecting on content, in practice, was not found to be noticeable in the data as they were collected in PISA.

Even these three scales overlap considerably. In practice, most tasks make many different demands on readers. The three aspects are conceived as interrelated and interdependent, and assigning a task to one or another of the scales is often a matter of fine discrimination about its salient features, and about the approach typically taken to it. Empirical evidence from the main study data was used to validate these judgements. Despite the interdependence of the three scales, they reveal interesting and useful distinctions between countries and among sub-groups within the countries.

Pragmatic and technical reasons also determined the use of only three aspects to describe proficiency scales. In 2003 and 2006, reading will be a minor domain and will therefore be restricted to about 30 items, which would be insufficient for reporting over five scales.

TASK VARIABLES

In developing descriptions of the conditions and features of tasks along each of the three scales, distinct, intersecting sets of variables associated with task difficulty seemed to be operating. These variables are based on the judgements by reading experts of the items that fall within each level band rather than on any systematic analysis, although systematic analyses will be made later.

The PISA definition of reading literacy builds, in part, on the IEA Reading Literacy Study (Elley, 1992), but also on IALS. It reflects the emphasis of the latter study on the importance of reading skills in active and critical participation in society. It was also influenced by current theories which emphasise the interactive nature of reading (Dechant, 1991; McCormick, 1988; Rumelhart, 1985), on models of discourse comprehension (Graesser, Millis and Zwaan, 1997; Kintsch and van Dijk, 1978; Van Dijk and Kintsch, 1983), and on theories of performance in solving reading tasks (Kirsch and Mosenthal, 1990). The definition of variables operating within the *reflection and evaluation* sub-scale is, we believe, PISA's major new contribution to conceptualising reading. PISA is the first large-scale study to attempt to define variables operating within the *reflection and evaluation* sub-scale and to propose characterising populations from this perspective in its reporting.

The apparently salient variables in each scale are described briefly below. It is important to remember that the difficulty of any particular item is conditioned by the interaction among all the variables.

TASK VARIABLES FOR THE COMBINED READING LITERACY SCALE

The overall proficiency scale for reading literacy covers three broad aspects of reading: retrieving, interpreting and reflecting upon and evaluating information. The proficiency scale includes tasks associated with each of these.

The difficulty of any reading task depends on an interaction between several variables. The type of process involved in retrieving, interpreting, or reflecting on and evaluating information is salient in relation to difficulty. The complexity and sophistication of processes range from making simple connections between pieces of information, to categorising ideas according to given criteria, to critically evaluating a section of text. The difficulty of retrieval tasks is associated particularly with the number of pieces of information to be included in the response, the number of criteria that the information must meet, and whether what is retrieved needs to be sequenced in a particular way. For interpretative and reflective tasks, the length, complexity and amount of text that needs to be assimilated particularly affect difficulty. The difficulty of items requiring reflection is also conditioned by the familiarity or specificity of the knowledge that must be drawn on from outside the text. For all aspects of reading, the tasks tend to be more difficult when there is no explicit mention of the ideas or information required to complete them, the required information is not prominent in the text, and much competing information is present.

TASK VARIABLES FOR THE RETRIEVING INFORMATION SUB-SCALE

Four important variables characterising the PISA *retrieving information* tasks were identified. They are outlined here and are incorporated in the proficiency scale description in Figure 32.

Type of retrieval

Type of retrieval is related to the type of match micro-aspect referred to in the reading framework for PISA (OECD, 1999a). *Locating* is the primary process used for tasks in this scale. Locating tasks require a reader to find and retrieve information in a text using criteria that are specified in a question or directive. The more criteria that need to be taken into account, the more the task will tend to be difficult. The reader may need to consult a text several times by cycling through it to find and retrieve different pieces of information. The more numerous the pieces of information to be retrieved, and whether or not they must be sequenced in a particular way, the greater the difficulty of the task.

Explicitness of information

Explicitness of information refers to the degree of literalness or explicitness in the task and in the text, and considers how much the reader must use inference to find the necessary information. The task becomes more difficult when the reader must infer what needs to be considered in looking for information, and when the information to be retrieved is not explicitly provided. This variable is also related to the type of match micro-aspect referred to in the reading framework for PISA. While retrieving information tasks generally require minimal inference, the more difficult tasks require some processing to match the requisite information with what is in the text, and to select relevant information through inference and prioritising.

Nature of competing information

Nature of competing information is similar to the plausibility of the distractors micro-aspect referred to in the reading framework for PISA. Information is competing when the reader may mistakenly retrieve it because it resembles the correct information in one or more ways. Within this variable, the prominence of the correct information also needs to be considered: it will be relatively easy to locate if it is in a heading, located near the beginning of the text, or repeated several times.

Nature of text

Nature of text refers to aspects such as text length and complexity. Longer and more complex texts are harder to negotiate than simpler and shorter texts, all other things being equal. Although *nature of text* is a variable in all scales, its characteristics as a variable and probably its importance differ in *retrieving information* and in the other two scales. This is probably because *retrieving information* tends to focus more on smaller details of text than *interpreting texts* and *reflection and evaluation* do. The reader therefore needs to take comparatively little account of the overall context (the text) in which the information is located, especially if the text is well structured and if the question or directive refers to it.

TASK VARIABLES FOR THE INTERPRETING TEXTS SUB-SCALE

A similar set of variables to those for *retrieving information* was identified for the PISA *interpreting texts* tasks. In some respects, the variables behave differently in relation to the *interpreting texts* sub-scale, as outlined here and incorporated in the scale description in Figure 33.

Type of interpretation

Type of interpretation is related to both the type of match and the type of information micro-aspects referred to in the reading framework for PISA. Several processes have been identified that form a hierarchy of complexity, and tend to be associated with increasing difficulty. At the easier end, readers need to *identify a theme or main idea*. More difficult tasks require *understanding relationships* within the text that are an inherent part of its organisation and meaning such as cause and effect, problem and solution, goal and action, claim and evidence, motive and behaviour, precondition and action, explanation for an outcome, and time sequence. The most difficult tasks are of two kinds: *construing meaning,* which requires the reader to focus on a word, a phrase or sentence, in order to identify its particular effect in context and may involve dealing with ambiguities or subtle nuances of meaning; and *analogical reasoning,* which requires *comparing* (finding similarities between parts of a text), *contrasting* (finding differences), or *categorising* ideas (identifying similarities and differences in order to classify information from within or relevant to the text). The latter may require either fitting examples into a category supplied in the text or finding textual examples of a given category.

Explicitness of information

Explicitness of information encompasses how much direction the reader is given in focusing the interpretation appropriately. The factors to be considered may be indicated explicitly in the item, and readily matched to one or more parts of the text. For a more difficult task, readers may have to consider factors that are not stated either in the item or the text. Generally, interpreting tasks require more inference than those in the *retrieving information* sub-scale, but there is a wide range of demand within this variable in the *interpreting texts* sub-scale.

The difficulty of a task is also conditioned by the number of factors that need to be considered, and the number of pieces of information that the reader needs to respond to the item. The greater the number of factors to consider or pieces of information to be supplied, the more difficult the task becomes.

Nature of competing information

Nature of competing information functions similarly to the variable with the same name in the *retrieving information* sub-scale. For interpreting items, however, explicit information is likely to compete with the implicit information required for the task.

Nature of text

Nature of text is relevant to the *interpreting texts* sub-scale in several ways. The familiarity of the topic or theme of the text is significant. Texts with more familiar topics and more personal themes tend to be easier to assimilate than those with themes that are remote from the reader's experience and that are more public or impersonal. Similarly, texts in a familiar form or genre are easier to manage than those in unfamiliar forms. The length and complexity of a text (or the part of it that needs to be considered) also play a role in the difficulty of a task. The more text the reader has to take into account, the more difficult a task is likely to be.

TASK VARIABLES FOR THE REFLECTION AND EVALUATION SUB-SCALE

Some of the variables identified as relevant to *retrieving information* and *interpreting texts* are also relevant to the PISA *reflection and evaluation* tasks, though operating differently to some extent. The *reflection and evaluation* dimension, however, is influenced by a wider range of task variables than the other reading aspects, as itemised here and incorporated in the scale description in Figure 34.

Type of reflection

Five reflecting processes were identified. The *reflection and evaluation* sub-scale associates each type of reflection with a range of difficulties, but on average, the types of reflection vary in complexity and tend to be associated with increasing difficulty.

Connecting is at the lowest level of reflection. A connection requires the reader to make a basic link between the text and knowledge from outside it. Connecting may involve demonstrating an understanding of a construct or concept underlying the text. It may be a matter of content, such as finding an example of a concept (*e.g.*, 'fact' or 'kindness'), or may involve demonstrating an understanding of the form or linguistic function of features of a text, such as recognising the purpose of conventional structures or linguistic features. For example, the task may require the reader to articulate the relationship between two parts of a text.

The following two types of reflection seem to be more difficult than connecting, but were found to be of similar difficulty.

Explaining involves going beyond the text to give reasons for the presence or purpose of text-based information or features that are consistent with the evidence presented in the text. For example, a reader may be asked to explain why there is a question on an employment application form about how far a prospective employee lives from the workplace.

When *comparing,* the reader needs to find similarities (or differences) between something in the text and something from outside it. In items described as involving comparing, for example, readers may be asked to compare a character's behaviour in a narrative with the behaviour of people they know; or to say whether their own attitude to life resembles that expressed in a poem. Comparisons become more demanding as the range of approaches from which the comparison can be made is more constricted and less explicitly stated, and as the knowledge to be drawn upon becomes less familiar and accessible.

The most difficult tasks involve either *hypothesising* or *evaluating.*

Hypothesising involves going beyond the text to offer explanations for text-based information or features, which are consistent with the evidence presented in the text. This type of reflection could be termed simply 'explaining' if the context is very familiar to the reader, or if some supporting information were supplied in the text. However, hypothesising tends to be relatively demanding because the reader needs to synthesise several pieces of information from both inside and outside the text, and to generate plausible conclusions rather than to retrieve familiar knowledge and apply it to the text. The degree to which signals are given about what kind of knowledge needs to be drawn on, and the degree of familiarity or concreteness of the knowledge, contribute to the difficulty of hypothesising tasks.

Evaluating involves making a judgement about a text as a whole or about some part or feature of it. This kind of critical thinking requires the reader to call upon an internalised hierarchy of values (good/bad; appropriate/inappropriate; right/wrong). In PISA items, the process of evaluating is often related to textual structure, style, or internal coherence. The reader may need to consider critically the writer's point of view or the text's stylistic appropriateness, logical consistency, or thematic coherence.

Nature of reader's knowledge

The *nature of reader's knowledge* brought to bear from outside the text, on a continuum from general (broad, diverse and commonly known) to specialised (narrow, specific and related to a particular domain), is important in reflecting tasks. The term 'knowledge' includes attitudes, beliefs and opinions as well as factual knowledge—any cognitive phenomenon that the reader may draw on or possess. The domain and reference point for the knowledge and experience on which the reader needs to draw to reflect upon the text contribute to the difficulty of the task. When the knowledge must be highly personal and subjective, there is a lower demand because there is a very wide range of appropriate responses and no strong external standard against which to judge them. As the knowledge to be drawn upon becomes more specialised, less personal and more externally referenced, the range of appropriate responses narrows. For example, if knowledge about literary styles or information about public events is a necessary prerequisite for a sensible reflection, the task is likely to be more difficult than a task that asks for a personal opinion about parental behaviour.

In addition, difficulty is affected by the extent to which the reader has to generate the terms of the reflection. In some cases, the item or the text fully define what needs to be considered in the course of the reflection. In other cases, readers must infer or generate their own set of factors as the basis for an hypothesis or evaluation.

Nature of text

Nature of text resembles the variable described for the *interpreting texts* sub-scale, above. Reflecting upon items that are based on simple, short texts (or simple short parts of longer texts) are easier than those based on longer, more complex texts. The degree of textual complexity is judged in terms of its content, linguistic form, or structure.

Nature of understanding of the text

Nature of understanding of the text is close to the 'type of match' micro-process described in the reading framework. It encompasses the kind of processing the reader needs to engage in before reflecting on the text. If the reflection is to be based on locating a small section of explicitly indicated text (*locating*), the task will tend to be easier than if it is based on a contradiction in the text that must first be inferred (*inferring a logical relationship*). The type of understanding of the text may entail partial or a broad, general understanding of the main idea. Reflecting items become more difficult as the reflection requires fuller, deeper and richer textual understanding.

RETRIEVING INFORMATION SUB-SCALE

The PISA 2000 *retrieving information* sub-scale is described in Figure 32.

	Distinguishing features of tasks at each level:	In a typical task at this level, the reader:
5	Tasks at this level require the reader to locate and possibly sequence or combine multiple pieces of deeply embedded information, some of which may be outside the main body of the text. Typically the content and form of the text are unfamiliar. The reader needs to make high-level inferences in order to determine which information in the text is relevant to the task. There is highly plausible and/or extensive competing information.	• Locates and combines two pieces of numeric information on a diagram showing the structure of the labour force. One of the relevant pieces of information is found in a footnote to the caption of the diagram. [Labour 3 *R088Q03*, score category 2]
4	Tasks at this level require the reader to locate and possibly sequence or combine multiple pieces of embedded information. Each piece of information may need to meet multiple criteria. Typically the content and form of the text are unfamiliar. The reader may need to make inferences in order to determine which information in the text is relevant to the task.	• Marks the positions of two actors on a stage diagram by referring to a play script. The two pieces of information needed are embedded in a stage direction in a long and dense text. [Amanda 4 *R216Q04*]
3	Tasks at this level require the reader to locate and in some cases recognise the links between pieces of information, each of which may be required to meet multiple criteria. Typically there is prominent competing information.	• Identifies the starting date of a graph showing the depth of a lake over several thousand years. The information is given in prose in the introduction, but the date is not explicitly marked on the graph's scale. The first marked date on the scale constitutes strong competing information. [Chad 3A *R040Q03A*] • Finds the relevant section of a magazine article for young people about DNA testing by matching with a term in the question. The precise information that is required is surrounded by a good deal of competing information, some of which appears to be contradictory. [Police 4 *R100Q04*]
2	Tasks at this level require the reader to locate one or more pieces of information, which may need to meet multiple criteria. Typically some competing information is present.	• Finds explicitly stated information in a notice about an immunisation program in the work place. The relevant information is near the beginning of the notice but embedded in a complex sentence. There is significant competing information. [Flu 2 *R077Q02*]
1	Tasks at this level require the reader to locate one or more independent pieces of explicitly stated information. Typically there is a single criterion that the located information must meet and there is little if any competing information in the text.	• Finds a literal match between a term in the question and the required information. The text is a long narrative; however, the reader is specifically directed to the relevant passage which is near the beginning of the story. [Gift 6 *R119Q06*] • Locates a single explicitly stated piece of information in a notice about job services. The required information is signalled by a heading in the text that literally matches a term in the question. [Personnel 1 *R234Q01*]
Below Level 1	Insufficient information to describe features of tasks at this level.	

Figure 32: The Retrieving Information Sub-Scale

INTERPRETING TEXTS SUB-SCALE

The PISA 2000 *interpreting texts* sub-scale is described in Figure 33.

	Distinguishing features of tasks at each level:	In a typical task at this level, the reader:
5	Tasks at this level typically require either construing of nuanced language or a full and detailed understanding of a text.	• Analyses the descriptions of several cases in order to determine the appropriate labour force status categories. Infers the criteria for assignment of each case from a full understanding of the structure and content of a tree diagram. Some of the relevant information is in footnotes and is therefore not prominent. [Labour 4 *R088Q04*, score category 2]
4	Tasks at this level typically involve either understanding and applying categories in an unfamiliar context; or construing the meaning of sections of text by taking into account the text as a whole. These tasks require a high level of text-based inference. Competing information at this level is typically in the form of ambiguities, ideas that are contrary to expectation, or ideas that are negatively worded.	• Construes the meaning of a sentence in context by taking into account information across a large section of text. The sentence in isolation is ambiguous and there are apparently plausible alternative readings. [Gift 4 *R119Q04*]
3	Tasks at this level require the reader to consider many elements of the text. The reader typically needs to integrate several parts of a text in order to identify a main idea, understand a relationship, or construe the meaning of a word or phrase. The reader may need to take many criteria into account when comparing, contrasting or categorising. Often the required information is not prominent but implicit in the text, and the reader may be distracted by competing information that is explicit in the text.	• Explains a character's behaviour in a given situation by linking a chain of events and descriptions scattered through a long story. [Gift 8 *R119Q08*] • Integrates information from two graphic displays to infer the concurrence of two events. The two graphics use different conventions, and the reader must interpret the structure of both graphics in order to translate the relevant information from one form to the other. [Chad 6 *R040Q06*]
2	Some tasks require inferring the main idea in a text when the information is not prominent. Others require understanding relationships or construing meaning within a limited part of the text, by making low-level inferences. Tasks at this level may involve forming or applying simple categories.	• Uses information in a brief introduction to infer the main theme of an extract from a play script. [Amanda 1 *R216Q01*]
1	Tasks at this level typically require inferring the main theme or author's purpose in a text about a familiar topic when the idea is prominent, either because it is repeated or because it appears early in the text. There is little if any competing information in the text.	• Recognises the main theme of a magazine article for teenagers about sports shoes. The theme is implied in the sub-heading and repeated several times in the body of the article. [Runners 1 *R110Q01*]
Below Level 1	Insufficient information to describe features of tasks at this level.	

Figure 33: The Interpreting Texts Sub-Scale

REFLECTION AND EVALUATION SUB-SCALE

The PISA 2000 *reflection and evaluation* sub-scale is described in Figure 34.

	Distinguishing features of tasks at each level:	In a typical task at this level, the reader:
5	Tasks at this level require critical evaluation or hypothesis, and may draw on specialised knowledge. Typically these tasks require readers to deal with concepts that are contrary to expectations, and to draw on a deep understanding of long or complex texts.	• Hypothesises about an unexpected phenomenon: that an aid agency gives relatively low levels of support to a very poor country. Takes account of inconspicuous as well as more obvious information in a complex text on a relatively unfamiliar topic (foreign aid) [Plan International 4B *R099Q4B*, score category 2] • Evaluates the appropriateness of an apparently contradictory section of a notice about an immunisation program in the workplace, taking into account the persuasive intent of the text and/or its logical coherence. [Flu 5 *R077Q05*]
4	Tasks at this level typically require readers to critically evaluate a text, or hypothesise about information in the text, using formal or public knowledge. Readers must demonstrate an accurate understanding of the text, which may be long or complex.	• Evaluates the writer's craft by comparing two short letters on the topic of graffiti. Readers need to draw on their understanding of what constitutes good style in writing. [Graffiti 6B *R081Q06B*]
3	Tasks at this level may require connections, comparisons and explanations, or they may require the reader to evaluate a feature of the text. Some tasks require readers to demonstrate a detailed understanding of the text in relation to familiar, everyday knowledge. Other tasks do not require detailed text comprehension but require the reader to draw on less common knowledge. The reader may need to infer the factors to be considered.	• Connects his/her own concepts of compassion and cruelty with the behaviour of a character in a narrative, and identifies relevant evidence of such behaviour in the text. [Gift 9 *R119Q09*, score category 2] • Evaluates the form of a text in relation to its purpose. The text is a tree diagram showing the structure of the labour force. [Labour 7 *R088Q07*]
2	Some tasks at this level require readers to make connections or comparisons between the text and outside knowledge. For others, readers need to draw on personal experience and attitudes to explain a feature of the text. The tasks require a broad understanding of the text.	• Compares claims made in two short texts (letters about graffiti) with his/her own views and attitudes. Broad understanding of at least one of the two letter writers' opinions needs to be demonstrated. [Graffiti 6A *R081Q06A*]
1	Tasks at this level require readers to make a simple connection between information in the text and common, everyday knowledge. The reader is explicitly directed to consider relevant factors in the task and in the text.	• Makes a connection by articulating the relationship between two parts of a single, specified sentence in a magazine article for young people about sports shoes. [Runners 6 *R110Q06*]
Below Level 1	Insufficient information to describe features of tasks at this level.	

Figure 34: The Reflection and Evaluation Sub-Scale

COMBINED READING LITERACY SCALE

The PISA 2000 *combined reading literacy* scale is described in Figure 35.

	Distinguishing features of tasks at each level:
5	The reader must: sequence or combine several pieces of deeply embedded information, possibly drawing on information from outside the main body of the text; construe the meaning of linguistic nuances in a section of text; or make evaluative judgements or hypotheses, drawing on specialised knowledge. The reader is generally required to demonstrate a full, detailed understanding of a dense, complex or unfamiliar text, in content or form, or one that involves concepts that are contrary to expectations. The reader will often have to make inferences to determine which information in the text is relevant, and to deal with prominent or extensive competing information.
4	The reader must: locate, sequence or combine several pieces of embedded information; infer the meaning of a section of text by considering the text as a whole; understand and apply categories in an unfamiliar context; or hypothesise about or critically evaluate a text, using formal or public knowledge. The reader must draw on an accurate understanding of long or complex texts in which competing information may take the form of ideas that are ambiguous, contrary to expectation, or negatively worded.
3	The reader must: recognise the links between pieces of information that have to meet multiple criteria; integrate several parts of a text to identify a main idea, understand a relationship or construe the meaning of a word or phrase; make connections and comparisons; or explain or evaluate a textual feature. The reader must take into account many features when comparing, contrasting or categorising. Often the required information is not prominent but implicit in the text or obscured by similar information.
2	The reader must: locate one or more pieces of information that may be needed to meet multiple criteria; identify the main idea, understand relationships or construe meaning within a limited part of the text by making low-level inferences; form or apply simple categories to explain something in a text by drawing on personal experience and attitudes; or make connections or comparisons between the text and everyday outside knowledge. The reader must often deal with competing information.
1	The reader must: locate one or more independent pieces of explicitly stated information according to a single criterion; identify the main theme or author's purpose in a text about a familiar topic; or make a simple connection between information in the text and common, everyday knowledge. Typically, the requisite information is prominent and there is little, if any, competing information. The reader is explicitly directed to consider relevant factors in the task and in the text.
Below Level 1	There is insufficient information to describe features of tasks at this level.

Figure 35: The Combined Reading Literacy Scale

CUT-OFF POINTS FOR READING

The definition of proficiency levels for reading is based on a bandwidth of 0.8 logits, and an RP level of 0.62 (see 'Defining Proficiency Levels' earlier in this chapter).

Using these criteria, Figure 36 gives the level boundaries for the three reading aspect scales and the *combined reading literacy* scale, based on the *PISA scale* with a mean of 500 and a standard deviation of 100 (see Chapter 13).

Boundary	Cut-Off Point on PISA Scale
Level 4 / Level 5	625.6
Level 3 / Level 4	552.9
Level 2 / Level 3	480.2
Level 1 / Level 2	407.5
Below Level 1 / Level 1	334.8

Figure 36: Combined Reading Literacy Scale Level Cut-Off Points

MATHEMATICAL LITERACY

WHAT IS BEING ASSESSED?

PISA's mathematical literacy tasks assess students' ability to recognise and interpret problems encountered in their world; to translate the problems into a mathematical context; to use mathematical knowledge and procedures from various areas to solve a problem within its mathematical context; to interpret results in terms of the original problem; and to reflect upon methods applied and communicate the outcomes.

In the PISA *mathematical literacy* scale, the key elements defining the increasing difficulty of tasks at successive levels are the number and complexity of processing or computation steps; connection and integration demands (from use of separate elements, to integration of different pieces of information, different representations, or different mathematical tools or knowledge); and representation, modelling, interpretation and reflection demands (from recognising and using a familiar, well-formulated model, to formulating, translating or creating a useful model within an unfamiliar context, and using insight, reasoning, argumentation and generalisation).

The factors that influence item difficulty, and therefore contribute to a definition of mathematical proficiency, include the following:

- *the kind and degree of interpretation and reflection required*, which includes the nature of demands arising from the context of the problem; the extent to which the mathematical demands of the problem are apparent or to which students must impose their own mathematical construction; and the extent to which insight, complex reasoning and generalisation are required; and
- *the kind and level of mathematical skill required*, which ranges from single-step problems requiring students to reproduce basic mathematical facts and simple computation processes to multi-step problems involving more advanced mathematical knowledge; and complex decision-making, information processing, and problem solving and modelling skills.

A single scale was proposed for PISA mathematical literacy. Five proficiency levels can be defined although an initial set of descriptions of three levels—lowest, middle, and highest—was developed for use in PISA 2000.

At the lowest level of proficiency that is described, students typically negotiate single-step processes that involve recognising familiar contexts and mathematically well-formulated problems, reproducing well-known mathematical facts or processes, and applying simple computational skills.

At higher levels of proficiency, students typically carry out more complex tasks involving more than a single processing step, and combine different pieces of information or interpret different representations of mathematical concepts or information, recognising which elements are relevant and important. To identify solutions, they typically work with given mathematical models or formulations, which are frequently in algebraic form, or carry out a small sequence of processing or a number of calculation steps to produce a solution.

At the highest level of proficiency that is described, students take a more creative and active role in their approach to solving mathematical problems. They typically interpret more complex information and negotiate a number of processing steps. They typically produce a formulation of a problem and often develop a suitable model that facilitates solving the problem. Students at this level typically identify and apply relevant tools and knowledge frequently in an unfamiliar context, demonstrate insight to identify a suitable solution strategy, and display other higher order cognitive processes such as generalisation, reasoning and argumentation to explain or communicate results.

Given that the amount of data available from the PISA 2000 study is limited because mathematics was a minor test domain, it was decided that it would be unwise to establish cut-off points between five levels.

The PISA 2000 *mathematical literacy* scale is described in Figure 37.

Highest Level Described

- Show insight in the solution of problems;
- Develop a mathematical interpretation and formulation of problems set in a real-world context;
- Identify relevant mathematical tools or methods for solution of problems in unfamiliar contexts;
- Solve problems involving several steps;
- Reflect on results and generalise findings; and
- Use reasoning and mathematical argument to explain solutions and communicate outcomes.

Middle Level Described

- Interpret, link and integrate different information in order to solve a problem;
- Work with and connect different mathematical representations of a problem;
- Use and manipulate given mathematical models to solve a problem;
- Use symbolic language to solve problems; and
- Solve problems involving a small number of steps.

Lowest Level Described

- Recognise familiar elements in a problem, and recall knowledge relevant to the problem;
- Reproduce known facts or procedures to solve a problem;
- Apply mathematical knowledge to solve problems that are simply expressed and are either already formulated in mathematical terms, or where the mathematical formulation is straightforward; and
- Solve problems involving only one or two steps.

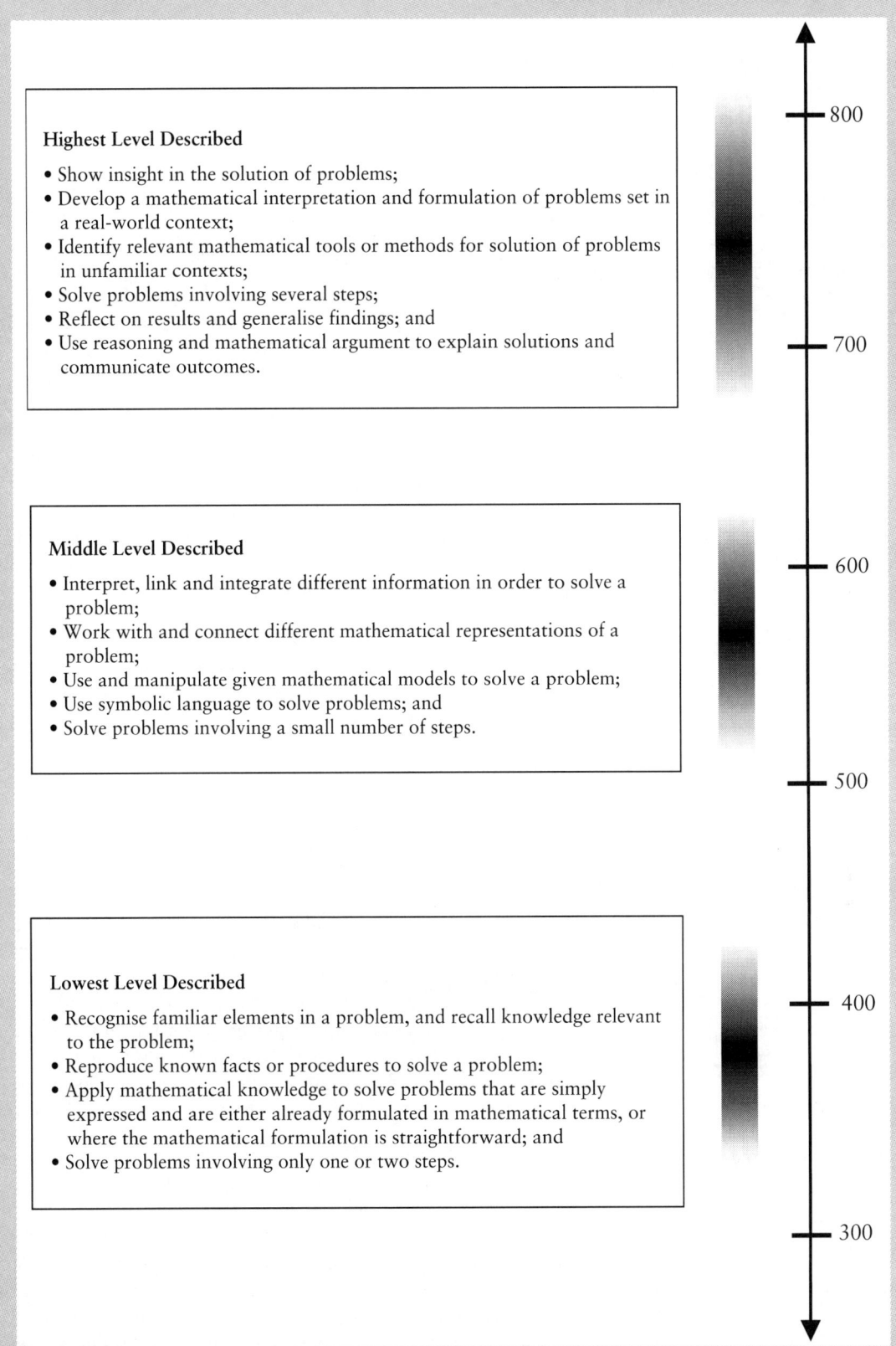

Figure 37: The Mathematical Literacy Scale

ILLUSTRATING THE PISA MATHEMATICAL LITERACY SCALE

The items from two different units (*Apples* and *Speed of Racing Car*) have been selected to illustrate the PISA mathematical literacy scale. Figure 38 shows where each item on the scale is located, and summarises the item to show how it illustrates the scale.

Item	PISA Scale	Comment
Apples M136Q03	732	Students are given a hypothetical scenario involving planting an orchard of apple trees in a square pattern, with a 'row' of protective conifer trees around the square. This item requires students to show insight into mathematical functions by comparing the growth of a linear function with that of a quadratic function. Students are required to construct a verbal description of a generalised pattern, and to create an argument using algebra. Students need to understand both the algebraic expressions used to describe the pattern and the underlying functional relationships in such a way that they can see and explain the generalisation of these relationships in an unfamiliar context. A chain of reasoning and communication of this reasoning in a written explanation is required.
Apples M136Q02	664	Students are given two algebraic expressions that describe the growth in the number of trees (apple trees and the protective conifers) as the orchard increases in size, and are asked to find a value for which the two expressions coincide. This item requires students to interpret expressions containing words and symbols—to link different representations (pictorial, verbal and algebraic) for two relationships (one quadratic and one linear). Students have to find a strategy for determining when the two functions will have the same solution (for example, by trial and error, or by algebraic means); and to communicate the result by explaining the reasoning and calculation steps involved.
Racing Car M159Q05	664	Students are given a graph showing the speed of a racing car as it progresses at various distances along a race track. For this item, they are also given a set of plans of hypothetical tracks and asked to identify which could have given rise to the graph. The item requires students to understand and interpret a graphical representation of a physical relationship (speed and distance of a car) and relate it to the physical world. Students need to link and integrate two very different visual representations of the progress of a car around a race track and to identify and select the correct option from among challenging alternatives.
Apples M136Q01	557	Students are given a hypothetical scenario involving planting an orchard of apple trees in a square pattern, with a 'row' of protective conifer trees around the square. They are asked to complete a table of values generated by the functions that describe the number of trees as the size of the orchard is increased. This item requires students to interpret a written description of a problem situation, to link this to a tabular representation of some of the information, and to recognise and extend a pattern. Students need to work with given models in order to relate two different representations (pictorial and tabular) of two relationships (one quadratic and one linear) to extend the pattern.

tem	PISA Scale	Comment
Racing Car M159Q01	502	Students are given a graph showing the speed of a racing car as it progresses at various distances along a race track. For this item they are asked to interpret the graph to find a distance that satisfies a given condition. The item requires students to interpret a graphical representation of a physical relationship (distance and speed of a car travelling on a track of unknown shape). Students need to interpret the graph by linking a verbal description with two particular features of the graph (one simple and straightforward, and one requiring a deeper understanding of several elements of the graph and what it represents), then identify and read the required information from the graph, selecting the best option from the given alternatives.
Racing Car M159Q03	423	In this item, students are asked to interpret the speed of the car at a particular point in the graph. The item requires students to read information from a graph representing a physical relationship (speed and distance of a car). Students need to identify the place in the graph referred to in a verbal description, recognise what is happening to the speed of the vehicle at that point, then select the best matching option from among given alternatives.
Racing Car M159Q02	412	This item asks students to read from the graph a single value that satisfies a simple condition. The item requires students to read information from a graph representing a physical relationship (speed and distance of a car). Students need to identify one specified feature of the graph (the display of speed), read directly from the graph a value that minimises the feature, then select the best match from among given alternatives.

Figure 38: Typical Mathematical Literacy Tasks

SCIENTIFIC LITERACY

WHAT IS BEING ASSESSED?

PISA's scientific literacy tasks assess students' ability to use scientific knowledge (understanding scientific concepts); to recognise scientific questions and to identify what is involved in scientific investigations (understanding the nature of scientific investigation); to relate scientific data to claims and conclusions (using scientific evidence); and to communicate these aspects of science.

In the PISA *scientific literacy* scale, the key elements defining the increasing difficulty of tasks at successive levels are the complexity of the concepts encountered, the amount of information given, the type of reasoning required, and the context and sometimes the format and presentation of the items. There is a progression of difficulty across tasks in the use of scientific knowledge involving:
- the recall of simple scientific knowledge, common scientific knowledge or given questions, variables or data;
- scientific concepts or questions and details of investigations; and
- elaborated scientific concepts or additional information or a chain of reasoning; through to simple scientific conceptual models or analysis of investigations or evidence for alternative perspectives.

The scientific proficiency scale is based on a definition of scientific literacy linked to four processes, as formulated in the PISA science framework (OECD, 1999a):
- *Understanding scientific concepts* concerns the ability to make use of scientific knowledge and to demonstrate an understanding of scientific concepts by applying scientific ideas, information, or appropriate concepts (not given in the stimulus or test item) to a given situation. This may involve explaining relationships, scientific events or phenomena or possible causes for the changes that are indicated, or making predictions about the effects of given changes or identifying the factors that would influence a given outcome.

Highest Level Described

- Create or use simple conceptual models to make predictions or give explanations;
- Analyse scientific investigations in relation to, for example, experimental design, identification of idea being tested;
- Relate data as evidence to evaluate alternative viewpoints or different perspectives; and
- Communicate scientific arguments and/or descriptions in detail and with precision.

Middle Level Described

- Use scientific concepts in making predictions or giving explanations;
- Recognise questions that can be answered by scientific investigation and/or identify details of what is involved in a scientific investigation; and
- Select relevant information from competing data or chains of reasoning in drawing or evaluating conclusions.

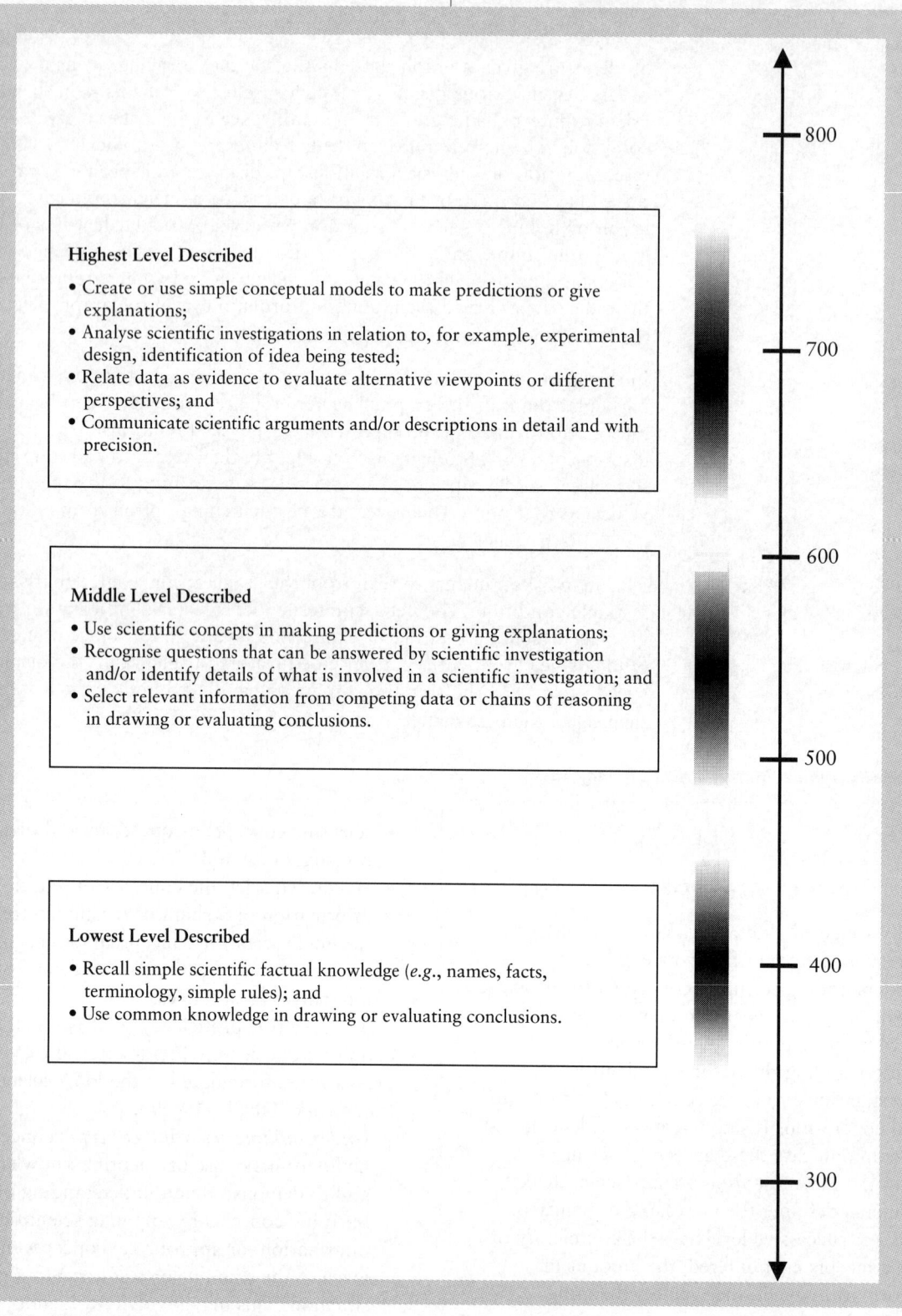

Lowest Level Described

- Recall simple scientific factual knowledge (*e.g.*, names, facts, terminology, simple rules); and
- Use common knowledge in drawing or evaluating conclusions.

Figure 39: The Scientific Literacy Scale

- *Understanding the nature of scientific investigation* concerns the ability to recognise questions that can be scientifically investigated and to be aware of what is involved in such investigations. This may involve recognising questions that could be or are being answered in an investigation, identifying the question or idea that was being (or could have been) tested in a given investigation, distinguishing questions that can and cannot be answered by scientific investigation, or suggesting a question that could be investigated scientifically in a given situation. It may also involve identifying evidence/data needed to test an explanation or explore an issue, requiring the identification or recognition of variables that should be compared, changed or controlled, additional information that would be needed, or action that should be taken so that relevant data can be collected.
- *Using scientific evidence* concerns the ability to make sense of scientific data as evidence for claims or conclusions. This may involve producing a conclusion from given scientific evidence/data or selecting the conclusion that fits the data from alternatives. It may also involve giving reasons for or against a given conclusion in terms of the data provided, or identifying the assumptions made in reaching a conclusion.
- *Communicating scientific descriptions or arguments* concerns the ability to communicate scientific descriptions, arguments and explanations to others. This involves communicating valid conclusions from available evidence/data to a specified audience. It may involve producing an argument or an explanation based on the situation and data given, or providing relevant additional information, expressed appropriately and clearly for the audience.

Developing the proficiency scale for science involved an iterative process that considered the theoretical basis of the science framework and the item analyses from the main study.

Consideration of the framework suggested a scale of scientific literacy which, at its lower levels, would involve being able to grasp easier scientific concepts in familiar situations such as recognising questions that can or cannot be decided by scientific investigation, recalling scientific facts, or using common scientific knowledge to draw conclusions.

Students at higher levels of proficiency would be able to apply more cognitively demanding concepts in more complex and occasionally unfamiliar contexts. This could involve creating models to make predictions, using data as evidence to evaluate different perspectives or communicating scientific arguments with precision.

The difficulty levels indicated by the analysis of the science items in PISA 2000 also gave useful information, which was considered along with the theoretical framework in developing scale descriptions.

Only limited data were available from the PISA 2000 study, where science was a minor test domain. For this reason, a strict definition of levels could not be confidently recommended. The precise definition of levels and investigation of sub-scales will be possible for PISA 2006, using the data from science as a major test domain.

The PISA 2000 *scientific literacy* scale is described in Figure 39.

ILLUSTRATING THE PISA SCIENTIFIC LITERACY SCALE

Several science items have been recommended for public release on the basis of the following criteria. In addition to indicating the assessment style used in PISA, these items provide a guide to the descriptive scientific proficiency scales. The selected items:

- exemplify the PISA philosophy of assessing the students' preparedness for future life rather than simply testing curriculum-based knowledge;
- cover a range of proficiency levels;
- give consistent, reliable item analyses and were not flagged as causing problems in individual countries;
- represent several formats: multiple-choice, short constructed-response, open response; and
- include some partial credit items.

The *Semmelweis* and *Ozone* units, containing a total of 10 score points, were released after PISA 2000. Characteristics of these units are summarised in Figures 40 and 41.

Semmelweis

The historical example about Semmelweis' discoveries concerning puerperal fever was chosen for several reasons:
- It illustrates the importance of systematic data collection for explaining a devastating phenomenon, the death of many women in maternity wards;
- It demonstrates the need to consider alternative explanations based on the data collected and on additional observations regarding the behaviour of the medical personnel;
- It shows how scientific reasoning based on evidence can refute popular beliefs that prevent a problem from being addressed effectively; and
- It allows students to expand on the example by bringing in their own scientific knowledge.

Unit Name	Unit Identification	Q#	Score	Location on PISA Scale	Scientific Process
Semmelweis	195	2	2	679	c
Semmelweis	195	2	1	651	c
Semmelweis	195	4	1	506	b
Semmelweis	195	5	1	480	a
Semmelweis	195	6	1	521	a

Note: The a, b, and c in the right-hand column refer to the scientific processes:
a = understanding scientific concepts; b = understanding the nature of scientific investigation; and c = using scientific evidence.

Figure 40: Characteristics of the Science Unit, Semmelweis

Sample Item S195Q02 (open constructed-response)

Sample Item S195Q02 is the first in a unit that introduces students to Semmelweis, who took up a position in a Viennese hospital in the 1840s and became puzzled by the remarkably high death rate due to puerperal fever in one of the maternity wards. This information is presented in text and graphs, and the suggestion is then made that puerperal fever may be caused by extraterrestrial influences or natural disasters—not uncommon thinking in Semmelweis' time. Semmelweis tried on several occasions to convince his colleagues to consider more rational explanations. Students are invited to imagine themselves in his position, and to use the data he collected to defend the idea that earthquakes are an unlikely cause of the disease. The graphs show a similar variation in death rate over time, and the first ward consistently has a higher death rate than the second ward. If earthquakes were the cause, death rates in both wards should be about equal. The graphs suggest that something having to do with the wards themselves would explain the difference.

To obtain full credit, students needed to refer to the idea that death rates in both wards should have been similar over time if earthquakes were the cause. Some students came up with answers that did not refer to Semmelweis' findings, but to a characteristic of earthquakes that made it very unlikely that they were the cause, such as that they are infrequent while the fever is constantly present. Others came up with very original well-taken statements such as 'if it were earthquakes, why do only women get the disease, and not men?' or ' if so, women outside the wards would also get that fever'. Although it could be argued that these students did not consider the data collected by Semmelweis, as the item asks, they were given partial credit because they demonstrated a certain ability to use scientific facts in drawing a conclusion.

This partial credit item is a good example of how one item can be used to exemplify two parts of the proficiency scale. The first score point is a moderately difficult item because it involves using scientific evidence to relate data systematically to possible conclusions using a chain of reasoning that is not given to the students. The second score point is at a higher level of proficiency because the students have to relate the data given as evidence to *evaluate* different perspectives.

Sample Item S195Q04 (multiple-choice)

Semmelweis gets an idea from his observations. Sample Item S195Q04 asks students to identify which from a set of ideas was most relevant to reducing the incidence of puerperal fever. Students need to put two pieces of relevant information from the text together: the behaviour of a medical student and the death of Semmelweis' friend from puerperal fever after dissection. This item exemplifies a low to moderate level of proficiency because it asks students to refer to given data or information to draw their conclusion.

Sample Item S195Q05 (open constructed-response)

Nowadays, most people are well aware that germs cause many diseases, and can be killed by heat. Perhaps not many people realise that routine procedures in hospitals make use of this to reduce risks of fever outbreak.

This item invites the student to apply the common scientific knowledge that heat kills bacteria to explain why these procedures are effective. This item is an example of a level of low to moderate difficulty.

Sample Item S195Q06 (multiple-choice)

Sample Item S195Q06 goes beyond the historical example to elicit common scientific knowledge needed to explain a scientific phenomenon. Students are asked to explain why antibiotics have become less effective over time. To respond correctly, they must know that frequent, extended use of antibiotics builds up strains of bacteria resistant to the antibiotics' initially lethal effects.

This item is located at a moderate level on the proficiency scale because it asks students to use scientific concepts (as opposed to common scientific knowledge, which is at a lower level) to give explanations.

Ozone

The subject of the *Ozone* unit is the effect on the environment of the depletion of the ozone layer, and is very important as it concerns human survival. It has received much media attention. The unit is significant too, because it points to the successful intervention by the international community at a meeting in Montreal—an early example of successful global consultation on matters that extend beyond national boundaries.

The text presented to the students sets the context by explaining how ozone molecules and the ozone layer are formed, and how the layer forms a protective barrier by absorbing ultra-violet radiation from the sun's rays. Both good and bad effects of ozone are described. The context of the items involves genuine, important issues, and gives the opportunity to ask questions about physical, chemical and biological aspects of science.

Sample Item S253Q01 (open constructed-response)

In the first *Ozone* sample item, the formation of ozone molecules is presented in a novel way. A comic strip shows three stages of oxygen molecules being split under the sun's influence and then recombined into ozone molecules. Students need to interpret this information and communicate it to a person with limited scientific knowledge. The intention is to assess students' ability to communicate their own interpretation, which requires an open-ended response format.

Many different responses can be given, but to gain full credit, students must describe what is happening in at least two of the three stages of the comic strip.

Unit Name	Unit Identification	Q#	Score	Location on PISA Scale	Scientific Process
Ozone	253	1	2	695	d
Ozone	253	1	1	641	d
Ozone	253	2	1	655	c
Ozone	253	5	1	560	a
Ozone	270	3	1	542	b

Note: The a, b, c, d in the right-hand column refer to the scientific processes: a = understanding scientific concepts; b = understanding the nature of scientific investigation; c = using scientific evidence; and d = communicating scientific descriptions or arguments.

Figure 41: Characteristics of the Science Unit, Ozone

Students who received partial credit for this item are regarded as working at a moderate to high level of proficiency because they could communicate a simple scientific description. Full credit requires more precision and detail—this is an example of the highest proficiency level.

Sample Item S253Q02 *(multiple-choice)*

Sample Item S253Q02 requires students to link part of the text to their own experience of weather conditions (thunderstorms occurring relatively close to Earth) in order to draw a conclusion about the nature of the ozone produced ('good' or 'bad'). The item requires drawing an inference or going beyond the stated information.

This is an example of an item at a moderate to high level of proficiency because students must relate data systematically to statements of possible conclusions using a chain of reasoning that is not specifically given to them.

Sample Item S253Q05 *(open constructed-response)*

In *Sample Item S253Q05*, students need to demonstrate specific knowledge of a possible consequence for human health of the depletion of the ozone layer. The *Marking Guide* is precise in demanding a particular type of cancer (skin cancer). This item is regarded as requiring a moderate level of proficiency because students must use a specific scientific concept in answering it.

Sample Item S270Q03 *(complex multiple-choice)*

The final *Ozone* sample item emphasises the international significance of scientific research in helping to solve environmental problems, such as the ones raised at the Montreal meeting. The item requires students to recognise questions that can be answered by scientific investigation and is an example of a moderate level of proficiency.

Chapter 17: Constructing and Validating the Questionnaire Indices

Wolfram Schulz

In several cases, the *raw* data from the context questionnaires were recoded or *scaled* to produce new variables, referred to as indices. Indices based on direct recoding of responses to one or more variables are called simple indices. Many PISA indices, however, have been constructed by applying a scaling methodology, and are referred to as complex indices. They summarise student or school representatives' (typically principals) responses to a series of related questions selected from larger constructs on the basis of theoretical considerations and previous research. Structural equation modelling was used to confirm the theoretically expected behaviour of the indices and to validate their comparability across countries. For this purpose, a model was estimated separately for each country and, collectively, for all OECD countries.[1]

This chapter describes the construction of all indices, both simple and complex. It presents the results of a cross-country validation of the student and school indices, and provides descriptive statistics for selected questionnaire variables. The analysis was done using Structural Equation Modelling (SEM) for a Confirmatory Factor Analysis (CFA) of questionnaire items.

CFA was used to validate the indices, and item response theory techniques were used to produce scale scores. An index involving multiple questions and student responses was scaled using the Rasch item response model, and the scale score is a weighted maximum likelihood estimate, referred to as a *Warm* estimator (Warm, 1985) (also see Chapter 9). Dichotomous response categories (*i.e.*, *yes/no*) produce only one parameter estimate (labelled 'Delta' in the figures reporting item parameters in this chapter). Rating scales allowing graded responses (*i.e.*, *never*, *some lessons*, *most lessons*, *every lesson*) produce both a parameter estimate and an estimate of the thresholds between *n* categories labelled 'Tau(1)', 'Tau(2)', etc. in the figures reporting item parameters in this chapter.

The scaling proceeded in three steps:

- Item parameters were estimated from calibration samples of students and schools. The student calibration sample consisted of sub-samples of 500 randomly selected students, and the school calibration sample consisted of sub-samples of 99 schools, from each participating OECD country.[2] Non-OECD countries did not contribute to the computation of the item parameters.

---

[1] The Netherlands was not included because of its low participation rate.

[2] For the international options, the item response theory indices were transformed using the same procedures as those applied to the other indices, but only OECD countries that had participated in the international options were included. For Belgium, only the Flemish Community chose to include the international options, and it was given equal weight and included. For the United Kingdom where only Scotland participated, the data were not included in the standardisation. The rationale was that in Belgium, the participating region represented half of the population whereas students in Scotland are only a small part of the student population in the United Kingdom.

- Estimates were computed for all students and all schools by anchoring the item parameters obtained in the preceding step.
- Indices were then standardised so that the mean of the index value for the OECD student population was zero and the standard deviation was one (countries being given equal weight in the standardisation process).

This item response theory approach was adopted for producing index 'scores', after validation of the indices with CFA procedures, because (i) it was consistent with the intention that the items simply be added together to produce a single index, and (ii) it provided an elegant way of dealing with missing item-response data.

VALIDATION PROCEDURES OF INDICES

Structural Equation Modelling (SEM) was used to confirm theoretically expected dimensions or to re-specify the dimensional structure. SEM takes the measurement error associated with the indicators into account and therefore provides more reliable estimates for the latent variables than classical psychometric methods like exploratory factor analyses or simple computations of alpha reliabilities.

Basically, in CFA with SEM, an expected covariance matrix is fitted to a theoretical factor structure by minimising the differences between an expected covariance matrix (Σ, based upon a given model) and the observed covariance matrix (S, computed from the data).

Measures for the overall fit of a model are then obtained by comparing the expected Σ matrix with the observed S matrix. If the differences are close to zero, then the model *fits the data*, while if they are rather large the model *does not fit the data* and some re-specification may be necessary or, if this is not possible, the theoretical model should be rejected. Generally, model fit indices are approximations and need to be interpreted with care. In particular, the chi-squared test statistic for the null hypothesis of $\Sigma=S$ becomes a rather poor fit measure with larger sample sizes because even small differences between matrices are given as significant deviations.

Though the assessment of model fit was based on a variety of measures, this report presents only the following two indices to illustrate the comparative model fits:

- The *Root Mean Square Error of Approximation* (RMSEA) measures the discrepancy per degree of freedom for the model (Browne and Cudeck, 1993). Values of 0.05 or less indicate a close fit, values of 0.08 or more indicate a reasonable to a large error of approximation and values greater than 1.0 should lead to the rejection of a model.
- The *Adjusted Goodness-of-Fit-Index* (AGFI) indicates the amount of variance in S explained with Σ. Values close to 1.0 indicate a good model fit.
- The difference between a specified model and a null model is measured by the *Normed Fit Index* (NFI), *Non-Normed Fit Index* (NNFI) and *Comparative Fit Index* (CFI). Like AGFI, values close to 1.0 for these three indices show a good model fit.

Additionally, the explained variance (or item reliability) in the manifest variables was taken as an additional indicator of model fit—*i.e.*, if the latent variables hardly explain any variance in the manifest variables, the assumed factor structure is not confirmed even if the overall model fit is reasonable.

Model estimation was done with LISREL (Jöreskog and Sörbom, 1993) using the STREAMS (Gustafsson and Stahl, 2000) interface program which gives the researcher the possibility of estimating models for groups of data (*e.g.*, different country data sets) and comparing the model fits across countries without needing to re-estimate the same model country-by-country. Model estimations were obtained using variance/covariance matrices.[3]

For each of the indices, the assumed model was estimated separately for each country and for the entire sample. In a few cases, the model had to be respecified; in some cases, where this was unsuccessful, only the results for the misfitting model are reported.

For the student data, the cross-country validation was based on the calibration sample.

---

[3] For ordinal variables, Jöreskog and Sörbom (1993) recommend using *Weighted Least Square Estimation* (WLS) with polychoric correlation matrices and its corresponding asymptotic covariance weight matrices instead of ML estimation with covariance matrices. As this procedure becomes computationally difficult with large amounts of data, the use of covariance matrices was chosen for the analysis of dimensionality reported here.

Here, the sample size was deemed appropriate for this kind of evaluation. For the school data, the complete school data set for each country was taken, given the small number of schools per country in the calibration sample.

INDICES

In the remainder of the chapter, simple index variables (those based on direct recoding of responses to one or more variables) are described first, followed by complex indices (those that have been constructed by applying IRT scaling methodology), first for students and second, for schools. Item parameter estimates are provided for each of the scaled indices.

STUDENT CHARACTERISTICS AND FAMILY BACKGROUND

Student age

The variable *AGE* gives the age of the student expressed in number of months and was computed as the difference between the date of birth and the middle date of the country's testing window.

Family structure

Students were asked to indicate who usually lives at home with them. The variable *FAMSTRUC* is based on the first four items of this question (*ST04Q01*, *ST04Q02*, *ST04Q03* and *ST04Q04*). It takes four values and indicates the nature of the student's family: (i) *single-parent family* (students who reported living with one of the following: mother, father, female guardian or male guardian); (ii) *nuclear family* (students who reported living with a mother and a father); (iii) *mixed family* (students who reported living with a mother and a male guardian, a father and a female guardian, or two guardians); and (iv) *other response combinations*.

Number of siblings

Students were asked to indicate the number of siblings older and younger than themselves, or the same age. *NSIB*, the total number of siblings, is derived from the three items of question *ST25Q01*.

Country of birth

Students were asked if they, their mother, and their father were born in the country of assessment or in another country. Responses were then grouped into: (i) students with *native-born* parents (students born in the country of the assessment, with at least one parent born in that country); (ii) *first-generation* students (students born in the country of the assessment but whose parents were both born in another country); and (iii) *non-native* students (students born outside the country of the assessment and whose parents were also born in another country). The variable is based on recoding *ST16Q01* (student), *ST16Q02* (mother) and *ST16Q03* (father).

Language spoken at home

Students were asked if the language spoken at home most of the time was the language of assessment, another official national language, another national dialect or language, or another language. The responses (to *ST17Q01*) were then grouped into two categories: (i) language spoken at home most of the time is different from the language of assessment, from other official national languages and from other national dialects or languages; and (ii) the language spoken at home most of the time is the language of assessment, is another official national language, or other national dialect or language.

Birth order

The birth order of the assessed student, *BRTHORD*, is derived from the variables *ST05Q01* (number of older siblings), *ST05Q02* (number of younger siblings) and *ST05Q03* (number of siblings of equal age). It is equal to 0 if the student is the only child, 1 if the student is the youngest child, 2 if the student is a middle child, and 3 if the student is the oldest child.

Socio-economic status

Students were asked to report their mother's and father's occupation, and to state whether each parent was: in full-time paid work; in part-time paid work; not working but looking for a paid job; or *other*. The open-ended responses were then coded in accordance with the International Standard Classification of Occupations (ISCO 1988).

The PISA International Socio-Economic Index of Occupational Status (*ISEI*) was derived from student responses on parental occupation. The index capture the attributes of occupations that convert parents' education into income, and were derived by the optimal scaling of occupation groups to maximise the indirect effect of education on income by occupation, and to minimise the direct effect of education on income net of occupation (both effects are net of age). For more information on the methodology, see Ganzeboom, de Graaf and Treiman (1992).

Data for mother's occupation, father's occupation and the student's expected occupation at the age of 30, obtained through questions *ST08Q01, ST09Q01, ST10Q01, ST11Q01* and *ST40Q01*, were transformed to *SEI* indices using the above procedures. The variables *BMMJ*, *BFMJ* and *BTHR* are the mother's *SEI*, father's *SEI* and student's self-expected *SEI*, respectively. Two new derived variables, *ISEI* and *HISEI*, were then computed from *BMMJ* and *BFMJ*. If *BFMJ* is available, *ISEI* is equal to *BFMJ*, while if it is not available but *BMMJ* is available, then *ISEI* is equal to *BMMJ*. *HISEI* corresponds to the higher value of *BMMJ* and *BFMJ*.[4]

Parental education

Students were asked to classify their mother's and father's highest level of education on the basis of national qualifications that were then coded according to the International Standard Classification of Education (ISCED, OECD, 1999*b*) to obtain internationally comparable categories of educational attainment. The resulting categories were: did not go to school; completed <ISCED Level 1 only (primary education)>; completed <ISCED Level 2 only (lower secondary education)>; completed <ISCED Level 3B or 3C only (upper secondary education, aimed in most countries at providing direct entry into the labour market)>; completed <ISCED Level 3A (upper secondary education, aimed in most countries at gaining entry into tertiary education)>; and completed <ISCED Level 5A, 5B or 6 (tertiary education)>.[5]

The educational level of the father and the mother were collected through two questions for each parent (*ST12Q01* and *ST14Q01* for the mother and *ST13Q01* and *ST15Q01* for the father). The variables in the database for mother's and father's highest level of education are labelled *MISCED* and *FISCED*.

Validating socio-economic status and parental education

In Canada, the Czech Republic, France and the United Kingdom, validity studies were carried out to test the reliability of student answers to the questions on their parents' occupations. Generally these studies indicate that useful data on parental occupation can be collected from 15-year-old students. Further details of the validity studies are presented in Appendix 4.

When reviewing the validity studies it should be kept in mind that 15-year-old students' reports of their parents' occupations are not necessarily less accurate than adults' reports of their own occupations. Individuals have a tendency to inflate their own occupations, especially when the data are collected by personal (including telephone) interviews. The correspondence between self-reports and proxy reports of husbands and wives is also imperfect. In addition, official records of a parent's occupation are arguably subject to greater sources of error (job changes, changes in coding schemes, etc.) than the answers of 15-year-olds.

---

[4] To capture wider aspects of a student's family and home background in addition to occupational status, the PISA initial report uses an index of economic, social and cultural status that is not in the international database. This index was created on the basis of the following variables: the International Socio-Economic Index of Occupational Status (*ISEI*); the highest level of education of the student's parents converted into years of schooling; the PISA index of family wealth; the PISA index of home educational resources; and the PISA index of possessions related to 'classical culture' in the family home. The *ISEI* represents the first principal component of the factors described above. The index was constructed to have a mean of 0 and a standard deviation of 1.

Among these components, the most commonly missing data relate to the International Socio-Economic Index of Occupational Status (*ISEI*), parental education, or both. Separate factor analyses were therefore undertaken for all students with valid data for: i) socio-economic index of occupational status, index of family wealth, index of home educational resources and index of possessions related to 'classical culture' in the family home; ii) years of parental education, index of family wealth, the index of home educational resources and index of possessions related to 'classical culture' in the family home; and iii) index of family wealth, index of home educational resources and index of possessions related to 'classical culture' in the family home. Students were then assigned a factor score based on the amount of data available. For this to be done, students had to have data on at least three variables.

[5] Terms in brackets < > were replaced in the national versions of the Student and School questionnaires by the appropriate national equivalent. For example, <qualification at ISCED level 5A> was translated in the United States into 'Bachelor's Degree, post-graduate certificate program, Master's degree program or first professional degree program'. Similarly, <classes in the language of assessment> in Luxembourg was translated into 'German classes' or 'French classes' depending on whether students received the German or French version of the assessment instruments.

The important issue here is the high correlation between parental occupation status derived from student and self-reports rather than the exact correspondence between ISCO occupational categories. For example, students' and parents' reports of a parent's occupation may result in it being coded to different ISCO categories but in very similar *SEI* scores.

In the PISA validity studies carried out in the four countries, the correlation of *SEI* scores between parental occupation as reported by students and by their parents was high, between 0.70 and 0.86. This correlation was judged to be high since the test/retest correlation of *SEI* from adults who were asked their occupation on two occasions over a short time period typically lies in this range.

The correspondence between broad occupational categories, which averaged about 70 per cent, was greater for some occupational groups (*e.g.* professionals) than others (*e.g.*, managers and administrators). Only 5 per cent of cases showed a large lack of correspondence, for example, between professionals and unskilled labourers.

Finally, the strength of the relationship between *SEI* and achievement was found to be very similar using *SEI* scores derived either from the students' or from parents' reports.

The desirability of coding to 4-digit ISCO codes versus 1 or 2-digit ISCO codes was also explored. *SEI* scores generated from one-digit ISCO codes (that is, only nine major groups) proved to substantially change the strength of the relationship between occupational status and achievement, usually reducing it but in some instances increasing it. The results of coding to only 2-digit ISCO codes were less clear. For the relationship between father's *SEI* and achievement, the correlations between *SEI* scores constructed from 2 or 4-digit ISCO codes were only slightly different. However with mother's *SEI*, sizeable differences did emerge for some countries, with differences of up to 0.05 in the correlation (or a 24 per cent attenuation). It is not immediately apparent why the correlation should change for mothers but not for fathers, but it is likely to be due to the greater clustering of women in particular jobs and the ability of 4-digit coding to distinguish high and low status positions within broad job groups. Since men's occupations are more evenly spread, the precision of 4-digit coding will have less of an impact.

Given the differences in the correlation between mother's *SEI* and achievement, it was preferable (and safer) to code the occupations to 4-digit ISCO codes. Additionally, converting already-coded occupations to 2-digit codes from 4-digit codes is quite a different exercise than directly coding the occupation to two digits. More detailed occupational coding is likely to increase the coder's familiarity and therefore accuracy with the ISCO coding schema.

PARENTAL INTEREST AND FAMILY RELATIONS
Cultural communication

The PISA index of *cultural communication* was derived from students' reports on the frequency with which their parents (or guardians) engaged with them in: discussing political or social issues; discussing books, films or television programmes; and listening to classical music. Frequency was measured on a five-point scale of *never or hardly ever*; *a few times a year*; *about once a month*; *several times a month*; and *several times a week*.

Scale scores are standardised *Warm* estimates. Positive values indicate a higher frequency of cultural communication and negative values indicate a lower frequency of cultural communication. The item parameter estimates used for the weighted likelihood estimation are given in Figure 42. For the meaning of delta and tau, see the third paragraph of this chapter.

	In general, how often do your parents:	Parameter Estimates				
		Delta	Tau(1)	Tau(2)	Tau(3)	Tau(4)
ST19Q01	discuss political or social issues with you?	-0.05	-0.59	0.43	-0.40	0.56
ST19Q02	discuss books, films or television programmes with you?	-0.68	-0.52	0.26	-0.32	0.58
ST19Q03	listen to classical music with you?	0.73	0.71	0.10	-0.60	-0.22

Figure 42: Item Parameter Estimates for the Index of Cultural Communication (CULTCOM)

Social communication

The PISA index of *social communication* was derived from students' reports on the frequency with which their parents (or guardians) engaged with them in the following activities: discussing how well they are doing at school; eating <the main meal> with them around a table; and spending time simply talking with them. Frequency was measured on a five-point scale of *never or hardly ever*; *a few times a year*; *about once a month*; *several times a month*; and *several times a week*.

Scale scores are standardised *Warm* estimates, where positive values indicate higher frequency of social communication and negative values indicate lower frequency of social communication. The item parameters used for the weighted likelihood estimation are given in Figure 43.

Family educational support

The PISA index of *family educational support* was derived from students' reports on how frequently the mother, father, or brothers and sisters worked with the student on what is regarded nationally as schoolwork. Students responded to each statement on a five-point scale with the following: *never or hardly ever*, *a few times a year*, *about once a month*, *several times a month* and *several times a week*.

Scale scores are standardised *Warm* estimates, where positive values indicate higher frequency of family (parents and siblings) support for the student's schoolwork while negative values indicate lower frequency. Item parameters used for the weighted likelihood estimation are given in Figure 44.

Cultural activities

The PISA index of *activities related to classical culture* was derived from students' reports on how often they had, during the preceding year: visited a museum or art gallery; attended an opera, ballet or classical symphony concert; or watched live theatre. Students responded to each statement on a four-point scale with: *never or hardly ever*, *once or twice a year*, *about three or four times a year*, and *more than four times a year*.

Scale scores are standardised *Warm* estimates where positive values indicate higher frequency and negative values indicate lower frequency of cultural activities during the year. Item parameters used for the weighted likelihood estimation are given in Figure 45.

	In general, how often do your parents:	Delta	Tau(1)	Tau(2)	Tau(3)	Tau(4)
ST19Q04	discuss how well you are doing at school?	0.052	-0.586	-0.012	0.069	0.53
ST19Q05	eat <the main meal> with you around a table?	-0.165	0.521	0.605	-0.504	-0.62
ST19Q06	spend time just talking to you?	0.113	0.011	0.143	-0.289	0.14

Figure 43: Item Parameter Estimates for the Index of Social Communication (SOCCOM)

	How often do the following people work with you on your <schoolwork>?	Delta	Tau(1)	Tau(2)	Tau(3)	Tau(4)
ST20Q01	Your mother	-0.24	-0.24	-0.07	-0.40	0.71
ST20Q02	Your father	0.01	-0.24	-0.13	-0.40	0.77
ST20Q03	Your brothers and sisters	0.24	0.22	-0.23	-0.38	0.39

Figure 44: Item Parameter Estimates for the Index of Family Educational Support (FAMEDSUP)

	During the past year, how often have you participated in these activities?	Delta	Tau(1)	Tau(2)	Tau(3)
ST18Q02	Visited a museum or art gallery.	-0.48	-1.54	0.77	0.77
ST18Q04	Attended an opera, ballet or classical symphony concert.	0.76	-0.46	0.52	-0.05
ST18Q05	Watched live theatre.	-0.28	-1.42	0.79	0.63

Figure 45: Item Parameter Estimates for the Index of Cultural Activities (CULTACTV)

Item dimensionality and reliability of 'parental interest and family relations' scales

Structural Equation Modelling confirmed the expected dimensional structure of the items used for the *parental interest and family relations* indices. All fit measures indicated a good model fit for the international sample (*RMSEA* = 0.045, *AGFI* = 0.97, *NNFI* = 0.93, and *CFI* = 0.95), and the estimated correlation between latent factors was highest between *CULTCOM* and *SOCCOM*, with 0.69, and lowest for *CULTACTV* and *FAMEDSUP*, with 0.17. For the country sub-samples, the *RMSEA* ranged between 0.032 and 0.071, showing that the dimensional structure was also confirmed across countries.

Table 74 shows the reliability for each of the *parental interest and family relations* variables for each participating country. Internal consistency is generally rather moderate but still satisfactory given the low number of items for each scale.

Table 74: Reliability of *Parental Interest and Family Relations* Scales

Country	CULTCOM	SOCCOM	FAMEDSUP	CULTACTV
Australia	0.62	0.58	0.66	0.60
Austria	0.55	0.53	0.70	0.66
Belgium	0.51	0.56	0.66	0.57
Canada	0.58	0.57	0.68	0.63
Czech Republic	0.53	0.57	0.63	0.64
Denmark	0.57	0.64	0.56	0.60
Finland	0.52	0.46	0.64	0.62
France	0.49	0.53	0.58	0.55
Germany	0.55	0.50	0.64	0.64
Greece	0.44	0.62	0.70	0.52
Hungary	0.50	0.58	0.65	0.66
Iceland	0.58	0.54	0.65	0.59
Ireland	0.53	0.56	0.69	0.54
Italy	0.49	0.55	0.59	0.57
Japan	0.59	0.59	0.71	0.50
Korea	0.63	0.67	0.74	0.67
Luxembourg	0.53	0.58	0.61	0.68
Mexico	0.50	0.72	0.66	0.62
New Zealand	0.57	0.56	0.69	0.59
Norway	0.60	0.65	0.69	0.60
Poland	0.57	0.63	0.66	0.68
Portugal	0.52	0.62	0.68	0.55
Spain	0.50	0.61	0.63	0.56
Sweden	0.58	0.57	0.60	0.63
Switzerland	0.58	0.47	0.66	0.60
United Kingdom	0.51	0.60	0.66	0.63
United States	0.63	0.68	0.69	0.65
Mean OECD countries	0.55	0.58	0.66	0.63
Brazil	0.57	0.65	0.67	0.54
Latvia	0.50	0.58	0.65	0.65
Liechtenstein	0.59	0.50	0.68	0.58
Russian Federation	0.49	0.62	0.67	0.68
Netherlands	0.54	0.64	0.67	0.59

Note: 'Mean OECD countries' does not include the Netherlands, which did not meet PISA's sampling standards.

FAMILY POSSESSIONS

Family wealth

The PISA index of *family wealth* was derived from students' reports on: (i) the availability in their home of a dishwasher, a room of their own, educational software, and a link to the Internet; and (ii) the numbers of cellular phones, televisions, computers, motor cars and bathrooms at home.

Scale scores are standardised *Warm* estimates, where positive values indicate more wealth-related possessions and negative values indicate fewer wealth-related possessions. The item parameters used for the weighted likelihood estimation are given in Figure 46.

Home educational resources

The PISA index of *home educational resources* was derived from students' reports on the availability and number of the following items in their home: a dictionary, a quiet place to study, a desk for study, text books and calculators.

Scale scores are standardised *Warm* estimates where positive values indicate possession of more educational resources and negative values indicate possession of fewer educational resources by the student's family. The item parameters used for the weighted likelihood estimation are given in Figure 47.

Possessions related to 'classical' culture in the family home

The PISA index of *possessions related to 'classical' culture in the family home* was derived from students' reports on the availability of the following items in their home: classical literature (examples were given), books of poetry and works of art (examples were given).

Scale scores are standardised *Warm* estimates, where positive values indicate a greater number of cultural possessions while negative values indicate fewer cultural possessions in the student's home. The item parameters used for the weighted likelihood estimation are given in Figure 48.

	In your home, do you have:	Delta	Tau(1)	Tau(2)	Tau(3)
ST21Q01	a dishwasher?	0.204			
ST21Q02	a room of your own?	-1.421			
ST21Q03	educational software?	0.085			
ST21Q04	a link to the Internet?	0.681			
	How many of these do you have at your home?				
ST22Q01	<Cellular> phone	0.225	-0.657	0.137	0.52
ST22Q02	Television	-1.332	-2.31	0.506	1.804
ST22Q04	Computer	1.133	-1.688	0.628	1.06
ST22Q06	Motor car	0.379	-1.873	0.262	1.611
ST22Q07	Bathroom	0.046	-3.364	0.973	2.391

Figure 46: Item Parameter Estimates for the Index of Family Wealth (WEALTH)

	In your home, do you have:	Delta	Tau(1)	Tau(2)	Tau(3)
ST21Q05	a dictionary?	-1.19			
ST21Q06	a quiet place to study?	0.08			
ST21Q07	a desk for study?	0.05			
ST21Q08	text books?	0.27			
	How many of these do you have at your home?				
ST22Q03	Calculator	0.79	-1.19	0.32	0.88

Figure 47: Item Parameter Estimates for the Index of Home Educational Resources (HEDRES)

	In your home, do you have:	Parameter Estimates Delta
ST21Q09	classical literature (*e.g.*, <Shakespeare>)?	0.14
ST21Q10	books of poetry?	0.04
ST21Q11	works of art (*e.g.*, paintings)?	-0.18

Figure 48: Item Parameter Estimates for the Index of Possessions Related to 'Classical Culture' in the Family Home (CULTPOSS)

Item dimensionality and reliability of 'family possessions' scales

Structural Equation Modelling largely confirmed the dimensional structure of the items on *family possessions*. For the international sample both *NNFI* and *CFI* were rather low (< 0.85) indicating a considerable lack of model fit, but *AGFI* (0.93) and *RMSEA* (0.063) showed a still acceptable fit. Estimated correlations between the latent factors were 0.40 for *WEALTH* and *HEDRES*, 0.21 for *WEALTH* and *CULTPOSS*, and 0.52 for *CULTPOSS* and *HEDRES*. The *RMSEA* measures for the country sub-samples ranged from 0.050 to 0.079.

Table 75 shows the reliability for each of the four *family possessions* variables for each participant. Whereas the reliability for *WEALTH* and *CULTPOSS* are reasonable, the internal consistency for *HEDRES* is rather low. Though the reliability of these indices might be considered lower than desirable, they were retained since they can be interpreted as simple counts of the number of possessions. The lower reliability simply suggests that these counts can be made up of very different subsets of items.

Table 75: Reliability of Family Possessions Scales

Country	WEALTH	HEDRES	CULTPOSS
Australia	0.66	0.43	0.64
Austria	0.62	0.28	0.57
Belgium	0.61	0.43	0.58
Canada	0.69	0.43	0.64
Czech Republic	0.67	0.38	0.54
Denmark	0.66	0.31	0.60
Finland	0.62	0.33	0.65
France	0.61	0.30	0.62
Germany	0.65	0.31	0.59
Greece	0.70	0.30	0.48
Hungary	0.70	0.27	0.55
Iceland	0.64	0.43	0.57
Ireland	0.66	0.35	0.58
Italy	0.67	0.22	0.56
Japan	0.50	0.20	0.60
Korea	0.61	0.17	0.54
Luxembourg	0.67	0.52	.067
Mexico	0.80	0.48	0.65
New Zealand	0.68	0.47	0.65
Norway	0.60	0.45	0.69
Poland	0.76	0.38	0.53
Portugal	0.75	0.29	0.61
Spain	0.67	0.26	0.60
Sweden	0.68	0.38	0.65
Switzerland	0.63	0.31	0.61
United Kingdom	0.65	0.46	0.66
United States	0.72	0.53	0.64
Mean OECD countries	0.70	0.36	0.59
Brazil	0.78	0.45	0.50
Latvia	0.68	0.32	0.57
Liechtenstein	0.60	0.41	0.56
Russian Federation	0.63	0.30	0.47
Netherlands	0.53	0.29	0.56

Note: 'Mean OECD countries' does not include the Netherlands, which did not meet PISA's sampling standards.

INSTRUCTION AND LEARNING
Instruction time

Three indices give the time in terms of number of minutes spent each week at school in the three assessed domains. The variables were labelled *RMINS* for reading courses, *MMINS* for mathematics courses and *SMINS* for science courses. They are simply the product of the corresponding item of student question 27 (*ST27Q01, ST27Q03, ST27Q05*) (number of class periods in <test language>, mathematics and science per week) and school question 6 (*SC06Q03*) (number of minutes per single class period).

Time spent on homework

The PISA index of *time spent on homework* was derived from students' reports on the amount of time they devoted to homework in the <test language>, in mathematics and in science. Students responded to this on a four-point scale: *no time*, *less than 1 hour a week*, *between 1 and 3 hours a week*, and *3 hours or more a week*.

Scale scores are standardised *Warm* estimates where positive values indicate more and negative values indicate less time spent on homework. The item parameters used for the weighted likelihood estimation are given in Figure 49.

Teacher support

The PISA index of *teacher support* was derived from students' reports on the frequency with which the teacher: shows an interest in every student's learning; gives students an opportunity to express opinions; helps students with their work; continues teaching until the students understand; does a lot to help students; and helps students with their learning. A four-point scale was used with response categories: *never*, *some lessons*, *most lessons* and *every lesson*.

Scale scores are standardised *Warm* estimates where positive values indicate higher levels and negative values indicate lower levels of teacher support. The item parameters used for the weighted likelihood estimation are given in Figure 50.

Achievement press

The PISA index of *achievement press* was derived from students' reports on the frequency with which, in their <test language> lesson, the teacher: wants students to work hard; tells students that they can do better; and does not like it when students deliver <careless> work; and students have to learn a lot. A four-point scale was used with response categories: *never*, *some lessons*, *most lessons* and *every lesson*.

	On average, how much time do you spend each week on homework and study in these subject areas?	Delta	Tau(1)	Tau(2)	Tau(3)
ST33Q01	<test language>	0.05	-2.59	-0.04	2.62
ST33Q02	<mathematics>	-0.23	-2.33	-0.01	2.34
ST33Q03	<science>	0.17	-2.04	0.02	2.02

Figure 49: Item Parameter Estimates for the Index of Time Spent on Homework (HMWKTIME)

	How often do these things happen in your <test language> lessons? The teacher:	Delta	Tau(1)	Tau(2)	Tau(3)
ST26Q05	shows an interest in every student's learning.	0.22	-1.78	0.36	1.42
ST26Q06	gives students an opportunity to express opinions.	-0.35	-1.80	0.35	1.45
ST26Q07	helps students with their work.	-0.04	-1.95	0.34	1.61
ST26Q08	continues teaching until the students understand.	-0.02	-1.97	0.31	1.66
ST26Q09	does a lot to help students.	-0.02	-2.15	0.30	1.86
ST26Q10	helps students with their learning.	0.20	-1.86	0.23	1.63

Figure 50: Item Parameter Estimates for the Index of Teacher Support (TEACHSUP)

Scale scores are standardised *Warm* estimates where positive values indicate higher levels and negative values indicate lower levels of achievement press. The item parameters used for the weighted likelihood estimation are given in Figure 51.

	How often do these things happen in your <test language> lessons?	Delta	Tau(1)	Tau(2)	Tau(3)
ST26Q02	The teacher wants students to work hard.	-0.37	-1.33	0.36	0.97
ST26Q03	The teacher tells students that they can do better.	0.22	-1.63	0.65	0.98
ST26Q04	The teacher does not like it when students deliver <careless> work.	0.19	-1.36	0.62	0.74
ST26Q15	Students have to learn a lot.	-0.04	-1.76	0.42	1.34

Figure 51: Item Parameter Estimates for the Index of Achievement Press (ACHPRESS)

Item dimensionality and reliability of 'instruction and learning' scales

Structural Equation Modelling confirmed the expected dimensional structure of the items used for the *instruction and learning* indices. All fit measures indicated a close model fit for the international sample (*RMSEA* = 0.046, *AGFI* = 0.97, *NNFI* = 0.96 and *CFI* = 0.97), and the estimated correlations between latent factors were 0.27 for *TEACHSUP* and *ACHPRESS*, 0.18 for *TEACHSUP* and *HMWKTIME*, and 0.15 for *ACHPRESS* and *HMWKTIME*. The *RMSEA* for the country sub-samples ranged between 0.043 and 0.080, showing that the dimensional structure was similar across countries.

Table 76 shows the reliability for each of the four *instruction and learning* variables for each participant. Internal consistency is high for both *HMWKTIME* and *TEACHSUP* but only moderate for *ACHPRESS*.

Table 76: Reliability of *Instruction and Learning* Scales

Country	HMWKTIME	TEACHSUP	ACHPRESS
Australia	0.81	0.90	0.53
Austria	0.57	0.87	0.59
Belgium	0.77	0.85	0.57
Canada	0.78	0.90	0.55
Czech Republic	0.72	0.80	0.67
Denmark	0.71	0.86	0.37
Finland	0.79	0.88	0.62
France	0.74	0.87	0.62
Germany	0.66	0.86	0.57
Greece	0.84	0.86	0.50
Hungary	0.69	0.85	0.54
Iceland	0.72	0.87	0.62
Ireland	0.78	0.89	0.50
Italy	0.70	0.85	0.51
Japan	0.86	0.89	0.47

Table 76 (cont.)

Country	HMWKTIME	TEACHSUP	ACHPRESS
Korea	0.88	0.83	0.38
Luxembourg	0.67	0.88	0.62
Mexico	0.74	0.83	0.49
New Zealand	0.80	0.89	0.51
Norway	0.82	0.88	0.60
Poland	0.79	0.86	0.61
Portugal	0.76	0.88	0.52
Spain	0.79	0.90	0.53
Sweden	0.74	0.88	0.55
Switzerland	0.68	0.86	0.55
United Kingdom	0.79	0.89	0.44
United States	0.77	0.91	0.54
Mean OECD countries	0.76	0.87	0.54
Brazil	0.80	0.86	0.47
Latvia	0.73	0.83	0.64
Liechtenstein	0.76	0.84	0.55
Russian Federation	0.80	0.84	0.53
Netherlands	0.69	0.82	0.49

Note: 'Mean OECD countries' does not include the Netherlands, which did not meet PISA's sampling standards.

SCHOOL AND CLASSROOM CLIMATE

Disciplinary climate

The PISA index of *disciplinary climate* summarises students' reports on the frequency with which, in their <test language> lesson: the teacher has to wait a long time for students to <quieten down>; students cannot work well; students don't listen to what the teacher says; students don't start working for a long time after the lesson begins; there is noise and disorder; and, at the start of class, more than five minutes are spent doing nothing. A four-point scale was used with response categories *never*, *some lessons*, *most lessons* and *every lesson*.

Scale scores are standardised *Warm* estimates where positive values indicate more positive perception of the disciplinary climate and negative values indicate less positive perception of the disciplinary climate. The item parameters used for the weighted likelihood estimation are given in Figure 52.

	How often do these things happen in your <test language> lessons?	Parameter Estimates			
		Delta	Tau(1)	Tau(2)	Tau(3)
ST26Q01	The teacher has to wait a long time for students to <quieten down>.	-0.26	-2.48	0.95	1.53
ST26Q12	Students cannot work well.	0.47	-2.52	1.02	1.50
ST26Q13	Students don't listen to what the teacher says.	0.11	-2.79	1.08	1.71
ST26Q14	Students don't start working for a long time after the lesson begins.	0.21	-2.23	0.76	1.47
ST26Q16	There is noise and disorder.	-0.10	-2.09	0.93	1.16
ST26Q17	At the start of class, more than five minutes are spent doing nothing.	-0.43	-1.56	0.72	0.84

Figure 52: Item Parameter Estimates for the Index of Disciplinary Climate (DISCLIM)

Teacher-student relations

The PISA index of *teacher-student relations* was derived from students' reports on their level of agreement with the following statements: students get along well with most teachers; most teachers are interested in students' well-being; most of my teachers really listen to what I have to say; if I need extra help, I will receive it from my teachers; and most of my teachers treat me fairly. A four-point scale was used with response categories *strongly disagree*, *disagree*, *agree* and *strongly agree*.

Scale scores are standardised *Warm* estimates where positive values indicate more positive perceptions of student–teacher relations and negative values indicate less positive perceptions of student–teacher relations. The item parameters used for the weighted likelihood estimation are given in Figure 53.

Sense of belonging

The PISA index of *sense of belonging* was derived from students' reports on whether their school is a place where they: feel like an outsider, make friends easily, feel like they belong, feel awkward and out of place, other students seem to like them, or feel lonely. A four-point scale was used with response categories: *strongly disagree*, *disagree*, *agree* and *strongly agree*.

Scale scores are standardised *Warm* estimates where positive values indicate more positive attitudes towards school and negative values indicate less positive attitudes towards school. The item parameters used for the weighted likelihood estimation are given in Figure 54.

Item dimensionality and reliability of 'school and classroom climate' scales

For the international sample, the Confirmatory Factor Analysis showed a good model fit with *RMSEA* = 0.053, *AGFI* = 0.95, *NNFI* = 0.92 and *CFI* = 0.94. The correlation between latent factors is -0.23 for *STUDREL* and *DISCLIM*, -0.09 for *BELONG* and *DISCLIM*, and 0.29 for *BELONG* and *STUDREL*. For the country sub-samples, the *RMSEA* ranged between 0.050 and 0.073, showing that the dimensionality structure is similar across countries.

Table 77 shows the reliability for each of the three *school and classroom climate* variables for each participating country. Internal consistency is very high for all three indices.

	How much do you disagree or agree with each of the following statements about teachers at your school?	Delta	Tau(1)	Tau(2)	Tau(3)
ST30Q01	Students get along well with most teachers.	0.22	-2.59	-0.76	3.35
ST30Q02	Most teachers are interested in students' well-being.	0.10	-2.48	-0.70	3.18
ST30Q03	Most of my teachers really listen to what I have to say.	0.14	-2.57	-0.53	3.09
ST30Q04	If I need extra help, I will receive it from my teachers.	-0.26	-2.20	-0.81	3.01
ST30Q05	Most of my teachers treat me fairly.	-0.20	-2.04	-0.96	3.00

Figure 53: Item Parameter Estimates for the Index of Teacher-Student Relations (STUDREL)

	My school is a place where:	Delta	Tau(1)	Tau(2)	Tau(3)
ST31Q01	I feel like an outsider (or left out of things). (rev.)	-0.57	-0.94	-0.68	1.62
ST31Q02	I make friends easily.	0.03	-1.83	-0.94	2.77
ST31Q03	I feel like I belong.	0.65	-1.49	-0.92	2.41
ST31Q04	I feel awkward and out of place. (rev.)	-0.18	-1.34	-0.56	1.89
ST31Q05	other students seem to like me.	0.59	-1.98	-1.27	3.25
ST31Q06	I feel lonely. (rev.)	-0.52	-1.18	-0.64	1.81

Note: Items marked 'rev.' had their response categories reversed before scaling.

Figure 54: Item Parameter Estimates for the Index of Sense of Belonging (BELONG)

Table 77: Reliability of *School and Classroom Climate* Scales

Country	DISCLIM	STUDREL	BELONG
Australia	0.84	0.83	0.83
Austria	0.81	0.80	0.80
Belgium	0.82	0.78	0.73
Canada	0.83	0.80	0.84
Czech Republic	0.81	0.77	0.69
Denmark	0.80	0.82	0.75
Finland	0.84	0.78	0.83
France	0.82	0.78	0.75
Germany	0.80	0.76	0.79
Greece	0.71	0.71	0.73
Hungary	0.84	0.77	0.76
Iceland	0.83	0.81	0.83
Ireland	0.86	0.77	0.84
Italy	0.82	0.75	0.72
Japan	0.80	0.85	0.78
Korea	0.81	0.82	0.69
Luxembourg	0.77	0.80	0.77
Mexico	0.70	0.70	0.71
New Zealand	0.85	0.78	0.83
Norway	0.83	0.82	0.82
Poland	0.81	0.78	0.68
Portugal	0.77	0.77	0.69
Spain	0.80	0.80	0.71
Sweden	0.82	0.81	0.81
Switzerland	0.77	0.82	0.75
United Kingdom	0.87	0.82	0.83
United States	0.83	0.83	0.86
Mean OECD countries	0.81	0.79	0.77
Brazil	0.76	0.76	0.77
Latvia	0.79	0.72	0.71
Liechtenstein	0.76	0.82	0.81
Russian Federation	0.80	0.70	0.71
Netherlands	0.83	0.73	0.76

Note: 'Mean OECD countries' does not include the Netherlands, which did not meet PISA's sampling standards.

READING HABITS

Engagement in reading

The PISA index of *engagement in reading* was derived from students' level of agreement with the following statements: I read only if I have to; reading is one of my favourite hobbies; I like talking about books with other people; I find it hard to finish books; I feel happy if I receive a book as a present; for me, reading is a waste of time; I enjoy going to a bookstore or a library; I read only to get information that I need; and I cannot sit still and read for more than a few minutes. A four-point scale was used with response categories *strongly disagree, disagree, agree* and *strongly agree*.

Scale scores are standardised *Warm* estimates where positive values indicate more positive attitudes towards reading and negative values indicate less positive attitudes towards reading. The item parameters used for the weighted likelihood estimation are given in Figure 55.

Reading diversity

The PISA index on *reading diversity* was derived from dichotomised student reports on how often (*never* to *a few times a year* versus *about once a month or more often*) they read: magazines, comic books, fiction, non-fiction books, email and web pages, and newspapers. It is interpreted as an indicator of the variety of student reading sources.

Scale scores are standardised *Warm* estimates where positive values indicate higher levels and negative values lower levels of reading diversity.

The item parameters used for the weighted likelihood estimation are given in Figure 56.

Item dimensionality and reliability of 'reading' scales

A CFA showed a still acceptable fit of the two-dimensional model for the international sample (*RMSEA* = 0.078, *AGFI* = 0.91, *NNFI* = 0.89 and *CFI* = 0.91), with a correlation between latent factors of 0.66. The *RMSEA* ranged between 0.046 and 0.127 across OECD countries. The lack of fit is largely due to the common variance between negatively phrased, and therefore, inverted, items, which is not explained in the model.

Table 78 shows the reliability for each of the four *reading* variables for each participating country. Reliability is generally rather low for *DIVREAD* but as this is a simple index measuring only the variation in reading material, the low internal consistency was not considered a major concern.

	How much do you disagree or agree with these statements about reading?	Delta	Tau(1)	Tau(2)	Tau(3)
ST35Q01	I read only if I have to. (rev.)	-0.42	-1.24	-0.18	1.42
ST35Q02	Reading is one of my favourite hobbies.	0.83	-1.61	-0.01	1.62
ST35Q03	I like talking about books with other people.	1.02	-1.82	-0.28	2.09
ST35Q04	I find it hard to finish books. (rev.)	-0.55	-1.45	-0.23	1.68
ST35Q05	I feel happy if I receive a book as a present.	0.54	-1.59	-0.52	2.11
ST35Q06	For me, reading is a waste of time. (rev.)	-0.91	-0.87	-0.67	1.54
ST35Q07	I enjoy going to a bookstore or a library.	0.45	-1.57	-0.36	1.92
ST35Q08	I read only to get information that I need. (rev.)	-0.05	-1.85	-0.05	1.90
ST35Q09	I cannot sit still and read for more than a few minutes. (rev.)	-0.91	-0.96	-0.46	1.42

Note: Items marked 'rev.' had their response categories reversed before scaling.

Figure 55: Item Parameter Estimates for the Index of Engagement in Reading (JOYREAD)

	How often do you read these materials because you want to?	Parameter Estimates Delta
ST36Q01	Magazines	-1.52
ST36Q02	Comic books	0.75
ST36Q03	Fiction (novels, narratives, stories)	0.60
ST36Q04	Non-fiction books	1.04
ST36Q05	Emails and Web pages	0.16
ST36Q06	Newspapers	-1.03

Note: Items were dichotomised as follows (0 = 1,2 = never or a few times a year); (1 = 3,4,5 = about once a month, several times a month or several times a week).

Figure 56: Item Parameter Estimates for the Index of Reading Diversity (DIVREAD)

Table 78: Reliability of *Reading Habits* Scales

Country	JOYREAD	DIVREAD
Australia	0.76	0.51
Austria	0.76	0.34
Belgium	0.74	0.55
Canada	0.77	0.50
Czech Republic	0.72	0.38
Denmark	0.75	0.58
Finland	0.75	0.43
France	0.71	0.54
Germany	0.76	0.40
Greece	0.66	0.48
Hungary	0.70	0.53
Iceland	0.72	0.48
Ireland	0.76	0.48
Italy	0.71	0.48
Japan	0.66	0.44
Korea	0.68	0.59
Luxembourg	0.71	0.53
Mexico	0.61	0.61
New Zealand	0.73	0.49
Norway	0.75	0.44
Poland	0.69	0.50
Portugal	0.70	0.50
Spain	0.70	0.53
Sweden	0.75	0.46
Switzerland	0.76	0.46
United Kingdom	0.75	0.50
United States	0.76	0.61
Mean OECD countries	0.72	0.50
Brazil	0.70	0.59
Latvia	0.64	0.44
Liechtenstein	0.73	0.50
Russian Federation	0.64	0.51
Netherlands	0.74	0.55

Note: 'Mean OECD countries' does not include the Netherlands, which did not meet PISA's sampling standards.

MOTIVATION AND INTEREST

The following indices were derived from the international option on Self-Regulated Learning, which about a quarter of the countries chose not to administer.

Instrumental motivation

The PISA index of *instrumental motivation* was derived from students' reports on how often they study to: increase their job opportunities; ensure that their future will be financially secure; and enable them to get a good job. A four-point scale was used with response categories *almost never*, *sometimes*, *often* and *almost always*.

Scale scores are standardised *Warm* estimates where positive values indicate higher levels and negative values indicate lower levels of endorsement of instrumental motivation for learning. The item parameters used for the weighted likelihood estimation are given in Figure 57.

Interest in reading

The PISA index of *interest in reading* was derived from student agreement with the three statements listed in Figure 58. A four-point scale was used with response categories *disagree*, *disagree somewhat*, *agree somewhat* and *agree*. For information on the conceptual underpinning of the index see Baumert, Gruehn, Heyn, Köller and Schnabel (1997).

Scale scores are standardised *Warm* estimates where positive values indicate higher levels and negative values indicate lower levels of interest in reading. The item parameters used for the weighted likelihood estimation are given in Figure 58.

How often do these things apply to you?		Delta	Tau(1)	Tau(2)	Tau(3)
CC01Q06	I study to increase my job opportunities.	0.04	-2.20	-0.01	2.20
CC01Q14	I study to ensure that my future will be financially secure.	0.26	-2.07	0.02	2.05
CC01Q22	I study to get a good job.	-0.30	-2.12	0.01	2.11

Figure 57: Item Parameter Estimates for the Index of Instrumental Motivation (INSMOT)

	How much do you disagree or agree with each of the following?	Parameter Estimates			
		Delta	Tau(1)	Tau(2)	Tau(3)
CC02Q06	Because reading is fun, I wouldn't want to give it up.	0.18	-1.55	-0.06	1.61
CC02Q13	I read in my spare time.	0.17	-1.45	-0.19	1.64
CC02Q17	When I read, I sometimes get totally absorbed.	-0.35	-1.40	-0.15	1.55

Figure 58: Item Parameter Estimates for the Index of Interest in Reading (INTREA)

Interest in mathematics

The PISA index of *interest in mathematics* was derived from students' responses to the three items listed in Figure 59. A four-point scale with the response categories *disagree, disagree somewhat, agree somewhat* and *agree* was used. For information on the conceptual underpinning of the index see Baumert, Gruehn, Heyn, Köller and Schnabel (1997).

Scale scores are standardised *Warm* estimates where positive values indicate a greater interest in mathematics and negative values a lower interest in mathematics. The item parameters used for the weighted likelihood estimation are given in Figure 59.

Item dimensionality and reliability of 'motivation and interest' scales

In a CFA, the fit for the three-dimensional model was acceptable ($RMSEA = 0.040$, $AGFI = 0.98$, $NNFI = 0.98$ and $CFI = 0.99$), and the correlation between the three latent dimensions was 0.13 for INTREA and INSMOT, 0.27 for INTMAT and INSMOT, and 0.11 for INTMAT and INTREA. Across countries, the *RMSEA* ranged between 0.014 and 0.074, which confirmed the dimensional structure for all countries.

Table 79 shows the reliability for each of the three *motivation and interest* variables for each participating country. For all three scales, the internal consistency is satisfactory across countries.

	How much do you disagree or agree with each of the following?	Parameter Estimates			
		Delta	Tau(1)	Tau(2)	Tau(3)
CC02Q01	When I do mathematics, I sometimes get totally absorbed.	-0.02	-1.55	-0.27	1.83
CC02Q10	Because doing mathematics is fun, I wouldn't want to give it up.	0.27	-1.30	-0.13	1.42
CC02Q21	Mathematics is important to me personally.	-0.25	-1.20	-0.28	1.48

Figure 59: Item Parameter Estimates for the Index of Interest in Mathematics (INTMAT)

Table 79: Reliability of *Motivation and Interest* Scales

COUNTRY	INSMOT	INTREA	INTMAT
Australia	0.83	0.83	0.72
Austria	0.81	0.84	0.72
Belgium (Fl.)	0.84	0.87	0.78
Czech Republic	0.81	0.86	0.68
Denmark	0.79	0.85	0.83
Finland	0.82	0.88	0.82
Germany	0.83	0.85	0.76
Hungary	0.85	0.87	0.75
Iceland	0.81	0.78	0.66
Ireland	0.85	0.84	0.71
Italy	0.84	0.82	0.72
Korea	0.72	0.82	0.83
Luxembourg	0.82	0.81	0.72
Mexico	0.69	0.61	0.51
New Zealand	0.85	0.83	0.75
Norway	0.83	0.85	0.79
Portugal	0.84	0.81	0.73
Sweden	0.85	0.75	0.77
Switzerland	0.78	0.84	0.77
United States	0.83	0.82	0.74
Mean OECD countries	0.82	0.83	0.75
Brazil	0.83	0.73	0.65
Latvia	0.69	0.75	0.72
Liechtenstein	0.83	0.84	0.73
Russian Federation	0.76	0.78	0.74
Netherlands	0.82	0.84	0.76
Scotland	0.79	0.86	0.72

Note: 'Mean OECD countries' does not include the Netherlands, which did not meet PISA's sampling standards. The Flemish Community of Belgium constitutes half of Belgium's population and has been given the status of a country for these analyses.

LEARNING STRATEGIES

Control strategies

The PISA index of *control strategies* was derived from students' responses to the five items listed in Figure 60. A four-point scale was used with the response categories *almost never*, *sometimes*, *often* and *almost always*. For information on the conceptual underpinning of the index see Baumert, Heyn and Köller (1994).

Scale scores are standardised *Warm* estimates where positive values indicate higher frequency and negative values indicate lower frequency of self-reported use of control strategies. The item parameters used for the weighted likelihood estimation are given in Figure 60.

	How often do these things apply to you? When I study,	Parameter Estimates			
		Delta	Tau(1)	Tau(2)	Tau(3)
CC01Q03	I start by figuring out exactly what I need to learn.	-0.13	-1.73	0.1	1.63
CC01Q13	I force myself to check to see if I remember what I have learned.	0.23	-1.75	0.23	1.52
CC01Q19	I try to figure out which concepts I still haven't really understood.	0.02	-2.43	0.22	2.21
CC01Q23	I make sure that I remember the most important things.	-0.54	-2.09	0.07	2.01
CC01Q27	and I don't understand something I look for additional information to clarify this.	0.43	-1.99	0.24	1.74

Figure 60: Item Parameter Estimates for the Index of Control Strategies (CSTRAT)

Memorisation

The PISA index of *memorisation strategies* was derived from students' reports on the four items in Figure 61. A four-point scale was used with the response categories *almost never*, *sometimes*, *often* and *almost always*. For information on the conceptual underpinning of the index see Baumert, Heyn and Köller (1994) and Pintrich *et al.* (1993).

Scale scores are standardised *Warm* estimates where positive values indicate higher frequency and negative values indicate lower frequency of self-reported use of memorisation as a learning strategy. Item parameters used for the weighted likelihood estimation are given in Figure 61.

Elaboration

The PISA index of *elaboration strategies* was derived from students' reports on the four items in Figure 62. A four-point scale with the response categories *almost never*, *sometimes*, *often* and *almost always* was used. For information on the conceptual underpinning of the index, see Baumert, Heyn and Köller (1994).

Scale scores are standardised *Warm* estimates where positive values indicate higher frequency and negative values indicate lower frequency of self-reported use of elaboration as a learning strategy. The item parameters used for the weighted likelihood estimation are given in Figure 62.

	How often do these things apply to you? When I study,	Parameter Estimates			
		Delta	Tau(1)	Tau(2)	Tau(3)
CC01Q01	I try to memorise everything that might be covered.	-0.26	-1.81	0.30	1.51
CC01Q05	I memorise as much as possible.	-0.10	-1.63	0.17	1.46
CC01Q10	I memorise all new material so that I can recite it.	0.62	-1.70	0.26	1.44
CC01Q15	I practise by saying the material to myself over and over.	-0.26	-1.57	0.22	1.35

Figure 61: Item Parameter Estimates for the Index of Memorisation (MEMOR)

	How often do these things apply to you? When I study,	Parameter Estimates			
		Delta	Tau(1)	Tau(2)	Tau(3)
CC01Q09	I try to relate new material to things I have learned in other subjects.	0.26	-2.39	0.20	2.20
CC01Q17	I figure out how the information might be useful in the real world.	0.32	-2.24	0.23	2.01
CC01Q21	I try to understand the material better by relating it to things I already know.	-0.40	-2.58	0.24	2.35
CC01Q25	I figure out how the material fits in with what I have already learned.	-0.18	-2.77	0.25	2.52

Figure 62: Item Parameter Estimates for the Index of Elaboration (ELAB)

How often do these things apply to you? When I study,		Parameter Estimates			
		Delta	Tau(1)	Tau(2)	Tau(3)
CC01Q07	I work as hard as possible.	0.09	-2.58	0.31	2.27
CC01Q12	I keep working even if the material is difficult.	0.33	-2.54	0.22	2.32
CC01Q20	I try to do my best to acquire the knowledge and skills taught.	-0.19	-2.82	0.15	2.68
CC01Q28	I put forth my best effort.	-0.23	-2.59	0.30	2.29

Figure 63: Item Parameter Estimates for the Index of Effort and Perseverance (EFFPER)

Effort and perseverance

The PISA index of *effort and perseverance* was derived from students' reports on the four items in Figure 63. A four-point scale with the response categories: *almost never, sometimes, often* and *almost always* was used.

Scale scores are standardised *Warm* estimates where positive values indicate higher frequency and negative values indicate lower frequency of effort and perseverance as a learning strategy.

The item parameters used for the weighted likelihood estimation are given in Figure 63.

Item dimensionality and reliability of 'learning strategies' scales

Table 80 shows the reliability of each of the four *learning strategies* variables for each participating country. For all four scales, the internal consistency is satisfactory across countries.

Table 80: Reliability of *Learning Strategies* Scales

Country	CSTRAT	MEMOR	ELAB	EFFPER
Australia	0.81	0.74	0.79	0.81
Austria	0.67	0.71	0.73	0.76
Belgium (Fl.)	0.69	0.76	0.77	0.78
Czech Republic	0.75	0.74	0.79	0.75
Denmark	0.70	0.63	0.75	0.76
Finland	0.77	0.71	0.79	0.78
Germany	0.73	0.73	0.75	0.77
Hungary	0.72	0.71	0.78	0.76
Iceland	0.72	0.70	0.76	0.77
Ireland	0.77	0.75	0.78	0.82
Italy	0.74	0.66	0.80	0.78
Korea	0.72	0.69	0.76	0.78
Luxembourg	0.77	0.77	0.76	0.78
Mexico	0.74	0.75	0.77	0.74
New Zealand	0.80	0.73	0.76	0.80
Norway	0.75	0.77	0.80	0.79
Portugal	0.77	0.73	0.74	0.78
Sweden	0.76	0.74	0.79	0.80
Switzerland	0.74	0.70	0.74	0.79
United States	0.83	0.77	0.80	0.83
Mean OECD countries	0.76	0.72	0.77	0.78
Brazil	0.77	0.67	0.73	0.77
Latvia	0.66	0.54	0.63	0.70

Table 80 (cont.)

Country	CSTRAT	MEMOR	ELAB	EFFPER
Liechtenstein	0.78	0.72	0.80	0.81
Russian Federation	0.71	0.56	0.77	0.76
Netherlands	0.70	0.65	0.75	0.77
Scotland	0.75	0.68	0.73	0.76

Note: 'Mean OECD countries' does not include the Netherlands, which did not meet PISA's sampling standards. The Flemish Community of Belgium constitutes half of Belgium's population and has been given the status of a country for these analyses.

LEARNING STYLE

Co-operative learning

The PISA index of *co-operative learning* was derived from student reports on the four items in Figure 64. A four-point scale with the response categories *disagree*, *disagree somewhat*, *agree somewhat* and *agree* was used. For information on the conceptual underpinning of the index, see Owens and Barnes (1992).

Scale scores are standardised *Warm* estimates where positive values indicate higher levels of self-perception of preference for co-operative learning and negative values lower levels of self-perception of this preference. The item parameters used for the weighted likelihood estimation are given in Figure 64.

Competitive learning

The PISA index of *competitive learning* was derived from students' responses to the items in Figure 65, which also gives item parameters used for the weighted likelihood estimation. A four-point scale with the response categories *disagree*, *disagree somewhat*, *agree somewhat* and *agree* was used. For information on the conceptual underpinning of the index, see Owens and Barnes (1992).

Scale scores are standardised *Warm* estimates where positive values indicate higher reported levels of self-perception of preference for competitive learning and negative values indicate lower levels of self-perception of this preference.

	How much do you disagree or agree with each of the following?	Delta	Tau(1)	Tau(2)	Tau(3)
CC02Q02	I like to work with other students.	-0.21	-0.85	-0.59	1.44
CC02Q08	I learn most when I work with other students.	0.74	-1.52	-0.11	1.63
CC02Q19	I like to help other people do well in a group.	-0.04	-1.29	-0.60	1.89
CC02Q22	It is helpful to put together everyone's ideas when working on a project.	-0.50	-1.03	-0.59	1.62

Figure 64: Item Parameter Estimates for the Index of Co-operative Learning (COPLRN)

	How much do you disagree or agree with each of the following?	Delta	Tau(1)	Tau(2)	Tau(3)
CC02Q04	I like to try to be better than other students.	0.19	-1.82	-0.09	1.91
CC02Q11	Trying to be better than others makes me work well.	0.28	-1.82	-0.29	2.10
CC02Q16	I would like to be the best at something.	-0.92	-1.10	-0.20	1.30
CC02Q24	I learn faster if I'm trying to do better than the others.	0.45	-1.99	-0.01	2.00

Figure 65: Item Parameter Estimates for the Index of Competitive Learning (COMLRN)

Item dimensionality and reliability of 'co-operative and competitive learning' scales

A CFA showed a poor fit for the initial model, which is largely due to a similar wording of items CC02Q02 and CC02Q08. After introducing a correlated error term for these items, the model fit was satisfactory for the international sample ($RMSEA = 0.048$, $AGFI = 0.98$, $NNFI = 0.97$ and $CFI = 0.98$). The $RMSEA$ ranged between 0.029 and 0.095 across countries, which confirmed the two-dimensional structure for the sub-samples.

Table 81 shows the reliability of the two *learning style* variables for each participant. The internal consistency for COPLRN is clearly lower than for COMLRN.

Table 81: Reliability of *Learning Style* Scales

Country	COPLRN	COMLRN
Australia	0.64	0.77
Austria	0.61	0.78
Belgium (Fl.)	0.59	0.77
Czech Republic	0.64	0.74
Denmark	0.60	0.81
Finland	0.67	0.80
Germany	0.68	0.75
Hungary	0.57	0.72
Iceland	0.64	0.79
Ireland	0.66	0.80
Italy	0.67	0.77
Korea	0.60	0.76
Luxembourg	0.73	0.75
Mexico	0.62	0.71
New Zealand	0.68	0.79
Norway	0.70	0.81
Portugal	0.64	0.79
Sweden	0.62	0.80
Switzerland	0.63	0.77
United States	0.77	0.78
Mean OECD countries	0.68	0.78
Brazil	0.59	0.73
Latvia	0.65	0.71
Liechtenstein	0.64	0.74
Russian Federation	0.66	0.72
Netherlands	0.60	0.81
Scotland	0.61	0.80

Note: 'Mean OECD countries' does not include the Netherlands, which did not meet PISA's sampling standards. The Flemish Community of Belgium constitutes half of Belgium's population and has been given the status of a country for these analyses.

SELF-CONCEPT

Self-concept in reading

The PISA index of *self-concept in reading* was derived from students' reports on the three items in Figure 66. A four-point scale was used with response categories *disagree*, *disagree somewhat*, *agree somewhat* and *agree*. For information on the conceptual underpinning of the index, see Marsh, Shavelson and Byrne (1992).

Scale scores are standardised *Warm* estimates where positive values indicate a higher level of self-concept in reading and negative values a lower level of self-concept in reading. The item parameters used for the weighted likelihood estimation are given in Figure 66.

Student self-concept in mathematics

The PISA index of *self-concept in mathematics* was derived from students' responses to the items in Figure 67. A four-point scale with the response categories *disagree*, *disagree somewhat*, *agree somewhat* and *agree* was used. For information on the conceptual underpinning of the index, see Marsh, Shavelson and Byrne (1992).

Scale scores are standardised *Warm* estimates where positive values indicate a greater self-concept in mathematics and negative values indicate a lower self-concept in mathematics. The item parameters used for the weighted likelihood estimation are given in Figure 67.

Student academic self-concept

The PISA index of *academic self-concept* was derived from student responses to the items in Figure 68, which gives item parameters used for the weighted likelihood estimation. A four-point scale with the response categories *disagree*, *disagree somewhat*, *agree somewhat* and *agree* was used. For information on the conceptual underpinning of the index, see Marsh, Shavelson and Byrne (1992).

Scale scores are standardised *Warm* estimates where positive values indicate higher levels of academic self-concept and negative values, lower levels of academic self-concept.

	How much do you disagree or agree with each of the following?	Parameter Estimates			
		Delta	Tau(1)	Tau(2)	Tau(3)
CC02Q05	I'm hopeless in <test language> classes. (rev.)	-0.52	-1.79	0.25	1.54
CC02Q09	I learn things quickly in <test language> class.	0.37	-2.21	-0.28	2.49
CC02Q23	I get good marks in <test language>.	0.15	-2.04	-0.42	2.45

Note: Items marked 'rev.' had their response categories reversed before scaling.

Figure 66: Item Parameter Estimates for the Index of Self-Concept in Reading (SCVERB)

	How much do you disagree or agree with each of the following?	Parameter Estimates			
		Delta	Tau(1)	Tau(2)	Tau(3)
CC02Q12	I get good marks in mathematics.	-0.48	-2.60	-0.36	2.96
CC02Q15	Mathematics is one of my best subjects.	0.36	-2.20	0.01	2.19
CC02Q18	I have always done well in mathematics.	0.12	-2.63	0.00	2.63

Figure 67: Item Parameter Estimates for the Index of Self-Concept in Mathematics (MATCON)

	How much do you disagree or agree with each of the following?	Parameter Estimates			
		Delta	Tau(1)	Tau(2)	Tau(3)
CC02Q03	I learn things quickly in most school subjects.	-0.13	-2.79	-0.41	3.20
CC02Q07	I'm good at most school subjects.	-0.02	-2.54	-0.39	2.93
CC02Q20	I do well in tests in most school subjects.	0.14	-2.59	-0.34	2.94

Figure 68: Item Parameter Estimates for the Index of Academic Self-Concept (SCACAD)

Item dimensionality and reliability of 'self-concept' scales

The dimensional structure of the items was confirmed by a CFA. The fit was acceptable for the international sample ($RMSEA = 0.073$, $AGFI = 0.95$, $NNFI = 0.95$ and $CFI = 0.97$). The correlation between latent factors was 0.09 between $MATCON$ and $SCVERB$, 0.56 between $MATCON$ and $SCACAD$, and 0.61 between $SCVERB$ and SCACAD. The $RMSEA$ ranged between 0.039 and 0.112 across countries, showing a variation in model fit. There was, however, only one country with a clearly poor fit for this model.

Table 82 shows the reliabilities of these country indices, which are satisfactory in almost all participating countries—the internal consistency of $SCVERB$ is below 0.60 in only one country.

Table 82: Reliability of *Self-Concept* Scales

Country	SCVERB	MATCON	SCACAD
Australia	0.76	0.85	0.74
Austria	0.81	0.88	0.76
Belgium (Fl.)	0.72	0.85	0.70
Czech Republic	0.74	0.84	0.76
Denmark	0.78	0.87	0.80
Finland	0.80	0.93	0.84
Germany	0.82	0.90	0.78
Hungary	0.66	0.87	0.73
Iceland	0.77	0.90	0.81
Ireland	0.79	0.87	0.77
Italy	0.82	0.87	0.74
Korea	0.68	0.89	0.78
Luxembourg	0.73	0.87	0.74
Mexico	0.52	0.84	0.71
New Zealand	0.81	0.88	0.79
Norway	0.74	0.90	0.85
Portugal	0.74	0.87	0.73
Sweden	0.75	0.88	0.81
Switzerland	0.75	0.88	0.74
United States	0.76	0.86	0.79
Mean OECD countries	0.75	0.88	0.79
Brazil	0.60	0.85	0.73
Latvia	0.67	0.85	0.66
Liechtenstein	0.73	0.84	0.77
Russian Federation	0.67	0.87	0.72
Netherlands	0.73	0.89	0.76
Scotland	0.81	0.87	0.74

Note: 'Mean OECD countries' does not include the Netherlands, which did not meet PISA's sampling standards. The Flemish Community of Belgium constitutes half of Belgium's population and has been given the status of a country for these analyses.

LEARNING CONFIDENCE

Perceived self-efficacy

The PISA index of *perceived self-efficacy* was derived from students' responses to the three items in Figure 69, which gives item parameters used for the weighted likelihood estimation. A four-point scale was used with response categories *almost never*, *sometimes*, *often* and *almost always*.

Scale scores are standardised *Warm* estimates where positive values indicate a higher sense of perceived self-efficacy and negative values, a lower sense of perceived self-efficacy.

	How often do these things apply to you?	Parameter Estimates			
		Delta	Tau(1)	Tau(2)	Tau(3)
CC01Q02	I'm certain I can understand the most difficult material presented in texts.	0.42	-2.77	0.45	2.32
CC01Q18	I'm confident I can do an excellent job on assignments and tests.	-0.26	-2.66	0.29	2.38
CC01Q26	I'm certain I can master the skills being taught.	-0.16	-2.86	0.26	2.6

Figure 69: Item Parameter Estimates for the Index of Perceived Self-Efficacy (SELFEF)

Control expectation

The PISA index of *control expectation* was derived from students' responses to the four items in Figure 70, which gives item parameters used for the weighted likelihood estimation. A four-point scale was used with response categories *almost never*, *sometimes*, *often* and *almost always*.

Scale scores are standardised *Warm* estimates where positive values indicate higher control expectation and negative values indicate lower control expectation.

Item dimensionality and reliability of 'learning confidence' scales

The CFA for the two-dimensional model showed an acceptable model fit for the international sample (*RMSEA* = 0.069, *AGFI* = 0.96, *NNFI* = 0.95 and *CFI* = 0.97). The correlation between the latent factors was as high as 0.93 but for conceptual reasons it was decided to keep two separate scales. The *RMSEA* for the country sub-samples ranged between 0.046 and 0.111.

Table 83 shows the reliability of each of the two *learning confidence* scales for each participating country. Internal consistency is good for both indices across countries.

	How often do these things apply to you?	Parameter Estimates			
		Delta	Tau(1)	Tau(2)	Tau(3)
CC01Q04	When I sit myself down to learn something really difficult, I can learn it.	-0.13	-2.25	0.34	1.90
CC01Q11	If I decide not to get any bad grades, I can really do it.	-0.09	-2.10	0.30	1.81
CC01Q16	If I decide not to get any problems wrong, I can really do it.	0.80	-2.44	0.35	2.09
CC01Q24	If I want to learn something well, I can.	-0.58	-2.49	0.29	2.20

Figure 70: Item Parameter Estimates for the Index of Control Expectation (CEXP)

Table 83: Reliability of *Learning Confidence* Scales

Country	SELFEF	CEXP
Australia	0.73	0.80
Austria	0.63	0.70
Belgium (Fl.)	0.64	0.72
Czech Republic	0.66	0.73
Denmark	0.72	0.75
Finland	0.77	0.81
Germany	0.67	0.71
Hungary	0.71	0.72
Iceland	0.79	0.78
Ireland	0.74	0.78
Italy	0.67	0.71
Korea	0.68	0.75
Luxembourg	0.67	0.74
Mexico	0.67	0.76
New Zealand	0.70	0.79
Norway	0.75	0.82
Portugal	0.69	0.75
Sweden	0.75	0.79
Switzerland	0.61	0.72
United States	0.77	0.79
Mean OECD countries	0.70	0.75
Brazil	0.66	0.72
Latvia	0.57	0.68
Liechtenstein	0.69	0.74
Russian Federation	0.67	0.70
Netherlands	0.63	0.70
Scotland	0.71	0.74

Note: 'Mean OECD countries' does not include the Netherlands, which did not meet PISA's sampling standards. The Flemish Community of Belgium constitutes half of Belgium's population and has been given the status of a country for these analyses.

COMPUTER FAMILIARITY OR INFORMATION TECHNOLOGY

The following indices were derived from the international option on Computer Familiarity, which was administered in almost two-thirds of the countries.

Comfort with and perceived ability to use computers

The PISA index of *comfort with and perceived ability to use computers* was derived from students' responses to the following questions: How comfortable are you using a computer? How comfortable are you using a computer to write a paper? How comfortable are you taking a test on a computer?, and If you compare yourself with other 15-year-olds, how would you rate your ability to use a computer? For the first three questions, a four-point scale was used with the response categories *very comfortable*, *comfortable*, *somewhat comfortable* and *not at all comfortable*. For the last question, a four-point scale was used with the response categories *excellent*, *good*, *fair* and *poor*. For information on the conceptual underpinning of the index, see Eignor, Taylor, Kirsch and Jamieson (1998).

Scale scores are standardised *Warm* estimates where positive values indicate a higher self-perception of computer abilities and negative values indicate a lower self-perception of computer abilities. The item parameters used for the weighted likelihood estimation are given in Figure 71.

Computer usage

The PISA index of *computer usage* was derived from students' responses to the six questions in Figure 72, which gives the item parameters used for the weighted likelihood estimation. A five-point scale with the response categories *almost every day*, *a few times each week*, *between once*

	How comfortable:	Delta	Tau(1)	Tau(2)	Tau(3)
IT02Q01	are you with using a computer?	-0.64	-1.71	0.01	1.70
IT02Q02	are you with using a computer to write a paper?	-0.26	-1.38	-0.13	1.51
IT02Q03	would you be taking a test on a computer?	0.50	-1.32	-0.11	1.43
IT03Q01	If you compare yourself with other 15-year-olds, how would you rate your ability to use a computer?	0.40	-2.52	-0.15	2.67

Note: All items were reversed for scaling.

Figure 71: Item Parameter Estimates for the Index of Comfort With and Perceived Ability to Use Computers (COMAB)

a week and *once a month*, *less than once a month* and *never* was used. For information on the conceptual underpinning of the index see Eignor, Taylor, Kirsch and Jamieson (1998).

Scale scores are standardised *Warm* estimates where positive values indicate higher frequency and negative values indicate lower frequency of computer use.

Interest in computers

The PISA index of *interest in computers* was derived from the students' responses to the four items in Figure 73, which gives item parameters used for the weighted likelihood estimation. A two-point scale with the response categories *yes* and *no* was used.

Scale scores are standardised *Warm* estimates where positive values indicate a more positive attitude towards computers and negative values, a less positive attitude towards computers.

Item dimensionality and reliability of IT-related scales

The three-dimensional model was confirmed by a CFA for the international sample (*RMSEA* = 0.070, *AGFI* = 0.92, *NNFI* = 0.91 and *CFI* = 0.91). The correlation between latent factors was 0.60 for *COMUSE* and *COMAB*, 0.59 for *COMATT* and *COMAB*, and 0.50 for *COMATT* and *COMUSE*. The *RMSEA* for the country sub-samples ranged between 0.049 and 0.095.

Table 84 shows the reliability for each of the three IT variables for each participant. Whereas internal consistency for *COMUSE* and *COMAB* is very high, *COMATT* has a somewhat lower but still satisfactory reliability in view of the fact that it consists of only four dichotomous items.

	How often do you use:	Delta	Tau(1)	Tau(2)	Tau(3)	Tau(4)
IT05Q03	the computer to help you learn school material?	-0.17	-0.92	-0.75	0.23	1.44
IT05Q04	the computer for programming?	0.35	-0.27	-0.47	-0.06	0.80
	How often do you use each of the following kinds of computer software?					
IT06Q02	Word processing (*e.g.*, Word® or Word Perfect®)	-0.71	-0.70	-1.18	0.24	1.64
IT06Q03	Spreadsheets (*e.g.*, Lotus® or Excel®)	0.23	-1.01	-0.60	0.17	1.44
IT06Q04	Drawing, painting or graphics	-0.10	-1.12	-0.38	0.22	1.28
IT06Q05	Educational software	0.40	-1.06	-0.48	0.21	1.33

Note: All items were reversed for scaling.

Figure 72: *Item Parameter Estimates for the Index of Computer Usage (COMUSE)*

		Parameter Estimates Delta
IT07Q01	It is very important to me to work with a computer.	0.53
IT08Q01	To play or work with a computer is really fun.	-1.28
IT09Q01	I use a computer because I am very interested in this.	0.11
IT10Q01	I forget the time, when I am working with the computer.	0.64

Note: All items were reversed for scaling.

Figure 73: *Item Parameter Estimates for the Index of Interest in Computers (COMATT)*

Table 84: Reliability of *Computer Familiarity* or *Information Technology* Scales

Country	COMAB	COMUSE	COMATT
Australia	0.84	0.81	0.69
Belgium (Fl.)	0.85	0.80	0.65
Canada	0.83	0.84	0.68
Czech Republic	0.85	0.79	0.60
Denmark	0.81	0.82	0.73
Finland	0.85	0.83	0.69
Germany	0.86	0.83	0.68
Hungary	0.72	0.76	0.69
Ireland	0.86	0.82	0.59
Luxembourg	0.87	0.85	0.71
Mexico	0.80	0.83	0.57
New Zealand	0.85	0.83	0.67
Norway	-	0.80	-
Sweden	0.79	0.83	0.68
Switzerland	0.86	0.82	0.73
United States	0.79	0.80	0.69
Mean OECD coun.	0.83	0.82	0.68
Brazil	0.87	0.81	0.51
Latvia	0.80	0.80	0.65
Liechtenstein	0.83	0.83	0.72
Russian Federation	0.83	0.83	0.76
Scotland	0.86	0.79	0.57

Note: *In Norway, only one item was included for the scale COMAB; no items were included for COMATT. The Flemish Community of Belgium constitutes half of Belgium's population and has been given the status of a country for these analyses.*

BASIC SCHOOL CHARACTERISTICS

The indices in this section were derived from the School Questionnaire.

Hours of schooling

The PISA index of *hours of schooling per year* was based on information provided by principals on: the number of instructional weeks in the school year; the number of <class periods> in the school week; and the number of teaching minutes in the average single <class period>. The index was derived from the product of these three factors, divided by 60, and has the variable label *TOTHRS*.

School type

A school was classified as either public or private according to whether a public agency or a private entity had the ultimate decision-making power concerning its affairs. A school was classified as public if the principal reported that it was managed directly or indirectly by a public education authority, government agency, or by a governing board appointed by government or elected by public franchise. A school was classified as private if the principal reported that it was managed directly or indirectly by a non-government organisation (*e.g.*, a church, a trade union, business or another private institution).

A distinction was made between *government-dependent* and *independent* private schools according to the degree of dependence on government funding. School principals were asked to specify the percentage of the school's total funding received in a typical school year from: government sources; student fees or school charges paid by parents; benefactors, donations, bequests, sponsorships or parental fund-raising; and other sources. Schools were classified as *government-dependent* private if they received 50 per cent or more of their core funding from government agencies and *independent* private if they received less than 50 per cent of their core funding from government agencies.

- SCHLTYPE is based on the question SC03Q01 and SC04Q01 to SC04Q04. This variable has the following categories:
  1=Private, government-independent;
  2=Private, government-dependent;
  3=Government.

School size

SCHLSIZE is the sum of questions SC02Q01 and SC02Q02, which ask for the total number of boys and the total number of girls enrolled as of March 31, 2000.

Percentage of girls

PCGIRLS is the ratio of the number of girls to the total enrolment (SCHLSIZE).

SCHOOL POLICIES AND PRACTICES

School and teacher autonomy

School principals were asked to report whether teachers, department heads, the school principal, an appointed or elected board, or higher level education authorities were primarily responsible for: appointing and dismissing teachers; establishing teachers' starting salaries and determining their increases; formulating and allocating school budgets; establishing student disciplinary and student assessment policies; approving students for admission; choosing textbooks; determining course content; and deciding which courses were offered.

The PISA index of *school autonomy* was derived from the number of categories that principals classified as not being a school responsibility (which were inverted before scaling).

Scale scores are standardised *Warm* estimates where positive values indicate higher levels and negative values indicate lower levels of school autonomy. The item parameters used for the weighted likelihood estimation are given in Figure 74.

The PISA index of *teacher autonomy* was derived from the number of categories that principals identified as being mainly the responsibility of teachers.

Scale scores are standardised *Warm* estimates where positive values indicate higher levels and negative values indicate lower levels of teacher participation in school decisions. The item parameters used for the weighted likelihood estimation are given in Figure 75.

	In your school, who has the main responsibility for: (not a school responsibility)	Parameter Estimates Delta
SC22Q01	hiring teachers?	-0.87
SC22Q02	firing teachers?	-1.49
SC22Q03	establishing teachers' starting salaries?	-3.65
SC22Q04	determining teachers' salary increases?	-3.49
SC22Q05	formulating the school budget?	-0.30
SC22Q06	deciding on budget allocations within the school?	2.00
SC22Q07	establishing student disciplinary policies?	3.67
SC22Q08	establishing student assessment policies?	1.91
SC22Q09	approving students for admittance to school?	0.53
SC22Q10	choosing which textbooks are used?	2.09
SC22Q11	determining course content?	-0.32
SC22Q12	deciding which courses are offered?	-0.09

Note: All items were reversed for scaling.

Figure 74: Item Parameter Estimates for the Index of School Autonomy (SCHAUTON)

In your school, who is primarily responsible for: (teachers)		Parameter Estimates Delta
SC22Q01	hiring teachers?	1.68
SC22Q02	firing teachers?	3.98
SC22Q03	establishing teachers' starting salaries?	4.27
SC22Q04	determining teachers' salary increases?	3.48
SC22Q05	formulating the school budget?	1.16
SC22Q06	deciding on budget allocations within the school?	-0.16
SC22Q07	establishing student disciplinary policies?	-2.85
SC22Q08	establishing student assessment policies?	-3.31
SC22Q09	approving students for admittance to school?	0.64
SC22Q10	choosing which textbooks are used?	-4.06
SC22Q11	determining course content?	-3.12
SC22Q12	deciding which courses are offered?	-1.73

Note: All items were reversed for scaling.

Figure 75: Item Parameter Estimates for the Index of Teacher Autonomy (TCHPARTI)

Item dimensionality and reliability of 'school and teacher autonomy' scales

A comparative CFA based on covariance matrices could not be completed for this index because in several countries there was no variance for some of the items used. This is plausible given that, depending on the educational system, schools and/or teachers never decide certain matters.

Table 85 shows the reliability for each *school and teacher autonomy* scale for each participating country. Not surprisingly, this varies considerably across countries.

Table 85: Reliability of *School Policies and Practices* Scales

Country	SCHAUTON	TCHPARTI
Australia	0.75	0.80
Austria	0.58	0.61
Belgium	0.61	0.59
Canada	0.75	0.71
Czech Republic	0.78	0.66
Denmark	0.62	0.78
Finland	0.67	0.65
France	0.78	0.63
Germany	0.81	0.75
Greece	0.87	0.49
Hungary	0.60	0.78
Iceland	0.64	0.62
Ireland	0.60	0.57
Italy	0.57	0.67
Japan	0.82	0.82
Korea	0.61	0.62
Mexico	0.83	0.61
New Zealand	0.11	0.74
Portugal	0.48	0.50
Spain	0.77	0.72
Sweden	0.69	0.76
Switzerland	0.74	0.68
United Kingdom	0.71	0.74
United States	0.78	0.82
Mean OECD countries	0.77	0.73
Brazil	0.82	0.66
Latvia	0.64	0.63
Liechtenstein	0.88	0.82
Russian Federation	0.61	0.38
Netherlands	0.41	0.77

Note: 'Mean OECD countries' does not include the Netherlands, which did not meet PISA's sampling standards. No results are available for Norway or Poland, and schools in Luxembourg all provided the same answers.

SCHOOL CLIMATE

School principals' perceptions of teacher-related factors affecting school climate

The PISA index of the *principals' perceptions of teacher-related factors affecting school climate* was derived from principals' reports on the extent to which 15-year-olds were hindered in their learning by: the low expectations of teachers; poor student-teacher relations; teachers not meeting individual students' needs; teacher absenteeism; staff resisting change; teachers being too strict with students; and students not being encouraged to achieve their full potential. The questions asked are shown in Figure 76. A four-point scale with the response categories *not at all*, *very little*, *to some extent* and *a lot* was used, and the responses were inverted before scaling.

Scale scores are standardised *Warm* estimates, where positive values indicate that teacher-related factors do not hinder the learning of 15-year-olds, whereas negative values indicate schools in which there is a perception that teacher-related factors hinder the learning of 15-year-olds. The item parameters used for the weighted likelihood estimation are given in Figure 76.

School principals' perceptions of student-related factors affecting school climate

The PISA index of the *principals' perceptions of student-related factors affecting school climate* was derived from principals' reports on the extent to which 15-year-olds were hindered in their learning by: student absenteeism; disruption of classes by students; students skipping classes; students lacking respect for teachers; the use of alcohol or illegal drugs; and students intimidating or bullying other students. A four-point scale with the response categories *not at all*, *very little*, *to some extent* and *a lot* was used, and the responses were inverted before scaling.

Scale scores are standardised *Warm* estimates, where positive values indicate that student-related factors do not hinder the learning of 15-year-olds, whereas negative values indicate schools in which there is a perception that student-related factors hinder the learning of 15-year-olds. The item parameters used for the weighted likelihood estimation are given in Figure 77.

	In your school, is the learning of <15-year-old students> hindered by:	Parameter Estimates			
		Delta	Tau(1)	Tau(2)	Tau(3)
SC19Q01	low expectations of teachers?	0.28	-2.15	-0.36	2.50
SC19Q03	poor student-teacher relations?	0.00	-2.45	0.77	1.68
SC19Q07	teachers not meeting individual students' needs?	-0.57	-2.81	-0.07	2.88
SC19Q08	teacher absenteeism?	-0.05	-2.50	0.31	2.18
SC19Q11	staff resisting change?	-0.21	-2.40	-0.23	2.63
SC19Q14	teachers being too strict with students?	0.85	-2.63	0.66	1.97
SC19Q16	students not being encouraged to achieve their full potential?	-0.30	-2.07	-0.05	2.13

Note: All items were reversed for scaling.

Figure 76: Item Parameter Estimates for the Index of Principals' Perceptions of Teacher-Related Factors Affecting School Climate (TEACBEHA)

	In your school, is the learning of <15-year-old students> hindered by:	Parameter Estimates			
		Delta	Tau(1)	Tau(2)	Tau(3)
SC19Q02	student absenteeism?	-1.02	-2.25	-0.07	2.31
SC19Q06	disruption of classes by students?	-0.62	-2.86	0.04	2.83
SC19Q09	students skipping classes?	-0.29	-2.24	0.1	2.14
SC19Q10	students lacking respect for teachers?	0.09	-2.8	0.19	2.61
SC19Q13	the use of alcohol or illegal drugs?	1.02	-1.68	0.82	0.86
SC19Q15	students intimidating or bullying other students?	0.82	-2.76	0.39	2.37

Note: All items were reversed for scaling.

Figure 77: Item Parameter Estimates for the Index of Principals' Perceptions of Student-Related Factors Affecting School Climate (STUDBEHA)

School principals' perception of teachers' morale and commitment

The PISA index of *principals' perception of teachers' morale and commitment* was derived from the extent to which school principals agreed with the statements in Figure 78, which gives the item parameters used for the weighted likelihood estimation. A four-point scale with the response categories *strongly disagree*, *disagree*, *agree* and *strongly agree* was used.

Scale scores are standardised *Warm* estimates, where positive values indicate a higher perception of teacher morale, and negative values a lower perception of teacher morale.

	Think about the teachers in your school. How much do you agree or disagree with the following statements?	Parameter Estimates			
		Delta	Tau(1)	Tau(2)	Tau(3)
SC20Q01	The morale of teachers in this school is high.	0.55	-2.45	-0.62	3.07
SC20Q02	Teachers work with enthusiasm.	0.07	-2.64	-1.05	3.70
SC20Q03	Teachers take pride in this school.	0.05	-2.32	-1.09	3.41
SC20Q04	Teachers value academic achievement.	-0.67	-1.16	-1.70	2.86

Figure 78: Item Parameter Estimates for the Index of Principals' Perceptions of Teachers' Morale and Commitment (TCMORALE)

Item dimensionality and reliability of 'school climate' scales

The model fit in a CFA was satisfactory for the international sample ($RMSEA = 0.071$, $AGFI = 0.91$, $NNFI = 0.89$ and $CFI = 0.91$). The correlation between latent factors was 0.77 for *TEACBEHA* and *STUDBEHA*, 0.37 for *TCMORALE* and *TEACBEHA*, and 0.23 for *TCMORALE* and *STUDBEHA*. For the country samples, the *RMSEA* ranged between 0.043 and 0.107.

Table 86 shows that the reliability for each of the *school climate* variables is high across countries.

Table 86: Reliability of *School Climate* Scales

Country	TEACBEHA	STUDBEHA	TCMORALE
Australia	0.86	0.86	0.74
Austria	0.73	0.75	0.69
Belgium	0.81	0.88	0.73
Canada	0.83	0.81	0.78
Czech Republic	0.78	0.76	0.70
Denmark	0.70	0.82	0.73
Finland	0.76	0.66	0.66
France	0.73	0.80	0.79
Germany	0.77	0.78	0.79
Greece	0.90	0.83	0.84
Hungary	0.80	0.83	0.71
Iceland	0.78	0.77	0.87
Ireland	0.81	0.81	0.81
Italy	0.87	0.81	0.80
Japan	0.82	0.85	0.89
Korea	0.82	0.78	0.87
Luxembourg	0.78	0.77	0.67
Mexico	0.89	0.88	0.87
New Zealand	0.82	0.78	0.84
Norway	0.78	0.76	0.76
Poland	0.73	0.82	0.59
Portugal	0.75	0.81	0.80
Spain	0.83	0.83	0.64
Sweden	0.76	0.74	0.75
Switzerland	0.77	0.83	0.74
United Kingdom	0.90	0.86	0.81
United States	0.86	0.74	0.88
Mean OECD countries	0.83	0.81	0.79
Brazil	0.85	0.84	0.83
Latvia	0.79	0.73	0.71
Liechtenstein	0.78	0.89	0.52
Russian Federation	0.79	0.80	0.74
Netherlands	0.79	0.85	0.60

Note: 'Mean OECD countries' does not include the Netherlands, which did not meet PISA's sampling standards.

SCHOOL RESOURCES

Quality of the schools' educational resources

The PISA index of the quality of a *school's educational resources* was based on the school principals' reports on the extent to which 15-year-olds were hindered in their learning by a lack of resources. The questions asked are shown in Figure 79, which gives item parameters used for the weighted likelihood estimation. A four-point scale with the response categories *not at all*, *very little*, *to some extent* and *a lot* was used and the responses were inverted before scaling.

Scale scores are standardised *Warm* estimates, where positive values indicate that the learning of 15-year-olds was not hindered by the (un)availability of educational resources. Negative values indicate the perception of a lower quality of educational materials at school.

Quality of the schools' physical infrastructure

The PISA index of the quality of a *school's physical infrastructure* was derived from principals' reports on the extent to which learning by 15-year-olds in their school was hindered by: poor condition of buildings; poor heating, cooling and/or lighting systems; and lack of instructional space (*e.g.*, classrooms). The questions are shown in Figure 80, which gives the item parameters used for the weighted likelihood estimation. A four-point scale with the response categories *not at all*, *very little*, *to some extent* and *a lot* was used and responses were reversed before scaling.

Scale scores are standardised *Warm* estimates, where positive values indicate that the learning of 15-year-olds was not hindered by the school's physical infrastructure, and negative values indicate the perception that the learning of 15-year-olds was hindered by the school's physical infrastructure.

Teacher shortage

The PISA index of *teacher shortage* was derived from the principals' view on how much 15-year-old students were hindered in their learning by the shortage or inadequacy of teachers in the <test language>, mathematics or science. The items are given in Figure 81, which shows the item parameters used for the weighted likelihood estimation. A four-point scale with the response categories *not at all*, *a little*, *somewhat* and *a lot* was used, and items were reversed before scaling.

	In your school, how much is the learning of <15-year-old students> hindered by:	Delta	Tau(1)	Tau(2)	Tau(3)
SC11Q04	lack of instructional material (*e.g.*, textbooks)?	0.76	-1.41	0.06	1.35
SC11Q05	not enough computers for instruction?	-0.30	-1.50	-0.18	1.67
SC11Q06	lack of instructional materials in the library?	0.10	-1.66	-0.11	1.76
SC11Q07	lack of multi-media resources for instruction?	-0.39	-1.79	-0.19	1.99
SC11Q08	inadequate science laboratory equipment?	-0.07	-1.51	-0.08	1.59
SC11Q09	inadequate facilities for the fine arts?	-0.09	-1.45	-0.07	1.51

Note: All items were reversed for scaling.

Figure 79: *Item Parameter Estimates for the Index of the Quality of the Schools' Educational Resources (SCMATEDU)*

	In your school, how much is the learning of <15-year-old students> hindered by:	Delta	Tau(1)	Tau(2)	Tau(3)
SC11Q01	poor condition of buildings?	0.09	-1.27	-0.47	1.75
SC11Q02	poor heating, cooling and/or lighting systems?	0.21	-1.36	-0.34	1.70
SC11Q03	lack of instructional space (*e.g.*, classrooms)?	-0.30	-1.18	-0.34	1.53

Note: All items were reversed for scaling.

Figure 80: *Item Parameter Estimates for the Index of the Quality of the Schools' Physical Infrastructure (SCMATBUI)*

Scale scores are standardised *Warm* estimates, where positive values indicate that the learning of 15-year-olds was not hindered by teacher shortage or inadequacy. Negative values indicate the perception that 15-year-olds were hindered in their learning by teacher shortage or inadequacy.

	In your school, is the learning of <15-year-old students> hindered by:	Delta	Tau(1)	Tau(2)	Tau(3)
SC21Q01	a shortage/inadequacy of teachers	-0.51	-2.25	0.16	2.08
SC21Q02	a shortage/inadequacy of <test language> teachers?	0.37	-1.64	0.18	1.46
SC21Q03	a shortage/inadequacy of <mathematics> teachers?	0.15	-1.68	0.09	1.60
SC21Q04	a shortage/inadequacy of <science> teachers?	-0.01	-1.61	0.02	1.59

Parameter Estimates

Note: All items were reversed for scaling.

Figure 81: Item Parameter Estimates for the Index of Teacher Shortage (TCSHORT)

Item dimensionality and reliability of 'school resources' scales

A CFA showed an acceptable model fit for the international sample (*RMSEA* = 0.077, *AGFI* = 0.91, *NNFI* = 0.93 and *CFI* = 0.94). The correlation between latent factors was 0.67 for *SCMATEDU* and *SCMATBUI*, 0.32 for *TCSHORT* and *SCMATBUI*, and 0.36 for TCSHORT and *SCMATEDU*. The *RMSEA* for the country samples ranged between 0.054 and 0.139.

Table 87 shows the reliability for each of the *school resources* scales (apart from computers, which are covered in the next section) for each participating country. Internal consistency is satisfactory across countries for all three scales (with the sole exception of *SCMATBUI* for Liechtenstein, where the number of schools was very small).

Table 87: Reliability of *School Resources* Scales

Country	SCMATEDU	SCMATBUI	TCSHORT
Australia	0.89	0.75	0.82
Austria	0.77	0.77	0.67
Belgium	0.86	0.73	0.83
Canada	0.87	0.80	0.87
Czech Republic	0.83	0.65	0.65
Denmark	0.79	0.70	0.76
Finland	0.84	0.82	0.72
France	0.83	0.72	0.88
Germany	0.86	0.78	0.84
Greece	0.84	0.91	0.95
Hungary	0.79	0.59	0.87
Iceland	0.80	0.71	0.83
Ireland	0.84	0.75	0.78
Italy	0.81	0.72	0.89
Japan	0.84	0.70	0.93

Table 87 (cont.)

Country	SCMATEDU	SCMATBUI	TCSHORT
Korea	0.86	0.75	0.93
Luxembourg	0.75	0.63	0.80
Mexico	0.88	0.81	0.91
New Zealand	0.87	0.82	0.90
Norway	0.86	0.77	0.88
Poland	0.84	0.79	0.88
Portugal	0.85	0.68	0.87
Spain	0.85	0.73	0.85
Sweden	0.83	0.79	0.87
Switzerland	0.79	0.68	0.74
United Kingdom	0.91	0.90	0.89
United States	0.77	0.73	0.85
Mean OECD countries	**0.85**	**0.79**	**0.88**
Brazil	0.87	0.83	0.88
Latvia	0.79	0.70	0.62
Liechtenstein	0.45	0.17	0.59
Russian Federation	0.78	0.77	0.85
Netherlands	0.89	0.80	0.82

Note: 'Mean OECD countries' does not include the Netherlands, which did not meet PISA's sampling standards.

Availability of computers

School principals provided information on the total number of computers available in their schools and more specifically on the number of computers: available to 15-year-olds; available only to teachers; available only to administrative staff; connected to the Internet; and connected to a local area network. Six indices of computer availability were prepared and included in the database:

- RATCOMP, which is the total number of computers in the school divided by the school enrolment size;
- PERCOMP1, which is the number of computers available for 15-year-olds (SC13Q02) divided by the total number of computers (SC13Q01);
- PERCOMP2, which is the number of computers available for teachers only (SC13Q03) divided by the total number of computers (SC13Q01);
- PERCOMP3, which is the number of computers available only for administrative staff (SC13Q04) divided by the total number of computers (SC13Q01);
- PERCOMP4, which is the number of computers connected to the Web (SC13Q05) divided by the total number of computers (SC13Q01); and
- PERCOMP5, which is the number of computers connected to a local area network (SC13Q06) divided by the total number of computers (SC13Q01).

Teacher qualifications

School principals indicated the number of full and part-time teachers employed in their schools and the numbers of: <test language> teachers, mathematics teachers and science teachers; teachers fully certified by the <appropriate national authority>; teachers with a qualification of <ISCED level 5A> in <pedagogy>, or <ISCED level 5A> in the <test language>, or <ISCED level 5A> in <mathematics>, or <ISCED level 5A> in <science>. Five variables were constructed:

- PROPQUAL, which is the proportion of teachers with an ISCED 5A qualification in pedagogy (SC14Q02) divided by the total number of teachers (SC14Q01);

- *PROPCERT*, which is the proportion of teachers fully certified by the appropriate authority (*SC14Q03*) divided by the total number of teachers (*SC14Q01*);
- *PROPREAD*, which is the proportion of test language teachers with an ISCED 5A qualification (*SC14Q05*) divided by the number of test language teachers (*SC14Q04*);
- *PROPMATH*, which is the proportion of mathematics teachers with an ISCED 5A qualification (*SC14Q07*) divided by the number of mathematics teachers (*SC14Q06*); and
- *PROPSCIE*, which is the proportion of science teachers who have an ISCED 5A qualification (*SC14Q09*) divided by the total number of science teachers (*SC14Q08*).

Student/teaching staff ratio

The *student/teaching staff ratio (STRATIO)* was defined as the number of full-time equivalent teachers divided by the number of students in the school. To convert head counts into full-time equivalents, a full-time teacher—employed for at least 90 per cent of the statutory time as a classroom teacher—received a weight of 1, and a part-time teacher—employed for less than 90 per cent of the time as a classroom teacher—received a weight of 0.5.

Class size

An estimate of *class size* was obtained from students' reports on the number of students in their respective <test language>, mathematics and science classes.

CHAPTER 18 INTERNATIONAL DATABASE

Christian Monseur

FILES IN THE DATABASE

The PISA international database consists of five data files: four student-level files and one school-level file. All are provided in text (or ASCII format) with the corresponding SAS® and SPSS® control files.

THE STUDENT FILES

Student and reading performance data files (filename: intstud_read.txt)

For each student who participated in the assessment, the following information is available:
- Identification variables for the country, school and student;
- The student responses on the three questionnaires, *i.e.*, the student questionnaire and the two international options: Computer Familiarity or Information Technology questionnaire (IT) and Cross-Curriculum Competencies questionnaire (CCC);
- The students' indices derived from the original questions in the questionnaires;
- The students' performance scores in reading;
- The student weights and a country adjustment factor for the reading weights; and
- The 80 reading Fay's replicates for the computation of the sampling variance estimates.

Student and mathematics performance data files (filename: intstud_math.txt)

For each student who was assessed with one of the booklets containing mathematics material, the following information is available:
- Identification variables for the country, school and student;
- The students' responses on the three questionnaires, *i.e.*, the student questionnaire and the two international options: Computer Familiarity or Information Technology questionnaire (IT) and Cross-Curriculum Competencies questionnaire (CCC);
- The students' indices derived from the original questions in the questionnaires;
- The students' performance scores in reading and mathematics;
- The student weights and a country adjustment factor for the mathematics weights; and
- The 80 reading Fay's replicates for the computation of the sampling variance estimates.

Student and science performance data files (filename: intstud_scie.txt)

For each student who was assessed with one of the booklets that contain science material, the following information is available:
- Identification variables for the country, school and student;
- The student responses on the three questionnaires, *i.e.*, the student questionnaire and the two international options: Computer Familiarity or Information Technology questionnaire (IT) and Cross-Curriculum Competencies questionnaire (CCC);
- The students' indices derived from the original questions in the questionnaires;
- The students' performance scores in reading and science;
- The student weights and a country adjustment factor for the science weights; and

- The 80 reading Fay's replicates for the computation of the sampling variance estimates.

THE SCHOOL FILE

The school questionnaire data file (filename: intscho.txt)

For each school that participated in the assessment, the following information is available:
- The identification variables for the country and school;
- The school responses on the school questionnaire; and
- The school indices derived from the original questions in the school questionnaire.
- The school weight.

THE ASSESSMENT ITEMS DATA FILE

The cognitive file (filename: intcogn.txt)

For each item included in the test, this file shows the students' responses expressed in a one-digit format. The items from mathematics and science used double-digit coding during marking[1]. A file including these codes was available to national centres.

RECORDS IN THE DATABASE

RECORDS INCLUDED IN THE DATABASE

Student level
- All PISA students who attended one of the two test (assessment) sessions.
- PISA students who only attended the questionnaire session are included if they provided a response to the father's occupation questions or the mother's occupation questions on the student questionnaire (questions 8 to 11).

School level
- All participating schools—that is, any school where at least 25 per cent of the sampled eligible students were assessed— have a record in the school-level international database, regardless of whether the school returned the school questionnaire.

RECORDS EXCLUDED FROM THE DATABASE

Student level
- Additional data collected by some countries for a national or international option such as a grade sample.
- Sampled students who were reported as not eligible, students who were no longer at school, students who were excluded for physical, mental or linguistic reasons, and students who were absent on the testing day.
- Students who refused to participate in the assessment sessions.
- Students from schools where less than 25 per cent of the sampled and eligible students participated.

School level
- Schools where fewer than 25 per cent of the sampled eligible students participated in the testing sessions.

REPRESENTING MISSING DATA

The coding of the data distinguishes between four different types of missing data:
- *Item level non-response*: 9 for a one-digit variable, 99 for a two-digit variable, 999 for a three-digit variable, and so on. Missing codes are shown in the codebooks. This missing code is used if the student or school principal was expected to answer a question, but no response was actually provided.
- *Multiple or invalid responses*: 8 for a one-digit variable, 98 for a two-digit variable, 998 for a three-digit variable, and so on. This code is used for multiple choice items in both test booklets and questionnaires where an invalid response was provided. This code is not used for open-ended questions.

---

[1] The responses from open-ended items could give valuable information about students' ideas and thinking, which could be fed back into curriculum planning. For this reason, the marking guides for these items in mathematics and science were designed to include a two-digit marking so that the frequency of various types of correct and incorrect response could be recorded. The first digit was the actual score. The second digit was used to categorise the different kings of response on the basis of the strategies used by the student to answer the item. The international database includes only the first digit.

- *Not applicable:* 7 for a one-digit variable, 97 for a two-digit variables, 997 for a three-digit variable, and so on for the student questionnaire data file and for the school data file. Code "n" is used for a one-digit variable in the test booklet data file. This code is used when it was not possible for the student to answer the question. For instance, this code is used if a question was misprinted or if a question was deleted from the questionnaire by a national centre. The "not-applicable" codes and code "n" are also used in the test booklet file for questions that were not included in the test booklet that the student received.
- *Not reached items:* all consecutive missing values starting from the end of each test session were replaced by the non-reached code, "r", except for the first value of the missing series, which is coded as missing.

HOW ARE STUDENTS AND SCHOOLS IDENTIFIED?

The student identification from the student files consists of three variables, which together form a unique identifier for each student:
- The country identification variable labelled COUNTRY. The country codes used in PISA are the ISO 3166 country codes.
- The school identification variable labelled SCHOOLID.
- The student identification variable labelled STIDSTD.

A fourth variable has been included to differentiate sub-national entities within countries. This variable (SUBNATIO) is used for four countries as follows:
- *Australia.* The eight values "01", "02", "03", "04", "05", "06", "07", "08" are assigned to the Australian Capital Territory, New South Wales, Victoria, Queensland, South Australia, Western Australia, Tasmania and the Northern Territory respectively.
- *Belgium.* The value "01" is assigned to the French Community and the value "02" is assigned to the Flemish Community.
- *Switzerland.* The value "01" is assigned to the German-speaking community, the value "02" is assigned to the French-speaking community and the value "03" is assigned to the Italian-speaking community.
- *United Kingdom.* The value "01" is assigned to Scotland, the value "02" is assigned to England and the value "03" is assigned to Northern Ireland.

The school identification consists of two variables, which together form a unique identifier for each school:
- The country identification variable labelled COUNTRY. The country codes used in PISA are the ISO 3166 country codes.
- The school identification variable labelled SCHOOLID.

THE STUDENT FILES

Two types of indices are provided in the student questionnaire files. The first set is based on a transformation of one variable or on a combination of the information included in two or more variables. Eight indices are included in the database from this first type. The second set is the result of a Rasch scaling and consists of weighted likelihood estimate indices. Fifteen indices from the student questionnaire, 14 indices from the international option on cross-curriculum competencies questionnaire and 3 indices from the international option on computer familiarity or information technology questionnaire are included in the database from this second type. For a full description of the indices and how to interpret them see the *Manual for the PISA 2000 database* (OECD, 2002a), also available through *www.pisa.oecd.org.*

Two types of estimates of student achievement are included in the student files for each domain (reading, mathematics and science) and for each subscale (retrieving information, interpreting texts and reflection and evaluation): a weighted likelihood estimate and a set of five plausible values. It is recommended that the set of plausible values be used when analysing and reporting statistics at the population level. The use of weighted likelihood estimates for population estimates will yield biased estimates. The weighted likelihood estimates for the domain scales were each transformed to a mean of 500 and a standard deviation of 100 by using the data of the participating OECD Member countries only[2]. These

---

[2] With the exception of the Netherlands, which did not reach the PISA 2000 sampling standards

linear transformations used weighted data, but the weights provided in the international database were transformed so that the sum of the weights per country was a constant. The same transformation was applied to the reading sub-scales. The linear transformation applied to the plausible values is based on the same rules as the ones used for the weighted estimates, except that the standardisation parameters were derived from the average of the mean and standard deviation computed from the five plausible values. For this reason, the means and variances of the individual plausible values are not exactly 500 and 100 respectively, but the average of the five means and the five variances is.

In the international data files, the variable called W_FSTUWT is the final student weight. The sum of the weights constitutes an estimate of the size of the target population, i.e., the number of 15-year-old students in that country attending school. In this situation large countries would have a stronger contribution to the results than small countries. These weights are appropriate for the analysis of data that have been collected from all assessed students, such as student questionnaire data, and reading performance data.

Because of the PISA test design, using the reading weights for analysing the mathematics or science data will overweight the students assessed with booklet zero (or SE Booklet) and therefore (typically) underestimate the results. To correct this over-weighting of the students taking the SE booklet, weight adjustment factors must be applied to the weights and replicates. Because of the need to use these adjustment factors in analyses, and to avoid accidental misuse of the student data, these data are provided in the three separate files:

- The file Intstud_read.txt comprises the reading ability estimates and weights. This file contains all eligible students who participated in the survey. As the sample design assessed reading by all students, no adjustment was needed;
- The file Intstud_math.txt comprises the reading and mathematics ability estimates. Weights and replicates in this file have already been adjusted by the mathematics adjustment factor. Thus, no further transformations of the weights or replicates are required by analysts of the data; and
- The file Intstud_scie.txt comprises the reading and science ability estimates. Weights and replicates in this file have already been adjusted by the science adjustment factor. Thus, no further transformations of the weights or replicates are required by analysts of the data.

For a full description of the weighting methodology, including the test design, calculation of the reading weights, adjustment factors and how to use the weights, see the *Manual for the PISA 2000 database* (OECD, 2002*a*), also available through *www.pisa.oecd.org*.

THE COGNITIVE FILES

The file with the test data *(filename: intcogn.txt)* contains individual students' responses to all items used for the international item calibration and in the generation of the plausible values. All item responses included in this file have a one-digit format, which contains the score for the student on that item.

The PISA items are organised into units. Each unit consists of a piece of text or related texts, followed by one or more questions. Each unit is identified by a short label and by a long label. The units' short labels consist of four characters. The first character is R, M or S respectively for reading, mathematics or science. The three next characters indicate the unit name. For example, R083 is a reading unit called 'Household'. The full item label (usually seven-digit) represents each particular question within a unit. Thus items within a unit have the same initial four characters: all items in the unit 'Household' begin with 'R083', plus a question number: for example, the third question in the 'Household' unit is R083Q03.

In this file, the items are sorted by domain and alphabetically by short label within domain. This means that the mathematics items appear at the beginning of the file, followed by the reading items and then the science items. Within domains, units with smaller numeric identification appear before those with larger identification, and within each unit, the first question will precede the second, and so on.

THE SCHOOL FILE

The school files contain the original variables collected through the school context questionnaire.

Two types of indices are provided in the

school questionnaire files. The first set is based on a transformation of one variable or on a combination of two or more variables. The database includes 16 indices from this first type. The second set is the result of a Rasch scaling and consists of weighted likelihood estimate indices. Eight indices are included in the database from this second type. For a full description of the indices and how to interpret them see the *Manual for the PISA 2000 database* (OECD, 2002*a*), also available through *www.pisa.oecd.org*.

The school base weight (WNRSCHBW), which has been adjusted for school non-response, is provided at the end of the school file. PISA uses an age sample instead of a grade sample. Additionally, the PISA sample of school in some countries included primary schools, lower secondary schools, upper secondary schools, or even special education schools. For these two reasons, it is difficult to conceptually define the school population, except that it is the population of schools with at least one 15-year-old student. While in some countries, the population of schools with 15-year-olds is similar to the population of secondary schools, in other countries, these two populations of schools are very different.

A recommendation is to analyse the school data at the student level. From a practical point of view, it means that the school data should to be imported into the student data file. From a theoretical point of view, while it is possible to estimate the per centage of schools following a specific school characteristic, it is not meaningful. Instead, the recommendation is to estimate the per centages of students following the same school characteristic. For instance, the per centages of private schools versus public schools will not be estimated, but the per centages of students attending a private school versus the per centage of students attending public schools will.

FURTHER INFORMATION

A full description of the PISA 2000 database and guidelines on how to analyse it in accordance with the complex methodologies used to collect and process the data is provided in the *Manual for the PISA 2000 database* (OECD, 2002*a*) also available through *www.pisa.oecd.org*

REFERENCES

Adams, R.J., Wilson, M.R. and Wang, W. (1997). The multidimensional random coefficients multinomial logit model. *Applied Psychological Measurement, 21*, 1-24.

Adams, R.J., Wilson, M.R. and Wu, M.L. (1997). Multilevel item response modeling: An approach to errors in variables regression. *Journal of Educational and Behavioral Statistics, 22*, 47-76.

Beaton, A.E. (1987). *Implementing the new design: The NAEP 1983-84 Technical Report*. (Report No. 15-TR-20). Princeton, NJ: Educational Testing Service.

Beaton, A.E., Mullis, I.V., Martin, M.O., Gonzalez, E.J., Kelly, D.L. and Smith, T.A. (1996). *Mathematics Achievement in the Middle School Years*. Chestnut Hill, MA: Center for the Study of Testing, Evaluation and Educational Policy, Boston College.

Baumert, J., Gruehn, S., Heyn, S., Köller, O. and Schnabel, K.U. (1997). *Bildungsverläufe und Psychosoziale Entwicklung im Jugendalter (BIJU): Dokumentation - Band 1*. Berlin: Max-Planck-Institut für Bildungsforschung.

Baumert, J., Heyn. S. and Köller, O. (1994). *Das Kieler Lernstrategien-Inventar*. Kiel: Institut für die Pädagogik der Naturwissenschaften an der Universität Kiel.

BMDP. (1992). BMDP Statistical Software. Los Angeles: Author.

Brennan, R.L. (1992). *Elements of Generalizability Theory*. Iowa City: American College Testing Program.

Browne, M.W. and Cudeck, R. (1993) Alternative Ways of Assessing Model Fit. In: K. Bollen and S. Long: *Testing Structural Equation Models*. Newbury Park: Sage.

Cochran, W.G. (1977). *Sampling Techniques* (3rd edition). New York: Wiley.

Cronbach, L.J., Gleser, G.C., Nanda, H. and Rajaratnam, N. (1972). *The Dependability of Behavioral Measurements: Theory of Generalizability for Scores and Profiles*. New York: Wileyand

Dale, E. and Chall, J.S. (1948). *A Formula for Predicting Readability*. Columbus: Bureau of Educational Research, Ohio State University.

Dechant, E. (1991). *Understanding and Teaching Reading: An Interactive Model*. Hillsdale, NJ: Lawrence Erlbaum.

De Landsheere, G. (1973). *Le test de closure, mesure de la lisibilité et de la compréhension*. Bruxelles: Nathan-Labor.

Eignor, D., Taylor, C., Kirsch, I. and Jamieson, J. (1998). *Development of a Scale for Assessing the Level of Computer Familiarity of TOEFL Students*. (TOEFL Research Report No. 60). Princeton, NJ: Educational Testing Service.

Elley, W.B. (1992). *How in the World do Students Read*. International Association for the Evaluation of Educational Achievement: The Hague

Flesch, R. (1949). *The Art of Readable Writing*. New York: Harper & Row

Fry, E.B. (1977). Fry's Readability graph: Clarification, validity and extension to level 17. *Journal of Reading, 20*, 242-252.

Ganzeboom, H.B.G., de Graaf, P.M. and Treiman, D.J. (1992). A standard international socio-economic index of occupational status. *Social Science Research, 21*, 1-56.

Gifi, A. (1990). *Nonlinear Multivariate Analysis*. New York: Wiley.

Graesser, A.C., Millis, K.K. and Zwaan, R.A. (1997). Discourse comprehension. *Annual Review of Psychology, 48*, 163-189.

Greenacre, M.J. (1984). *Theory and Applications of Correspondence Analysis*. London: Academic Press.

Gustafsson, J.E. and Stahl, P.A. (2000). *STREAMS User's Guide, Version 2.5 for Windows*. Mölndal Sweden: MultivariateWare.

Henry, G. (1975). *Comment mesurer la lisibilité*. Bruxelles: Nathan-Labor.

Hambleton, R., Merenda, P. and Spielberger, C.D. (in press). *Adapting Educational and Psychological Tests for Cross-Cultural Assessment*. Hillsdale, NJ: Lawrence Erlbaum.

International Assessment of Educational Progress. (1992). *Learning Science*. Princeton, NJ: Educational Testing Service.

International Labour Organisation. (1990). *International Standard Classification of Occupations: ISCO-88*. Geneva: Author.

Jöreskog, K.G. and Sörbom, D. (1993). *LISREL8 User's Reference Guide*. Chicago: Scientific Software International.

Judkins, D.R. (1990). Fay's Method for Variance Estimation. *Journal of Official Statistics*, 6(3), 223-239.

Kintsch, W. and van Dijk, T. (1978). Toward a model of text comprehension and production. *Psychological Review*, 85, 363-394.

Kirsch, I. and Mosenthal, P. (1990). Exploring Document Literacy: Variables underlying the performance of young adults. *Reading Research Quarterly*, 25, 5-30

Kish, L. (1965). *Survey Sampling*. New York: Wiley.

Longford, N.T. (1995). *Models of Uncertainty in Educational Testing*. New York: Springer-Verlag.

Macaskill, G., Adams, R.J. and Wu, M.L. (1998). Scaling methodology and procedures for the mathematics and science literacy, advanced mathematics and physics scales. In: M. Martin and D.L. Kelly (eds.) *Third International Mathematics and Science Study, Technical Report Volume 3: Implementation and Analysis*. Chestnut Hill, MA: Center for the Study of Testing, Evaluation and Educational Policy, Boston College.

McCormick, T.W. (1988). *Theories of Reading in Dialogue: An Interdisciplinary Study*. New York: University Press of America.

McCullagh, P. and Nelder, J.A. (1983). *Generalized Linear Models* (2nd edition). London: Chapman and Hall.

Marsh, H.W., Shavelson, R.J. and Byrne, B.M. (1992). A multidimensional, hierarchical self-concept. In: R.P. Lipka and T.M. Brinthaupt (eds.), *Studying the Self: Self-perspectives Across the Life-Span*. Albany: State University of New York Press.

Mislevy, R.J. (1991). Randomization-based inference about latent variables from complex samples. *Psychometrika*, 56, 177–196.

Mislevy, R.J. and Sheehan, K.M. (1987). Marginal estimation procedures. In: A.E. Beaton (ed.), *The NAEP 1983-1984 Technical Report*. (Report No. 15-TR-20). Princeton, NJ: Educational Testing Service, 293-360.

Mislevy, R.J. and Sheehan, K.M. (1989). Information matrices in latent-variable models. *Journal of Educational Statistics*, 14(4), 335-350.

Mislevy, R.J., Beaton, A.E., Kaplan, B. and Sheehan, K.M. (1992). Estimating population characteristics from sparse matrix samples of item responses. *Journal of Educational Measurement*, 29, 133–161.

Nishisato, S. (1980). *Analysis of Categorical Data: Dual Scaling and its Applications*. Toronto: University of Toronto Press.

Oh, H.L. and Sheuren, F.J. (1983). Weighting Adjustment for Unit Nonresponse. In: W.G. Madow, I. Olkin and D. Rubin (eds.) *Incomplete Data in Sample Surveys, Vol. 2: Theory and Bibliographies*. New York: Academic Press, 143-184.

Organisation for Economic Co-Operation and Development (1999a). *Measuring Student Knowledge and Skills: A New Framework for Assessment*. Paris: OECD Publications.

Organisation for Economic Co-Operation and Development (1999b). *Classifying Educational Programmes. Manual for ISCED-97 Implementation in OECD Countries*. Paris: OECD Publications.

Organisation for Economic Co-Operation and Development (2000). *Literacy in the Information Age*. Paris: OECD Publications.

Organisation for Economic Co-Operation and Development (2001). *Knowledge and Skills for Life: First Results from PISA 2000*. Paris: OECD Publications.

Organisation for Economic Co-Operation and Development (2002a). *Manual for the PISA 2000 Database*. Paris OECD Publications.

Organisation for Economic Co-Operation and Development (2002b). *Sample Tasks from the PISA 2000 Assessment*. Paris OECD Publications.

Owens, L. and Barnes, J. (1992). *Learning Preferences Scales*. Hawthorn, Vic.: Australian Council for Educational Research.

Peschar, J.L. (1997). *Prepared for Life? How to Measure Cross-Curricular Competencies*. Paris: OECD Publications.

Pintrich, P.R., Smith, D.A.F., Garcia, T. and McKeachie, W.J. (1993). Reliability and predictive validity of the Motivated Strategies for Learning questionnaire (MLSQ). *Educational and Psychological Measurement*, 53, 801-813.

Robitaille, D.F. and Garden, R.A. (eds.) (1989). *The IEA Study of Mathematics II: Contexts and Outcomes of School Mathematics*. Oxford: Pergamon Press.

Rubin, D.B. (1987). *Multiple Imputations for Non-Response in Surveys*. New York: Wiley.

Rumelhart, D.E. (1985). Toward an interactive model of reading. In: H. Singer, and R.B. Ruddell (eds.), *Theoretical models and the processes of reading* (3rd edition). Newark, DE: International Reading Association.

Rust, K. (1985). Variance estimation for complex estimators in sample surveys. *Journal of Official Statistics*, *1*(4), 381-397.

Rust, K.F. and Rao, J.N.K. (1996). Variance estimation for complex surveys using replication techniques. *Statistical Methods in Medical Research*, *5*(3), 283-310.

Särndal, C.E., Swensson, B. and Wretman, J. (1992). *Model Assisted Survey Sampling*. New York: Springer-Verlag.

Searle, S.R. (1971). *Linear Models*. New York: Wiley.

Shao, J. (1996). Resampling methods in sample surveys (with discussion). *Statistics*, 27, 203-254.

Sirotnik, K. (1970). An analysis of variance framework for matrix sampling. *Educational and Psychological Measurement*, 30, 891-908.

Spache, G. (1953). A new readability formula for primary grade reading materials. *Elementary School Journal*, 55, 410-413.

Thorndike, R.L. (1973). *Reading Comprehension Education in Fifteen Countries*. Uppsala: Almqvist & Wiksell.

Travers, K.J. and Westbury, I. (eds.) (1989). *The IEA Study of Mathematics I: Analysis of Mathematics Curricula*. Oxford: Pergamon Press.

Van Dijk, T.A. and Kintsch, W. (1983). *Strategies of Discourse Comprehension*. Orlando: Academic Press.

Verhelst, N.D. (2000). *Estimating Variance Components in Unbalanced Designs*. (R&D Notities, 2000-1). Arnhem: Cito Group.

Warm, T.A. (1985). *Weighted maximum likelihood estimation of ability in Item Response Theory with tests of finite length*. (Technical Report CGI-TR-85-08). Oklahoma City: U.S. Coast Guard Institute.

Westat (2000). *WesVar 4.0 User's Guide*. Rockville, MD: Author.

Wolter, K.M. (1985). *Introduction to Variance Estimation*. New York: Springer-Verlag.

Wu, M.L. (1997). The developement and application of a fit test for use with generalised item response model. Masters of Education Dissertation. University of Melbourne.

Wu, M.L., Adams, R.J. and Wilson, M.R. (1997). *ConQuest: Multi-Aspect Test Software* [computer program]. Camberwell, Vic.: Australian Council for Educational Research.

APPENDIX 1: SUMMARY OF PISA READING LITERACY ITEMS

Identification Number	Name	Source	Language in which Submitted	Sub-Scale	Cluster	International Per Cent Correct	Difficulty	Tau-1	Tau-2	Tau-3	Threshold 1	Threshold 2	Threshold 3
R040Q02	Lake Chad	ACER	English	Retr. inf.	R9	64.82 (0.39)	-0.221				478		
R040Q03A	Lake Chad	ACER	English	Retr. inf.	R9	50.39 (0.39)	0.459				540		
R040Q03B	Lake Chad	ACER	English	Refl. & eval.	R9	36.58 (0.34)	1.123				600		
R040Q04	Lake Chad	ACER	English	Int. texts	R9	76.94 (0.28)	-1.112				397		
R040Q06	Lake Chad	ACER	English	Int. texts	R9	56.44 (0.37)	0.106				508		
R055Q01	Drugged Spiders	Cito	English	Int. texts	R5	83.79 (0.22)	-1.377				373		
R055Q02	Drugged Spiders	Cito	English	Refl. & eval.	R5	52.93 (0.27)	0.496				543		
R055Q03	Drugged Spiders	Cito	English	Int. texts	R5	60.57 (0.29)	0.067				504		
R055Q05	Drugged Spiders	Cito	English	Int. texts	R5	77.45 (0.26)	-0.877				419		
R061Q01	Macondo	ACER	Spanish	Int. texts	R6	65.98 (0.29)	-0.112				488		
R061Q03	Macondo	ACER	Spanish	Int. texts	R6	62.33 (0.27)	0.005				499		
R061Q04	Macondo	ACER	Spanish	Int. texts	R6	68.36 (0.26)	-0.313				470		
R061Q05	Macondo	ACER	Spanish	Refl. & eval.	R6	54.25 (0.33)	0.499				544		
R067Q01	Aesop	Greece	Greek	Int. texts	R5	88.35 (0.19)	-1.726				341		
R067Q04	Aesop	Greece	Greek	Refl. & eval.	R5	54.31 (0.22)	0.516	-0.456	0.456		479	611	
R067Q05	Aesop	Greece	Greek	Refl. & eval.	R5	62.48 (0.29)	0.182	0.482	-0.482		487	543	
R070Q02	Beach	Cito	English	Retr. inf.	R1	52.74 (0.32)	0.485				542		
R070Q03	Beach	Cito	English	Retr. inf.	R1	70.46 (0.25)	-0.487				454		
R070Q04	Beach	Cito	English	Refl. & eval.	R1	17.52 (0.22)	2.581				733		
R070Q07T	Beach	Cito	English	Int. texts	R1	54.35 (0.26)	0.428	-0.122	0.122		488	586	
R076Q03	Iran Air	Cito	English	Retr. inf.	R5	68.58 (0.30)	-0.284				473		
R076Q04	Iran Air	Cito	English	Int. texts	R5	53.88 (0.28)	0.475				542		
R076Q05	Iran Air	Cito	English	Retr. inf.	R5	52.61 (0.28)	0.528				546		
R077Q02	Flu	ACER	English	Retr. inf.	R9	70.02 (0.34)	-0.607				443		
R077Q03	Flu	ACER	English	Refl. & eval.	R9	44.28 (0.34)	0.706	0.798	-0.798		542	583	
R077Q04	Flu	ACER	English	Int. texts	R9	53.34 (0.32)	0.247				521		
R077Q05	Flu	ACER	English	Refl. & eval.	R9	30.73 (0.29)	1.521				637		
R077Q06	Flu	ACER	English	Int. texts	R9	44.68 (0.40)	0.699				562		
R081Q01	Graffiti	Finland	Finnish	Int. texts	R1	76.34 (0.23)	-0.852				421		
R081Q02	Graffiti	Finland	Finnish	Int. texts	R1								
R081Q05	Graffiti	Finland	Finnish	Int. texts	R1	52.65 (0.26)	0.475				542		
R081Q06A	Graffiti	Finland	Finnish	Refl. & eval.	R1	67.14 (0.26)	-0.303				471		
R081Q06B	Graffiti	Finland	Finnish	Refl. & eval.	R1	44.75 (0.31)	0.906				581		
R083Q01	Household Work	ACER	English	Int. texts	R6	66.36 (0.28)	-0.163				484		

Identification Name Number		Source	Language in which Submitted	Sub-Scale	Cluster	International Per Cent Correct	Difficulty	Item Parameters Tau-1	Tau-2	Tau-3	Thresholds 1	2	3
R083Q02	Household Work	ACER	English	Retr. inf.	R6	85.12 (0.21)	-1.422				369		
R083Q03	Household Work	ACER	English	Retr. inf.	R6	80.53 (0.23)	-1.036				404		
R083Q04	Household Work	ACER	English	Int. texts	R6	68.06 (0.28)	-0.198				480		
R083Q06	Household Work	ACER	English	Refl. & eval.	R6	47.17 (0.32)	0.845				575		
R086Q04	If	ACER	English	Refl. & eval.	R4	29.00 (0.24)	1.791				661		
R086Q05	If	ACER	English	Int. texts	R4	83.48 (0.22)	-1.367				374		
R086Q07	If	ACER	English	Refl. & eval.	R4	72.74 (0.26)	-0.683				436		
R088Q01	Labour	N Z'land	English	Int. texts	R9	62.76 (0.34)	-0.235				477		
R088Q03	Labour	N Z'land	English	Retr. inf.	R9	45.97 (0.27)	0.658	-0.578	0.578		485	631	
R088Q04T	Labour	N Z'land	English	Int. texts	R9	39.20 (0.25)	1.117	-1.336	1.336		473	727	
R088Q05T	Labour	N Z'land	English	Refl. & eval.	R9	68.83 (0.32)	-0.588				445		
R088Q07	Labour	N Z'land	English	Refl. & eval.	R9	61.62 (0.37)	-0.135				486		
R091Q05	Library	ACER	English	Retr. inf.	R3	85.78 (0.21)	-1.484				363		
R091Q06	Library	ACER	English	Int. texts	R3	86.42 (0.18)	-1.597				353		
R091Q07B	Library	ACER	English	Refl. & eval.	R3	79.45 (0.21)	-1.039				404		
R093Q03	News Agencies	Denmark	Danish	Int. texts	R5	74.69 (0.26)	-0.563				447		
R093Q04	News Agencies	Denmark	Danish	Int. texts	R5								
R099Q02	Plan International	ACER	English	Int. texts	R7								
R099Q03	Plan International	ACER	English	Int. texts	R7								
R099Q04B	Plan International	ACER	English	Refl. & eval.	R7	10.66 (0.16)	2.916	-0.316	0.316		705	822	
R100Q04	Police	Belgium	French	Retr. inf.	R6	61.13 (0.29)	0.178				515		
R100Q05	Police	Belgium	French	Int. texts	R6	58.26 (0.28)	0.217				518		
R100Q06	Police	Belgium	French	Int. texts	R6	80.24 (0.24)	-1.012				406		
R100Q07	Police	Belgium	French	Int. texts	R6	80.65 (0.24)	-1.065				402		
R101Q01	Rhino	Sweden	Swedish	Int. texts	R1	54.92 (0.30)	0.457				540		
R101Q02	Rhino	Sweden	Swedish	Int. texts	R1	86.11 (0.17)	-1.627				350		
R101Q03	Rhino	Sweden	Swedish	Refl. & eval.	R1	63.93 (0.28)	-0.082				491		
R101Q04	Rhino	Sweden	Swedish	Int. texts	R1	78.32 (0.26)	-1.002				407		
R101Q05	Rhino	Sweden	Swedish	Int. texts	R1	47.41 (0.30)	0.800				571		
R101Q08	Rhino	Sweden	Swedish	Int. texts	R1	55.81 (0.28)	0.380				533		
R102Q01	Shirts	Cito	English	Int. texts	R4	81.10 (0.24)	-1.306				380		
R102Q04A	Shirts	Cito	English	Int. texts	R4	36.00 (0.29)	1.206				608		
R102Q05	Shirts	Cito	English	Int. texts	R4	41.80 (0.30)	0.905				581		
R102Q06	Shirts	Cito	English	Refl. & eval.	R4	33.44 (0.25)	1.481				633		
R102Q07	Shirts	Cito	English	Int. texts	R4	85.23 (0.22)	-1.566				356		
R104Q01	Telephone	N Z'land	English	Retr. inf.	R6	82.63 (0.23)	-1.235				386		

Appendices

Identification Number	Name	Source	Language in which Submitted	Sub-Scale	Cluster	International Per Cent Correct	Difficulty	Tau-1	Tau-2	Tau-3	Threshold 1	Threshold 2	Threshold 3
R104Q02	Telephone	New Zealand	English	Retr. inf.	R6	41.30 (0.29)	1.105				599		
R104Q05	Telephone	New Zealand	English	Retr. inf.	R6	28.89 (0.18)	1.875	-0.914	0.914		574	764	
R104Q06	Telephone	New Zealand	English	Retr. inf.	R6	79.51 (0.22)	-0.931				414		
R110Q01	Runners	Belgium	French	Int. texts	R8	84.50 (0.24)	-1.561				356		
R110Q04	Runners	Belgium	French	Retr. inf.	R8	78.84 (0.27)	-1.166				392		
R110Q05	Runners	Belgium	French	Retr. inf.	R8	76.21 (0.24)	-1.025				405		
R110Q06	Runners	Belgium	French	Refl.&eval	R8	77.78 (0.23)	-1.059				402		
R111Q01	Exchange	Finland	Finnish	Int. texts	R4	63.87 (0.28)	-0.053				494		
R111Q02B	Exchange	Finland	Finnish	Refl.&eval	R4	34.14 (0.24)	1.365	-0.554	0.554		551	694	
R111Q04	Exchange	Finland	Finnish	Retr. inf.	R4	77.70 (0.25)	-0.868				419		
R111Q06B	Exchange	Finland	Finnish	Refl.&eval	R4	44.42 (0.29)	0.808	0.828	-0.828		552	592	
R119Q01	Gift	USA	English	Int. texts	R3	73.46 (0.23)	-0.563				447		
R119Q04	Gift	USA	English	Int. texts	R3	40.38 (0.30)	1.149				603		
R119Q05	Gift	USA	English	Refl.&eval	R3	37.10 (0.25)	1.226	0.030	-0.030		567	652	
R119Q06	Gift	USA	English	Retr. inf.	R3	85.29 (0.22)	-1.448				367		
R119Q07	Gift	USA	English	Int. texts	R3	42.81 (0.26)	1.031	-0.216	0.216		539	645	
R119Q08	Gift	USA	English	Int. texts	R3	56.64 (0.28)	0.338				529		
R119Q09T	Gift	USA	English	Refl.&eval	R3	63.98 (0.28)	0.116	0.450	-0.450		480	537	
R120Q01	Student Opinions	ACER	English	Int. texts	R7	57.89 (0.25)	0.202				517		
R120Q03	Student Opinions	ACER	English	Int. texts	R7	43.04 (0.25)	1.004				590		
R120Q06	Student Opinions	ACER	English	Refl.&eval	R7	61.33 (0.25)	0.105				508		
R120Q07T	Student Opinions	ACER	English	Refl.&eval	R7	71.82 (0.24)	-0.629				441		
R122Q01A	Justart	ACER	English		R5								
R122Q01B	Justart	ACER	English		R5								
R122Q01C	Justart	ACER	English		R5								
R122Q02	Justart	ACER	English	Refl.&eval	R5	59.82 (0.29)	0.138				511		
R122Q03T	Justart	ACER	English	Retr. inf.	R5	43.48 (0.25)	0.894	-0.029	0.029		535	625	
R216Q01	Amanda & the Duchess	France	French	Int. texts	R9	73.54 (0.36)	-0.833				423		
R216Q02	Amanda & the Duchess	France	French	Refl.&eval	R9	44.22 (0.41)	0.690				561		
R216Q03T	Amanda & the Duchess	France	French	Int. texts	R9	43.90 (0.35)	0.751				567		
R216Q04	Amanda & the Duchess	France	French	Retr. inf.	R9	36.61 (0.35)	1.206				608		
RR216Q06	Amanda & the Duchess	France	French	Int. texts	R9	67.10 (0.32)	-0.474				455		

Identification Number	Name	Source	Language in which Submitted	Sub-Scale	Cluster	International Per Cent Correct	Difficulty	Tau-1	Tau-2	Tau-3	1	2	3
R219Q01E	Employment	IALS	IALS	Retr. inf.	R1	69.94 (0.27)	-0.550				448		
R219Q01T	Employment	IALS	IALS	Int. texts	R1	57.37 (0.31)	0.278				524		
R219Q02	Employment	IALS	IALS	Refl. & eval.	R1	76.24 (0.27)	-0.917				415		
R220Q01	South Pole	France	French	Retr. inf.	R7	46.03 (0.31)	0.785				570		
R220Q02B	South Pole	France	French	Int. texts	R7	64.49 (0.30)	-0.144				485		
R220Q04	South Pole	France	French	Int. texts	R7	60.67 (0.28)	0.163				513		
R220Q05	South Pole	France	French	Int. texts	R7	84.88 (0.21)	-1.599				353		
R220Q06	South Pole	France	French	Int. texts	R7	65.54 (0.27)	-0.172				483		
R225Q01	Nuclear	IALS	IALS	Int. texts	R2								
R225Q02	Nuclear	IALS	IALS	Int. texts	R2	70.77 (0.25)	-0.313				470		
R225Q03	Nuclear	IALS	IALS	Retr. inf.	R2	89.87 (0.17)	-1.885				327		
R225Q04	Nuclear	IALS	IALS	Retr. inf.	R2	75.80 (0.28)	-0.663				438		
R227Q01	Optician	Switzerland	German	Int. texts	R4	57.65 (0.34)	0.196				516		
R227Q02T	Optician	Switzerland	German	Retr. inf.	R4	59.58 (0.20)	0.045	-1.008	1.008		401	604	
R227Q03	Optician	Switzerland	German	Refl. & eval.	R4	55.58 (0.32)	0.295				525		
R227Q04	Optician	Switzerland	German	Int. texts	R4	69.85 (0.28)	-0.216	0.457	-0.457		450	507	
R227Q06	Optician	Switzerland	German	Retr. inf.	R4	74.29 (0.26)	-0.916				415		
R228Q01	Guide	Finland	Finnish	Int. texts	R7	67.24 (0.27)	-0.335				468		
R228Q02	Guide	Finland	Finnish	Int. texts	R7	59.36 (0.23)	0.194				516		
R228Q04	Guide	Finland	Finnish	Int. texts	R7	57.03 (0.30)	0.247				521		
R234Q01	personnel	IALS	IALS	Retr. inf.	R2	85.14 (0.20)	-1.487				363		
R234Q02	personnel	IALS	IALS	Retr. inf.	R2	31.76 (0.28)	1.728				655		
R236Q01	newrules	IALS	IALS	Int. texts	R8	47.88 (0.31)	0.660				558		
R236Q02	newrules	IALS	IALS	Int. texts	R8	25.52 (0.25)	1.873				669		
R237Q01	Hiring Interview	IALS	IALS	Retr. inf.	R8	59.59 (0.26)	-0.005				498		
R237Q03	Hiring Interview	IALS	IALS	Int. texts	R8	57.60 (0.30)	0.132				510		
R238Q01	Bicycle	IALS	IALS	Retr. inf.	R2	65.07 (0.30)	-0.092				490		
R238Q02	Bicycle	IALS	IALS	Int. texts	R2	49.46 (0.27)	0.722				564		
R239Q01	Allergies/Explorers	IALS	IALS	Int. texts	R8	52.38 (0.30)	0.469				541		
R239Q02	Allergies/Explorers	IALS	IALS	Retr. inf.	R8	66.78 (0.27)	-0.257				475		
R241Q01	Warrantyhotpoint	IALS	IALS	Retr. inf.	R2								
R241Q02	Warrantyhotpoint	IALS	IALS	Int. texts	R2	57.59 (0.30)	0.432				538		
R245Q01	Movie Reviews	IALS	IALS	Retr. inf.	R2	72.69 (0.25)	-0.556				448		
R245Q02	Movie Reviews	IALS	IALS	Int. texts	R2	66.63 (0.28)	-0.043				494		
R246Q01	Contactemployer	IALS	IALS	Retr. inf.	R8	75.08 (0.29)	-0.805				425		
R246Q02	Contactemployer	IALS	IALS	Retr. inf.	R8	31.96 (0.31)	1.560				640		

Appendices

APPENDIX 2: SUMMARY OF PISA MATHEMATICAL LITERACY ITEMS

Identification Number	Name	Source	Language in which Submitted	Cluster	International Per Cent Correct	Difficulty	Tau-1	Tau-2	Tau-3	Thresholds 1	2	3
M033Q01	A View Room	Cito	Dutch	M3	74.03 (0.27)	-1.520				442		
M034Q01T	Bricks	Cito	Dutch	M3	38.72 (0.28)	0.459				593		
M037Q01T	Farms	Cito	Dutch	M1	60.96 (0.42)	-0.867				492		
M037Q02T	Farms	Cito	Dutch	M1	55.16 (0.32)	-0.453				524		
M124Q01	Walking	Cito	Dutch	M1	34.41 (0.40)	0.536				599		
M124Q03T	Walking	Cito	Dutch	M1	18.89 (0.25)	1.276	-0.258	0.169	0.089	600	659	708
M136Q01T	Apples	Cito	Dutch	M2	49.14 (0.28)	-0.139				548		
M136Q02T	Apples	Cito	Dutch	M2	24.88 (0.26)	1.255				655		
M136Q03T	Apples	Cito	Dutch	M2	13.19 (0.18)	1.820	0.385	-0.385		672	723	
M144Q01T	Cube Painting	USA	English	M1	63.86 (0.33)	-1.012				481		
M144Q02T	Cube Painting	USA	English	M1	26.26 (0.32)	1.090				641		
M144Q03	Cube Painting	USA	English	M1	76.82 (0.33)	-1.815				420		
M144Q04T	Cube Painting	USA	English	M1	37.31 (0.38)	0.431				591		
M145Q01T	Cubes	Cito	Dutch	M3	58.28 (0.32)	-0.559				516		
M148Q01T	Continent Area	Sweden	Swedish	M2	19.33 (0.20)	1.474	-0.138	0.138		629	712	
M148Q02T	Continent Area	Sweden	Swedish	M2	61.57 (0.28)	-0.686				506		
M150Q01	Growing Up	Cito	Dutch	M2	69.36 (0.26)	-1.129	-0.502	0.502		415	529	
M150Q02T	Growing Up	Cito	Dutch	M2	45.79 (0.29)	0.009				559		
M150Q03T	Growing Up	Cito	Dutch	M2	60.46 (0.34)	-0.745				501		
M155Q01	Population Pyramids	Cito	Dutch	M3	59.49 (0.32)	-0.643	0.481	-0.481		486	532	
M155Q02T	Population Pyramids	Cito	Dutch	M3	14.54 (0.22)	1.718	0.229	-0.229		660	719	
M155Q03T	Population Pyramids	Cito	Dutch	M3	51.33 (0.27)	-0.230				541		
M155Q04T	Population Pyramids	Cito	Dutch	M3	67.22 (0.33)	-0.851				492		
M159Q01	Racing Car	Austria	German	M4	83.71 (0.26)	-2.037				403		
M159Q02	Racing Car	Austria	German	M4	82.81 (0.22)	-1.897				413		
M159Q03	Racing Car	Austria	German	M4	28.34 (0.33)	1.266				655		
M159Q05	Racing Car	Austria	German	M4	58.48 (0.32)	-0.233				537		
M161Q01	Triangles	USA	English	M4	26.31 (0.24)	1.328	-0.360	0.360		609	710	
M179Q01T	Robberies	TIMSS	English	M4	37.81 (0.28)	0.477				595		
M192Q01T	Containers	Germany	German	M3	19.92 (0.25)	1.858				700		
M266Q01T	Carpenter	ACER	English	M4	54.17 (0.31)	-0.130				548		
M273Q01T	Pipelines	Czech Rep.	Czech	M4								

APPENDIX 3: SUMMARY OF PISA SCIENTIFIC LITERACY ITEMS

Identification Number	Name	Source	Language in which Submitted	Cluster	International Per Cent Correct	Difficulty	Tau-1	Tau-2	Tau-3	Thresholds 1	2	3
S114Q03T	Greenhouse	Cito	English	S1	56.79 (0.35)	-0.373				520		
S114Q04T	Greenhouse	Cito	English	S1	39.29 (0.30)	0.377	-0.050	0.050		545	645	
S114Q05T	Greenhouse	Cito	English	S1	24.60 (0.32)	1.307				688		
S128Q01	Cloning	Cito	French	S2	61.64 (0.28)	-0.557				502		
S128Q02	Cloning	Cito	French	S2	45.38 (0.28)	0.284				586		
S128Q03T	Cloning	Cito	French	S2	61.16 (0.27)	-0.527				505		
S129Q01	Daylight	ACER	English	S4	38.75 (0.33)	0.620				619		
S129Q02T	Daylight	ACER	English	S4	17.82 (0.25)	1.497	0.673	-0.673		682	732	
S131Q02T	Good Vibrations	ACER	English	S2	50.51 (0.28)	0.028				560		
S131Q04T	Good Vibrations	ACER	English	S2	24.74 (0.24)	1.438				701		
S133Q01	Research	USA	English	S1	56.22 (0.33)	-0.356				522		
S133Q03	Research	USA	English	S1	42.24 (0.30)	0.313				589		
S133Q04T	Research	USA	English	S1	43.25 (0.34)	0.250				582		
S195Q02T	Semmelweis' Diary	Cito	Dutch	S3	24.95 (0.26)	0.946	1.273	-1.273		638	666	
S195Q04	Semmelweis' Diary	Cito	Dutch	S3	63.33 (0.27)	-0.643				493		
S195Q05T	Semmelweis' Diary	Cito	Dutch	S3	67.58 (0.29)	-0.900				467		
S195Q06	Semmelweis' Diary	Cito	Dutch	S3	60.04 (0.27)	-0.494				508		
S209Q01T	Tidal Power	ACER	English	S3	43.31 (0.32)	0.346				592		
S209Q02T	Tidal Power	ACER	English	S3	40.01 (0.33)	0.419				599		
S213Q01T	Clothes	Australia	English	S1	75.41 (0.31)	-1.484				409		
S213Q02	Clothes	Australia	English	S1	48.29 (0.27)	0.026				560		
S252Q01	South Rainea	Korea	Korean	S3	71.98 (0.24)	-1.123				445		
S252Q02	South Rainea	Korea	Korean	S3	54.59 (0.26)	-0.176				540		
S252Q03T	South Rainea	Korea	Korean	S3	28.37 (0.30)	0.978	0.609	-0.609		628	682	
S253Q01T	Ozone	Norway	Norwegian	S4	34.78 (0.32)	0.849				642		
S253Q02	Ozone	Norway	Norwegian	S4	53.79 (0.32)	-0.108				547		
S253Q05	Ozone	Norway	Norwegian	S4	88.27 (0.20)	-2.491				308		
S256Q01	Spoons	TIMSS	English	S1	73.41 (0.29)	-1.250				432		
S268Q01	Algae	Sweden	Swedish	S4	39.83 (0.38)	0.578				615		
S268Q02T	Algae	Sweden	Swedish	S4	57.39 (0.41)	-0.236				534		
S268Q06	Algae	Sweden	Swedish	S4	59.28 (0.29)	-0.460				511		
S269Q01	Earth's Temperature	Cito	Dutch	S2	41.36 (0.31)	0.497				607		
S269Q03T	Earth's Temperature	Cito	Dutch	S2	35.30 (0.31)	0.712				629		
S269Q04T	Earth's Temperature	Cito	Dutch	S2	56.42 (0.34)	-0.287				529		
S270Q03T	Ozone	Belgium	French	S4								

Appendices

APPENDIX 4: THE VALIDITY STUDIES OF OCCUPATION AND SOCIO-ECONOMIC STATUS (SUMMARY)

As part of the field trial, informal validity studies were conducted in Canada, the Czech Republic, France and the United Kingdom. These studies addressed the question of how well 15-year-olds could be expected to report the occupations of their parents.

CANADA

The Canadian study found the following correlation results:
- between achievement and mother's occupation reported by student: 0.24;
- between achievement and mother's occupation reported by mother in 80 per cent of cases and father in 20 per cent of cases: 0.20;
- between achievement and father's occupation reported by student: 0.21; and
- between achievement and father's occupation reported by father in 20 per cent of cases and mother in 80 per cent of cases: 0.29.
(It should be noted that 80 per cent of the responses here are proxy data.)

CZECH REPUBLIC

The correlations between student and parent-reported parental occupational status (SEI) in the study in the Czech Republic were:
- for mothers 0.87; and
- for fathers 0.85.

FRANCE

The extent of agreement between the students' and the parents' reports of the parents' occupations in France, grouped by ISCO Major Group, is shown in Table 88. This table could call the accuracy of student's reports of their parents' occupations into question. However, two important factors should be noted. First, the table includes non-response, which necessarily decreases the level of agreement. Non-response by parents ranged from 2 per cent to over 10 per cent for the *Manager* group. Second, the responses not in agreement were clustered around the main diagonal. So, for example,

Table 88: Validity Study Results for France

ISCO Major Group	Group	Mother % Agreement with Parent	Mother Number	Father % Agreement With Parent	Father Number
1000	Legislators, Senior Officials, Managers	39	26	44	87
2000	Professionals	74	88	69	87
3000	Technicians, Associate Professionals	62	125	50	126
4000	Clerks	69	137	43	35
5000	Service/Sales	63	110	62	38
6000	Agricultural/Primary Industry	75	8	85	39
7000	Craft and Trades	64	17	76	130
8000	Operators, Drivers	67	22	58	66
9000	Elementary Occupations	57	57	43	37
Total			711		711

of students who responded that their father was in the *Craft and Trades* group, 76 per cent of the fathers put their occupation in the same category and 11 per cent were in the next category (*Operators*). Of students who indicated that their mothers were professionals, their answers were confirmed by their mothers in 74 per cent of cases and another 19 per cent were self-reported para-professionals. Although students who indicated that their father's occupation was in the manager group had this confirmed by their fathers in only 44 per cent of cases, another 30 per cent of the fathers were self-reported professionals and para-professionals. Third, there were very few irreconcilable dis-agreements. For example, in the previous example, no father whose child classified him as a Manager self-reported himself in major groups 6 to 9. Similarly, of fathers reported as professionals by their children, very few (0.5 per cent) indicated that they worked as operatives or unskilled labourers.

UNITED KINGDOM

In the study carried out in the United Kingdom, SEI scores of parents' occupations were developed from 3-digit ISCO codes.

The correlations based on the SEI scores of occupations reported by students and parents were:
- for mothers 0.76; and
- for fathers 0.71.

The extent of agreement between the students' and the parents' reports of the parents' occupations, grouped by ISCO Major Group, is shown in Table 89 for the United Kingdom study.

Correlations based on the SEI scores developed from the three-digit ISCO Codes were:
- between achievement and mother's occupation reported by student: 0.32;
- between achievement and mother's self-reported occupation: 0.25;
- between achievement and father's occupation reported by student: 0.36; and
- between achievement and father's self-reported occupation: 0.38.

Table 89: Validity Study Results for the United Kingdom

ISCO Major Group	Group	Mother % Agreement with Parent	Mother Number	Father % Agreement With Parent	Father Number
1000	Legislators, Senior Officials, Managers	53	34	55	71
2000	Professionals	94	69	82	44
3000	Technicians, Associate Professionals	40	25	60	30
4000	Clerks	64	74	50	12
5000	Service/Sales	73	67	69	13
6000	Agricultural/Primary Industry	0	1	0	1
7000	Craft and Trades	20	5	68	41
8000	Operators, Drivers	83	6	71	21
9000	Elementary Occupations	60	20	56	9
Total			309		246

APPENDIX 5: THE MAIN FINDINGS FROM QUALITY MONITORING OF THE PISA 2000 MAIN STUDY

Not all pieces of information gathered by School Quality Monitors (SQMs) or National Centre Quality Monitors (NCQMs) are used in this report. Items considered relevant to data quality and to conducting the testing sessions are included here in the section on SQM reports. A more extensive range of information is included in the section on NCQM reports.

SCHOOL QUALITY MONITOR REPORTS

A total of 103 SQMs submitted 893 reports that were processed by the Consortium. These came from 31 national centres (including the two linguistic regions of Belgium, which are counted as two national centres in these analyses). The form of the reports from one country was not amenable to data entry and they were therefore not included in the quality monitoring analyses.

Administration of Tests and Questionnaires in Schools

SQMs were asked to record the time at key points before, during and after the administration of the tests and questionnaires. The times, measured in minutes, were transformed into duration to the nearest minute for:

- *Cognitive Blocks One and Two:* Time taken for the first and second parts of the assessment booklet (referred to in these analyses as 'cognitive blocks') considered separately (should each equal 60 minutes if PISA procedures were completely followed);

- *Questionnaire:* Time taken for the Student Questionnaire;

- *Student working time:* Time taken for the first and second cognitive blocks plus the questionnaire (that is, total time spent by students in working on PISA materials). It was expected that this would be around 150 minutes, excluding breaks between sessions and time spent by the Test Administrator giving instructions for conducting the session; and

- *Total duration*: Time from the entrance of the first student to the exit of the last student, which provides a measure of how long PISA took out of a student's school day.

Duration of cognitive blocks

The mean duration of each of the first and second cognitive blocks was 60 minutes. Totals of 97 and 93 per cent of schools, respectively, completed the first and second blocks in 60±2 minutes. For each block, only 1 per cent of schools took more than 62 minutes, three of these using 70 minutes for the first block and two using more than 70 minutes for the second block (longest time was 79 minutes). Just over 2 per cent of schools for the first block and 6 per cent for the second block took less than 58 minutes.

There was a group of 20 schools from one country that took only 50 minutes to complete the second block, which points to a systematic error in administration procedures. Follow-up of other schools that finished early revealed that the students had either lost interest or had given up because they found the test too difficult. Some commented that the students gave up because they were unfamiliar with the format of the complex multiple-choice items.

In an attempt to explain the times in excess of 62 minutes, cross-tabulations were constructed of the time variable with the 'general disruption' variable (Q28), and with the 'detection of defective booklets' variable (Q34). None of the schools where the time exceeded 62 minutes was reported to have had these problems.

Duration of Student Questionnaire session

The mean duration of the Student Questionnaire session was 36 minutes. A total of 39 per cent of schools took 30 minutes to complete the questionnaire. By 40 minutes, 77 per cent of schools visited by SQMs had completed the questionnaire. The minimum time taken to complete the session was 17 minutes (at one school), and the maximum was 95 minutes (also at one school). Figure 82 shows the statistics and histogram summarising these data.

No school was reported as having the questionnaire session and the cognitive block sessions on different days.

Duration of student working time

This section is concerned with the time students spent working on PISA materials, excluding breaks between sessions and time spent by the Test

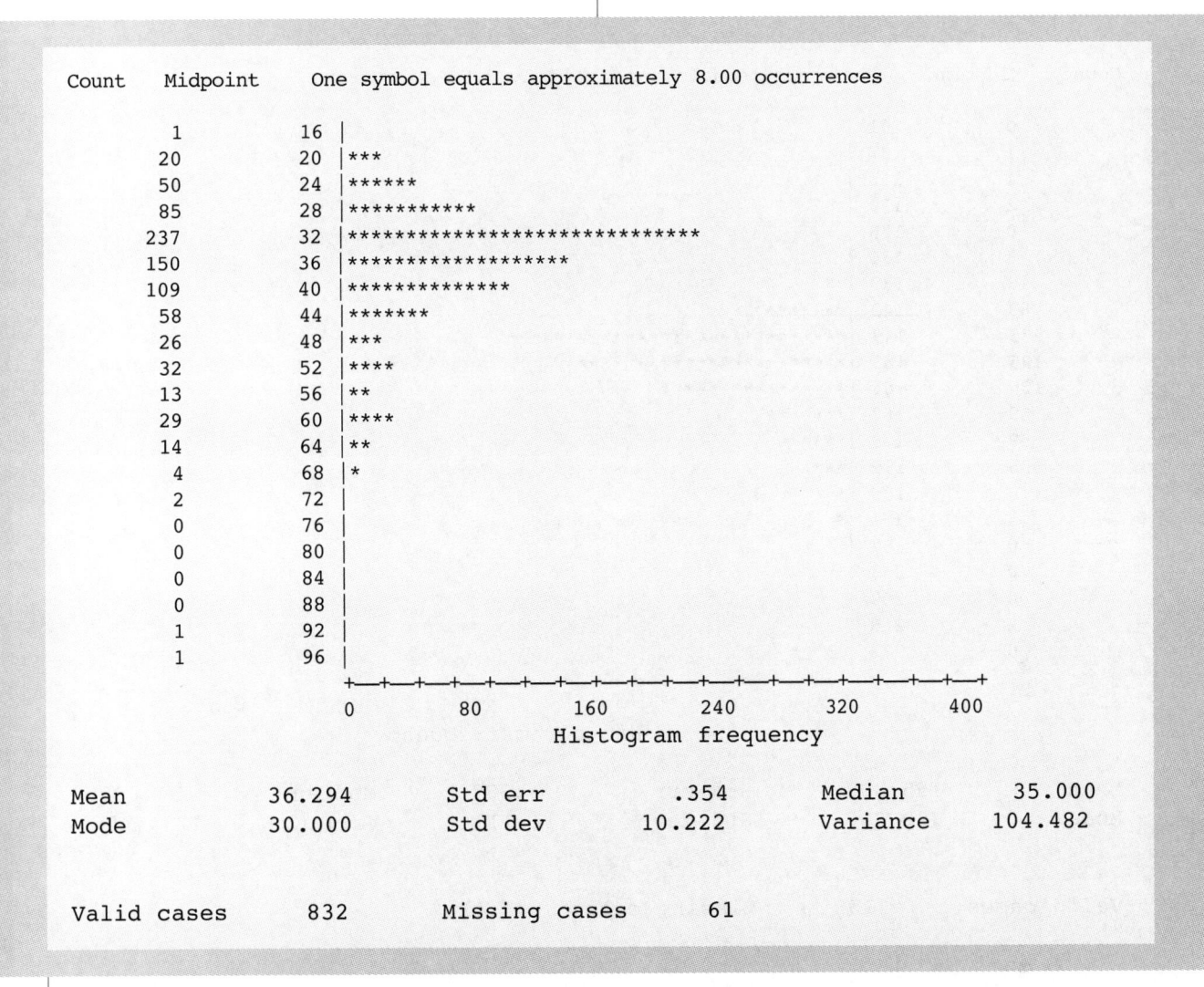

```
Count    Midpoint     One symbol equals approximately 8.00 occurrences

    1       16   |
   20       20   |***
   50       24   |******
   85       28   |**********
  237       32   |*****************************
  150       36   |******************
  109       40   |**************
   58       44   |*******
   26       48   |***
   32       52   |****
   13       56   |**
   29       60   |****
   14       64   |**
    4       68   |*
    2       72   |
    0       76   |
    0       80   |
    0       84   |
    0       88   |
    1       92   |
    1       96   |
                 +----+----+----+----+----+----+----+----+----+----+
                 0        80       160      240      320      400
                                Histogram frequency

Mean           36.294     Std err        .354      Median      35.000
Mode           30.000     Std dev      10.222      Variance   104.482


Valid cases      832     Missing cases    61
```

Figure 82: Duration of Questionnaire Session, Showing Histogram and Associated Summary Statistics

Administrator giving instructions for the session. It was expected that this time would be around 150 minutes. About 15 per cent of schools took 150 minutes, and about 24 per cent took less than 150 minutes. Thus, the majority of schools (about 60 per cent) took longer than was expected—although only a third took longer than 155 minutes and the percentage drops rapidly beyond 160 minutes. Most of the additional time was taken up in completing the Student Questionnaire. The inclusion of various national and international options with the questionnaire makes it difficult to establish the reasons for the long duration of the working period for many schools. Figure 83 shows the statistics and histogram summarising these data.

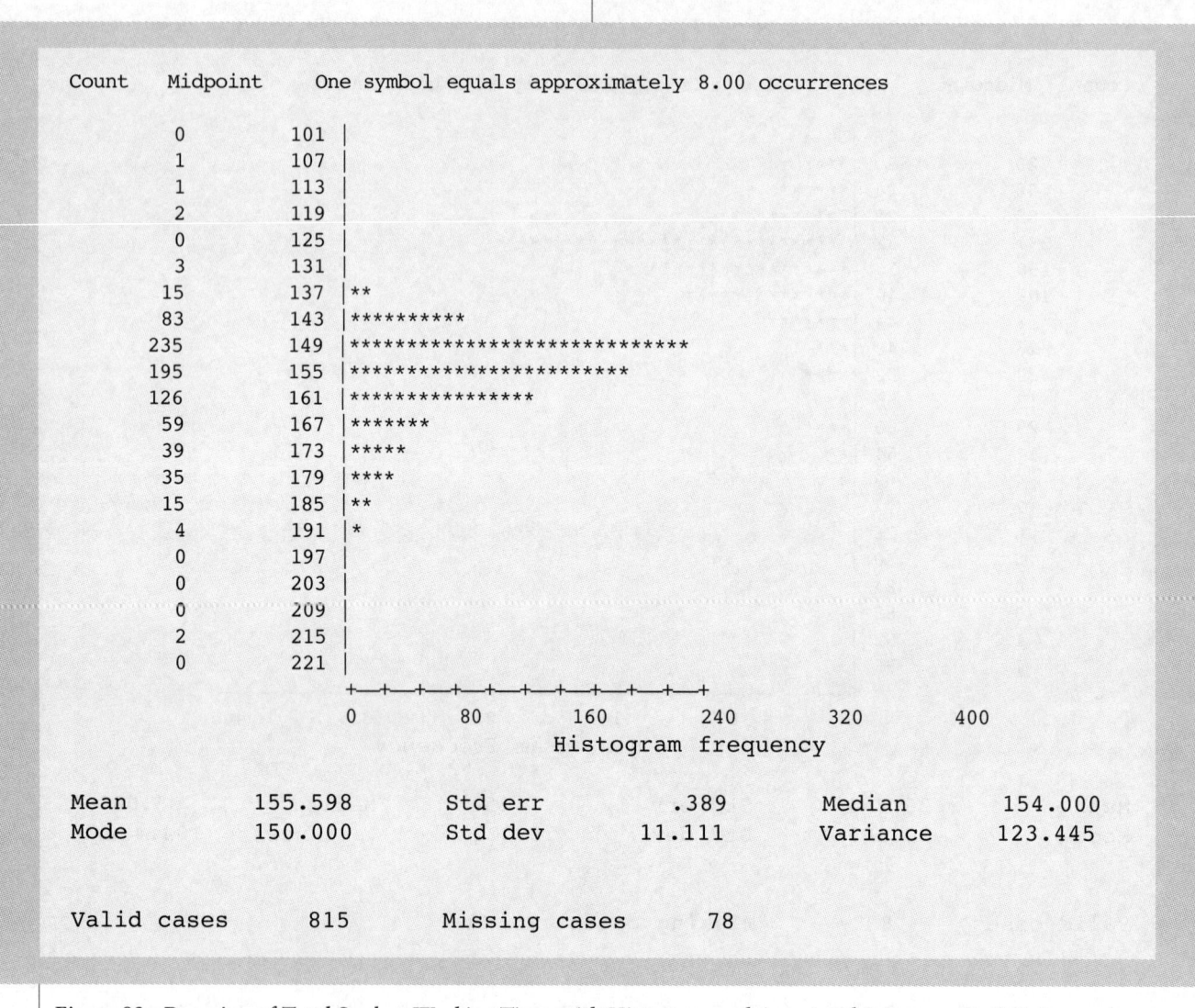

```
Count    Midpoint     One symbol equals approximately 8.00 occurrences

    0       101    |
    1       107    |
    1       113    |
    2       119    |
    0       125    |
    3       131    |
   15       137    |**
   83       143    |**********
  235       149    |*****************************
  195       155    |************************
  126       161    |****************
   59       167    |*******
   39       173    |*****
   35       179    |****
   15       185    |**
    4       191    |*
    0       197    |
    0       203    |
    0       209    |
    2       215    |
    0       221    |
                   +----+----+----+----+----+----+
                   0    80   160  240  320  400
                          Histogram frequency

Mean         155.598     Std err        .389    Median    154.000
Mode         150.000     Std dev      11.111    Variance  123.445


Valid cases      815     Missing cases    78
```

Figure 83: Duration of Total Student Working Time, with Histogram and Associated Summary Statistics

Total duration of PISA in the school

The mean duration from the entrance to the test room to the exit of the last student was 205 minutes (about three and one-half hours), with a median of 200 minutes and mode of 195 minutes. There were noteworthy extremes. At one extreme, the entire PISA exercise took 75 minutes—in schools using the SE booklet, who were only required to complete one hour of testing. At the other extreme, some schools took more than 300 minutes (over five hours). These long periods were due to extended breaks between the two parts of the test, or between the testing and questionnaire sessions (in some cases as long as 90 minutes), or both. The very long breaks were mostly taken in only one country.

PREPARATION FOR THE ASSESSMENT

Conditions for the test and questionnaire sessions

Generally, the data from the SQM reports suggest that the preparations for the PISA sessions went well and test room conditions were adequate. Most of the 7 per cent of cases where SQMs commented that conditions were less than adequate were because the testing room was too small.

Introducing the study

A script for introducing PISA to the students was provided in the *Test Administrator's Manual*. While a small amount of latitude was permitted to suit local circumstances, *e.g.*, in the way encouragement was given to students concerning the importance of participating in PISA, TAs were reminded to follow the script as closely as feasible. From the SQM reports, it appears that TAs took this advice seriously. Almost 80 per cent of those visited by SQMs followed the script exactly, with about 18 per cent making minor adjustments and only 2 per cent reported as paraphrasing the script in a major way. While the number of major adjustments is small (about 20 cases), it is enough to assume that insufficient emphasis may have been given to this aspect in the TA training.

BEGINNING THE TESTING SESSIONS

Of more importance is the accuracy with which the TAs read the instructions for the first and second parts of the testing session. Question 12 in the box below pertained to the first part of the session.

Almost all TAs followed the script of the Cognitive Blocks section of the manual for giving the directions, the examples and the answers to the examples, prior to beginning the actual test. The number of major additions and deletions would be a concern if they pertained to these aspects, but, given that they mostly related to whether students should stay in the testing room after finishing and were spread through about half the countries, it is unlikely these departures from the script would have had much effect on achievement, except possibly in one country where no script was provided to TAs.

Corresponding statistics for the second part of the testing session showed that a higher percentage (83) of TAs followed the instructions verbatim, with smaller numbers of adjustments to the script. Numbers of major adjustments were about the same as for the first part of the session. Again, adjustments to the script usually involved paraphrasing, but this occurred often enough that it seems that not enough emphasis was put during TA training on the need for adhering accurately to the script.

CONDUCTING THE TESTING SESSIONS

In assessing how TAs recorded information, monitored the students, and ended the first and second cognitive block sessions, the SQMs overwhelmingly judged that the sessions were conducted according to PISA procedures. Information on timing and attendance was not recorded in only five cases. About 5 per cent of TAs were reported as remaining at their desks during the session rather than walking around to monitor students as they worked, but some commented that the students were so well behaved that there was no need to walk around. In all but six instances in the first session and 14 in the second, students stopped work promptly when the TA said it was time to stop.

At the end of the first and second parts of the testing session, close to 85 per cent of the TAs

---

Q 12 Did the Test Administrator read the directions, the examples and the answer to the examples from the Script of the Cognitive Blocks exactly as it is written?

Yes	705 (79.8%)	
No	178 (20.2%)	If no, did the Test Administrator make:
Minor additions	136 (15.2%)	
Major additions	23 (2.6%)	
Minor deletions	81 (9.1%)	
Major deletions	11 (1.2%)	
Missing	10 (1.1%)	

If major additions or deletions were made, please describe:

No explanations were given by the SQMs for the major deletions, but it is likely that they arose when Test Administrators paraphrased instructions. Nearly all of the major deletions occurred because the Test Administrator said that students could leave when they had finished, when the instructions said they should remain in the room. This occurred in 17 different countries.

were reported as having followed the script exactly as it was written. Other cases involved some paraphrasing of the script (*e.g.*, reminding students to complete the Calculator Use question at the end of their test booklet), and all but a very small number were considered to be minor. Of serious concern, however, is the country where no script was provided to TAs.

THE STUDENT QUESTIONNAIRE SESSION

Although TAs and their assistants were encouraged to assist students in answering questions in the questionnaire, about the same percentage as for the cognitive sessions read the script exactly as it was written and seemed to perceive the session as rule-bound. In about 100 cases the TAs paraphrased the script, but in a further 20 cases the TAs substituted their own instructions entirely. In some of these instances (both types), the important instructions that students could ask for help if they had difficulties and that their answers would not be read by school staff were missed. These omissions represent a serious deviation from PISA procedures and are thus a concern in relation to the accuracy of students' responses.

Most TAs realised that time constraints for completing the questionnaire did not need to be rigorously imposed. Because of this flexibility, the timing procedures were less closely monitored than they were for the cognitive blocks.

GENERAL QUESTIONS CONCERNING THE ASSESSMENT

This section of the appendix describes general issues concerning how PISA sessions were conducted, such as:
- frequency of interruptions;
- orderliness of the students;
- evidence of cheating;
- how appropriately the TA answered questions;
- whether any defective books were detected and whether their replacement was handled appropriately;
- whether any late students were admitted; and
- whether students refused to participate.

The SQMs' responses to some of these are shown in the boxes below and some comments are made following the boxes.

Q 28 Were there any general disruptions to the session that lasted for more than one minute (e.g., alarms, announcements, changing of classes, etc.)?

Yes	99 (11.1%) If yes, specify.
	Most disruptions occurred because of noise—either from bells ringing, music lessons, the playground, or students changing classes.
No	792 (88.9%)
Missing	2 (0.2%)

Q 29 Generally, were the students orderly and cooperative?

Yes	836 (94.6%)
No	48 (5.4%)
Missing	9 (1.0%)

> **Q 32 Was there any evidence of students cheating during the assessment session?**
>
> Yes   42 (4.7%)
>
> **If yes, describe this evidence.**
>
> Most of the evidence to do with cheating concerned students exchanging booklets, asking each other questions and showing each other their answers. Some students checked with their neighbour to see if they had the same test booklets. Most incidences reported by School Quality Monitors seem to have been relatively minor infringements.
>
> No   847 (95.3%)
>
> Missing 4 (0.4%)

> **Q 36 Did any students refuse to participate in the assessment after the session had begun?**
>
> Yes   48 (5.4%)
>
> No   837 (94.6%)
>
> Missing 8 (0.9%)

These data suggest that very high proportions of students who participated in the PISA tests and questionnaires did so in a positive spirit. Students refused to participate after the session had started in only a small percentage of sessions. While cheating was reported to have occurred in 42 of the observed sessions, it is difficult to imagine why students would try to cheat given that they knew that they had different test booklets. This item was included in the SQM observation sheet because there were relatively high levels of cheating reported in the field trial. It is unlikely that the cheating offences reported by the SQMs would have had much influence on country results and rankings, though they possibly affected the results of a few individual students.

More than 95 per cent of TAs were reported as responding to students' questions appropriately during the test and questionnaire administration.

In 28 cases, TAs were observed to admit late students after the testing had begun, which was clearly stated in their manual as unacceptable. Though low in incidence, this represented a violation of PISA procedures and may not have received sufficient emphasis in TA training.

Defective test booklets were detected in close to 100 (about 11 per cent) of the SQM visits. These were replaced appropriately in half the cases, but in the other half the correct procedure was not followed. In five cases, where there were 10 or more defective booklets, the TA may not have had enough spare copies to distribute according to the specified procedure, though subsequent investigation showed that in two of these cases the booklets were replaced correctly. In the majority of cases, only one or two booklets were defective. (Items that were missing from test booklets or questionnaires were coded as *not administered* and therefore did not affect results.)

SUMMARY

The data from the SQMs support the view that, in nearly all of the schools that were visited, PISA test and questionnaire sessions were conducted in an orderly fashion and conformed to PISA procedures. The students also seem to have participated with good grace judging by the low level of disruption and refusal. This gives confidence that the PISA test data were collected under near-optimal conditions.

INTERVIEW WITH THE PISA SCHOOL CO-ORDINATOR

School Quality Monitors conducted an interview with the PISA School Co-ordinators to try and establish problems experienced by schools in conducting PISA, including:

- How well the PISA activities went at the school;
- How many schools refused to have a make-up session;
- If there were any problems co-ordinating the schedule for the assessment;
- If there were any problems preparing an accurate list of age-eligible students;
- If there were any problems in making exclusions of sampled students;
- If the students received practice on PISA-like questions before the PISA assessment; and
- How many students refused to participate in the PISA tests prior to testing.

SQMs were advised that they should treat the interview as a fairly informal 'conversation', since it was judged that this would be less likely to be seen as an imposition on teachers. The quality of the data from these interviews was good, judging by their completeness and detail.

Responses from the interviews are summarised in Table 90.

The PISA activities appeared to have gone well in the vast majority of schools visited by the SQMs. The problems that did exist related to clashes with examinations or the curriculum, or lack of time to organise the testing. Given the demands of the sampling procedures on many schools, the relatively long time during which students were needed, and the possibility that in some countries the Student Questionnaire could be seen as controversial, this result is a very positive endorsement of the procedures put in place by National Centres.

Only 10 of the almost 900 schools that SQMs visited refused to conduct a make-up session if one was required. Generally, the schools visited had no difficulties co-ordinating the schedule for the assessment. This may suggest that the role of the School Co-ordinator was important in helping to place PISA into the school, and that it successfully achieved its objectives.

It was expected that preparing the list of age-eligible students might be a problem for schools, particularly those without computer-based records. However, only a small minority of the schools visited by the SQMs said that they had experienced problems.

It had also been anticipated that excluding sampled students might be a problem for schools. The evidence here shows that only a small minority of the schools visited by the SQMs had problems. This finding is consistent with the NCQM reports where only five NPMs anticipated that schools would have problems. (However, it is also possible that exclusions were seen not to be problematic because they were not taken seriously. Caution is therefore advised in interpreting these results.)

Very few schools had used questions similar to those found in PISA for practice before assessment day. This is a positive finding since it implies that rehearsal effects were probably minimal.

Student refusals prior to the testing day were widely distributed among schools, with one notable exception, as shown in Table 91. Further investigation showed that this school was in a country where a national option meant that more than 35 students could be sampled. All other schools from this country had low levels of refusal.

Table 90: Responses to the School Co-ordinator Interview

Interview question	Yes (%)	No (%)	Missing (%)
In your opinion, did the PISA activities go well at your school?	91	5	4
Were there any problems co-ordinating the schedule for the assessment?	11	85	4
Did you have any problems preparing an accurate list of age-eligible students?	7	90	3
Did you have any problems making exclusions after you received the list of sampled students?	5	90	5
Did the students get any practice on questions like those in PISA before their assessment day?	4	91	5
Did any students refuse to take the test prior to the testing?	22	76	2

Table 91: Numbers of Students per School Refusing to Participate in PISA Prior to Testing

Number of Students Per School	Frequency
1	88
2	47
3	18
4	14
5	7
6	7
7	4
9	4
10	2
11	1
12	1
44	1

NATIONAL CENTRE QUALITY MONITOR REPORTS

NCQMs interviewed 29 NPMs. This report does not include Australia, Japan or the United States, where the Consortium was responsible in whole or in part for PISA activities. Seven NCQMs collected the data. Most interviews lasted about two hours.

STAFFING

Test Administrators

Three-quarters of the NPMs thought that it was easy to find TAs as described by the PISA guidelines. Of the remaining countries, two stated that they would have problems because of a general lack of qualified people interested in the job. Two countries reported that budget concerns made it difficult to find appropriate people. Five countries noted that it was necessary to use school staff, and that there was, therefore, a chance that the Test Administrator *might* be a teacher of some of the students. However, this was not expected to happen often. This is backed up by the responses to Question 5, where no country expected to have to use teachers of sampled students routinely.

The National Centre or NPM in 25 countries directly or indirectly trained the TAs. Two countries contracted this training out. Sometimes the National Centre would only train regional staff, who would then train the TAs working locally.

The International Project Centre has established the following criteria for Test Administrators:

It is <u>required</u> that the Test Administrator NOT be the reading, mathematics, or science instructor of any students in the sessions he or she will administer for PISA;

It is <u>recommended</u> that the Test Administrator NOT be a member of the staff of any school where he or she will administer PISA; and

It is <u>preferable</u> that the Test Administrator NOT be a member of the staff of any school in the PISA sample.

Q 4   How easy was it to comply with these criteria? If NOT easy, why not?
          Easy   20
          Not Easy   8
          No Response/NA   1

Q 5   Who will be Test Administrators for the main study?
          NPM/National Centre staff   2
          Regional/District   4
          External contractor   7
          Teacher of students   0
          Other school staff   9
          Other   7

SCHOOL QUALITY MONITORS

Several countries found it difficult to recruit SQMs primarily because the NPM believed that the Consortium had not provided an adequate job description. Three countries noted that it was difficult to find interested people that spoke either English or French, and a further three countries noted that it was hard to find qualified people interested in or independent of the national centre.

Q 14 How easy was it to find School Quality Monitors?		
Easy	15	
Not Easy	13	If NOT easy, why not?
		Need better job description — 6
		Lack English/French — 3
		Qualified – no interest/time — 2
		Qualified – not independent of national centre — 1

MARKERS

Countries planned to use several sources for recruiting markers. Most planned to use teachers or retired teachers who were familiar with 15-year-olds and the subject matter taught to them. Thirteen countries intended to use university students (mainly graduate-level in education). Five countries planned to use national centre staff. A few countries planned on using scientists or research staff as markers.

ADMINISTRATIVE ISSUES

Obtaining permission from schools

Thirteen NPMs indicated that it had been difficult to obtain schools' participation in PISA in their country. Four said that money or in-kind contributions to the school were used to encourage participation. In one country speeches were made to teacher and parent groups, and in another a national advertisement to promote PISA was used. Several countries provided brochures and other information to schools, and at least one country used a public website. Letters of support from Ministries of Education were noted to be useful in some instances. Telephone calls and personal meetings with school and regional staff were also common.

Unannounced visits by School Quality Monitors

PISA procedures for School Quality Monitors' visits to schools required that the visits be unannounced. This was expected to pose problems in several countries, but in practice it was a problem in only three, where unannounced visits to schools are not permitted.

Security and confidentiality

All countries took the issue of confidentiality seriously. Nearly all required a pledge of confidentiality and provided instructions on maintaining confidentiality and security. Of the

---

The markers of PISA tests:

- must have a good understanding of mid-secondary level mathematics and science OR <test language>; and
- understand secondary level students and the ways that students at this level express themselves.

Q 49 Do you anticipate or did you have any problems recruiting the markers who will meet these criteria? If yes, what are these problems?

Yes	8	Seven of these 'yes' responses were due to a 'lack of qualified/available staff'. Two countries cited cost or other factors as reasons for having difficulties recruiting markers.
No	19	
No response/NA	2	

Q 50 Who will be the markers (that is, from what pool will the markers be recruited)?

	First	Source	Second
Third National Centre staff	0	5	0
Teachers/Professional Educators	25	0	2
University students	3	1	1
Scientists/researchers	1	1	2
Other	0	1	1
No response/NA	0	0	0

29 respondents, 16 intended to send school packages of materials direct to TAs, nine were planning to send them to the relevant school, and four had arranged to send them to regional ministry or school inspectors' premises for collection by the TA.

Most countries said that the materials could not be inventoried without breaking the seal, either because they were wrapped in paper or more commonly were sealed in boxes with instructions not to open them until testing. These countries had not followed the suggestion in the *NPM Manual* that packages be heat-sealed in clear plastic, allowing booklets to be counted without the seal being broken.

Q 12	What are you doing to keep the materials secure?
	At the National Centre
	All countries reported good security including confidentiality pledges, locked rooms/secured buildings, and instructions about confidentiality and security. All of the National Centres were used to dealing with embargoed and secure material.
	While in the possession of the Test Administrator
	Most countries used staff who were familiar with test security and confidentiality. This issue was also emphasised at Test Administrator training.
	While in the possession of the School Co-ordinator
	In these cases, the material was sealed and the School Co-ordinator given instructions on handling the material. Materials were not to be opened until the morning of testing.

Student Tracking Forms

Student Tracking Forms are among the most important administrative tools in PISA. It was important to know if NPMs, TAs and SCs found them amenable to use. Replies pointed to a need to simplify the coding scheme for documenting student exclusions and to give thought to translation issues.

Q 17	Does the Student Tracking Form provided by the Consortium meet the needs in your country?
	Yes 22
	No 7
	If no, how did you modify the form to better meet your needs?
	Three countries indicated that they had problems entering the exclusions. Other problems mentioned were: problems trans-lating the text into the country's lang-uage, problems adding a tenth booklet and problems adding additional columns. One country thought the process was too complicated in general.

TRANSLATION AND VERIFICATION

The quality of data from a study like PISA depends considerably on the quality of the instruments, which in turn depend largely on the quality of translation. It was very important to the project to know that National Centres were able to follow the translation guidelines and procedures appropriately. By and large the translation quality objectives were met, as shown by the NPMs' responses to the following questions.

Eight countries listed time pressure as the main problem with international verification. Two

Q 28	Were the guidelines (for translation and verification) clear?
	Yes 24
	No 1
	No response/NA 4

Q 30	How much did the international verification add to the workload in the main study? If a lot, explain.
	Not much 17
	A lot 10
	No response/NA 2

Q 33	Did the remarks of the verifier significantly improve the national version for the field trial? If no, what were the problems?
	Yes 14
	No 11
	No response/NA 4

> **Q 34** Did the remarks of the verifier significantly improve the national version for the <u>main study</u>? If no, what were the problems?
>
> | | |
> |---|---|
> | Yes | 12 |
> | No | 13 |
> | No response/NA | 4 |

expressed by ten of the countries who responded that significant improvements were not made was that not many changes were made in any case. This is what would be hoped after the experiences of the field trial. However, a small number of countries did indicate some problems.

> **Q 55** Do you have any comments about manuals and other materials at this time?
>
> **NPM Manual**
> Comments offered=17
> No comments offered=12
>
> Thought manual good/adequate = 7
> Concerned about the lateness of receiving manual = 2
> Manual needs to be simplified or made clearer = 8
>
> **SC Manual**
> Comments offered=17
> No comments offered=12
>
> Thought manual good/adequate = 5
> Manual needs to be simplified or made clearer = 11
> Manual needs checklist or more examples (especially non-English/French) = 1
>
> **TA Manual**
> Comments offered=16
> No comments offered=13
>
> Thought manual good/adequate=4
> Manual needs to be simplified or made clearer=11
> Manual needs checklist or more examples (especially non-English/French) = 1
>
> **Marking Guide**
> Comments offered=16
> No comments offered=13
>
> Thought Guide good/adequate = 11
> Guide needs to be simplified or made clearer = 2
> Guide needs checklist or more examples (especially non-English/French) = 1
> Other comments = 2
>
> **Sampling Manual**
> Comments offered=16
> No comments offered=13
>
> Thought manual good/adequate = 12
> Manual needs to be simplified or made clearer = 4
>
> **Translation Guidelines**
> Comments offered=11
> No comments offered18
>
> Thought Guidelines good/adequate = 10
> Guidelines need to be simplified or made clearer = 1
>
> **Other**
> Comments offered=6
> No comments offered=23
>
> Thought good/adequate = 2
> Manual needs to be simplified or made clearer = 4
> (Other comments referred to the KeyQuest Manual and were noted earlier in the report in the section on the Student Tracking Form and sampling.)

commented on the cost of verification procedures. The 11 NPMs who said that there was no significant improvement in the national version for the field trial also noted that they had experienced few initial problems. No country felt that the verifiers had made errors, but at least one mentioned that they did not always agree with or accept the verifier's suggestions.

Slightly fewer countries indicated that there were significant improvements in their national versions for the main study. Again, the reason

ADEQUACY OF THE MANUALS

One aim of the NCQM visits was to collect suggestions from NPMs about areas in which the various PISA manuals could be improved. Seventeen of the NPMs offered comments, which are tabulated in the box below.

The format of some of the manuals clearly needs to be simplified. A problem for many NPMs was keeping track of and following revisions, especially while translations were in progress.

CONCLUSION

In general, the NCQM reports point to a strong organisational base for the conduct of PISA. National Centres were, in the main, well organised and had a good understanding of the following aspects:
- appointing and training Test Administrators;
- appointing SQMs;
- organising for marking and appointing markers;
- security of PISA materials;
- the Student Tracking Form and sampling issues; and
- translation (where appropriate) and verification of materials, although concerns were expressed about how much work was involved and some disagreement with decisions made during this process was indicated.

APPENDIX 6: ORDER EFFECTS FIGURES

Table 92: Item Assignment to Reading Clusters

No.	1	2	3	4	5	6	7	8	9
1	R219Q01T	R245Q01	R091Q05	R227Q01	R093Q03	R061Q01	R228Q01	R110Q01	R077Q02
2	R219Q01E	R245Q02	R091Q06	R227Q02T	R055Q01	R061Q03	R228Q02	R110Q04	R077Q03
3	R219Q02	R225Q02	R091Q07B	R227Q03	R055Q02	R061Q04	R228Q04	R110Q05	R077Q04
4	R081Q01	R225Q03	R119Q09T	R227Q04	R055Q03	R061Q05	R099Q04B	R110Q06	R077Q05
5	R081Q05	R225Q04	R119Q01	R227Q06	R055Q05	R083Q01	R120Q01	R237Q01	R077Q06
6	R081Q06A	R238Q01	R119Q07	R086Q05	R122Q02	R083Q02	R120Q03	R237Q03	R216Q01
7	R081Q06B	R238Q02	R119Q06	R086Q07	R122Q03T	R083Q03	R120Q06	R236Q01	R216Q02
8	R101Q01	R234Q01	R119Q08	R086Q04	R067Q01	R083Q04	R120Q07T	R236Q02	R216Q03T
9	R101Q02	R234Q02	R119Q04	R102Q01	R067Q04	R083Q06	R220Q01	R246Q01	R216Q04
10	R101Q03	R241Q02	R119Q05	R102Q04A	R067Q05	R100Q04	R220Q02B	R246Q02	R216Q06
11	R101Q04			R102Q05	R076Q03	R100Q05	R220Q04	R239Q01	R088Q01
12	R101Q05			R102Q06	R076Q04	R100Q06	R220Q05	R239Q02	R088Q03
13	R101Q08			R102Q07	R076Q05	R100Q07	R220Q06		R088Q04T
14	R070Q02			R111Q01		R104Q01			R088Q05T
15	R070Q03			R111Q02B		R104Q02			R088Q07
16	R070Q04			R111Q04		R104Q05			R040Q02
17	R070Q07T			R111Q06B		R104Q06			R040Q03A
18									R040Q03B
19									R040Q04
20									R040Q06

Table 92 shows the assignment of items to each of the nine reading clusters. Figures 84 to 92 represent the complete set of plots of order effects in the booklets. There is one figure for each cluster. In the legend, the first digit after 'Pos.' shows whether the cluster was in the first or second half of the booklet, and the second digit shows the cluster's position in the booklet half. For example, Pos. 2.1 means that the cluster was the first one in the second half of the booklet indicated in brackets.

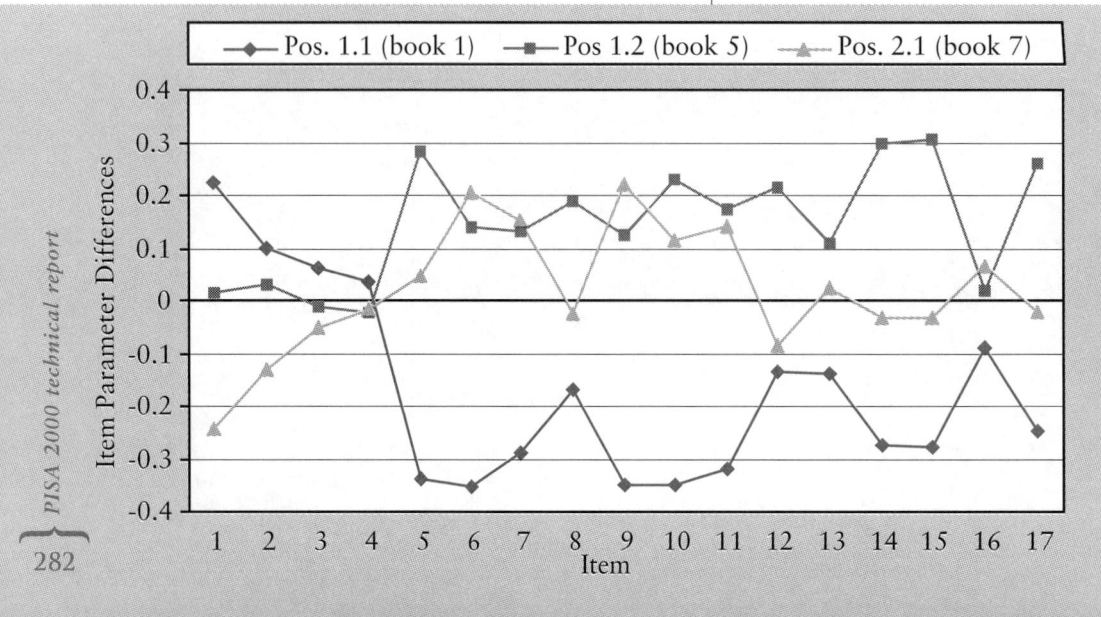

Figure 84: Item Parameter Differences for the Items in Cluster One

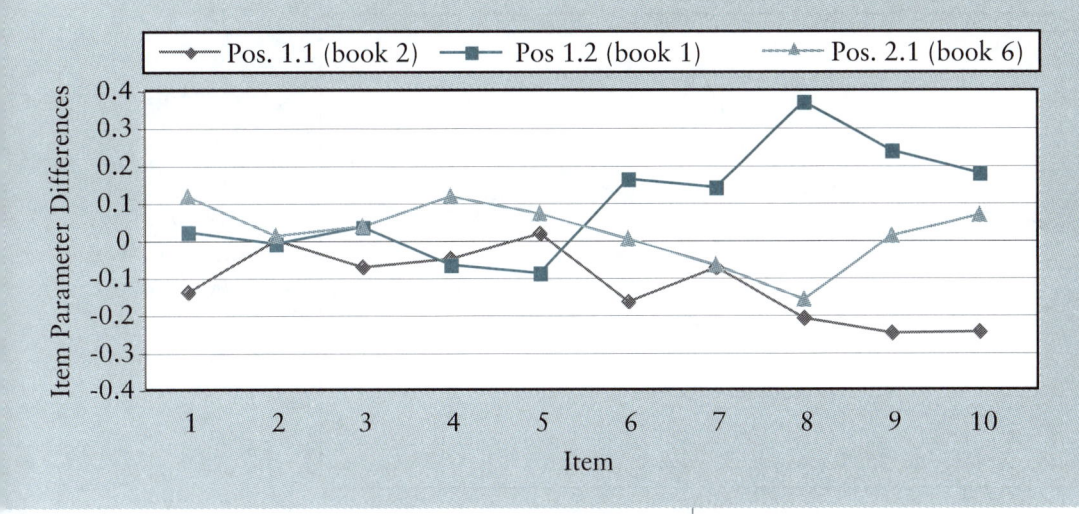

Figure 85: Item Parameter Differences for the Items in Cluster Two

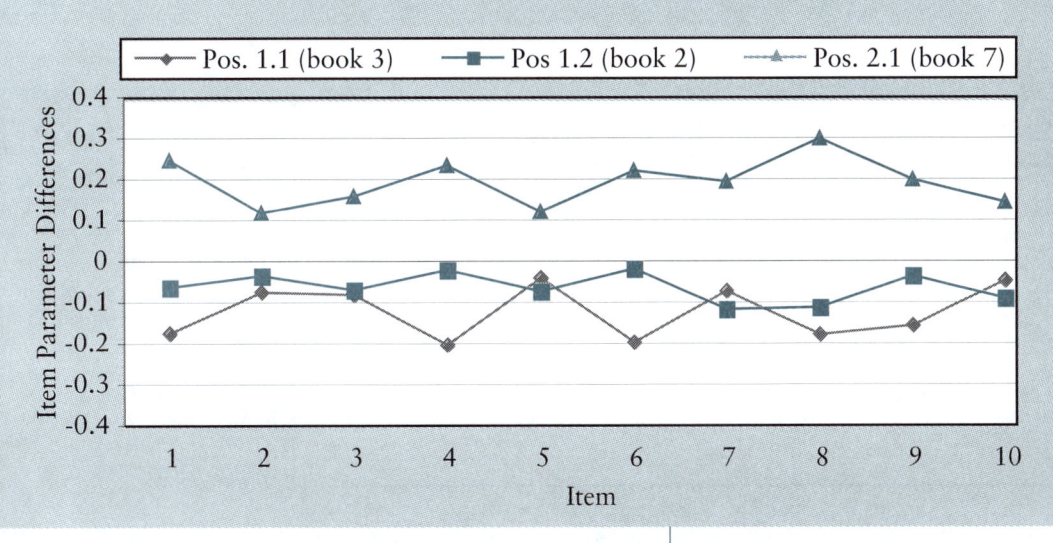

Figure 86: Item Parameter Differences for the Items in Cluster Three

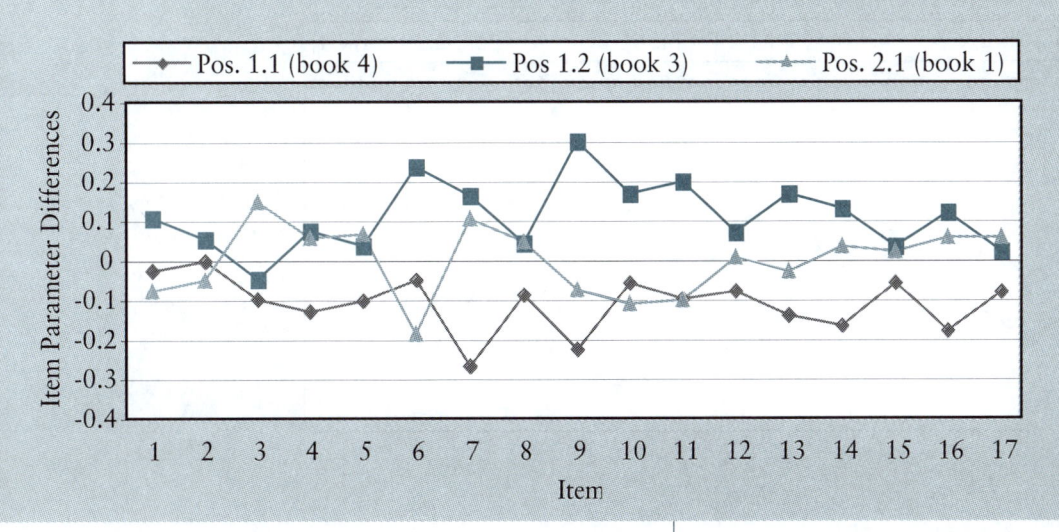

Figure 87: Item Parameter Differences for the Items in Cluster Four

Appendices

283

Figure 88: Item Parameter Differences for the Items in Cluster Five

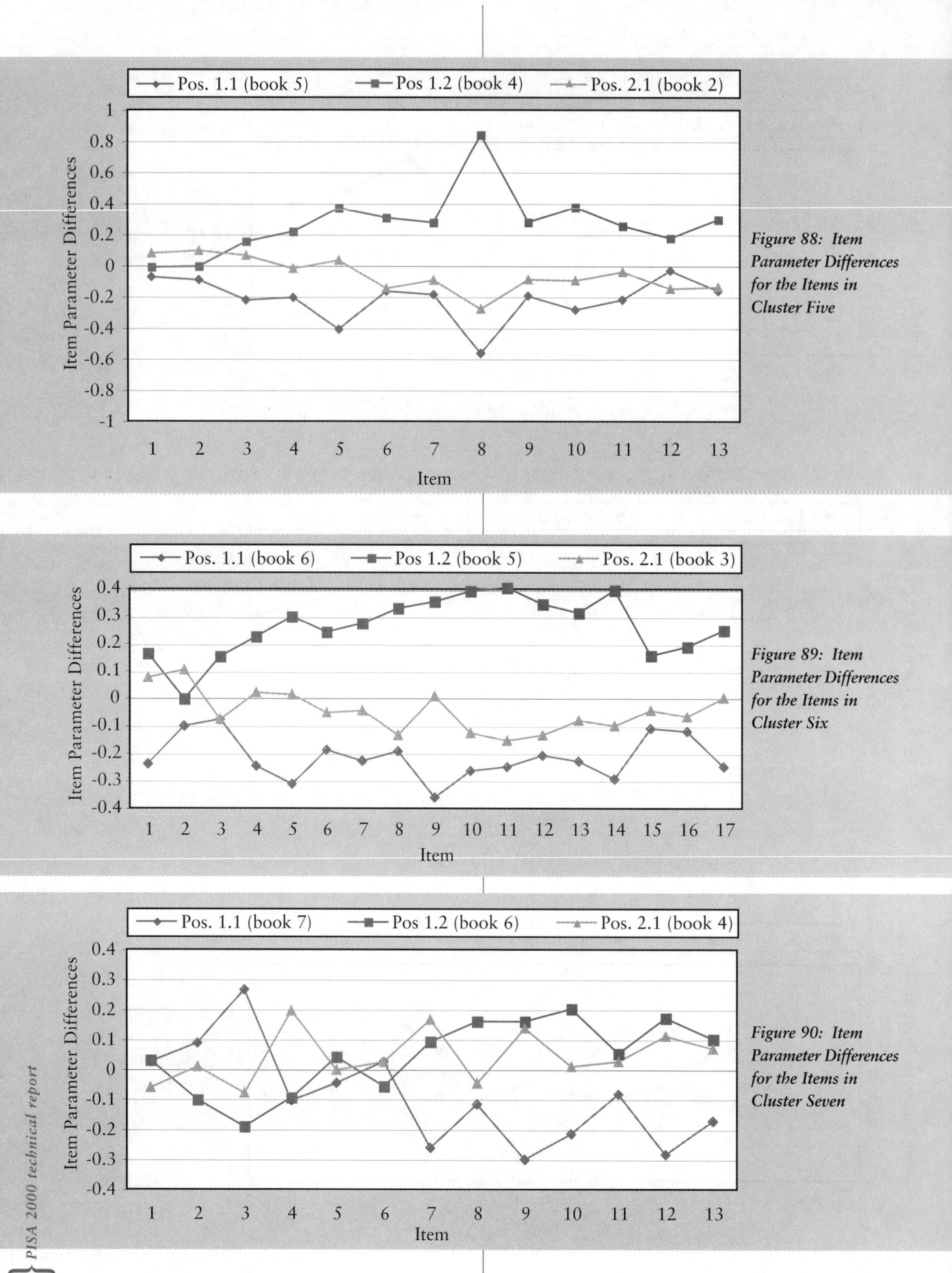

Figure 89: Item Parameter Differences for the Items in Cluster Six

Figure 90: Item Parameter Differences for the Items in Cluster Seven

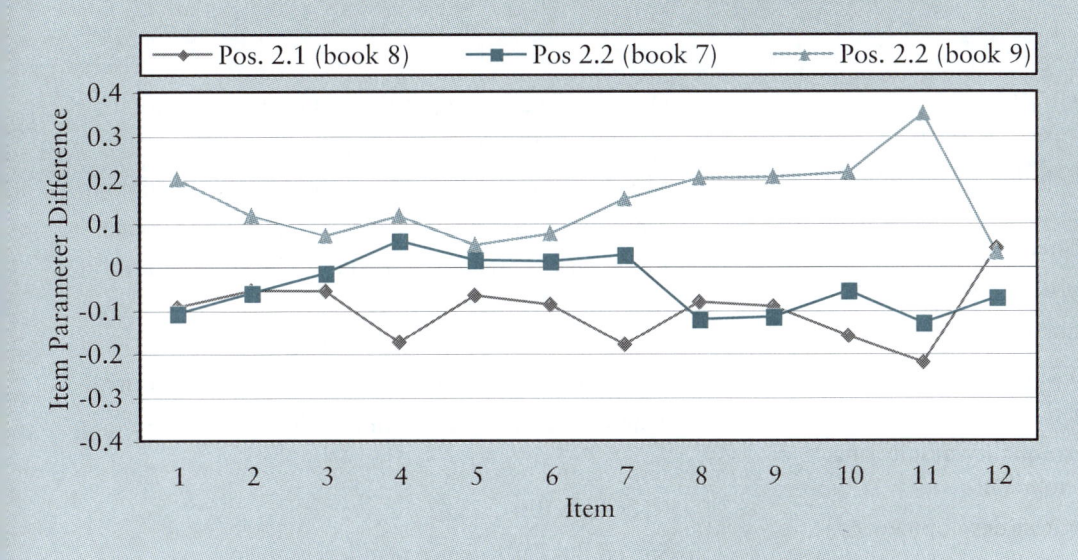

Figure 91: Item Parameter Differences for the Items in Cluster Eight

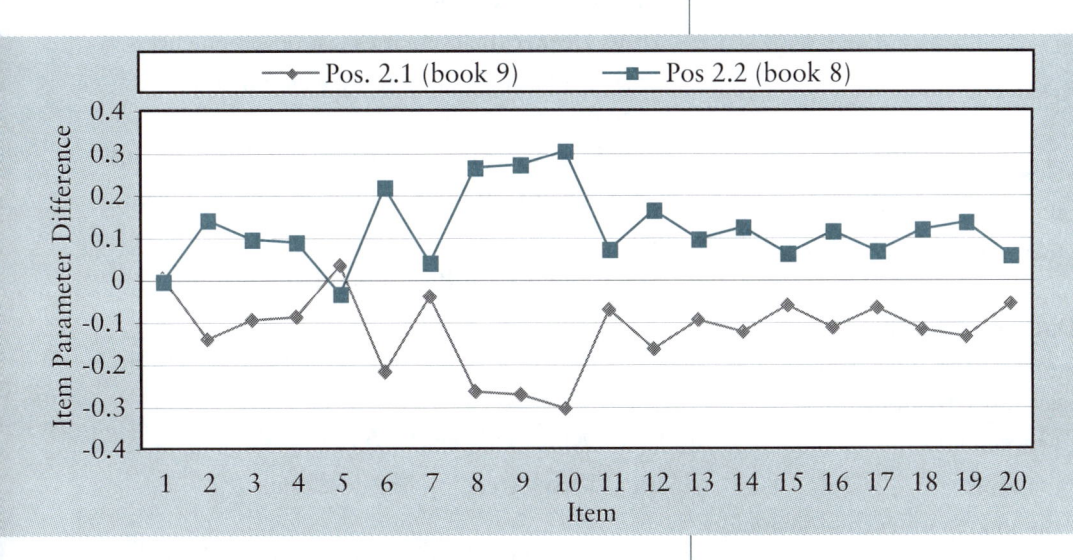

Figure 92: Item Parameter Differences for the Items in Cluster Nine

APPENDIX 7: PISA 2000 EXPERT GROUP MEMBERSHIP AND CONSORTIUM STAFF

PISA CONSORTIUM

AUSTRALIAN COUNCIL FOR EDUCATIONAL RESEARCH

Ray Adams (Project Director of the PISA Consortium)
Alla Berezner (data processing, data analysis)
Claus Carstensen (data analysis)
Lynne Darkin (reading test development)
Brian Doig (mathematics test development)
Adrian Harvey-Beavis (quality monitoring, questionnaire development)
Kathryn Hill (reading test development)
John Lindsey (mathematics test development)
Jan Lokan (quality monitoring, field procedures development)
Le Tu Luc (data processing)
Greg Macaskill (data processing)
Joy McQueen (reading test development and reporting)
Gary Marks (questionnaire development)
Juliette Mendelovits (reading test development and reporting)
Christian Monseur (Director of the PISA Consortium for data processing, data analysis, quality monitoring)
Gayl O'Connor (science test development)
Alla Routitsky (data processing)
Wolfram Schulz (data analysis)
Ross Turner (test analysis and reporting co-ordination)
Nikolai Volodin (data processing)
Craig Williams (data processing, data analysis)
Margaret Wu (Deputy Project Director of the PISA Consortium)

WESTAT

Nancy Caldwell (Director of the PISA Consortium for field operations and quality monitoring)
Ming Chen (sampling and weighting)
Fran Cohen (sampling and weighting)
Susan Fuss (sampling and weighting)
Brice Hart (sampling and weighting)
Sharon Hirabayashi (sampling and weighting)
Sheila Krawchuk (sampling and weighting)
Dward Moore (field operations and quality monitoring)
Phu Nguyen (sampling and weighting)
Monika Peters (field operations and quality monitoring)
Merl Robinson (field operations and quality monitoring)
Keith Rust (Director of the PISA Consortium for sampling and weighting)
Leslie Wallace (sampling and weighting)
Dianne Walsh (field operations and quality monitoring)
Trevor Williams (questionnaire development)

CITOGROEP

Steven Bakker (science test development)
Bart Bossers (reading test development)
Truus Decker (mathematics test development)
Erna van Hest (reading test development and quality monitoring)
Kees Lagerwaard (mathematics test development)
Gerben van Lent (mathematics test development)
Ico de Roo (science test development)
Maria van Toor (office support and quality monitoring)
Norman Verhelst (technical advice, data analysis)

EDUCATIONAL TESTING SERVICE

Irwin Kirsch (reading test development)

OTHER EXPERTS

Marc Demeuse (quality monitoring)
Harry Ganzeboom (questionnaire development)
Aletta Grisay (technical advice, data analysis, translation, questionnaire development)
Donald Hirsch (editorial review)
Erich Ramseier (questionnaire development)
Marie-Andrée Somers (data analysis and reporting)
Peter Sutton (editorial review)
Rich Tobin (questionnaire development and reporting)
J. Douglas Willms (questionnaire development, data analysis and reporting)

READING FUNCTIONAL EXPERT GROUP

Irwin Kirsch (Chair) (Educational Testing Service, United States)
Marilyn Binkley (National Center for Educational Statistics, United States)
Alan Davies (University of Edinburgh, United Kingdom)
Stan Jones (Statistics Canada, Canada)
John de Jong (Language Testing Services, The Netherlands)
Dominique Lafontaine (Université de Liège Sart Tilman, Belgium)
Pirjo Linnakylä (University of Jyväskylä, Finland)
Martine Rémond (Institut National de Recherche Pédagogique, France)
Ryo Watanabe (National Institute for Educational Research, Japan)
Prof. Wolfgang Schneider (University of Würzburg, Germany)

MATHEMATICS FUNCTIONAL EXPERT GROUP

Jan de Lange (Chair) (Utrecht University, The Netherlands)
Raimondo Bolletta (Istituto Nazionale di Valutazione, Italy)
Sean Close (St Patrick's College, Ireland)
Maria Luisa Moreno (IES "Lope de Vega", Spain)
Mogens Niss (IMFUFA, Roskilde University, Denmark)
Kyungmee Park (Hongik University, Korea)
Thomas A. Romberg (United States)
Peter Schüller (Federal Ministry of Education and Cultural Affairs, Austria)

SCIENCE FUNCTIONAL EXPERT GROUP

Wynne Harlen (Chair) (University of Bristol, United Kingdom)
Peter Fensham (Monash University, Australia)
Raul Gagliardi (University of Geneva, Switzerland)
Svein Lie (University of Oslo, Norway)
Manfred Prenzel (Universität Kiel, Germany)
Senta Raizen (National Center for Improving Science Education (NCISE), United States)
Donghee Shin (Dankook University, Korea)
Elizabeth Stage (University of California, United States)

CULTURAL REVIEW PANEL

Ronald Hambleton (Chair) (University of Massachusetts, United States)
David Bartram (SHL Group plc, United Kingdom)
Sunhee Chae (KICE, Korea)
Chiara Croce (Ministero della Pubblica Istruzione, Direzione Generale degli Scambi Culturali, Italy)
John de Jong (Language Testing Services, The Netherlands)
Jose Muniz (University of Oviedo, Spain)
Yves Poortinga (Tilburg University, The Netherlands)
Norbert Tanzer (University of Graz, Austria)
Pierre Vrignaud (INETOP - Institut National pour l'Enseignement Technique et l'Orientation Professionnelle, France)
Ingemar Wedman (University of Stockholm, Sweden)

TECHNICAL ADVISORY GROUP

Geoff Masters (Chair) (ACER, Australia)
Ray Adams (ACER, Australia)
Pierre Foy (Statistics Canada, Canada)
Aletta Grisay (Belgium)
Larry Hedges (The University of Chicago, United States)
Eugene Johnson (American Institutes for Research, United States)
John de Jong (Language Testing Services, The Netherlands)
Keith Rust (WESTAT, USA)
Norman Verhelst (Cito group, The Netherlands)
J. Douglas Willms (University of New Brunswick, Canada)

APPENDIX 8: CONTRAST CODING FOR PISA-2000 CONDITIONING VARIABLES

Conditioning Variables	Variable Name (s)	Variable Coding	Contrast Coding
Sex - Q3	ST03Q01	1 <Female>	-1
		2 <Male>	1
		Missing	0
Mother - Q4a	ST04Q01	1 Yes	10
		2 No	01
		Missing	00
Female Guardian - Q4b	ST04Q02	1 Yes	10
		2 No	01
		Missing	00
Father - Q4c	ST04Q03	1 Yes	10
		2 No	01
		Missing	00
Male Guardian - Q4d	ST04Q04	1 Yes	10
		2 No	01
		Missing	00
Brothers - Q4e	ST04Q05	1 Yes	10
		2 No	01
		Missing	00
Sisters - Q4f	ST04Q06	1 Yes	10
		2 No	01
		Missing	00
Grandparents - Q4g	ST04Q07	1 Yes	10
		2 No	01
		Missing	00
Others - Q4h	ST04Q08	1 Yes	10
		2 No	01
		Missing	00
Older - Q5a	ST05Q01	1 None	10
		2 One	20
		3 Two	30
		4 Three	40
		5 Four or more	50
		Missing	11
Younger - Q5b	ST05Q02	1 None	10
		2 One	20
		3 Two	30
		4 Three	40
		5 Four or more	50
		Missing	11
Same age - Q5c	ST05Q03	1 None	10
		2 One	20
		3 Two	30
		4 Three	40
		5 Four or more	50
		Missing	11

Conditioning Variables	Variable Name (s)	Variable Coding	Contrast Coding
Mother currently doing - Q6	ST06Q01	1 Working full-time <for pay>	1000
		2 Working part-time <for pay>	0100
		3 Not working, but looking...	0010
		4 Other (*e.g.*, home duties, retired)	0001
		Missing	0000
Father currently doing - Q7	ST07Q01	1 Working full-time <for pay>	1000
		2 Working part-time <for pay>	0100
		3 Not working, but looking...	0010
		4 Other (*e.g.*, home duties, retired)	0001
		Missing	0000
Mother's secondary educ - Q12	ST12Q01	1 No, she did not go to school	10000
		2 No, she completed <ISCED level 1> only	01000
		3 No, she completed <ISCED level 2> only	00100
		4 No, she completed <ISCED level 3B, 3C> only	00010
		5 Yes, she completed <ISCED 3A>	00001
		Missing	00000
Father's secondary educ - Q13	ST13Q01	1 No, he did not go to school	10000
		2 No, he completed <ISCED 1 1> only	01000
		3 No, he completed <ISCED 2> only	00100
		4 No, he completed <ISCED 3B, 3C> only	00010
		5 Yes, he completed <ISCED 3A>	00001
		Missing	00000
Mother's tertiary educ - Q14	ST14Q01	1 Yes	10
		2 No	01
		Missing	00
Father's tertiary educ - Q15	ST15Q01	1 Yes	10
		2 No	01
		Missing	00
Country of birth, self - Q16a	ST16Q01	1 <Country of Test>	10
		2 Another Country	01
		Missing	00
Country of birth, Mother - Q16b	ST16Q02	1 <Country of Test>	10
		2 Another Country	01
		Missing	00
Country of birth, Father - Q16c	ST16Q03	1 <Country of Test>	10
		2 Another Country	01
		Missing	00

Conditioning Variables	Variable Name (s)	Variable Coding	Contrast Coding
Language at home - Q17	ST17Q01	1 <Test language>	1000
		2 <Other official national languages>	0100
		3 <Other national dialects or languages>	0010
		4 <Other languages>	0001
		Missing	0000
Movies - Q18a	ST18Q01	1 Never or hardly ever	10
		2 Once or twice a year	20
		3 About 3 or 4 times a year	30
		4 More than 4 times a year	40
		Missing	41
Art gallery - Q18b	ST18Q02	1 Never or hardly ever	10
		2 Once or twice a year	20
		3 About 3 or 4 times a year	30
		4 More than 4 times a year	40
		Missing	11
Pop Music - Q18c	ST18Q03	1 Never or hardly ever	10
		2 Once or twice a year	20
		3 About 3 or 4 times a year	30
		4 More than 4 times a year	40
		Missing	11
Opera - Q18d	ST18Q04	1 Never or hardly ever	10
		2 Once or twice a year	20
		3 About 3 or 4 times a year	30
		4 More than 4 times a year	40
		Missing	11
Theatre - Q18e	ST18Q05	1 Never or hardly ever	10
		2 Once or twice a year	20
		3 About 3 or 4 times a year	30
		4 More than 4 times a year	40
		Missing	11
Sport - Q18f	ST18Q06	1 Never or hardly ever	10
		2 Once or twice a year	20
		3 About 3 or 4 times a year	30
		4 More than 4 times a year	40
		Missing	41
Discuss politics - Q19a	ST19Q01	1 Never or hardly ever	10
		2 A few times a year	20
		3 About once a month	30
		4 Several times a month	40
		5 Several times a week	50
		Missing	11

Conditioning Variables	Variable Name (s)	Variable Coding	Contrast Coding
Discuss books - Q19b	ST19Q02	1 Never or hardly ever	10
		2 A few times a year	20
		3 About once a month	30
		4 Several times a month	40
		5 Several times a week	50
		Missing	51
Listen classics - Q19c	ST19Q03	1 Never or hardly ever	10
		2 A few times a year	20
		3 About once a month	30
		4 Several times a month	40
		5 Several times a week	50
		Missing	11
Discuss school issues - Q19d	ST19Q04	1 Never or hardly ever	10
		2 A few times a year	20
		3 About once a month	30
		4 Several times a month	40
		5 Several times a week	50
		Missing	51
Eat <main meal> - Q19e	ST19Q05	1 Never or hardly ever	10
		2 A few times a year	20
		3 About once a month	30
		4 Several times a month	40
		5 Several times a week	50
		Missing	51
Just talking - Q19f	ST19Q06	1 Never or hardly ever	10
		2 A few times a year	20
		3 About once a month	30
		4 Several times a month	40
		5 Several times a week	50
		Missing	51
Mother - Q20a	ST20Q01	1 Never or hardly ever	10
		2 A few times a year	20
		3 About once a month	30
		4 Several times a month	40
		5 Several times a week	50
		Missing	11
Father - Q20b	ST20Q02	1 Never or hardly ever	10
		2 A few times a year	20
		3 About once a month	30
		4 Several times a month	40
		5 Several times a week	50
		Missing	11

Conditioning Variables	Variable Name (s)	Variable Coding	Contrast Coding
Siblings - Q20c	ST20Q03	1 Never or hardly ever 2 A few times a year 3 About once a month 4 Several times a month 5 Several times a week Missing	10 20 30 40 50 11
Grandparents - Q20d	ST20Q04	1 Never or hardly ever 2 A few times a year 3 About once a month 4 Several times a month 5 Several times a week Missing	10 20 30 40 50 11
Other relations - Q20e	ST20Q05	1 Never or hardly ever 2 A few times a year 3 About once a month 4 Several times a month 5 Several times a week Missing	10 20 30 40 50 11
Parents' friends - Q20f	ST20Q06	1 Never or hardly ever 2 A few times a year 3 About once a month 4 Several times a month 5 Several times a week Missing	10 20 30 40 50 11
Dishwasher - Q21a	ST21Q01	1 Yes 2 No Missing	10 01 00
Own room - Q21b	ST21Q02	1 Yes 2 No Missing	10 01 00
Educat software - Q21c	ST21Q03	1 Yes 2 No Missing	10 01 00
Internet - Q21d	ST21Q04	1 Yes 2 No Missing	10 01 00
Dictionary - Q21e	ST21Q05	1 Yes 2 No Missing	10 01 00
Study place - Q21f	ST21Q06	1 Yes 2 No Missing	10 01 00
Desk - Q21g	ST21Q07	1 Yes 2 No Missing	10 01 00

Conditioning Variables	Variable Name (s)	Variable Coding	Contrast Coding
Text books - Q21h	ST21Q08	1 Yes	10
		2 No	01
		Missing	00
Classic literature - Q21i	ST21Q09	1 Yes	10
		2 No	01
		Missing	00
Poetry - Q21j	ST21Q10	1 Yes	10
		2 No	01
		Missing	00
Art works - Q21k	ST21Q11	1 Yes	10
		2 No	01
		Missing	00
Phone - Q22a	ST22Q01	1 None	10
		2 One	20
		3 Two	30
		4 Three or more	40
		Missing	21
Television - Q22b	ST22Q02	1 None	10
		2 One	20
		3 Two	30
		4 Three or more	40
		Missing	41
Calculator - Q22c	ST22Q03	1 None	10
		2 One	20
		3 Two	30
		4 Three or more	40
		Missing	41
Computer - Q22d	ST22Q04	1 None	10
		2 One	20
		3 Two	30
		4 Three or more	40
		Missing	21
Musical instruments - Q22e	ST22Q05	1 None	10
		2 One	20
		3 Two	30
		4 Three or more	40
		Missing	11
Car - Q22f	ST22Q06	1 None	10
		2 One	20
		3 Two	30
		4 Three or more	40
		Missing	21
Bathroom - Q22g	ST22Q07	1 None	10
		2 One	20
		3 Two	30
		4 Three or more	40
		Missing	21

Conditioning Variables	Variable Name (s)	Variable Coding	Contrast Coding
<Extension> - Q23a	ST23Q01	1 No, never	10
		2 Yes, sometimes	20
		3 Yes, regularly	30
		Missing	11
<Remedial> in <test lang> - Q23b	ST23Q02	1 No, never	10
		2 Yes, sometimes	20
		3 Yes, regularly	30
		Missing	11
<Remedial> in other subjects - Q23c	ST23Q03	1 No, never	10
		2 Yes, sometimes	20
		3 Yes, regularly	30
		Missing	11
Skills training - Q23d	ST23Q04	1 No, never	10
		2 Yes, sometimes	20
		3 Yes, regularly	30
		Missing	11
In <test language> - Q24a	ST24Q01	1 No, never	10
		2 Yes, sometimes	20
		3 Yes, regularly	30
		Missing	11
In other subjects - Q24b	ST24Q02	1 No, never	10
		2 Yes, sometimes	20
		3 Yes, regularly	30
		Missing	11
<Extension> - Q24c	ST24Q03	1 No, never	10
		2 Yes, sometimes	20
		3 Yes, regularly	30
		Missing	11
<Remedial> in <test language> - Q24d	ST24Q04	1 No, never	10
		2 Yes, sometimes	20
		3 Yes, regularly	30
		Missing	11
<Remedial> in other subjects - Q24e	ST24Q05	1 No, never	10
		2 Yes, sometimes	20
		3 Yes, regularly	30
		Missing	11
Skills training - Q24f	ST24Q06	1 No, never	10
		2 Yes, sometimes	20
		3 Yes, regularly	30
		Missing	11
<Private tutoring> - Q24g	ST24Q07	1 No, never	10
		2 Yes, sometimes	20
		3 Yes, regularly	30
		Missing	11

Conditioning Variables	Variable Name (s)	Variable Coding	Contrast Coding
School program - Q25	ST25Q01	1 <ISCED 2A>	100000
		2 <ISCED 2B>	010000
		3 <ISCED 2C>	001000
		4 <ISCED 3A>	000100
		5 <ISCED 3B>	000010
		6 <ISCED 3C>	000001
		Missing	000000
Teachers wait long time - Q26a	ST26Q01	1 Never	10
		2 Some lessons	20
		3 Most lessons	30
		4 Every lesson	40
		Missing	21
Teachers want students to work - Q26b	ST26Q02	1 Never	10
		2 Some lessons	20
		3 Most lessons	30
		4 Every lesson	40
		Missing	41
Teachers tell students do better - Q26c	ST26Q03	1 Never	10
		2 Some lessons	20
		3 Most lessons	30
		4 Every lesson	40
		Missing	21
Teachers don't like - Q26d	ST26Q04	1 Never	10
		2 Some lessons	20
		3 Most lessons	30
		4 Every lesson	40
		Missing	21
Teachers show interest - Q26e	ST26Q05	1 Never	10
		2 Some lessons	20
		3 Most lessons	30
		4 Every lesson	40
		Missing	41
Teachers give opportunity - Q26f	ST26Q06	1 Never	10
		2 Some lessons	20
		3 Most lessons	30
		4 Every lesson	40
		Missing	41
Teachers help with work - Q26g	ST26Q07	1 Never	10
		2 Some lessons	20
		3 Most lessons	30
		4 Every lesson	40
		Missing	41
Teachers continue teaching - Q26h	ST26Q08	1 Never	10
		2 Some lessons	20
		3 Most lessons	30
		4 Every lesson	40
		Missing	31

Conditioning Variables	Variable Name (s)	Variable Coding	Contrast Coding
Teachers do a lot to help - Q26i	ST26Q09	1 Never	10
		2 Some lessons	20
		3 Most lessons	30
		4 Every lesson	40
		Missing	31
Teachers help with learning - Q26j	ST26Q10	1 Never	10
		2 Some lessons	20
		3 Most lessons	30
		4 Every lesson	40
		Missing	31
Teachers check homework - Q26k	ST26Q11	1 Never	10
		2 Some lessons	20
		3 Most lessons	30
		4 Every lesson	40
		Missing	21
Students cannot work well - Q26l	ST26Q12	1 Never	10
		2 Some lessons	20
		3 Most lessons	30
		4 Every lesson	40
		Missing	21
Students don't listen - Q26m	ST26Q13	1 Never	10
		2 Some lessons	20
		3 Most lessons	30
		4 Every lesson	40
		Missing	21
Students don't start - Q26n	ST26Q14	1 Never	10
		2 Some lessons	20
		3 Most lessons	30
		4 Every lesson	40
		Missing	21
Students learn a lot - Q26o	ST26Q15	1 Never	10
		2 Some lessons	20
		3 Most lessons	30
		4 Every lesson	40
		Missing	31
Noise & disorder - Q26p	ST26Q16	1 Never	10
		2 Some lessons	20
		3 Most lessons	30
		4 Every lesson	40
		Missing	21
Doing nothing - Q26q	ST26Q17	1 Never	10
		2 Some lessons	20
		3 Most lessons	30
		4 Every lesson	40
		Missing	21

Conditioning Variables	Variable Name (s)	Variable Coding	Contrast Coding
Number in < test language> - Q27a	ST27Q01	1 2 ... 90 Missing	010 020 ... 900 041
Usual in <test lang> - Q27aa	ST27Q02	1 Yes 2 No Missing	10 01 00
Number in Mathematics - Q27b	ST27Q03	1 2 ... 90 Missing	010 020 ... 900 041
Usual in Mathematics - Q27bb	ST27Q04	1 Yes 2 No Missing	10 01 00
Number in Science - Q27c	ST27Q05	1 2 ... 90 Missing	010 020 ... 900 041
Usual in Science - Q27cc	ST27Q06	1 Yes 2 No Missing	10 01 00
In < test language> - Q28a	ST28Q01	1 2 ... 90 Missing	010 020 ... 900 251
In Mathematics - Q28b	ST28Q02	1 2 ... 90 Missing	010 020 ... 900 241
In Science - Q28c	ST28Q03	1 2 ... 90 Missing	010 020 ... 900 241
Miss school - Q29a	ST29Q01	1 None 2 1 or 2 3 3 or 4 4 5 or more Missing	10 20 30 40 11

Conditioning Variables	Variable Name (s)	Variable Coding	Contrast Coding
<Skip> classes - Q29b	ST29Q02	1 None	10
		2 1 or 2	20
		3 3 or 4	30
		4 5 or more	40
		Missing	11
Late for school - Q29c	ST29Q03	1 None	10
		2 1 or 2	20
		3 3 or 4	30
		4 5 or more	40
		Missing	11
Well with teachers - Q30a	ST30Q01	1 Strongly disagree	10
		2 Disagree	20
		3 Agree	30
		4 Strongly agree	40
		Missing	31
Interested in students - Q30b	ST30Q02	1 Strongly disagree	10
		2 Disagree	20
		3 Agree	30
		4 Strongly agree	40
		Missing	31
Listen to me - Q30c	ST30Q03	1 Strongly disagree	10
		2 Disagree	20
		3 Agree	30
		4 Strongly agree	40
		Missing	31
Give extra help - Q30d	ST30Q04	1 Strongly disagree	10
		2 Disagree	20
		3 Agree	30
		4 Strongly agree	40
		Missing	31
Treat me fairly - Q30e	ST30Q05	1 Strongly disagree	10
		2 Disagree	20
		3 Agree	30
		4 Strongly agree	40
		Missing	31
Feel an outsider - Q31a	ST31Q01	1 Strongly disagree	10
		2 Disagree	20
		3 Agree	30
		4 Strongly agree	40
		Missing	11
Make friends - Q31b	ST31Q02	1 Strongly disagree	10
		2 Disagree	20
		3 Agree	30
		4 Strongly agree	40
		Missing	31

Conditioning Variables	Variable Name (s)	Variable Coding	Contrast Coding
Feel I belong - Q31c	ST31Q03	1 Strongly disagree 2 Disagree 3 Agree 4 Strongly agree Missing	10 20 30 40 31
Feel awkward - Q31d	ST31Q04	1 Strongly disagree 2 Disagree 3 Agree 4 Strongly agree Missing	10 20 30 40 11
Seem to like me - Q31e	ST31Q05	1 Strongly disagree 2 Disagree 3 Agree 4 Strongly agree Missing	10 20 30 40 31
Feel lonely - Q31f	ST31Q06	1 Strongly disagree 2 Disagree 3 Agree 4 Strongly agree Missing	10 20 30 40 11
Don't want to be - Q31g	ST31Q07	1 Strongly disagree 2 Disagree 3 Agree 4 Strongly agree Missing	10 20 30 40 21
Feel Bored - Q31h	ST31Q08	1 Strongly disagree 2 Disagree 3 Agree 4 Strongly agree Missing	10 20 30 40 21
I complete on time - Q32a	ST32Q01	1 Never 2 Sometimes 3 Most of the time 4 Always Missing	10 20 30 40 31
I do watching TV - Q32b	ST32Q02	1 Never 2 Sometimes 3 Most of the time 4 Always Missing	10 20 30 40 21
Teachers grade - Q32c	ST32Q03	1 Never 2 Sometimes 3 Most of the time 4 Always Missing	10 20 30 40 21

Conditioning Variables	Variable Name (s)	Variable Coding	Contrast Coding
I finish at school - Q32d	ST32Q04	1 Never	10
		2 Sometimes	20
		3 Most of the time	30
		4 Always	40
		Missing	21
Teachers comment on - Q32e	ST32Q05	1 Never	10
		2 Sometimes	20
		3 Most of the time	30
		4 Always	40
		Missing	21
Is interesting - Q32f	ST32Q06	1 Never	10
		2 Sometimes	20
		3 Most of the time	30
		4 Always	40
		Missing	21
Is counted in <mark> - Q32g	ST32Q07	1 Never	10
		2 Sometimes	20
		3 Most of the time	30
		4 Always	40
		Missing	21
Homework <test language> - Q33a	ST33Q01	1 No time	10
		2 Less than 1 hour a week	20
		3 Between 1 and 3 hours a week	30
		4 3 hours or more a week	40
		Missing	31
Homework <maths> - Q33b	ST33Q02	1 No time	10
		2 Less than 1 hour a week	20
		3 Between 1 and 3 hours a week	30
		4 3 hours or more a week	40
		Missing	31
Homework <science> - Q33c	ST33Q03	1 No time	10
		2 Less than 1 hour a week	20
		3 Between 1 and 3 hours a week	30
		4 3 hours or more a week	40
		Missing	31
Read each day - Q34	ST34Q01	1 I do not read for enjoyment	10
		2 30 minutes or less each day	20
		3 More than 30 minutes to less than 60 minutes each day	30
		4 1 to 2 hours each day	40
		5 More than 2 hours each day	50
		Missing	21
Only if I have to - Q35a	ST35Q01	1 Strongly disagree	10
		2 Disagree	20
		3 Agree	30
		4 Strongly agree	40
		Missing	21

Conditioning Variables	Variable Name (s)	Variable Coding	Contrast Coding
Favourite hobby - Q35b	ST35Q02	1 Strongly disagree	10
		2 Disagree	20
		3 Agree	30
		4 Strongly agree	40
		Missing	21
Talking about books - Q35c	ST35Q03	1 Strongly disagree	10
		2 Disagree	20
		3 Agree	30
		4 Strongly agree	40
		Missing	21
Hard to finish - Q35d	ST35Q04	1 Strongly disagree	10
		2 Disagree	20
		3 Agree	30
		4 Strongly agree	40
		Missing	21
Feel happy - Q35e	ST35Q05	1 Strongly disagree	10
		2 Disagree	20
		3 Agree	30
		4 Strongly agree	40
		Missing	31
Waste of time - Q35f	ST35Q06	1 Strongly disagree	10
		2 Disagree	20
		3 Agree	30
		4 Strongly agree	40
		Missing	21
Enjoy library - Q35g	ST35Q07	1 Strongly disagree	10
		2 Disagree	20
		3 Agree	30
		4 Strongly agree	40
		Missing	31
For information - Q35h	ST35Q08	1 Strongly disagree	10
		2 Disagree	20
		3 Agree	30
		4 Strongly agree	40
		Missing	21
Few minutes only - Q35i	ST35Q09	1 Strongly disagree	10
		2 Disagree	20
		3 Agree	30
		4 Strongly agree	40
		Missing	21
Magazines - Q36a	ST36Q01	1 Never or hardly ever	10
		2 A few times a year	20
		3 About once a month	30
		4 Several times a month	40
		5 Several times a week	50
		Missing	51

Conditioning Variables	Variable Name (s)	Variable Coding	Contrast Coding
Comics - Q36b	ST36Q02	1 Never or hardly ever 2 A few times a year 3 About once a month 4 Several times a month 5 Several times a week Missing	10 20 30 40 50 11
Fiction - Q36c	ST36Q03	1 Never or hardly ever 2 A few times a year 3 About once a month 4 Several times a month 5 Several times a week Missing	10 20 30 40 50 21
Non-fiction - Q36d	ST36Q04	1 Never or hardly ever 2 A few times a year 3 About once a month 4 Several times a month 5 Several times a week Missing	10 20 30 40 50 11
E-mail & Web - Q36e	ST36Q05	1 Never or hardly ever 2 A few times a year 3 About once a month 4 Several times a month 5 Several times a week Missing	10 20 30 40 50 31
Newspapers - Q36f	ST36Q06	1 Never or hardly ever 2 A few times a year 3 About once a month 4 Several times a month 5 Several times a week Missing	10 20 30 40 50 51
How many books at home - Q37	ST37Q01	1 None 2 1-10 books 3 11-50 books 4 51-100 books 5 101-250 books 6 251-500 books 9 More than 500 books Missing	10 20 30 40 50 60 70 51
Borrow books - Q38	ST38Q01	1 Never or hardly ever 2 A few times per year 3 About once a month 4 Several times a month Missing	10 20 30 40 11

Conditioning Variables	Variable Name (s)	Variable Coding	Contrast Coding
How often use school library - Q39a	ST39Q01	1 Never or hardly ever 2 A few times a year 3 About once a month 4 Several times a month 5 Several times a week Missing	10 20 30 40 50 11
How often use computers - Q39b	ST39Q02	1 Never or hardly ever 2 A few times a year 3 About once a month 4 Several times a month 5 Several times a week Missing	10 20 30 40 50 21
How often use calculators - Q39c	ST39Q03	1 Never or hardly ever 2 A few times a year 3 About once a month 4 Several times a month 5 Several times a week Missing	10 20 30 40 50 51
How often use Internet - Q39d	ST39Q04	1 Never or hardly ever 2 A few times a year 3 About once a month 4 Several times a month 5 Several times a week Missing	10 20 30 40 50 11
How often use science labs - Q39e	ST39Q05	1 Never or hardly ever 2 A few times a year 3 About once a month 4 Several times a month 5 Several times a week Missing	10 20 30 40 50 11
Calculator Use	Caluse	1 'No calculator' 2 'A simple calculator' 3 'A scientific calculator' 4 'A programmable calculator' 5 'A graphics calculator' Missing	10 20 30 40 50 11
Booklet	BookID	0 1 2 3 4 5 6 7 8 9	000000000 100000000 010000000 001000000 000100000 000010000 000001000 000000100 000000010 000000001

Conditioning Variables	Variable Name (s)	Variable Coding	Contrast Coding
Mother's main job	BMMJ	1	010
		2	020
		...	
		90	900
		missing	500
Father's main job	BFMJ	1	010
		2	020
		90	900
		missing	501

Multi-column entries without over-bars indicate multiple contrasts. Barred columns are treated as one contrast.

APPENDIX 9: SAMPLING FORMS

| PISA Sampling Form 1 | Time of Testing and Age Definition |

See Section 3.1 of School Sampling Manual.

PISA Participant: _____

National Project Manager: _____

1. Beginning and ending dates of assessment _____ 2000 to _____ 2000

2. Please confirm that the assessment start date is after the first three months of the academic year.
   ☐ Yes
   ☐ No

3. Students who will be assessed were born between _____ and _____
   　　　　　　　　　　　　　　　　　　　　　　　　　　　　　D D M M Y Y　　D D M M Y Y

4. As part of of the PISA sampling process for your country, will you be selecting students other than those born between the dates in 3) above? (For example students in a particular grade, no matter what age.)
   ☐ No
   ☐ Yes (please describe the additional population):

| PISA Sampling Form 2 | National Desired Target Population |

See Section 3.2 of School Sampling Manual.

PISA Participant: _____

National Project Manager: _____

1. Total national population of 15-year-olds:　　　　　　　　　　　　　　　[a]

2. Total national population of 15-year-olds enrolled in educational institutions:　[b]

3. Describe the population(s) to be omitted from the national desired target population (if applicable).
_____
_____

4. Total enrolment omitted from the national desired target population　　　[c]
   (corresponding to the omissions listed in the previous item):

5. Total enrolment in the national desired target population:　　　　　　　[d]
   box [b] - box [c]

6. Percentage of coverage in the national desired target population:　　　　[e]
   (box [d] / box [b]) x 100

7. Describe your data source (Provide copies of relevant tables): _____
_____
_____

| PISA Sampling Form 3 | National Defined Target Population |

See Section 3.3 of School Sampling Manual.

PISA Participant: _____

National Project Manager: _____

1. Total enrolment in the national desired target population: [a]
   From box [d] on Sampling Form 2

2. School-level exclusions:

Description of exclusions	Number of schools	Number of students
TOTAL		[b]

Percentage of students not covered due to school-level exclusions: ____ %
(box [b] / box [a]) x 100

3. Total enrolment in national defined target population before within-school   [c]
   exclusions: box [a] - box [b]

4. Within-school exclusions:

Description of exclusions	Expected number of students
TOTAL	[d]

Expected percentage of students not covered due to within-school exclusions: ____ %
(box [d] / box [a]) x 100

5. Total enrolment in national defined target population: [e]
   (box [a] − (box [b] + box [d])

6. Coverage of national desired target population: [f]
   (box [e] / box [a]) x 100

7. Describe your data source (Provide copies of relevant tables): _____
_____
_____

PISA Sampling Form 4	Sampling Frame Description

See Sections 5.2 – 5.4 of School Sampling Manual.

PISA Participant: _____

National Project Manager: _____

1. Will a sampling frame of geographic areas be used?
   - [ ] Yes   Go to 2
   - [ ] No   Go to 5

2. Specify the PSU Measure of Size to be used.
   - [ ] 15-year-old student enrolment
   - [ ] Total student enrolment
   - [ ] Number of schools
   - [ ] Population size
   - [ ] Other (please describe): _____
   _____

3. Specify the school year for which enrolment data will be used for the PSU Measure of Size:

4. Please provide a preliminary description of the information available to construct the area frame, **Please consult with Westat for support and advice in the construction and use of an area-level sampling frame.** _____
   _____

5. Specify the school estimate of enrolment (ENR) of 15-year-olds that will be used.
   - [ ] 15-year-old student enrolment
   - [ ] Applying known proportions of 15-year-olds to corresponding grade level enrolments
   - [ ] Grade enrolment of the modal grade for 15-year-olds
   - [ ] Total student enrolment, divided by number of grades

6. Specify the year for which enrolment data will be used for school ENR. _____

7. Please describe any other type of frame, if any, that will be used. _____
   _____

PISA Sampling Form 5 — Excluded Schools

See Section 5.5 of School Sampling Manual.

PISA Participant: _____

National Project Manager: _____

Use additional sheets if necessary

School ID	Reason for exclusion	School ENR

| PISA Sampling Form 6 | Treatment of Small Schools |

See Section 5.7 of School Sampling Manual.

PISA Participant: _____

National Project Manager: _____

1. Enrolment in small schools:

Type of school based on enrolment	Number of schools	Number of students	Percentage of Total enrolment
Enrolment of 15-year-old students < 17			[a]
Enrolment of 15-year-old students ≥ 17 and < 35			[b]
Enrolment of 15-year-old students ≥ 35			[c]
TOTAL			100%

2. If the sum of the percentages in boxes [a] and [b] is less than 5%, AND the percentage in box [a] is less than 1%, then all schools should be subject to normal school sampling, with no explicit stratification of small schools required or recommended.

    (box [a] + box [b]) < 5% and box [a] < 1%?   ☐ Yes   or   ☐ No
    ⇓
    Go to 6.

3. If the sum of the percentages in boxes [a] and [b] is less than 5%, BUT the percentage in box [a] is 1% or more, a stratum for very small schools is needed. Please see section 5.7.2 to determine an appropriate school sample allocation for this stratum of very small schools.

    (box [a] + box [b]) < 5% and box [a] ≥ 1%?   ☐ Yes   or   ☐ No
    ⇓
    Form an explicit stratum of very small
    schools and record this on Sampling Form 7.

4. If the sum of the percentages in boxes [a] and [b] is 5% or more, BUT the percentage in box [a] is less than 1%, an explicit stratum of small schools is required, but no special stratum for very small schools is required. Please see Section 5.7.2 to determine an appropriate school sample allocation for this stratum of small schools.

    (box [a] + box [b]) ≥ 5% and box [a] < 1%?   ☐ Yes   or   ☐ No
    ⇓
    Form an explicit stratum of small schools and
    record this on Sampling Form 7. Go to 6.

5. If the sum of the percentages in boxes [a] and [b] is 5% or more, AND the percentage in box [a] is 1% or more, an explicit stratum of small schools is required, AND an explicit stratum for very small schools is required. Please see section 5.7.2 to determine an appropriate school sample allocation for these strata of moderately small and very small schools.

    (box [a] + box [b]) ≥ 5% and box [a] ≥ 1%?   ☐ Yes   or   ☐ No
    ⇓
    Form an explicit stratum of moderately small schools
    and an explicit stratum of very small schools, and record
    this on Sampling Form 7.

6. If the percentage in box [a] is less than 0.5%, then these very small schools can be excluded from the national defined target population only if the total extent of school level exclusions of the type mentioned in 3.3.2 remains below 0.5%. If these schools are excluded, be sure to record this exclusion on Sampling Form 3, item 2.

    box [a] < 0.5%?   ☐ Yes   or   ☐ No
    ⇓ Excluding very small schools?   ☐ Yes   or   ☐ No

PISA Sampling Form 7 — Stratification

See Section 5.6 of School Sampling Manual.

PISA Participant: _____

National Project Manager: _____

Explicit Stratification

1. List and describe the variables used for explicit stratification.

	Explicit stratification variables	Number of levels
1		
2		
3		
4		
5		

2. Total number of explicit strata: _____

(Note: if the number of explicit strata exceeds 99, the PISA school coding scheme will not work correctly. See Section 6.6. Consult Westat and ACER.)

Implicit Stratification

3. List and describe the variables used for implicit stratification in the order in which they will be used (i.e., sorting of schools within explicit strata).

	Implicit stratification variables	Number of levels
1		
2		
3		
4		
5		

| **PISA Sampling Form 8** | | | **Population Counts by Strata** | |

See Section 5.9 of School Sampling Manual.

PISA Participant: _____

National Project Manager: _____

Use additional sheets if necessary

(1)	(2)	(3)	(4)	(5)
		\multicolumn{3}{c}{Population Counts}	
		Schools	\multicolumn{2}{c}{Students}	
Explicit Strata	Implicit Strata		ENR	MOS

PISA Sampling Form 9 — Sample Allocation by Explicit Strata

See Section 6.2 of School Sampling Manual.

PISA Participant: _____

National Project Manager: _____

Use additional sheets if necessary

(1) Explicit Strata	(2) Stratum Identification	(3) % of eligible students in population	(4) No. of schools in population	(5) Sample Allocation — Schools	(6) Sample Allocation — Students	(7) % of eligible students expected in sample

PISA Sampling Form 10	**School Sample Selection**

See Section 6.3 of School Sampling Manual.

PISA Participant: _____

National Project Manager: _____

Explicit Stratum: _____   Stratum ID _____

S	**D**	**I**	**RN**
[a] Total Measure of Size	[b] Desired Sample Size	[c] Sampling Interval	[d] Random Number

Use additional sheets if necessary

(1) Line Numbers	(2) Selection Numbers

PISA Sampling Form 11 — School Sampling Frame

See Sections 6.4 - 6.6 of School Sampling Manual.

PISA Participant: _____

National Project Manager: _____

Explicit Stratum: _____   Stratum ID _____

Use additional sheets if necessary

(1) School List Identification	(2) Implicit Stratum	(3) MOS	(4) Cumulative MOS	(5) Sample Status	(6) PISA School Identification

APPENDIX 10: STUDENT LISTING FORM

Page __ of __

School Identification: _____   Country Name: _____

School Name: _____   List Prepared By: _____

Address: _____   Telephone Number: _____

_____   Date List Prepared: _____

_____   Total Number Students Listed: _____

> **DIRECTIONS:** PLEASE COMPLETE COLUMNS A, B, C AND D, FOR EVERY STUDENT <BORN IN 1984>.
>
> Include students who may be excluded from other testing programs, such as some students with disabilities or limited language proficiency. Detailed instructions and information about providing computer-generated lists are on the other side of this page.

For Sampling Only		(A) Student's Name	(B)	(C)	(D)
Selected Student (Enter "S")	Line #	(First Middle Initial Last)	Grade	Sex (M / F)	Birth Date (mm/yy)

A. Instructions for Preparing a List of Eligible Students

1. Please prepare a list of **ALL students <born in 1984. . .NPM must insert eligibility criteria>** using the most current enrolment records available.

2. Include on the list students who typically may be excluded from other testing programs (such as some students with disabilities or limited language proficiency).

3. Write the name for each eligible student. Please also specify current grade, sex, and birth date for each student.

4. If confidentiality is a concern in listing student names, then a unique student identifier may be substituted. Because some students may have the same or similar names, it is important to include a birth date for each student.

5. The list may be computer-generated or prepared manually using the PISA Student Listing Form. A Student Listing Form is on the reverse side of these instructions. You may copy this form or request copies from your National Project Manager.

6. If you use the Student Listing Form on the reverse side of this page, do **not** write in the "For Sampling Only" columns.

7. Send the list to the National Project Manager (NPM) to arrive no later than <insert DATE>. Please address to the NPM as follows: <insert name and mailing address>

B. Suggestions for Preparing Computer-Generated Lists

1. Write the school name and address on list.

2. List students in alphabetical order.

3. Number the students.

4. Double-space the list.

5. Allow left-hand margin of at least two inches.

6. Include the date the printout was prepared.

7. Define any special codes used.

8. Include preparer's name and telephone number.

APPENDIX 11: STUDENT TRACKING FORM

Country Name: _____ Stratum Number: _____
School Name: _____ School ID: _____

Page ___ of ___

SAMPLING INFORMATION

(A) Number of Students Aged 15	(B) Number of Students Listed for Sampling	(C) Sample Size	(D) Random Number	(E) Sampling Interval	(F) First Line Number Selected [(Box D X Box E) + 1]
			0.___		

(1) ID	(2) Line Number (Sample)	(3) Student Name	(4) Grade	(5) Gender (M/F)	(6) Birth Date (MM-YY)	(7) Excluded Code	(8) Booklet Number	(9) Original Session P1 / P2 / SQ	(10) Follow-up Session P1 / P2 / SQ
1									
2									
3									
4									
5									
6									
7									
8									
9									
10									
11									
12									
13									
14									
15									

EXCLUSION CODES (Col. 7)
1 = Functionally disabled
2 = Educable mentally retarded
3 = Limited test language proficiency
4 = Other

PARTICIPATION CODES (Cols. 9&10)
0 = Absent
1 = Present
8 = Not applicable, *i.e.*, excluded, no longer in school, not age eligible

PISA STUDENT TRACKING FORM
(continued)

Country Name: _____ Stratum Number: _____

School Name: _____ School ID: _____

Page ___ of ___

(1) ID	(2) Line Number (Sample)	(3) Student Name	(4) Grade	(5) Gender (M/F)	(6) Birth Date (MM-YY)	(7) Excluded Code	(8) Booklet Number	(9) Original Session P1 / P2 / SQ	(10) Follow-up Session P1 / P2 / SQ
16									
17									
18									
19									
20									
21									
22									
23									
24									
25									
26									
27									
28									
29									
30									
31									
32									
33									
34									
35									

Appendices

APPENDIX 12: ADJUSTMENT TO BRR FOR STRATA WITH ODD NUMBERS OF PRIMARY SAMPLING UNITS

Splitting an odd-sized sample into unequal half-samples without adjustment results in positively biased estimates of variance with BRR. The bias may not be serious if the number of units is large and if the sample has a single-stage design. If, however, the sample has a multi-stage design and the number of second-stage units per first-stage unit is even moderately large, the bias may be severe. The following adjustment, developed by David Judkins of Westat, removes the bias.

The n_h units in each stratum are divided into half-samples. Without loss of generality, assume that the first half-sample is the smaller of the two if the number of sample units in a stratum is odd. For PISA, n_h = 2 or 3. Let u_h=least integer greater than or equal to $n_h/2$ (u_h = 1 or 2 for PISA), ℓ_h=greatest integer less than or equal to $n_h/2$ (ℓ_h = 1 for PISA), $0 \leq k < 1$ be the Fay factor (k=0.5 for PISA) and $d_{ht} = \pm 1$ according to a rule such that $\sum d_{ht} d_{h't} = 0$ for $h \neq h'$ (as is obtained from a Hadamard matrix of appropriate size).

Then the replication factors for the first and second half-samples are:

$$1 + d_{ht}(1-k)\sqrt{\frac{u_h}{\ell_h}} \text{ and } 1 - d_{ht}(1-k)\sqrt{\frac{\ell_h}{u_h}}. \tag{89}$$

Hence for PISA, if $n_h = 2$, the replication factors are $1 + d_{ht}/2$ and $1 - d_{ht}/2$, that is 1.5 and 0.5, or 0.5 and 1.5, for the first and second half-samples respectively. If $n_h = 3$, the replication factors are:

$$1 + \left(d_{ht}/\sqrt{2}\right) \text{ and } 1 - \left(d_{ht}/2\sqrt{2}\right), \tag{90}$$

that is, 1.7071 and 0.6464, or 0.2929 and 1.3536, where the first factor in each case is the one that applies to the single PSU in the first half-sample, while the second factor applies to the two PSUs in the second half-sample.

Proof

Let x_{hi} be an unbiased estimate of the characteristic of interest for the i-th unit in the h-th stratum. Let $x = \sum_h \sum_i x_{hi}$ be the full sample estimate. Let δ_{hi1} and δ_{hi2} denote membership of half-samples 1 and 2 respectively. Let L be the number of strata and T be the number of replicates (T=80 for PISA). Let

$$\alpha_h = \sqrt{\frac{u_h}{\ell_h}}.$$

Then

$$\begin{aligned}\hat{v} &= \frac{1}{(1-k)^2} \frac{1}{T} \sum_{t=1}^{T} \left\{ \sum_{h=1}^{L} \left[(1 + d_{ht}(1-k)\alpha_h) \sum_{i=1}^{n_h} \delta_{hi1} x_{hi} + \left(1 - d_{ht}\frac{(1-k)}{\alpha_h}\right) \sum_{i=1}^{n_h} \delta_{hi2} x_{hi} \right] - x \right\}^2 \\ &= \frac{1}{(1-k)^2} \frac{1}{T} \sum_{t=1}^{T} \left\{ \sum_{h=1}^{L} \left[d_{ht}(1-k)\alpha_h \sum_{i=1}^{n_h} \delta_{hi1} x_{hi} - d_{ht}(1-k)\frac{1}{\alpha_h} \sum_{i=1}^{n_h} \delta_{hi2} x_{hi} \right] \right\}^2 \\ &= \frac{1}{T} \sum_{t=1}^{T} \left\{ \sum_{h=1}^{L} d_{ht} \left[\alpha_h \sum_{i=1}^{n_h} \delta_{hi1} x_{hi} - \frac{1}{\alpha_h} \sum_{i=1}^{n_h} \delta_{hi2} x_{hi} \right] \right\}^2\end{aligned} \tag{91}$$

Given the balancing property of $\{d_{ht}\}$, this simplifies to:

$$\hat{v} = \frac{1}{T}\sum_{t=1}^{T}\sum_{h=1}^{L}d_{ht}^2\left[\alpha_h\sum_{i=1}^{n_h}\delta_{hi1}\,x_{hi} - \frac{1}{\alpha_h}\sum_{i=1}^{n_h}\delta_{hi2}\,x_{hi}\right]^2$$

$$= \sum_{h=1}^{L}\left[\alpha_h\sum_{i=1}^{n_h}\delta_{hi1}\,x_{hi} - \frac{1}{\alpha_h}\sum_{i=1}^{n_h}\delta_{hi2}\,x_{hi}\right]^2 . \quad (92)$$

For convenience, rewrite the simplified $\hat{v}$ as:

$$\hat{v} = \sum_{h=1}^{L}\left(\hat{x}_{h1} - \hat{x}_{h2}\right)^2 . \quad (93)$$

To prove unbiasedness, note that $E(\hat{x}_{h1}) = \alpha_h \ell_h X_h = X_h\sqrt{u_h \ell_h}$, where $X_h = E(x_{hi})$ (assuming identical distribution within stratum), and that:

$$E(\hat{x}_{h2}) = \frac{1}{\alpha_h}u_h X_h = X_h\sqrt{u_h \ell_h} = E(\hat{x}_{h1}). \quad (94)$$

Note furthermore that under simple random sampling *with* replacement,

$$\begin{aligned}Var(\hat{x}_{h1}) &= \alpha_h^2 \ell_h \sigma_h^2, \text{ where } \sigma_h^2 = Var(x_{hi}) \\ &= u_h \sigma_h^2 \text{ and} \\ Var(\hat{x}_{h2}) &= \frac{1}{\alpha_h^2}u_h \sigma_h^2 \\ &= \ell_h \sigma_h^2.\end{aligned} \quad (95)$$

Thus,

$$\begin{aligned}E(\hat{v}) &= \sum_{h=1}^{L}E(\hat{x}_{h1} - \hat{x}_{h2})^2 = \sum_{h=1}^{L}\left[Var(\hat{x}_{h1}) + Var(\hat{x}_{h2})\right] \\ &= \sum_{h=1}^{L}(u_h + \ell_h)\sigma_h^2 \\ &= \sum_{h=1}^{L}n_h \sigma_h^2,\end{aligned} \quad (96)$$

which is the true sampling variance of x.

Imprimé en France, JOUVE, 11, bd de Sébastopol, 75001 Paris - FRANCE
N° 315576M. Dépôt légal : Novembre 2002